D0778656

WITHDRAWN
UTSA Libraries

LEWIS NAMIER

A BIOGRAPHY

LEWIS NAMIER
A BIOGRAPHY

JULIA NAMIER

London
OXFORD UNIVERSITY PRESS
NEW YORK TORONTO
1971

Oxford University Press, Ely House, London W.1

GLASGOW NEW YORK TORONTO MELBOURNE WELLINGTON
CAPE TOWN SALISBURY IBADAN NAIROBI DAR ES SALAAM LUSAKA ADDIS ABABA
BOMBAY CALCUTTA MADRAS KARACHI LAHORE DACCA
KUALA LUMPUR SINGAPORE HONG KONG TOKYO

ISBN 0 19 211706 8

© Lady Namier 1971

*Printed in Great Britain by
The Camelot Press Ltd., London and Southampton*

CONTENTS

v

CONTENTS

LIST OF ILLUSTRATIONS

vii

PREFACE

Lewis Namier and I met in the autumn of 1942. London, already much scarred by the Blitz, was to suffer even worse destruction before the war ended and Lewis went north. Like the masonry and window glass, old conventions and habits came to be strewn about us more thickly as the war years swept by. But we had sensed mankind's indestructibly resilient creative powers pushing through the rubble, shaping new ways in it and of it. Until he was bombed out we lived near enough to each other for him to walk over in an air-raid if so determined; and if another air-raid caught up with him while he was with me, it offered a good reason to outstay his usual time of about two hours. There was hardly a topic we did not talk of at length in the black-out; to find very soon that the differences and similarities between us were exactly right to stimulate interest and sympathy. He being by far the better speaker, my part came to be that of a one-woman chorus listening, witnessing, reacting to his entrancing monologues. When he spoke volubly of himself it was clear that in this man of pronounced male characteristics the female element, too, sought expression. Talking of himself, he gave himself.

L—his signature in letters to close friends—was a person so paradoxical that in the months of heightened introspection preceding his death he summed himself up as perverse. Small wonder that even I had understood him fully only a few weeks earlier. Yet from the start the urge to understand and be understood had fuelled his dynamism; while the range of his communicative powers had been well indicated by the difference between his manner when giving a public lecture and when impressing on the minds of an intimate company some story or episode. From the rostrum he addressed an audience assumed to be sensitive, exacting, and alert. He might stress a sentence by a change of intonation or a fleeting smile or frown. But little more. And the repressed fireworks of gestures, quips, witticisms made for muscular, tense clarity of exposition. But when he reclined in an easy

ix

chair and let himself go, his sparkling, often startling, words were amplified with mimicry and expressive movements of the whole body as he unforgettably enacted an episode in which he had taken part or at which he had been present. In such dramatic sketches, whole groups of people came alive in the mind's eye of anyone who looked and listened. In a related context a pupil speaks of L's conversation having had a 'Homeric quality' in so far as he would often 'add in parenthesis some delightful apophthegm' after the mention of a man or a place. And the same pupil (John R. G. Tomlinson) defines L's Jewish stories, picked up from pukka Jews like Chaim Weizmann or Shmarya Levin, as 'parables really' drawn with 'delighted animation' and infallible subtlety from a great fund in order to flash colour on to some 'point of the moment' and give it depth. Recently too, one of L's 'nieces by adoption'—Rosemary Mitchison, a granddaughter of his revered tutor A. L. Smith—wrote to say she had taken two girls to the *Merchant of Venice* which none of them had seen. 'At one time Shylock starts telling a story. I sat in astonishment. It was as if Shakespeare had been listening to Uncle Lewis.'

Reasonably chary when confronting opponents, he showed them only the brilliance of his mind, never the vigour of his illuminating imagination. Unless fully at ease, he held its flights strictly under control. But proven friendship led to stupendous ventures with him in his world of imaginative symbolism as well as to the discovery of his mind's most subtle elegancies, each revealing in its own way his finely wrought personality.

The sweep of L's spirit and the vistas of his thought, together with precise observation of minute detail, at once spellbound me. But I was next struck by the purity of his intentions, and realized he was a man without guile. Guilelessness is seldom found alongside a piercing intellect; and not till after we were married, in 1947, and I grew attentive even to the inflections of his moods, could I measure how keenly perceptive and how richly endowed with gifts of unflinching analysis a guileless man can be. The more L revealed himself, the more incontrovertible became this rare association of gifts. And yet he was implacably stern too: owing to an equally rare awareness, at all times and in all circumstances, of the direst human derelictions and the loftiest peaks of human achievement. By these extremes he judged action and inaction, failure and success, his own and those of others. It made of him a man humble before God; but intolerant of puerile standards and of all humbug.

From the first time L came to see me he clamoured to be understood. But his significant, wide-ranging self-revelations were, of course, highly haphazard. I began to grasp the precise order of some sequences of events only fifteen months before his death when, under strong provocation from abroad where all kinds of untruths were being circulated, he entrusted me with writing his biography. From then on he spoke consecutively of his ancestry, birth, boyhood, undergraduate years, and the years up to World War I.

In the last weeks of his life, while sorting out for my future use some of his old and incredibly jumbled papers, he would constantly step into my room to add an unforgettable touch to some episode or event. When he died I knew of him all he thought important; but much remained pell-mell. After his death I spent years gathering in and studying documents to solve the jigsaw puzzles I was left with—the placing of every incident where it belonged in the seventy-two years of his crowded life. After much checking and cross-checking I am satisfied that I have got right even the most tricky sequences; and that this biography presents his life such as he deemed it to have been. If any fact is at all distorted, it was unconsciously shifted from true by him, owing to the mental process he called 'telescoping'—an effect of time on memory.

When the hour came for me to plan the biography, three abundant sources of material were to hand: my notes of L's recollections expounded with meticulous precision in the last year and a quarter of his life; documents long kept by him or gathered in by me after his death from far and wide; and my vivid memories of living alongside him in the last thirteen years. Though the three sources have been freely used throughout, his own recollections predominate up to his first year in Balliol; with the letters written to me by men who were up at Oxford with him in the years 1908–11 documentary evidence starts predominating and does so till 1942; after that our shared experiences, as remembered by me, are increasingly important. Because of the three different sources, the biography has been divided into three parts. But the material, while prompting the division, also precluded the division from being kept to rigorously. For one thing, L's active interest in psychoanalysis—dating from 1922—had not only pushed back his childhood memories to the age of about two; it had entwined all his memories with a caustic self-analysis nowhere more apparent than in his letters to me. Leaving for Manchester University before Lent term 1945 he had asked me not to destroy any of them since he would be writing much about his educational and literary work; when he retired from his chair in 1953, he took the batch from me to place among his own papers.

Even before I had reached the preliminary sketches for L's university years, I had to consider my proper approach to him as historian. His mind and method I knew well. On some points he had deliberately instructed me; others I had imbibed when, sauntering into my room to puzzle things out, he sat down to debate aloud, with himself, a variety of linked problems. But of the opinions, convictions, and theories of other historians I knew, and still know, very little.

As time passed and it became clear that L. B. Namier would remain a historian's historian, I came to think it best for me to communicate his enthusiasm for certain historical problems and to indicate his approach to them, but to abstain from classifying him or evaluating his position in the hierarchy of historians. This I leave to experts, offering them what only I know.

I wish to thank the British Academy for allotting me a grant to ease my expenses on this work; the Trustees of the Rhodes Trust for allowing me to read their files on their Trust's grants to L. B. Namier for the completion of his eighteenth-century books; the Polish Library in London and its Librarian for help with Polish material I hold, or lacked and needed; and the Central Zionist Archives in Jerusalem for microfilm of documents written by Namier or relevant to his service as Political Secretary to the Jewish Agency in London.

My thanks are also due to the late Michael Dugdale for permission to quote from his mother's diaries and from her letters to my husband throughout their long friendship, and to the literary executors of Sir James Headlam-Morley for permission to quote from his letters to my husband, written in 1919. For help in checking and cross-checking facts and dates relating to the family background, L's childhood, and his youth, I am indebted chiefly to his sister, his paternal aunt Mrs. Henry Landau, and his cousin Mrs. Maximilian Schutz. Nor can I omit to thank all who have allowed me to use their family documents, and those who on their own initiative have sent me excerpts or photostats of documents written by my husband, or relevant to him, and chanced upon by them in obscure or not easily accessible archives. My gratitude goes to every one of these generous helpers whether known to me personally or only by name.

CHRONOLOGICAL TABLE

1888   (27 June) Born at Wola Okrzejska (in Russian Poland) into the Bernsztajn vel Niemirowski family.

1890   The family moves to Kobylowloki in Austrian Poland.

1896   They move to Nowosiolka Skalacka, near the Russian frontier.

1898   First major quarrel between father and son, over decision to have the children educated at home, not at the local school.

1906   Matriculates. The family moves to Koszylowce.

1906–7 Attends Lausanne University.

1907–8 Attends the London School of Economics. Joins the Fabian Society.

1908   Enters Balliol College.

1910   Changes his name to Lewis Bernstein Naymier.

1911   Achieves a first class degree in Modern History.

1913   Becomes a British subject. Changes the spelling of his name to Namier. In the U.S.A. on his father's business; writes articles for *American Leader*; begins to collect eighteenth-century material.

1914   Returns to England. In Oxford begins a book on the emergence of the U.S. at the collapse of the first British Empire. Lectures to the W.E.A. Joins the army.

1915   Discharged from army at the request of the Foreign Office, to join Wellington House, an Intelligence Bureau.

1917   Marries Clara Sophia Edeleff-Poniatowska.

1918   Appointed to the Political Intelligence Department of the Foreign Office.

1920   Returns to Oxford. Gives lectures and tutorials. Writes 'The Downfall of the Habsburg Monarchy'.

1921   Deserted by his wife. Becomes representative in Prague of a cotton business. Appointed *Manchester Guardian Commercial*'s reporter in Vienna.

1922   Disinherited by his father's will. Never goes home again.

1924   Returns to London. Writes 'The Electoral Structure of England', and 'Why Men Went into Parliament'.

1925   Deflected into writing articles and book reviews for weekly journals.

1929   *The Structure of Politics at the Accession of George III* published. Becomes member of the Committee on the Records of Past Members of the House of Commons (a project which was shelved at the end of the 1930s). Joins the Zionist Organization as Political Secretary to its Jewish Agency in London.

1930   *England in the Age of the American Revolution* published. Takes part in drafting the MacDonald Letter to Dr. Weizmann.

1931   *Skyscrapers* published. Becomes Professor of Modern History at Manchester University.

1933   In free time resumes work at the Jewish Agency to rescue and re-establish German-Jewish scholars and students.

1934   Gives Ford Lectures, 'The Cabinet in the Eighteenth Century'.

1935   'From Vienna to Versailles' appears in *The Nineteenth Century and After*.

1937   *Additions and Corrections to Sir John Fortescue's Edition of the Correspondence of King George III* (Vol. I) published.

1938   Starts to write contemporary European history.

1939   Takes part in the St. James's Palace tripartite Conference between the Government, Arabs, and Jews. Seconded for liaison work between the Foreign Office/Colonial Office and the Zionist Organization. *In the Margin of History* published.

1940   Starts a comparative and critical analysis of various official pre-war collections of documents—'Coloured Books'.

1942   *Conflicts* published.

1944   Delivers the Raleigh Lecture, '1948: The Revolution of the Intellectuals'.

1945   Resumes university duties. Expands his Raleigh Lecture for publication. First wife dies.

1947   Delivers the Waynflete Lectures, 'The German Problem in 1848–50'. *Facing East* published. Marries the author.

1948   Takes Sabbatical leave. *Diplomatic Prelude* (which includes 'Coloured Books') published. Delivers in Rome the Academia dei Lincei lecture, 'Nationality and Liberty'. Elected honorary Fellow of Balliol College.

1949   Returns to his university duties.

1950   *Europe in Decay* published.

1951   Appointed member of the Editorial Board of the revived History of Parliament, and editor of three volumes—section 1750–90.

1952   *In the Nazi Era* published. Delivers Romanes Lecture, 'Monarchy and the Party System'. Knighted. Awarded an honorary D.Litt. by the University of Durham. Delivers the Creighton Lecture (London University), 'Some Basic Factors of Nineteenth-Century European History'.

1953   Delivers to the Royal Academy of Arts a lecture, 'King George III: A Study of Personality'. Retires from his professorship. Delivers four lectures on France 1815–51 to Alexandra College, Dublin.

1955   Awarded D.Litt. by Oxford University.

1956   Receives in Balliol College a book of essays presented to him by sixteen leading English historians. Awarded an honorary degree by Rome University.

1957   Awarded honorary Litt. D. by Cambridge University. Works on the History of Parliament. Revises *The Structure of Politics* for its second edition. Assigned £4,000 a year for four years by the Rockefeller Foundation to direct research.

1958   Visits Israel as a member of the Board of Editors for the Weizmann Papers.

1959   Delivers in Cambridge the Leslie Stephen Lecture, 'Charles Townshend: His Character and Career'.

1960   Awarded a D.C.L. by the Chancellor of the University of Oxford. Works on biography of Charles Townshend, and on the revision of *England in the Age of the American Revolution*. Dies in London (August).

PART I

EARLY YEARS

CHAPTER ONE

Ancestry and Birth

Lewis Namier was the only son and younger child of Joseph Bernsztajn vel Niemirowski and his wife Ann. The marriage was celebrated in 1885 when Joseph was twenty-seven years old and his bride seventeen. Both were children of polonized Jews but there the similarity of background stopped. L's grandfathers had little in common.

L's paternal grandfather, Jacob Bernsztajn, was a revolutionary after the nineteenth-century manner, a romantic Polish nationalist, a fairly successful Warsaw banker, and the descendant of many notable men of learning. Associates made much of the fact that his forebears had belonged to a group of Jews so polonized by the nineteenth century that, after the Napoleonic wars, they were singled out by special decree as sufficiently well established and well known locally to warrant their being granted full rights of landownership. Whatever the disabilities of other Jews, this particular group could thereafter buy or sell land, inherit, or leave it by testament. The locality of their privileges was known as Congress Poland at that time (1815–63) of Poland's periodic carvings-up and regroupings. It included Warsaw, where Joseph —Jacob's second son and Lewis's father—was born. The family prided itself above all on the number of scholars through whom their ancestry could be traced to the Talmudic Era. Yet the greatest of them was a modern man, Ezekiel Landau of Prague. Born in 1713 Ezekiel died in 1773, having written many works of which one, *Noda bi-Yehuda*, is still classed as an important contribution to the 'later medieval Responsa literature'.[1] At what time and how the family were forbidden to continue using their old name of Niemirowski and were compelled to substitute Bernsztajn is by now untraceable. But in the view of an expert, Professor Stanislaw Kot, it was most likely to have been in the second

[1] Isidor Epstein: *Judaism*, London, Penguin Books, 1959.

3

half of the eighteenth century when much of Poland was being fiercely Germanized. What is known of the tenacious stock indicates that they somehow contrived to have 'vel Niemirowski' inserted in important documents after the imposed name; that the resentment against the imposition fluctuated from generation to generation without ever drying up; and that in Jacob, L's grandfather, it broke out with a new twist.

Jacob was born in Vinnitsa in the Government of Podolye, at that time part of Russian Poland. But he lived most of his life in Warsaw where he owned considerable property and ran his own banking house. His bottled-up exasperation against the imposed name led him through one thing and another (and because oppressors are easily interchangeable) to revolt against the Russian regime, grown markedly harsh after the nationalist insurrection of 1830. For taking part in the second revolt or revolution of the nineteenth century, that of 1863, Jacob was imprisoned though not deported. Kept in custody for more than a year he suffered considerable physical deterioration, and the family fortune never quite recovered, not even after his release. Yet on his many children from their earliest years, Jacob and his wife Balbina—mother of thirteen children—continually impressed exacting standards of behaviour and appearance. Touches of ceremony abounded in their household habits, blending well with the children's education—the best Warsaw could offer. The boys graduated at the university, the girls were chiefly taught at home by a selection of first-rate teachers. All spoke French and German fluently, and English after a fashion. There was much playing of the piano and other musical instruments. Vacations were spent some miles to the east of Warsaw at Wola Okrzejska, a country house in the district of Lukov, Government of Sedlets, bought by Jacob's father from Bishop Ciechanowski, an uncle of Henryk Sienkiewicz—author of *Quo Vadis*. Situated in country that would have been monotonous but for its woods and streams, Wola was much loved by the family. But perhaps there were too few acres to it or its soil was poor or else it was mismanaged—financially it was a constant disappointment and sometimes a burden.

From the point of view of scholarship the family of L's paternal grandmother, Jacob's second or, possibly, third wife, was even

more highly and widely esteemed in Jewish circles than her husband's. Balbina was a direct descendant of the most renowned
eighteenth-century Jew, Eliyahu ben-Solomon, Gaon[1] of Vilna
(1720–97). Described by Isidor Epstein as 'the greatest intellectual
and spiritual force of Rabbinic Judaism since Maimonides', the
Gaon was an unconventional traditionalist round whom legends
collected during his lifetime. Meticulous bookish learning seems
to have developed in him a piercing insight into human situations.
His profession, as it were, was the pondering of the Talmud and
the elucidation of the Torah, the Law. His vocation was to find
for life's concrete riddles—when put to him—a 'true' yet sensible
answer: one that was in perfect accord with his people's ancient
and elaborate Law, but at the same time, in its modern context,
humane. Between him and the Hassidic rabbis hostility was acute
and unrelenting. Though interested in secular studies in so far as
they could throw some light on the Torah, he was opposed to all
philosophizing, and his interpretation of texts was untainted by
casuistry. He refused all rabbinical office; yet thousands of Jews,
at a loss for practical solutions in tune with godly wisdom, diligently sought his guidance.

Balbina herself was a worldly-wise, somewhat pompous,
domestic tyrant who, as a matter of course, took over the reins
from her dying husband. The eldest son was already stricken by
the disease of which he was to die a few years later. And Joseph,
who at this juncture should have been accepted as head of the
family, was easily outshone by his mother, with her regal carriage
and forceful personality. Yet strikingly able and well-groomed to
a nicety, a Pole with a Russian cast and speaking Russian like a
native, Joseph, the full-voiced young advocate, looked forward
to a brilliant career. Tall and slender, with a long narrow finely-
featured face and aquiline nose, he was not unlike his mother,
though in him her eagle pride was toned down to a softer, more
sheep-like hubris. And while her flashing eyes could pierce, his
bulged slightly, and easily changed from mild to supercilious. He
had inherited his mother's Van Dyck hands; but none of her
steely resilience. Lank sandy hair was soon to recede from his
already too high forehead. He looked overbred; and for a Jew,

---

[1] The title of a Jewish leader among East European Jews.

his background was glamorous. By contrast that of his bride was earthy.

Ann's father, Maurice Theodor Sommersztajn, was a hard-headed, self-made man, owner of prosperous estates in the district of Trembowla in Eastern Galicia, also known as the Western Ukraine. Ann, his eldest surviving child, spoke of him to her own children years later as a cautious man of vision, one whose acts of daring were thought out with care. He had ploughed up on a large scale some hitherto uncultivated portions of the steppe lands of the Pantalicha region—a grandiose project successfully carried through. Well-informed in his own chosen sphere, Theodor was a go-ahead agriculturalist, but otherwise had no learning.

Ann's education at Dresden had been cut short by her mother's death. Summoned home, she returned to be entrusted with responsibility for her brother and two sisters, and to play with great pleasure the lady of her father's houses: the country house at Darachow and the town house at Tarnopol (later, chief town of the province). Father and daughter resembled each other enough to enjoy the dissimilarities in their upbringing; and the new domestic arrangements worked well until he decided to remarry. Incensed at the idea of submitting to a stepmother, whoever she might be, Ann made up her mind to leave and run a house of her own. For this—given the time and place—she, too, had to get married. Able, accomplished in the art of home-building and the craft of home-management, mentally alert and warm-hearted though shrewd, she was widely appreciated. But she was plain: stocky, plump, and almost swarthy. Well-wishers could only stress the intelligence of her magnificent eyes. Luckily her dowry was good.

On some important issues Joseph and his bride were in immediate agreement. Both belonged to what can be called, in the context of their lives, the tradition of Jacob Bernsztajn. Like him, they identified themselves with the nation in whose midst they lived. They were Poles. But outstripping him in the logic of their behaviour, they had no use at all for Jewish observances; while the Polish customs of the Roman Church, widespread and deep-rooted in the nation, seemed to them acceptable as a matter of course. Religious enthusiasm, whatever its source, they dismissed as bad taste—an attitude usual at that time among any

Roman Catholic Poles they were likely to mix with. Religion was for them no serious issue, only a churchy complex of loved customs. The whys and wherefores you left to the priests whose business it was to know and disentangle, to speak of the faith and be stirred by it. Lay enthusiasm for religion, as distinct from nationalism, was viewed with marked distaste, amused or prim. The young couple's dismissal of it was prim, and their firm intention was to merge easily and happily with friends, servants, and neighbours without obscuring their own Jewish descent of which both were proud—Joseph because of his lineage, Ann because of her father. To them their stepping out together into a new life seemed the obvious moment to make their position clear and to cut themselves loose officially from meaningless Jewish usages grown irksome. But Balbina—supported by Theodor's mature, traditionally educated bride—thought otherwise. At once the issue cast a shadow; it fell between the two older women on the one side and the young couple on the other. This shadow darkened round Ann, as neither of the women was concerned with Joseph: Ann's step-mother finding him unimportant, and his own mother considering him above censure.

At the wedding Balbina stole the show. Her approach was dynastical. Her son—a male descendant of the Gaon—was being married to a motherless girl; soon he would have male descendants; and their link with the Gaon would be through her. She insisted on meticulous traditional observances. And even in Theodor's house at the wedding feast of sumptuous rejoicing, her mind and hand were felt and known as omnipresent and decisive. After the honeymoon—Verona, Venice, and Florence—the young couple settled down in Warsaw, not far from Balbina's observant eye. Months passed and there was no pregnancy. Was the girl barren? The tragic element in the lives so attentively scrutinized, eluded her. She saw only an unattractive daughter-in-law, increasingly reticent, almost—she feared—becoming hard. Of the girl's loneliness and humiliation no rumour reached her. That her son was spending his nights away from home she was never to know. Ann alone could have disclosed the truth, and she spoke of it only once, more than twenty years later, to her own son returned from Oxford during a long vacation.

With the pitiless self-appraisal of the proud who have grown perceptive, Ann told Lewis that, knowing herself to be plain, she would not have thought it unnatural to be neglected for another woman whom she would have imagined as lovely, seductive, and experienced beyond compare. But Joseph's barren infatuation, or 'adultery' as she put it, was too degrading to mention to anyone but her son. Joseph was a gambler. Almost nightly till dawn he could be found at a select club where they punted high. Fluctuating luck kept his passion keen but, on balance, he lost heavily. What was worse, his ability to concentrate on anything but the cards was being undermined, his nerves were on edge.

Yet a day came when the family were told Ann was expecting. And in due course, in July 1887, she was delivered of a robust girl whom young and old agreed to call Theodora—suitable enough for Maurice Theodor's granddaughter. But Joseph remained tense and difficult. He was hard up. Sleepless nights were telling on his work. Briefs were no longer coming in. Moreover, the shrewd Theodor had so far handed over only half his daughter's dowry.

Soon Ann was again pregnant. Balbina, sharing the conviction of many mothers of large families, was certain she knew the sex of the child: it was to be a boy. His birth ought to have taken place in Warsaw where she could have seen that all was done as it should be. But at that moment her predominant concern was not with her future grandson but with two of her sons: the eldest, plodding through the last stages of his fatal illness, and Joseph who clearly was not well and was apparently working too hard to no profit. The family therefore decided that Joseph, his wife, and daughter would give up their Warsaw house and move to Wola. It would be good for his health and he would in time take over the estate's management to make of it, at last, a profitable concern. He would wind up his practice in Warsaw and free himself from an occupation now considered by his mother too demanding on his delicate constitution. The country air and quiet would ease his nervous strain and bring prosperity, health, and happiness to the little family.

Things did not work out as planned. Under Ann's supervision the domestic upheaval proceeded according to schedule but Joseph's disentanglements were slowed down by many snags. In the end he moved his family to Wola, saw them comfortably installed, and returned to Warsaw. To-ing and fro-ing became his habit until, as summer advanced, the estate and Ann needed his presence at all times.

In her eighth month of pregnancy Ann, heavy and weary, kept much to her own rooms and the nursery. Downstairs Joseph had congenial company. The estate agent, Baron Kurela—a great horseman and ready gambler—was almost at his beck and call. And Chan Girey, a former Russian military attaché in Paris, had come for a long visit. In France he had got through more money than he could afford and was now doing penance by living in retirement on his fine 'donation' estate: given him by the Russians after confiscation from a deported Polish family. By his immediate neighbours he was severely ostracized; and when he went to the local races for the first time he was ignored by all except Joseph who had known and liked him for some years. Having greeted each other, the two walked about a good deal together and talked with animation. Girey, found to be even more amusing than before, was pressed to come and stay at Wola whenever he chose, for as long as he liked.

After midsummer the fine weather broke. Rain came down in torrents. The men downstairs played taroc, a fashionable card game for three. On 26 June the sun gleamed fiercely but fitfully. Windows had to be shut against blood-hungry insects. It was steaming hot. Kurela had driven over in his calèche drawn by a fine new pair recently arrived from their native steppe lands further south. He persuaded Ann to come for a drive. Before the rain she had been driving out daily though with less spirited horses and a less dashing driver. First all went well. But as they skirted a wood the horses took fright. Foaled and trained in open grassland they were unused to clear-cut hopping shadows cast by leaves torn at by a gusty wind. The road forked and Kurela, his self-confidence undisturbed, turned into the mellow and more even shade of the wood. Horseflies pounced. Stung, the horses bolted. Full-speed, the calèche hurtled against a large tree. Ann was badly thrown.

By the time she was back in her room the birthpangs had

9

started. Joseph sent his carriage for the doctor. Women of the household and some older bodies from the neighbourhood flocked in. Not until the next day, 27 June, was Ann's ordeal over. The child was a puny boy, presumed dead and put on one side. All attention was fixed on the mother. When the doctor was satisfied that she was no longer in immediate danger, the women began to drift away. One of them stopped beside the naked newborn child. She thought she heard it squeak, lifted it up, and found that its naked shrivelled body, though cold, had not the coldness, nor the stiffness, of death. The doctor's attention was now drawn to the boy and, having done all that could be of any use, he decided to stay at Wola as long as either patient might need him. For the next few days he joined the card game and played whist downstairs.

CHAPTER TWO

Grief and Delight
1888–1896

Ann soon recovered from her misadventure; but the child remained a weakling. Because of him there was much letter-writing between Wola and Warsaw, Warsaw and Darachow, Darachow and Wola. Blame was laid on this person and that, advice was given of one sort and another. Balbina insisted that the boy be named Jacob—the correct name for the eldest son of the family. Ann answered that his name was Ludwik. Why Ludwik? Because Ann had long liked it. Robust and resilient, secure in her isolation, she was quietly taking charge while her husband went about justifying with rhetorical utterances his policy of drift.

The physical reason for Joseph's apathy was never established. But he was an intermittently sick man. For the next year or two, some undefined ailment seemed to drain away his energy, while a severe ulceration of the gums increased his irritability. As the autumn of 1888 drew near he was more loath to take over the estate management from Kurela. Again on the pretext of winding up his practice he went to Warsaw. Again he could be seen at the club. On one occasion, when staying with his mother who had severely taken him to task for indifference to family traditions, he went and registered that his son had been born in their house and had been given the name of Ludwik—two correct statements. But he amplified the entries to read: in his mother's *Warsaw* house; and named—*according to the Jewish rite*. When in later years it was demanded of him why he did this, Joseph raised his eyebrows and said he had been very ill, very tired, and intolerably nagged at by two intense women in disaccord. Besides, unless the child had been born in Warsaw there would have been no good reason for registering him there, and Joseph wanted to be through with the whole business. Above all he wanted peace.

But peace he did not get. Ann had to be told. She *was* told, and in a flash of anger she accepted her father's pressing invitation to come to Darachow. His comfortable wife—Theodor wrote—wanted more and more children about her. She was good at tending the sick too. Ann herself, if not the children, would be looked after at Darachow far better than at Wola. Up to her moment of anger Ann had avoided accepting her father's invitations without ever actually refusing. Hostility to her stepmother had not decreased with the heaping up of difficulties in her own married life, but her father, when compared with her husband, towered, a giant of a man.

With Ann's letter written, events took their course. The journey was a nightmare. In Warsaw there was much criticism of her actions and there were disparaging looks directed at her son, only slightly softened by the popularity of Theodora's glossy ginger locks and winning ways. Worse was to come. Up to their departure from Warsaw Ann and the children had at least been well cared for. Between Warsaw and Tarnopol she changed trains twice, alone, with an infant in her arms and by her side a child whom she often had to carry too. One evening a Russian general was put into their compartment. While playing bears and bisons with the little girl he had been good company, but as the night wore on he cursed the boy whose whimpering kept him awake. Whimpers changed to howls, and the child vomited.

At some moment that night L must have had a severe shock which later blended with visual impressions retold, vividly and often, by others in his presence. For years the Russian general recurred in his nightmares. A big red face, moustache and eyebrows abristle, china-blue eyes grown circular with anger. The petrifying red thing took shape somewhere above L's head and came down with inexorable deliberation. The fierce eyebrows changed to long coppery sparks, the eyes grew rounder, the moustache made menacing noises that merged into the howls of a trapped animal aware of being in mortal peril. Only gradually did L come to recognize the howls for his own.

At Tarnopol they were met by Theodor and two servants, a man and a maid. The station-master escorted them from the platform to their carriages. For Ann the ease and geniality, the energy and the determination to forge ahead which were personified in her father blended happily with the wide-open, well-known landscape they drove through. And for a while she had Theodor to herself—the children followed with the servants in the second carriage. The immensity of level land, rippling rather than rolling, was capped by sky that curved down steeply to touch the wind-blown earth at a distance natural to the beholder's eye unhindered by ridge or building. It can be a relief after much turmoil to let the eyes find their natural limit wherever they turn.

Darachow engulfed them in flabby embraces and then separated them immediately, each into his own niche. Ann's relationship with her stepmother shaped badly; even worse than it had with Balbina. Theodor was the one man—the one person—with whom she had ever wanted to be alone to the exclusion of all others. And in the next two years, while she remained the loving yet unwilling inmate of his home run by a usurper, her jealousy reached its peak. For all that, the years of attrition were formative: of Ann as wife, mother, and home-maker; of Joseph as husband, father, and manager of agricultural estates. True, he lived in his mother's Warsaw house, visiting Wola only to supervise the reorganization she wanted there. Her eldest son had died, and Balbina now was sole proprietress with full rights of disposal. But whether in Warsaw or the country nearby, Joseph was merely winding up his past while he ripened into full manhood. Gradually he came to prefer Ann's steering to Balbina's. As to the children, Theodora's looks had always appealed to him; and a son was a son.

The trend of things to come met Joseph with vigour only when he went south to see his wife and children. As the months ticked by he went more often and stayed longer. Theodor, loving his eldest daughter with a passionate concern that in a lesser man might have acquired incestuous overtones, used—at every opportunity—his knowledge of the Ukrainian earth and climate, of men and their affairs, and also his peculiar wisdom and authoritarian charm, to train her mate, Joseph, in the things he himself was able to transmit. Owing to him, at the end of the two unsatisfactory years, Joseph could move his family from Darachow to Kobylowloki (which can be translated as Mare's Portages), another estate recently bought by Theodor, deeper down in the steppes to the south.

In later years L traced his first feelings of acute emotional distress to the long drive away from the known house, in an unknown direction along execrable roads. He understood only that they were taking him away from Thérèse, his mother's young sister, as fair and gentle as Ann was dark and stern. For two summers at Darachow and two winters at Tarnopol, Thérèse comforted the child when nightmares or illness made of him a nuisance to all but her. When paroxysms of the whooping-cough had suffocated him, it was she who carried him about, crooning over him even in the dead of night. And it must have been she who, intuitively grasping a basic need and delight of his, often put him on top of a cupboard where he would sit for hours looking down on the people below, observing them. 'Even now', added the friend (Mrs. Edgar Dugdale) who in 1941 recorded his account of it, 'he is never so happy as when looking at the world from a hilltop.'

As the reunited parents and their children started on the long drive to Kobylowloki, Ann promised her sobbing son that Thérèse would be following immediately. Joseph said she would often come to stay. L believed neither. They failed to communicate the sense of confidence and comfort which flowed to him from her. In the unfamiliar house his longing for Thérèse increased, and his estrangement from his parents hardened. Yet in the next three years she came more than once to Kobylowloki. And every time before she arrived he was sick with apprehension that she would not reach them; and no sooner had she left than he wept till he vomited again, in a paroxysm of acute despair.

Kobylowloki was a seedy one-storey farmhouse barely large enough to hold the family and its several servants. But for its outhouses and labourers' quarters it stood alone, in open steppe land, miles away from any civilized centre or household. Its amenities were few. The parents accepted life there as a period of probation. They were determined to succeed and both had much to do. Ann strove against great odds to make the house comfortable and to keep the quarrels between servants and labourers from growing into dangerous feuds. The situation and its imperative demands brought out and developed her ability to deal with people. She was respected and obeyed. As Theodor had given her a well-stocked medicine chest, the sick and the accident-prone came to rely on her skill. Wherever she went she was closely followed by her labrador, accepted even by the two cows she had singled out for the children—the servants' children as well as her own. Soon she asked Theodor for veterinary manuals, textbooks, primers, and before long was handling sick animals also.

Joseph, in a grim mood, set about proving his worth to Ann, Theodor, and himself. He succeeded remarkably well whether sowing and reaping wheat, barley, and oats, or planting and lifting potatoes (grown chiefly for alcohol). Deprived of the more usual forms of gambling he took to sowing white clover on a large scale for seed—Australia was an inexhaustible market. If extreme heat swooped down to brood over the steppe at the wrong time, the whole crop was a dead loss. But if all went well, the returns were magnificent. It was worth the risk. It was his only flutter. And he had a run of lucky years.

The preoccupations of Joseph and Ann left the children much to themselves and the house-servants. Theodora, with premature poise and self-assurance, stepped into the daytime emptiness where Thérèse should have been. Artistically gifted, she drew her brother into her rich life of play and fantasy; and renamed him Ulu (pronounced Ooloo) which soon caught on even in the wider family circles. But her brother's secret life was unknown to her. A new, shapeless nightmare had begun to haunt him. Time and again, at the brink of sleep he was engulfed in a certitude that he could not accept: Thérèse was about to be irreparably snatched away. He came to fear the approach of sleep, strove to keep awake, failed, and was overcome by an involved despair that even the howling Russian general had never evoked. On the following day L was dull and languid. And his indifference to his sister, his parents, and the household, engendered in him a poignant sense of failure.

Yet despite L's nightmares and ill-health, and his father's fits of depression and increasing hypochondria, life at Kobylowloki was not all gloom for the children. Beyond the stables and the cowhouse was a pond where they learned first to slide then to skate, and in mild winter weather were allowed to spend as many day-light hours as they liked. In the next year L began unforgettably to register visual impressions: snow falling thick and fast on his coat and upturned face; the intricate monochrome patterns drawn on windows by frost; a French print, clear and dark against the pale wall of his room—soldiers in French uniform holding a redoubt against invading Germans. He also began to keep a mental register of unforgettable rebuffs. On a summer day of brilliant sunlight, at some distance from the house, he saw a bank smothered in pink daisies. Amazed at their colour L picked a large handful and ran home. He found Ann at last, preoccupied as usual. Stretching up to her his offering, he explained his wonder that his daisies were not white. But all Ann could see was a limp bunch of field flowers. She told the child not to be silly and ordered him to throw his weeds on the dust heap. As she hurried away the grip of his hot hands, which had tightened round the posy on the way home and during his efforts to find his mother, loosened. He trampled the heads and stalks into the dust. It took L almost a lifetime to forgive the grief and insult of that hour. But in his last years any flowers placed in his room (whether tulips or roses, cyclamen or gloxinias, and regardless of their colour) he called 'my pink daisies'. He had succeeded in weaving with wry affection into his later life even this earliest and most bitter rebuff. But the immediate impact had led to a resolute withdrawal. And in the days of long lamplight that followed his fourth birthday he taught himself to read while his sister painted with fiery zeal.

Left alone for most of the time, the children were now and then attentively listened to. One overheard conversation was remembered verbatim as typical of both. L must have been again pondering his estrangement from the family and asking himself why he was with them at all. He formulated his perplexity carefully and safely, saying something like: 'I wonder how people's children come to be with them.' His sister brightly answered: 'But Ulu, haven't you seen pictures of storks, each one carrying a child in its beak?' 'Silly Dziunia,' retorted L, 'a painter saw a stork, then he saw a child and put them together, that's all.'

Even more exciting than falling snow, frost abstracts, bright flowers, or pictures of men in action, was the appearance at

Kobylowloki of new faces. First came Ella, the illegitimate child of a Moravian peasant-woman and a local magnate. Unpolished, but a kindly girl full of common sense, having in addition the qualities which combine to make an excellent nurse, and being also naturally good with children, she was engaged to look after L and Theodora and to teach them German. She did more. In helping L to understand the core of Christian devotion without caring a rap for denominational distinctions, and in developing his deep sympathy for the fears and joys of animals—horses especially—she was one of the chief formative forces in his early life.

For a while Joseph's mind, too, was on horses. Having decided that the children should learn riding he undertook to teach them. The sturdy Ukrainian horse is rather small, and exceptionally small ones can be found. Throughout the steppe lands—and in the whole of Russia, too, before the proletarian revolution—peasant boys rode self-taught, barefoot and bareback on horses absurdly large for them, using as chief points of control their inner ankle-bones. Of L and Theodora no such feats were asked; and Joseph had a sense of style. But teaching bored him and he soon handed them over to the head stable-boy who was delighted, but too often engaged on other work in the good hours of the better days. Neither L nor Theodora learnt much riding at Kobylowloki, but it was there—in the open steppes—that they came to know and understand horses.

Ella's arrival was soon followed by the frequent appearance of a young man, a school teacher, whom Ann had persuaded to ride over from the village, where he lived and taught, to give lessons to her children. He found the farouche boy reading books beyond his age with ease and interest, but Theodora was hardly able to read at all. While she plodded along, L wandered off to the stables mostly with Ella who patronized one of the younger boys. On some occasions the child was put on his honour to keep near the horses and left with no close supervision until called back to the schoolroom. During these solitary moments in the stables L found in the horses outstanding differences of character, developed a personal approach to each one, and dreamed up an adventurous association with a great mare of which he spoke to me with

awe shortly before his death. Ella and the stable-boys must have
been transmitting to the children legends about magic horses
reputed, in the wide band of Siberian, Russian, and Ukrainian
steppe lands, to be a child's best friend. But though L's attention
was, on the whole, turning outward, his secret emotional life was
moving to a new crisis.

Thérèse—more lovely than before, excited and exciting—came
for a few days. L was perplexed: there were whisperings, incomprehensible allusions, sentences suddenly broken off, warning
glances. There was suppressed laughter. She took him, dazed, to
her room, seated him cosily in her lap and, with many endearments and little caresses, said she was about to be married to a
man in Vienna who would become L's uncle and whom he must
love very much because she did. In Vienna she would live in a
fine house where lots of little Ulus of her own would come to her.
And all of them would love him, the first Ulu, very much. He
listened in silence, waited a little, slipped off her knee and went
off for comfort to the stables. L's nightmares of formless fore-
boding having proved to be concrete foreknowledge, they continued for life. He hung his heart upon a weeping willow tree and
resigned himself to being thwarted in love, one way or another.

The outrageous information that marriage would bring lots of
little Ulus to Thérèse in Vienna was quickly followed by the
enigmatic parental announcement that Balbina, their father's
mother, had died in Warsaw. How did one die in Warsaw? If a
horse was injured in a way Ann could not put right, the head
stable-boy shot it. In a quick sharp spell of winter weather a small
bird, thickly blanketed in hoar-frost, had been inadvertently
kicked by one of the children. Died on the wing, Ella had said. It
lay stiff, on its back, with claws changed to little black hooks that
broke with hardly a snap when you tried to unbend them. A
stable-boy would not have shot Balbina. Was she lying stiff on a
large white bed with unbending, hooked, dark fingers which
would break if touched? The parents were unconcerned. Balbina's
death brought them certain sums of money and this they liked.
Only a younger sister of Joseph's was sad: about to be married
she had to put off her wedding day. No little Ulus there for a
time.

In due course the wedding was celebrated at Lwow, the administrative centre for the whole of Galicia and a fine, ancient city. The parents had to attend. With them they took L and Theodora accompanied by Ella. For the children, aged six and seven, it was the first railway journey which they later remembered. But L's wide-eyed pleasure was not unmixed. Traces of a mild epidemic of cholera still persisted in the region and, throughout the absence from home, Joseph fussed a great deal over food and drinking water. As for Ann, she once again was unwittingly tactless. While the train swung them to its soothing rhythm between Tarnopol and Lwow, L was for the first time aware of hearing her story about the Russian general—an angry fuss-pot more ridiculous than frightening, a silly old gentleman whom they had met on another railway journey, years earlier. To have his fearful vision casually exteriorized and made trite was to L a shock and an outrage. Reeling at the blow he failed for a while to regain his balance.

Of the wedding he remembered only being kept on a strict diet and having frequent new nightmares. Weary and fed up he tried to induce restful sleep by spinning thoughts about attractive people in pleasant situations. Recently a project had been discussed—that he might go to the village school. He thought of it as an escape from a cage. And at Lwow he dreamed up a lovely young teacher, not unlike Thérèse, who knew the answer to all his questions and never snubbed him like Ann, never wittily turned his questions to ridicule as Joseph liked to do. For a while L slept well, and woke happy. But on one restless night a whistling wind blew the lovely teacher down on to deep snow. Stretching up her hands which stiffened and turned black, she died. For some time L was morose, being certain that he never would go to the village school. Yet he did have one day of unspoilt enjoyment during that visit away from home. It was spent by the family in the outer suburbs of Lwow at an exhibition hinged on the eighteenth-century national hero Kosciuszko: 1894 was the centenary of Raclawice, his spectacular victory over the Russian army. Joseph, moved to oratory, used the occasion to speak of his own father who had sacrificed health and money to much the same cause at a later date. L's imagination stirred. Voices called to him, faces moved towards him out of the past. He began to wonder about the people who had lived before his grandparents; people who had done things which still mattered—to his parents and him.

About his not escaping from Kobylowloki to have lessons with the village boys L's premonitions again proved true. Theodor decided to move his daughter's family to a better property in a more accessible and civilized region. The children's education was one reason for it; his increasing confidence in Joseph was another. Already he was giving his son-in-law the interest on the second half of Ann's dowry, though he still held the capital. Of his new plan for them the travellers heard on the way home. Filled with expectation they reached Kobylowloki in an unsettled mood. But life lagged behind the drive of their desires, and they lived on in gloomy isolation for another two years, undertaking nothing new, just jogging along.

The tiresome delay was nobody's choice, nobody's fault. Theodor had carefully singled out as desirable—and most suitable for his daughter and Joseph—a fairly large estate, Nowosiolka Skalacka, containing four excellent farms and forest land with commercial possibilities. It lay some twenty miles northeast of Darachow, very near the Russian frontier, and had once formed part of a vast domain belonging to a family allied to the last king of Poland. But for many decades a Jewish family of businessmen, the Rosenstocks, had been buying up, bit by bit, any Galician land that the voluntarily expatriate Princes Poniatowski wished to sell. Nowosiolka had been held by the Rosenstocks for quite a while when Theodor, not averse to pressing a bargain, began urgently to want it. Kobylowloki under Joseph's management had reached a point of perfection that could be followed by recession. It was ripe for the market. But what to do with the family, grown restive? Joseph longed for work of greater scope and for exciting recreation in congenial company. Ann planned reconstructions and large-scale redecorations of the desirable rambling house of Nowosiolka. Theodora dreamed of painting seriously, with a properly trained teacher. L was champing to get to school. He might start at Skalat (so large a village that it was almost a town) or at Trembowla (quite a town) and, in either case, go on to the classical gymnasium at Tarnopol. This roughly corresponded to the best of English grammar schools, but its certificate—if he there completed his studies—would open the university to him with no further tests, written or oral. Yet Ella was, for once, the most absent-minded and harassed member of the household. Increasingly bothered by a perplexity of suitors she had turned down all but the most eligible, and still was left with three. It was typical of the region that the richest suitor was a Roman Catholic, the next in importance a Protestant (not exactly of the same sect as Ella's mother), and the third a member of the Ruthenian Church (of the Eastern Rite). The first was a well-to-do farmer, but an occasional heavy drinker and then inclined to beat up anyone within reach; the second, sober, stern, and intent on bettering himself in his trade, had insisted a little too much that he would never reproach Ella for being the child of a peasant-woman's irregular and transient association with a man far above her station; the third, with a heart of gold, was a happy-go-lucky younger son of a family long connected with horse-breeding under the patronage of a great local family largely responsible for introducing English stock into the Pantalicha. A brilliant dancer, he also sang solo parts in the church choir but, delighted with his lot, lacked drive.

Unconventionally and more wisely than she knew, Ella made of L her confidant and revealed to him (unaware of doing so) that there could be practical considerations for, and against, a marriage regarded as a problem—possibly difficult but not insoluble. L, keenly interested and mustering in his mind combinations of advantages and disadvantages for Ella's happiness, found himself in need of more and more concrete information. But the weighing of facts, whatever their number, proved to be inconclusive; and Ella soon turned for additional guidance to religion. At home she prayed for the right inspiration and, when this seemed uncertain or slow to come, took to going to church. In the absence of a Protestant chapel in the region, she went to the nearest church of the Roman Catholics or of the Ruthenians. Neither was near, but both could be reached in the vehicle put by Ann at Ella's disposal to this end—a light, one-horse trap, easily transferred from wheels to runners in winter. Whichever man she married, Ella would as a matter of course become a parishioner where he was; that she should know more of both Churches was all to the good. On her drives she always took with her L, and sometimes Theodora too. The boy and his nurse soon agreed that the Eastern Church—small, dark, and uncluttered with pews—seemed better to serve their purpose. Through the silent congregation, standing or kneeling, they would thread their way to a large ikon of the Mother of Jesus—Ella felt her problem to be essentially a woman's and to be best dealt with by the greatest of women. As they took up their position at a foot or two from the ikon, the pool of candlelight floating between them and the image would flicker, casting quick little shadows on the enigmatic ancient face whose eyelids and lips would seem to move. Ella prayed fervently. L prayed hard; and under inexpert guidance soon turned the Virgin Mary into an object of almost exclusive, passionate devotion.

In the end the departure from Kobylowloki was hurried. A buyer, having agreed to pay a handsome price, insisted on moving in while Rosenstock still refused to sell Nowosiolka but, pressed to do so, suggested instead a ten years' lease which Theodor might then prolong for another five. Although not the bargain Theodor had been waiting for, it was not a bad offer in the circumstances. He agreed, and the family's pent-up energies broke into a spurt of agitation. It was the summer of 1896.

Nowosiolka's dilapidated mansion filled with workmen while the family prepared to settle down for the rest of the building season in a half-timbered forester's lodge near by. For L the move was more than a change: it was a spate of revelations. The lodge stood just inside a plantation of fine mature oaks, some of which were being felled. Their first impact on him continued vivid to his death. The sight, the smell, the sounds, the presence of trees never ceased to evoke in L a sense of wonder; and the most moving friendship of his old age was largely based on a shared enthusiasm for them.

Stirred to life by new impressions, questions burgeoned in his mind. As no one appeared anxious to discuss with him these matters of moment, he took to puzzling out the answers for himself. The genesis of wind intrigued him. In the steppes it was invigorating, scented with flowers or grasses, unless, thick with dust or snow, it obscured the sight and tickled the nose and throat. At Nowosiolka it blew softly when the great trees gently waved their top branches and it blew strong when they tossed about, creaking with the effort. L had noticed Thérèse and seen others use their fans on hot still days; he concluded it was the trees that generated the wind by a vast concerted movement. Later, as the autumn hardened into winter, he observed a crust of ice forming on puddles and then noticed that the water under the crust had disappeared, leaving an empty space between the thin sheet of ice and the ground. If you stamped on the ice it broke, tumbling down in fragments to the bottom of what had been a pool. He concluded that the internal heat of the earth dried up the water when a spot was isolated from cold air by a blanket of ice, however thin.

Soon after their arrival at the lodge and right into early autumn, the children went for long walks, their first. Usually they were accompanied by Ella, several large dogs left behind by the forester on holiday, and a man detailed to watch over them. In the open steppes limitless to the eye, no one went for walks, but in the shady woodlands of Nowosiolka walking was a pleasure. And sometimes the children and servants, enraptured with movement and discovery, forgot the hour. On their return they might easily find a meal served and Joseph, watch in hand, pacing the dining-room floor. To him food was increasingly important while life's minutiae swelled into obsessions. On every possible occasion he insisted that hands should be scrubbed and mouths rinsed, hats worn against the sun however weak, and mufflers against the wind however gentle. He ordered that rooms should be aired while no one was there, yet windows be promptly shut if anyone entered. With his hypochondria noticeably fanning out, he lived in horror of anyone's illness or death, dwelt on his own imminent demise and, with meticulous grandiloquence, explained the reasons for his strict orders.

From the start his children had been unlike each other. At Nowosiolka their difference in character and temperament became striking, with their reaction to Joseph serving as catalyst. Theodora, seeing her father with his watch in hand, would run forward to beg his forgiveness with a pretty display of amused affection—

she did not take his foibles too seriously and loved him none the less; L would stop, scowl, and slowly walk off to wash before being told to. Already a pattern of relationships could have been traced. It was to endure. Until Joseph's death between the two World Wars he and his daughter greatly enjoyed each other's company; while father and son seemed to have been foredoomed to jar on each other's nerves.

In the period of transition, while living in the oak wood, the children's greatest joy was visiting on foot a distant orchard where—in a cluster of huts linked together by passages snugly boarded up or only floored and roofed over—lived a gnarled old bee-keeper with shaven chin, a splendid moustache and fuzzy side-whiskers. In his strange assortment of clothes he cut a romantic figure and, having served as a soldier in foreign parts when young, had many a tall story. Yet the children liked him chiefly because they found his life sad: his betrothed had died while he was away and he lived alone, calling his bees his children but loving children even more than bees. He would feed L and Theodora on honey and plums, cherries, pears, or whatever fruit was in season. Between keeping them agape with his tales, true or invented, he would discuss in clipped undertones with Ella and the manservant matters of common interest such as the mating of his two bitches with this or that dog they had brought along. L, attentive on the outskirts of their talking, learnt about the customs on which was based the disposal of puppies from mixed unions, between a bitch and a dog of different households. Everything he heard or saw, there or elsewhere, was food for his mind.

Ella's first move to start on the way home was the cue for a tussle in the orchard that soon became traditional. The bee-keeper would attempt to fill the pockets of his guests with choice fruits; they waved him back—already they had had more than enough. He tried to slip in here and there one more plum or pear; they shrilly protested, zig-zagging backwards, cavorting away to the gate. Later, near home (because unsure of Joseph) the children would force themselves to gobble up their fruit; and L vividly remembered its being more tasty, more juicy and aromatic, than any eaten sedately in the orchard. Yet as he hurriedly munched and swallowed, he sadly foresaw another attack of indigestion from which Theodora, to his mortification, seemed immune.

The days were drawing in, the nights were growing cold, the forester was coming back from his holiday in Canada, but the workmen were far from finished with their tasks at the big house. Again Theodor came to the rescue: Ella and the children had best come to stay with him in town, while the parents roughed it in the few rooms by now completely ready, and the house-servants made the best of a fluid situation bound to get better from day to day or, at least, from week to week. Anyhow the forester, a valuable man, was on no account to be hindered in his work, or upset.

Much as L liked living in the oak wood, a visit to Tarnopol (and without his parents) delighted him. He was so keyed up for enjoyment that when Theodor suggested taking him into the Pantalicha to look over with a master's eye the horses, cattle, donkeys, and goats, about to be rounded up for moving into winter quarters, anticipation robbed him of sleep. Dismayed, he felt an irritable langour creep over him. Setting his teeth, with an energy akin to despair he steeled himself to stifle it and miss nothing, to enjoy every minute of the rare event.

On their drive through the muddy little towns of Skalat and Trembowla to Darachow, grandfather and grandson discovered each other and liked what they found. Darachow's stolid squat house, enlarged by the unusual absence of shrill voices and patter-ing feet, received—as into a cup held ready—the shy new friend-ship of the old man and the small boy. After a night of sleep so heavy he might have been drugged, L woke early, alert and excited though vaguely indisposed. At the first glimmer, in a cold world emerging out of darkness into light and warmth—a world of flat grey shapes that bulged as they gained colour—the two drove out again, in happy silence, their backs to the rising sun.

Grass lands are not spectacular. But those who know them well find differences between one region and another. The Pantalicha was as unlike the country round Kobylowloki as flat grass land could be; and it still was, in the last century, the most impressive part of Strussow—a vast complex of steppes that took its name from (or gave it to) the Sturs, Polish knights of considerable antiquity, later supplanted by the aristocratic Baworowskis out of

whose hands the territory began to slip piecemeal. A flat water-
shed, rising high between the Strypa and the Seret, two sizeable
rivers, it then still was cut across, or meandered through, by slow
streams inclined to spread into lakes, ponds, marshes, and bog.
Rehman, who devoted many years to its exploration, classified
the Pantalicha as belonging to the system of grass lands which
stretches across Eastern Europe right away into Siberia. In many
parts of it he found a Siberian grass (*Sonecillus glauca Cass.*) locally
called *starczik*. And everywhere was an abundance of flowers and
grasses. The vast, well-watered table-land curved down to its two
dominant rivers in wide sweeps, steep to begin with but presently
flattening out. Men kept to the river banks which they cultivated
and had dotted about with crouched dwellings. The raised flat
land was left to the huge untended herds of horses and long-
horned dun cattle (Poles have described their colour to me as
café-au-lait, ranging from much coffee and little milk to much
milk and little coffee); there they roamed from spring to autumn,
trampling, fouling, destroying the lush plant life as they went.

Theodor's strong pair of horses easily drew his spacious
wooden cart up into the table-land. The wide expanses touched
off in L the sort of experience a fledgling must have when it first
spreads its wings. He was intoxicated, exhilarated, and felt dizzy,
but on reaching the herds he was all attention, and Theodor,
noting his intelligent interest, was well pleased. Catching sight
more than once of his grandfather's approving glance, L glowed
with a satisfaction new to him. But at noon, when the men squatted
down in small groups round bonfires and he found himself sitting
fairly near Theodor yet with his back to him, L took advantage of
this to refuse all but liquid food. He felt too sluggish to move
unless prodded, and far below the root of his tongue was a
thickening which swelled into a dull ache at every gulp. He was
going through the final stages of a steeply rising fever. His basically inert body was yet jerked into febrile activity by his darting
adventurous mind, close-bound to his senses with their painfully
heightened response to challenge or irritation. As grandfather and
grandson presently moved on to other herds, the thickening rose
higher in L's throat and stifled him. He no longer could give full-
voiced answers to full-voiced remarks, yet continued resolutely

to move about on foot whenever Theodor did, and avidly to look and listen, and to store in his tenacious mind whatever he saw or heard. When the last lot of cattle had been sized up and the cart-horses' heads were turned for home L swooned off. He lay in a huddle at the bottom of the cart—unsprung but with an abundance of soft hay firmly packed between its floor and the thick heavy carpet on which Theodor sat and L dozed. As Theodor spoke L came to. In measured words the old man declared his approval of the day, rounding off with an announcement that was a promise. At the age of ten L would come to live at the Tarnopol house during term time. His morning walk to the gymnasium and the walk back in time for a late lunch should keep him fit, however arduous his studies. This crowning joy of a memorable day opened in L's mind a floodgate through which words began to rush. But his throat, acting independently, held back the flood. Only a very few heavy ones pushed through. Himself a man of monosyllables by preference, though a dab at commercial patter, Theodor once again approved, and confirmed it by clamping a heavy, protective hand on the boy's shoulder.

When they reached Darachow L was in no condition to move or speak. They carried him into the house. By candlelight Theodor and his servant realized how ill the child was. They wrapped him in blankets and sheepskin rugs. Horses that had been resting for the long drive to Tarnopol on the following day were at once harnessed to the barouche. And immediately after a hurried meal Theodor and his man started out on their night journey, taking it in turns to bear the main weight of the boy, wrapped like a mummy. He was big and heavy for his age.

The doctor said it was diphtheria, and the household was at once adjusted to provide reasonable isolation for a child seen as a source of danger. Days later L apprehended in quick succession the bliss of tranquillity, a smell of medicine and disinfectant, and the sustaining presence of Ella. He knew himself to be well cared for and happy, but the thread of lucidity, too weak to endure, dissolved. After a while another formed, to the modulations of Ann's voice. She stood in the doorway. Her arms were round Ella who was weeping, but her words sped past Ella, to him. He was their treasure, she could never thank Ella enough. Ella, between

27

sobs, repeated that she was not really crying, that she was crying because of relief, that it was too much to know the child was out of danger and to have Ann there, thanking her so kindly, and taking Theodora back to Nowosiolka—such an easing of responsibilities. L's eyes were on Ann. In a voice betraying emotion, she said the doctor had advised her not to come near L but that he would soon be strong enough for Ella to bring him home. Leaving, she blew him a kiss.

Throughout convalescence L felt he was emerging from an ancient, fossilized cocoon of unhappiness. Life smiled on him. Ella was even more kind and understanding than before. Affectionate messages from Theodor came up to him regularly, together with tit-bits from other members of the household. Everyone seemed to rejoice that he should be alive, still among them and on the mend, while at Nowosiolka Ann was giving special attention to the decoration of his room and growing impatient for his return. For the first time her son realized that she loved him with a robust tenderness not unlike Theodor's. His recovery was spectacular.

At last pronounced fit for the journey, L was received at Nowosiolka in a mood resembling a family party; only that he was immediately put to bed. Next morning he woke early, delighted that the first thing his eyes should rest on was the print of French soldiers defending their redoubt. Almost at once Ann crept in, straight from bed, wrapped in a flowing garment that fell round her in pale, soft folds. Seeing her son awake she hurried forward and clasped him in her arms. As he snuggled up to her she murmured words of endearment he did not remember having heard from her before. As Ann matured and gained the assurance that her marriage was not a dismal failure, she came to resemble, in certain little things, her sister Thérèse.

CHAPTER THREE

Wings and Feelers
1896–1906

With Kobylowloki a thing of the past, the parents' period of probation was over; and at Nowosiolka they found a steady bond in knowing they had made good together. The children, irrepressibly bounding into life, cried out for civilized surroundings where fully and comfortably to develop, and they fed back in return, to the household that was shaping them, a certain measure of zestful fearlessness and steely drive. The zestful fearlessness came more noticeably from Theodora while the steely drive sprang in larger measure from the delicate boy. Perseverance despite all odds often marks an especially gifted child. None the less, sharing everything, each child seemed to acquire the characteristic quality of the other.

That winter, too, in their new home the parents found a common interest for their hours of leisure. They began building up a library noted nine years later by Stanislaw Kot for—among other rare books—its fine full edition of General Montecuculi's works on military science, geometry, history, and architecture. The best of the suitable rooms was chosen for the library by Joseph with help from all. As months and years went by, the book-lined walls came to reflect, with surprising accuracy, the mind and interests of each member of the family. There was a family likeness throughout the collection but there were also many pronounced, possibly irreconcilable, differences. And while the four minds were discovering one another as they gravitated towards the library, each pair of book-collectors—the young and the old—found within itself a community of interests but considerable divergencies in taste. Less overtly, two criss-cross friendships began to form at Nowosiolka: of father and daughter, and mother and son. These complex relations, and the involved tensions generated by them, drew the family into a unified entity that had still been dormant, or rudimentary, at Kobylowloki where each member coped singly with strains and stresses fostered by the general situation. Besides, for the next ten years the children's education was their own and their elders' engrossing concern.

Under Austrian law, in Galicia as elsewhere, every child was obliged to attend school from the age of about seven, and L had grounds to hope that he might at once go to a local primary school. But Joseph would not hear of it. From the pinnacles of his Warsaw education he looked askance at Ukrainian lower-grade schooling and despised the pupils' manners and tone. To L's distress the law on education allowed parents to have their children taught at home provided certain formalities were observed and the instruction was up to standard. The formalities were easy to observe and Joseph's children received a grounding in all subjects superior to that offered by the State. But, inclined to argue, and to elaborate his arguments till sheer accumulation made them sound incontrovertible, Joseph querulously pointed out time and again that L's poor health was the ultimate reason for his being kept at home—the well-being of others mattered quite as much as his. This the boy passionately resented. When small he had seldom been among children because of frequent stomach trouble and vomiting. Soon after his recovery from diphtheria he developed an almost chronic inflammation of the eyelids, and blockages in the nose which would today no doubt be diagnosed as severe sinus trouble. More often than not he felt stupefied by dull pain in the head and face. Joseph quickly talked himself into believing these symptoms to be infectious, yet he insisted that the surgical knife, expertly used, would free L of all discomfort and make him fit at last to mix with rough little boys. The drastic character of surgery fascinated Joseph. To him the irreversible removal of an evil thing appeared unquestionably good. He took to musing aloud about a visit to Vienna: only the two of them, he and the boy, who might be operated upon.

The effect on L was disastrous. Not only did he feel once again singled out as unfit to mix with children of his own age and sex, but his bodily suffering was now used to hinder his development into a socially adequate boy. Coddled to distraction, he increas-

1. L's paternal grandmother, Balbina

2. L's maternal grandfather, Theodor Sommersztajn

ingly yearned for the rough and tumble of classmates who, in their harsh unthinking way, might well have knocked out of him his tendency to exaggerate daily vexations which piled up into violent resentments akin to hate. He had to a high degree the gift, possessed by more children than is realized, of ardently seeking situations that might well be painful but could prove salutary in the long run.

But no, instead of being encouraged to become more independent through contact with other boys, L was further exasperated by yet another parental reason for keeping him at home. Most of the lower-grade schoolboys spoke Ukrainian among themselves though instruction at school was in Polish. Joseph, easily intoxicated by the flow of words, was intellectually fascinated by languages and knew more than one: Polish spoken in his home and that of his parents; Russian, the official language in the days and places of his own schooling; German, the language of the Austro-Hungarian Empire; English and French, deemed great because of their literary and legal traditions. But Ukrainian was to him no language at all. To make this clear he solemnly forbade his children to pick it up from anyone, especially from the servants whose native tongue it was. Later L put down to this interdict—or parental fad—a 'certain, conditioned' deafness as he called it, a distressing habit of hearing without taking in conversations of which he was, so to speak, forbidden to grasp the meaning. He also traced to those years his passionate siding with the 'Ruthenians', or Ukrainians,[1] when their attrition became a feature of Polish politics in 1919.

Meantime, in the new year of 1897, under pressure from Theodor, it was decided at Nowosiolka that on reaching the age of eleven and ten both children would regularly be staying with him at Tarnopol in order to attend the best schools in the district: Theodora the girls' gymnasium, L the boys'. Mina, Theodor's wife, jibbed at the idea but he remained firm. He wanted his grandchildren there, and have them he would. When she protested too much he silenced her by remarking that he anyway meant to leave his town house to his eldest daughter together with enough capital to run two households—a decision he had made known to

[1] See Appendix for an explanation of the terms 'Ruthenian' and 'Ukrainian'.

Ann some time earlier. Shocked to her financial core Mina was filled with wild apprehension for the security of her own children whose numbers had been steadily increasing at the rate of one a year. The alarm resounded throughout her family. Aunts, uncles, and the remotest cousins stirred, prophesying disaster now that the dangerous Ann and her detestable son—unaccountably loved by Theodor—had moved nearer to the moneyed man. And while the touching friendship between grandfather and grandson increased, relations between the two families grew strained.

While waiting for his tenth birthday, L was developing his ability to enjoy private happiness despite all odds. Of the present he accepted with full relish only the outdoor life that he and Theodora led. As the family doctor wished him to read less and be out more, there came to Nowosiolka among other educators a retired cavalry officer. From him the children learnt, during long hours which would otherwise have been spent at lessons, the correct essentials of riding and as much expert skating as any child could wish for. Under his supervision, in the summer of 1897, they explored on horseback virtually the whole neighbourhood. Before the summer was over they began to compete with each other in jumping ditches and other natural obstacles, and, when alone together, dared each other to do more than their instructor would have thought wise. Only snow, once again falling thick on stretches of freezing mud, finally put a stop to their riding. In a matter of days they had turned into skating enthusiasts. But Theodor, looking ahead to a new open season, sent word that he intended to give them a horse each, to own and to cherish.

After Christmas Ella had a second bout of churchgoing. Her former suitors, fed up with her indecisions, had made other arrangements and had withdrawn from her sphere of preoccupations. But in Skalat lived a well-to-do artisan tradesman, a widower with one small daughter. As the little girl and Ella had fallen for each other almost at sight, the child's father was quick to conclude that marriage with the rich children's nurse would solve his problems beautifully. She once again felt uncertain; yet she now apparently needed only persuasion, and time in which to assimilate it.

The large Ruthenian church of Saints Cosmo and Damian

stood at a short distance from land farmed by Joseph on the town side of his property. Once again, Ella and L took up their station in front of a favourite ikon. But it was now L who bought the votive candles and fixed them securely into the ample, worn sockets, which, if a candle was not to topple over, had first to be half-filled with little drips of melted wax. To his almost forgotten adoration he returned with new fervour, more mature and even slightly reasoned. On the surface of his life were his conflicts with Joseph, his new friendships with Theodor and Ann, his love-hate for Theodora, and his dread of not being an ordinary boy fit to mix with others; yet below the surface was the enigma of God, accepted as loving and just, but obviously doing nothing about much that was outrageous in L's life. Between these two regions— oddly torn apart—dwelt the Virgin, immeasurably hurt yet giving comfort, sorely deprived yet bestowing on all who asked for it an understanding which turned devotion to her into forgiveness of others. L had recognized in himself a reluctance to forgive, and he had become hazily aware that to escape a subtle distortion he must learn to forgive through being forgiven.

About this time both children began to suspect that all was not well with their mother. She was getting fat and, once again, irritable. She wanted to be everywhere yet stayed much in her room, and Ella showed unusual concern for her. At Cosmo and Damian's L was told in whispers to pray for Ann's health, for the welfare of a little stranger and his mother, and for families with little children on the way. He thought Ella meant children travelling about, perhaps with a grandfather, and wondered—he would have much preferred that to staying at home.

On the day Ann had her miscarriage the children's instructor kept them out of the house for as long as he could, skating on the distant lake. After dusk, excited as well as pleasantly tired, they romped home to be told in hushed voices that Ann had been taken ill, that three doctors were there, and no noise was to be made. The library was the best place for them. In the last half-year L had been taking down from Ann's shelves books on animals, vines and fruit-trees, and from Joseph's, books on philosophy. He had also glanced through a handsome illustrated quarto of *The Decameron,* but this he dismissed as monotonous, even tedious;

whereas certain little books on gaming and the art of winning he studied carefully. Whatever he understood in any book he never forgot, and throughout the harassment of his mother's long incomprehensible illness, enjoyed many animated discussions on a variety of topics with the doctors who came and went. One of them, something of a local champion, L beat more than once at chess.

While Ann's life was still in the balance a confidential messenger arrived, bidding Joseph hurry to Tarnopol where Theodor, critically ill, needed help to make a testament leaving Ann the bulk of his fortune. Without hesitation Joseph sent the man back to say he could not think of leaving Ann's bedside for the three days or so the visit would entail. She was at death's door, and if she died he and his sorrowing children would hardly survive. Of what use was money to them now?

Before Ann recovered, Theodor had died intestate and she inherited only her due. Under Austrian law legacies were divided into as many equal parts as there were children, each of whom yearly gave a surviving mother an appointed portion of his inheritance. A depression like the old gloom of Kobylowloki settled on Nowosiolka. Ann was slow to get back her energy and the little she did muster was squandered, with Joseph's help, on regrets about the irremediable past and fear of more ill luck to come.

L's tenth birthday, the date most eagerly looked forward to in his short life, was a disaster. He raised with his father the matter of arrangements for going to the Tarnopol gymnasium. Mina could not be asked to have Theodor's grandchildren in her house: rumours that her relatives had disgracefully thwarted his last efforts to get in a lawyer—so that Ann might inherit more than her share—aggravated the mutual enmity of the two households. Gossip, busily retold, had led to a breakdown of communications. Where in Tarnopol could L and Theodora stay while things tided over? The answer was nowhere.

Seething with rage L flung himself into protracted arguments with Joseph. Never had they spoken to each other so much, so often, or for so long. Never again were they to face each other in so down-to-the-bone yet flamboyant a series of encounters in which they exposed, rather than formulated, the incompatibility of their wishes and the divergence of their judgements on what was right or wrong. Neither forgave or forgot the words hurled at or by him in that summer's clash. Fertile ground for new animosities, it was fed for years by streams of anger flowing back to keep its insults green.

In the course of the most bitter show-down of them all, L was told off-hand—merely to support some point Joseph was pressing home—that no one in the family was a Christian nor even a Jew, in the religious sense. Yet, entered as a Jew in the Warsaw books, L was obliged to stick to the fiction. His was a somewhat delicate situation. But it did not matter. The prevalent local leniency, which older people would have condemned as laxity, made it easy to avoid any tinge of unpleasantness. For some sort of examination in religion he would have to sit at some time, but local priests and rabbis were amenable to reason; everything would run smoothly and no one would be any the wiser. He must only obey implicitly those who understood the situation better than he could, those who were intent on doing everything for the best, his best, and were dexterous at handling affairs. The right approach was to consider the course they were following as a somewhat tricky piece of daily routine. All L had to remember was his rather unusual position of being neither a Christian nor a Jew, in short his being 'nothing'.

To L's dismay Ann wearily, but firmly, supported Joseph. In a leap of impassioned indignation against his universe L unleashed his imagination. He saw his parents wantonly wrenching him away from Christ, his anchor of security, and away from Christ's mother, his one source of comfort, and he rebelled. Never again did he go to church with Ella. He dismissed from his mind all thought of God and was glad to see every trace of his religious feeling wither. When the thunderous acrimony died down he was left without respect for his parents and bereft of their celestial counterparts' protection. Most importantly, Joseph affirmed his son to be nothing. 'Nothing . . . nothing' resounded in the child's mind and reverberated in his memory opening up for him a numinous void. Whether in him or round him, it remained with L for life.

Theodora, no less amazed than L to learn that they were not Christians, treated the revelation with customary common sense. At some opportune moment she would join the Church together with the whole family since they all meant to, though no one had got down to it. As to school, she was glad rather than sorry to continue riding, skating, and painting for much of the day. In time, she took it, her brother and she would sit for their examinations at Tarnopol as did most of the richer landowners' children without ever having attended school. The two would pass brilliantly. Nothing could be simpler or nicer. She failed to see why he made a fuss.

Theodora was totally unable to grasp that her brother felt bereft to the point of channelling his abilities and imagination into plans of escape from under the paternal roof. With Theodor's loving support gone, Ann siding with Joseph, and the ghastly void looming where a naïve, hodge-podge religion had been, there was nothing to hope for at Nowosiolka. But the romantic solution was not followed through. Instead, the entire family, with Ella and two menservants, spent five winter months (1898-9) in the Alps at Merano in a cosy Tyrolean house on a sunny hillside. Their financial situation was good. Ann's money—the second half of her dowry, handed over together with her portion of the inheritance—made a tidy sum. It was wise to spend generously on restoring her health. And, in the long run, everyone benefited from the change.

Up to the midsummer upheaval L's life had been—as he later saw it—three-quarters private, interior, and one-quarter communal, shared with others. At Merano he strove to stifle as much as he could of that in him which was incommunicable; and soon his readjustment was speeded up by the parents' deciding to leave the children and servants among the snowhills and descend alone into Italy. They were away for over two months, revisiting Verona, Venice, and the lakes. Here and there they lingered in casinos and tried their luck at the tables. Joseph was cautious. He accepted a limit for his losses, and, when he won, quietly carried away his luck-money. Ann had become his mascot; but while his appreciation of her increased, so did his fear of losing her. He hovered about, murmuring pained requests that she should avoid all possibility of accidents and infections, otherwise, he said, anxiety would drive him to an early grave.

During the parents' absence in Italy the children and servants drew closer together. The local language being German, not Polish, all drifted into speaking Ukrainian among themselves. For once, too, the hour of meals was flexible. Daylight being obviously precious, the easy-going adults minded little when exactly their charges ate, or what, so long as they had plenty of it; and appetites were vast. L's health improved, he felt at ease and was happy. Later he counted the unsupervised yet pampered months at Merano as the best of his childhood. By the time the parents rejoined them he could even accept his father's foibles more lightly, if a shade ironically. In the following weeks, while Theodora's painting entered a romantic phase, L's taste for caricature surfaced and established itself. He was never to be any good with a pencil, but his minute observation was true, and his visual juxtapositions and conclusions were startling. His wit was never banal, nor was it ever vulgar—its bite went too deep for that.

To Nowosiolka the family returned early in spring, refreshed, and relieved that father and son should have apparently buried their hatchets. Much ingenuity was deployed and energy was lavishly spent on new arrangements for the children's education. Ann took in hand the general planning and left to Joseph the painstaking elaboration of the details he so much enjoyed. She had realized that above all her son needed for daily companion a gifted mentor, able to develop his intellectual abilities and the physical prowess he aspired to. The task of finding the right man she delegated to Joseph who, after widespread inquiries, introduced into her presence Edmond Weissberg—a freelance journalist soon to be known as the brilliant leader-writer E. Borecki. Brawny, fair-haired, and so good-looking that Theodora some years later made him pose for a much admired prize-winning picture of Wagner's Siegfried, Weissberg was an all-round athlete (though chiefly a pugilist) with a well-equipped mind and courage bordering on effrontery. Ann, at first glance taken aback by such good looks, soon warmed to him. She had made up her mind that the children's happiness depended on the family being from now on definitely recognized as of Jewish descent, with strong Christian sympathies and Polish enthusiasms. In the children's tutor she was lucky to find a man of good Jewish stock, with a knowledge of Polish history and literature rare even in the circles where he moved, and a remarkable grasp of the complexities that bedevilled Austrian domestic politics. Passionately ethical, deeply concerned with every manner of underdog who came to his notice, he took religion to be nonsense which yet had its uses as a potent tranquillizer for the feeble-minded and the hopelessly under-privileged—exactly her own views.

Weissberg's ability in handling adolescents and his dexterity in arranging the lives of others to their satisfaction won the children over in no time. They accepted him as a heaven-sent agent, made specially to suit their needs and having nothing in common with the ordinary dim teachers and governesses who came and went and changed endlessly. For a time he was the dominant influence in L's life, and Ella, now at a loose end, soon came to feel that, for her, marriage was the right course.

Ann declared herself Ella's mother by proxy. The girl, already an old spinster by local standards, was being married from her house. The marriage settlement was gone into with care, and presents which amounted to a handsome dowry were showered upon the bride. At Ann's suggestion, too, certain alterations were made in the widower's solid one-storey house and his unsatisfactory garden. In the next four or five years L often rode over to see Ella. He was careful to admire, at the appropriate season, the rich garlands of cobheads or tobacco leaves hung out to dry on the pale blue outer walls—a dash of blue in the whitewash was the sign of a house-proud owner.

During these visits and the meditative rides home, L often pondered the degradation that marriage could bring to a good and conscientious woman. It was coarsening Ella, narrowing down her sphere of interests to a trumpery routine till there was no possible topic of conversation with her beyond a purely matter-of-fact exchange of inquiries and information. Yet she had an adequate servant-girl whom she had trained in much of the domesticity she had herself learnt from Ann. The trouble rested with her husband, his relatives, and friends—their minds were rough and narrow. Once again, and as before unknown to her,

Ella's life and personality were affecting the mind and character of the boy. They were building up in him an intense sympathy for the submerged and inarticulate part of the population whose vision was sadly limited. Later he put his compassion into words: 'We who talk much are unable to gauge the effect of reticence forced upon those whom life makes dumb.' Her spoilt life also increased his sense of guilt when his first marriage foundered.

None the less Weissberg's was now the chief influence, and under his attentive eye, L was encouraged to wrestle and spar with boys of his own size. Sometimes a few rode out together, and L would gallop away ahead of them to a hilltop. Waiting to be joined he observed the wide horizon and noted details with such care that years later, in June 1919, he could write in derisive anger of a mis-statement by the English representative on an unofficial Allied Commission that was moving between Warsaw and Galicia, 'His statement is a ridiculous mare's nest. . . . He claims to have been to Tarnopol and Skalat and that he knows "there are no windmills". Even in such factual detail he is inaccurate. . . .' There follows a lyrical passage on the exact position of a 'beautiful windmill'. Yet Ann, though satisfied with Weissberg's steering of her children, was not happy. Joseph obstinately refused to give her the details of dangerous financial operations he was probing or letting himself be drawn into. His avowed reason—to spare her the worries that he himself suffered—was probably true. But clear-minded, straightforward and courageous as she was, his upset mien, evasions and heavy sighs kept her in a turmoil of anxiety at least equal to his own. Of this the children got only the backwash. True, L keenly observed the symptoms. But even he was being diverted. Branch-railways were modifying social intercourse. Staying away from home was becoming somewhat less of an event, shorter visits were coming in, and the children's expeditions to Tarnopol, when the time came for them to sit for their yearly pass-certificates at the gymnasium, were relatively easy. But not for long was this enough for Theodora and L. Full of pent-up restlessness they wanted to get away, to know other people, other lands, the tang of a different life. For reasons of his own, Joseph fell in with his children's mood. Financial dreams were leading his mind to Vienna. Preoccupied with his health, he had arranged to see there several famous doctors, and had decided it was time, too, for L to have the best possible opinion on the blockage in his nose and about his eyelids, still periodically inflamed.

In the winter of 1902–3 the family were in Vienna for over two months—staying chiefly with relations—while the children's tutor returned to Lwow to play a more active part in running a young socialist group called Mlodziez and a political journal called *Promien* (the Sunray). On L, his tutor's political involvements left an indelible mark. A perceptive child, he had noted, early on, the distinctions between Poles and Ruthenians. Under his father's roof, in the neighbouring villages, and wherever he went in Galicia, he distinguished the one from the other as a matter of course. They spoke different languages, worshipped in separate churches, dressed differently on festive days. Their songs and the traditional decorative detail on their clothes, household vessels, or farm implements, were not the same—most Poles recognizing those of the Ruthenians as more colourful. Necessity had spun between the two nations a fine fabric of conventions which blurred or cushioned unpleasantness at the junctions or overlappings of interests. Yet many edges remained dangerously jagged. Hoary resentments were continually increased by new rancours, and on both sides grudges were piling up. To L's untutored perception of the sullen enmity smouldering between the two interlocked ethnic groups, each devoted to its ancient ways but jostling the other at lamentably close quarters, Weissberg added an informed awareness of political and economic conflicts between the owners of the land (almost exclusively Poles in that region) and the tillers of the soil (almost exclusively Ruthenians). Polish socialist preoccupations and problems, as they were in the days of his boyhood, were to colour L's political outlook for life.

Whatever elaborations of thought he reached in time, all stemmed in some circuitous way from the convictions of Weissberg, the brilliant publicist steeped in the Galician-Polish mood prevalent at the turn of the century. The general political and economic assumptions were Marxist, but the urgent concern was with agrarian reform—the righting of the dispossessed native Ruthenian peasantry's wrongs; a concern which was reinforced by a mounting sense of outrage at vast acres too often seen to be mismanaged by the stewards of absentee landlords. The cumulative regional irritation—which overstressed the significance of occupational, traditional, and linguistic differences—had long been feeding separatist dreams. Given that all Polish lands (in Prussia, Russia, and Austria-Hungary) would one day revert to the Poles, would it not be just for tracts of land tilled by Ruthenians to form a separate state, with laws better suited to the Ruthenian peasants, not exclusively to their Polish landlords? Under Weissberg's tutoring L's socialism and nationalism acquired a romantic fervour; yet tutor and pupil continued firmly to believe in the importance of establishing a democratic legislation by strictly democratic means. Both were fundamentally law-abiding men. It is true that when the Polish Socialist Party (P.P.S.) gained nation-wide importance it developed some highly questionable off-shoots. That, however, was in the unforeseeable future; and the young socialist group that L was about to join remained, while he had anything to do with it, absolutely true to the P.P.S.'s basic ideals of total ethnic equality among nationalities headed and guided by the Poles. The principles were already laid down clearly. Their application was hopefully left to the emerging national leaders.

Like the Polish land itself, political parties were hobbled by circumstances beyond any patriot's control; and active political leaders had to be daring conspirators to achieve any measure of nation-wide repute. Brilliant organizing abilities alone could hardly captivate the dismembered nation's imagination. Naturally enough, the first political hero to fire L's imagination was Joseph Pilsudski, future Marshal and Polish Prime Minister, a romantic revolutionary nationalist. Later, in England, influenced by Fabians and others, L's socialism was to move toward aspirations for a Welfare State under Tory administration; but for the organic quality of a people's self-expression in its entire way of life he retained a passionate and sensitive admiration. The Dual Monarchy supplied him with much food for thought on the subject.

From about 1905 L began to find inconsistencies in the

programme of East European socialists. On the one hand they preached national self-determination as the due of every group that ardently wished to set itself free; on the other hand they proclaimed the 'universalism' (the one-ness) of all the dispossessed—a great body of people whose most ardent wishes were assumed to be identical. L's discernment of the inconsistency started that year, but only found its full expression forty-three years later, in a lecture ('Nationality and Liberty') delivered in Rome. But long before that he had realized that Austria-Hungary was irrevocably distintegrating into a multitude of conflicting peoples, to each of whom the land itself was the most important factor of the situation. Too many groups of men had been confusingly strewn about for too long over a vast area. The economic interests of certain groups and regions had cut across the passionate determination of each group to continue living, thinking, speaking, singing, and decorating its life in its own loved, time-honoured, customary way. Every people, he concluded, should have its own land where it can develop its genius in a manner suited to its own mind and heart. But how to achieve it? At the time of his first Vienna visit, L's aspiration was—like Weissberg's—that resurgent Poland should be administered by socialists with firm liberal intentions. But the visit itself he remembered, almost exclusively, for its unrelieved physical distress.

At once Joseph took his son to a renowned nose-and-throat specialist, and then to a highly recommended oculist. Both were devotees of surgery, men after his own heart. The boy's eyelids were operated upon and a crooked bone was removed from his nose. When all was over, one eyelid remained slightly distorted, giving the upper line of his eye a Mongolian tilt; and after a few years the unsupported flesh of his nose began to droop. By the time old age had come he used special nostril-props at night to prevent the collapsed flesh from blocking his nose and forcing open his mouth. If it did open, a sucking roar at once woke him. Already in his Vienna bed, lying in a darkened room and readjusting the icebags on his face, he suspected that the indignities and pain which Joseph and his cronies were inflicting upon him would prove worse than useless. Ann shared his misgivings; and although both maintained the strictest reticence on the matter, they again warmed to each other.

Theodora was the only one fully to enjoy the stay in Vienna. Before leaving Nowosiolka she had arranged through her aunt Thérèse to join a select private academy of art, and there she spent a few hours almost every day. Soon she found congenial company for going the round of museums and exhibitions, and by the time she left had formed one true friendship. Marie Beer, in her early twenties, was about to become engaged to a young officer. The Beers, like the Bernsztajns, were of pure Jewish stock, but it was Marie's great-grandfather who had lopped himself off the ancestral tree; her grandfather, a Roman Catholic as a matter of course, felt Austrian to the core. Marie, well set up, with fine features, an abundance of yellow hair, bright blue eyes, and a rosy complexion, had one lasting defect. Owing to a congenital malformation of a hip she walked with a slight limp and refused to dance or skate, but otherwise she carried it off well, was amusing, witty, and so brilliant a linguist that she counted on earning handsome pin-money before long by translating French and English novels into German. Painting and the study of art she had taken up with a view to achieving a home decorated and furnished with tempered originality. Theodora was immensely impressed and, bubbling with excitement, would invade L's sick-room for a while every day to talk of painting, pictures, the beauty of Vienna, and Marie. Irritated by such exuberance, L dubbed her new friend 'your chocolate-box Miss' whom he declared to be a stuck-up goose more likely than not. But as he mocked, curiosity stirred in him, and when they left for home without his having caught even a glimpse of Marie, he was rather cross.

No sooner had the children settled down to their old ways at Nowosiolka than Weissberg sprung a surprise on them. He was thinking vaguely of getting married, and for a variety of reasons had decided to devote his energies chiefly to municipal work in one of the larger townships. Of a sudden L was intellectually aware of the impermanence, the fluidity of human relations, and was brushed against by renewed panic emanating from his numinous void.

For his replacement Weissberg recommended a singularly

gifted young man—Adam (alias Arian) Heilpern, yet another polonized Jew. In the previous year Heilpern had graduated at the philosophical faculty of Lwow University and was currently writing his doctoral thesis for the University of Vienna. In it he dealt with matters important to the study of Slavonic languages— a field of learning on which he was to leave his mark while continuing fairly active in home politics. As a schoolboy he had joined the young socialist group and remained Weissberg's fast friend and supporter despite their diverging careers. His own chief enthusiasm was for teaching. In time he founded a Primary Schools' Association at Skalat and, in 1930, was appointed headmaster of the second Tarnopol gymnasium. But while still young he also delighted in exercising other abilities which struck rigorists as unsuited to his scholarly aspirations and official personality. He was known throughout Galicia for breaking in, with steely good-humour, the most intractable horses. If you had a really difficult one, you handed it over to him. And he was reputed to transfer his skills easily to a variety of tasks, concentrating on almost anything with admirable results. Of this gift he made good use during the Nazi rule in Vienna. Though no great musician he combined his early musical training with his dexterity in order to make violins. Secreted away under the roof of a house belonging to steadfast friends, he made there fiddle after fiddle which his protectors sold for a good price. They never got into trouble over him, and he survived the persecution and slaughter with his health impaired only by years of scanty food and a complete lack of outdoor exercise. When communications with England reopened, he wrote to L from Silesia telling of the general position, his own experiences, and Weissberg's violent death after many acts of hair-raising effrontery in the Resistance. Edmond, who changed his name to Wielinski during the 1918 de-Germanization of Poland, had been, some time between the two World Wars, deputy-mayor of Lodz. Because he had been well known as a Jew before 1918, his nordic looks and Polish name were of little use to him under the Nazis. Yet so convincing was his swagger, so brilliant his planning and plotting, so swift were his decisions and actions, that the enemy did him to death only in the last, most gruesome, months of their pervasive presence.

In the spring of 1903—with the tragedies to come still veiled—
Ann persuaded Weissberg to see L and Theodora through their
summer examinations while she set Heilpern to work on his thesis
comfortably, in the Nowosiolka library. Next, with her support,
Weissberg managed to persuade Joseph not to drag the boy off
to Vienna for more tinkering with his nose and eyelids, but to
let him go for a mountain holiday with his tutors into the Tatra
range of the Carpathians. To L's delight Joseph agreed, and at
Zakopane the two men applied themselves to freeing the boy
from tangles which hindered his development.

They were strange companions. Weissberg—on the large side
and almost dashing, with his brilliant grasp of political situations
and a jovial readiness for political adventure. Heilpern—tiny,
wiry, with a long pale face, eyes so mild that he had been nick-
named Jesusik, yet possessed by a veritable passion for language
and teaching. And L—the tormented adolescent in whom both
men had recognized an intellect superior to theirs. His gratitude
to both was great. As for Heilpern's so-called incongruities of
disposition, to L they were endearing. Men and women unconventionally put together already attracted him.

After some climbing, fairly stiff by the standards of the day, the
three bumped into a pair of more advanced climbers descending
from greater altitudes. Marian Kukiel (later C.G.S. to General
Sikorski) and Stanislawa Beres, recently engaged to be married,
were young socialists well known to Weissberg. Mountaineering
was at once given up in favour of animated discussions. For hours
on end the five walked about the airy lower slopes, absorbed in
topics of vital interest to them. It was in the Tatra, rather than at
Nowosiolka in the preceding months, that L's attitude to Weissberg and Heilpern defined itself, and that his taste for politics
acquired a new coherence. By the time the five tore themselves
away from the lovely leafiness of foothills overshadowed by
towering gaunt grey crags of granite and overlooked by higher,
paler snow-edged ranges, L was a different boy. Broader and
stronger, overtly resolute and much less moody.

Disentanglement from the family skein continued at Nowosiolka. The Vienna specialists, told about the dismal results of

their operations, had spoken enthusiastically to Joseph about certain corrective little incisions still to be made here and there. Convinced that they were right, he put their case to the family. But L, aware of discreet support from his mother and Heilpern, felt detached and listened to the brilliant performance with genuine, if amused, admiration. He was enjoying Joseph's mind, far superior to his own. Its misuse he judged to be deplorable. But then, to what use should a good mind be put? Heilpern was carefully laying the foundations of L's imaginative grasp of semantics based on a mass of sound evidence gathered in from the great family of Slavonic languages. As the new interest grew, L's fear of Joseph left him. Unable to dissuade his father from planning further tinkering with his face, L decided to play for time. Procrastination would be his course. There could be no immediate visit to Vienna anyhow. Lessons tied him to Nowosiolka and, since Heilpern would go from him one day as Weissberg had already gone, L was intent on absorbing his tutor's Vienna thesis, and much of the material it was based on, while the author and he lived under one roof. Besides, engaged in spreading the young socialists' nets in the neighbourhood and collecting their subscriptions, on that score too he wanted no disturbance. But as he deftly played for time, the situation, inseparable from his new attitude to life, sparked off in him a sense of urgency—a feeling for opportunities not to be missed: time was inexorable, destined to draw away into the irretrievable past all events, all situations, while each specific opportunity was still forming. A man's life was a race against time. Although disturbing, this had its compensations. Affecting all men, it made even Joseph manageable. Later, L's overwhelming sense of time's swift retrocession increased till it acquired the concreteness of physical sensations. More than once, when decisive and sustained action was imperative, he felt paralysed by too clear an awareness of time's implacable course. But while new, his vision of a moment's singular immediacy helped him to master situations as they came along.

When Heilpern's academic interests next took him to Lwow, L asked to go too. Was it not best for him to hand over personally his list of young socialists and the money he had raised? And

3b. A family portrait

3a. L and his sister as infants

4a. The house at Koszylowce (pronounced Koshilovtsi), restored after World War I

4b. Koszylowce outbuildings

was not this a splendid opportunity to visit the university with Heilpern, and be shown round by him? Joseph thought not, yet in the end waived his objections. Chuckling, L set off with Heilpern, to visit more than once the young Kukiels in their Lwow home; and that year his friendship with the couple was cemented. Yet, for all L's self-congratulations, Joseph's assent was not caused by his son's clever handling of him. The agreement between Rosenstock and Theodor—which had devolved upon Ann—was running out. Joseph could have renewed it. But since the glum days at Kobylowloki, he hankered after a place of his own and, with his credit and reputation much improved, was looking about for a more attractive and larger estate. There were several possibilities and he foresaw many absences from home. The pleasant prospect reduced somewhat even his cantankerous anxiety over L's inadequacies.

For relaxation in the family circle Joseph devised a new conversational game. L and he would choose a suitable subject, each define his position regarding its more important aspects and, towards the end of a meal, start a formal disputation. Those present were asked to listen carefully and later, in the study or library, declare which of the two they sided with and why. Joseph's brilliance at the game astonished everyone. L was invariably beaten, but, already haunted by a suspicion of his father's weaknesses, was glad to lose.

Some time earlier Joseph had introduced into the Nowosiolka routine a simpler intellectual exercise. Being supreme at mental calculation—able to resolve in next to no time the most elaborate and intricate sums—he greatly enjoyed putting L through his paces and spurring him on to count better and more quickly. Now, with the winding up of Nowosiolka in view, Joseph took L into his confidence, explained his method of accountancy, and showed him the books. The object was to give his son practical instruction in the management of a medium-sized, mixed agricultural estate. Of this L quickly grasped the pattern but, with his innate flair for the exact relation between minute facts and their general setting, he also perceived, almost at once, how his father's meticulous concentration on every split farthing left gaps through which thousands could slip. Astounded, he pointed out his discovery, only to have it brushed aside as irrelevant. (When telling me of this, L summed up his distress with a bitter: '*Vive la bagatelle,* as usual!')

From journeys in search of his dream-estate Joseph brought home tales of widespread excitement. The Russo-Japanese war, calamitous for Poland's oppressor, was raising hopes of speedy liberation. Secret political groups, endemic for a hundred years, were stirring throughout Poland. Grown more active, they were breaking cover. The fashionable craze among the young was for shooting and marksmanship. It affected L, whom Joseph forbade handling any weapon till he had finished school and was eighteen. But, with his father's wasted brilliance forever dangling before his mind's eye and his own feeling for the evanescence of opportunities heightened, L dismissed the prohibition as not serious. He resumed visiting his old friend the bee-keeper. They talked of politics, wars, and weapons. They handled a few of these weapons and L was shown how to fire an old blunderbuss, with a deafening detonation and a vicious kick. He minded the kick even more than the noise, but persisted. Gradually his delicate eardrums were damaged, especially the right one. The range of his hearing decreased but he became a good marksman, and proud of it. Yet the surreptitious act rankled. More upright than most men, he deeply resented having a furtive action imposed upon him. That it was imposed he did not doubt, and the old animosity flared up: Joseph was a lightweight. Lightweights in positions of power generated corruption. They were a menace.

Into this turmoil the late summer of 1904 brought a romantic interlude. A year earlier, when L and his tutors were in the Tatra, the rest of the family had enjoyed a more conventional holiday. Using Vienna for base, they had travelled in many directions, often taking with them Marie Beer. Good at planning and arranging things, she proved to be a delightful companion. Joseph thought her quite lovely, she listened so well. Ann, impulsively taken into the girl's confidence, felt protective and, after returning home, continued to give advice by letter. But in the early winter Marie went down with meningitis, was despaired of, and recovered very slowly. Months lapsed before her correspondence with Nowosiolka was resumed and, after a couple of exploratory notes, mother and daughter pressed her to come for a long stay when fit for the journey.

Along roads mantled with dust inches thick, L and Theodora drove out to fetch Marie from the station. At last he was to see in the flesh the buxom, almost brash, young woman whom he had clearly visualized when others spoke of her. But to Theodora's shouts of greeting there stepped down on to the platform a willowy girl, slightly awkward in her movements, tired, and looking rather lost. Luckily for him Theodora had everything under control. Giving orders right and left she led them out of the station—not too quickly, Marie was rather slow. In the carriage, sitting opposite the two girls, L gradually regained his composure. A mannerism of Marie's held his attention. Every now and then she would raise her gloved hand, press her fingertips to her forehead above the right eyebrow, and slowly draw them outward, as though discarding persistent pain or a haunting thought. By her side Theodora scintillated as she chatted away.

Ann's warm-hearted greeting worked as a cordial. Marie was to do exactly as she wished: Nowosiolka was a very special convalescent home, she their sole patient and loved by all. The following weeks proved Ann to be right. Marie regained her liveliness and put on weight, and everyone there loved her. L, swept off his feet by a great upsurge of devotion, sat gazing at her across the table until the impact of Theodora's mocking eyes broke the spell. He frowned at his sister, dropped his head and stared at his plate, but not for long. Again he looked across, felt riveted, and again Theodora interfered. At the centre of his plate was a large magenta cabbage-rose. A garland of small ones encircled the edge. He came to detest large flower decorations in the middle of plates, and when we set up house together I was careful that none should be there to disturb him. Between meals Heilpern generously praised Marie's intelligence and courage, deplored her delicate health, and urged L to make himself of use to her in any little way he could. But Theodora was always hanging about with her knowing look and derisive smile—a symbol of the rabble that can only mock. What could he do, tongue-tied and grief-stricken by this, his only lifelong love, foredoomed, misunderstood, and worthy of ranking with the greatest unrequited love sung by man.

49

She was invariably kind to him, without condescension, though in a rather absent-minded way which made the gulf between them even greater.

Marie had left after the snow had fallen. But L's sadness persisted all winter and merged into a new family conflict. Joseph, by now satisfied that his son could be trained in the art of sifting evidence and that the boy's oratory—though not a patch on his own—stood a chance of being improved to a standard of excellence, wished him in due course to read law at Lwow University. But L thought science would serve his purpose better. He was searching for a clue to men's actions or, rather, to the obvious motives that prompt those actions. Science might give him the answer, the law could not. Besides, hopeless though his love was, Marie would have to be impressed one day by unexpectedly hearing of him from admiring strangers. He had to do something impressive quickly, in a universally important field. Here again science could serve his purpose, the law could not. Moreover there were only three faculties at Lwow—philosophy (which included philology), medicine, and law. He could study medicine there and then specialize in biophysics. But for training in other fields of science he would have to go elsewhere, perhaps Paris—a delightful prospect. Father and son talked much round the core of the matter, each seeing the justice of his own position with increasing clarity, till the boy felt all discussion to be useless. But his fit of despondency coincided with Joseph's finding at last the right property: Koszylowce (pronounced Koshilovtsi) some sixty miles south-west of Nowosiolka and about two hundred north-west of the Black Sea, on a high plateau above the river Dzurin, a northern confluent of the Dniester. Its manor house and farm buildings were in good repair, and its black earth would grow almost any worthwhile crop. True, to conclude the deal he would have to raise a considerable sum of money, in other words pull off certain complicated financial transactions. His mind fully occupied with these, he lost interest even in the future profession of his son who, relieved, concentrated on his examinations and on grasping the last, finest points of his tutor's thesis. Heilpern, having received his Vienna doctorate, was nominated headmaster of a boys' school at Yaslo, and was to leave Nowosiolka before long.

Joseph's financial schemes and deals took him to Vienna in the early autumn of 1905. He wanted his wife and daughter there to soothe and brace him, and spoke again of L's eyelids needing urgent attention. But the old oculist had died and the new one, much younger and reputed to be even more brilliant and go-ahead, thought the incisions had been a dreadful mistake. Cauterization, followed by common-sense treatments, would have been the thing. And the nose specialist, seeing that L had not responded to his operation, agreed that cauterization might now do the trick. No use crying over spilt milk. The boy had paid his dime to the glory of progress, and there was nothing more to be said.

L, eager to escort Theodora and Marie on their jaunts about Vienna, suppressed the quips which came bubbling up to sparkle on the surface of his mind. Joseph, delighted to detect no bitterness for once, responded with an act of generosity. While they were there L might buy himself a shotgun. If he promised not to neglect his lessons, he might learn to shoot before his eighteenth birthday. In no time L fell in love with Vienna—Marie's true ambience. Ann, Theodora, even Thérèse, were there incidentally, and so was he. But Marie and Vienna belonged together, and suited him to perfection. Their mood was light-hearted, verging on the flippant, but poignant all the same because of doleful undertones always muffled, never stifled.

Effervescent wit and song rose spontaneously at every turn, but they were cultivated and blended together with clear-sighted deliberation in order to be flung negligently over doom-laden realities repugnant to the fluent idiom of the day. In the streets, the gardens, the theatre, L picked up the art of laughing off inexpressible calamities; and rapturously responding to the new verbal challenge, he scattered everywhere his own scintillating contributions. Yet some Viennese features he found distasteful. Its baroque architecture had, for him, clear affinities with Theodora and certain paternal relations whom he lumped together and dismissed as elaborate—a term of extreme aesthetic condemnation.

On one of the family's last days in Vienna Heilpern called. He was concerned about L's Greek—it could do with a bit of polishing though there was no doubt of his passing the final school examinations in the following summer. Recently in Lwow,

Heilpern had run into the ideal coach—Stanislaw Kot, a graduate of Cracow University, who was to make a corner in the history of Poland's Protestant sects and, at the height of his career, rise to be Polish Ambassador, first to the Kremlin and then to Rome. Unlike Heilpern and Weissberg, Kot was the son of Polish peasants. True to type he was a stocky, determined man, hard-working, imaginative and with a ribald sense of humour. Heilpern's suggestion that he should enjoy an exhilarating rest while coaching, for a couple of months, the brilliant son of a Galician landowner, did not attract him. He agreed under pressure, but refused to commit himself for more than a month; yet having arrived at Nowosiolka early in October, he stayed on almost to the end of the year.

Kot's change of heart was largely due to Ann. She, never having known a time of loveliness or self-appreciative desirability, had matured early into a matron of great dignity. Nowosiolka was proving itself worthy of her abilities and efforts. Members of its household, and chance visitors too, basked in the generous warmth of her perceptive appreciation of them. The prevalent happy restraint in words, tone, and manner which emanated from her but seemed to the young self-imposed, heightened the general sense of security under her roof, and led many to seek her advice. There was much coming and going in Nowosiolka at this time. All topics were broached, many were discussed with passion, yet none touched even the fringes of impropriety. Theodora was always there, and the men's innate courtesy—activated by Ann in those who were staying in the house or had dropped in for a meal—sharpened their ability to talk freely without embarrassing the daughter of the house or giving umbrage to their revered hostess—the benevolent matriarch of Nowosiolka.

Kot, when off duty, burrowed happily in the library, admired Theodora's painting, listened to her playing his favourite pieces on the piano, and cautioned L on his neglect of the absolutely unavoidable religious studies. L laughed off criticism and warning. He had got the measure of the examining rabbis. Their chief question was always about some personage whom they thought great. Whoever he was, L would dismiss him with a few pleasing

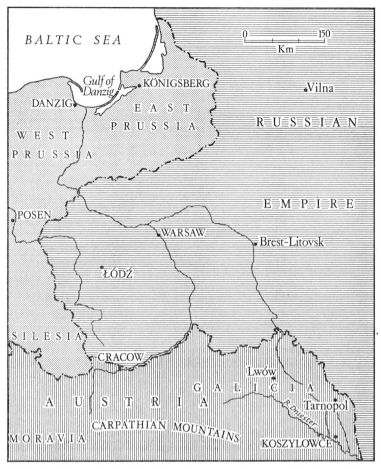

Poland, 1863–1918, showing Koszylowce near the eastern borders of the
Austro-Hungarian Empire

resonant generalizations and swing over to the one man of whom
he knew pretty well everything—King David. With earnest zest
he talked at length on little known details which astonished
and charmed his listeners. The trick had never failed and he was
sure it would serve him once again. He refused to waste time
(his fugitive time) on dull remote men or issues while engrossed in
comparing Plato—the persuasive authoritarian—with John Stuart
Mill whom Joseph revered as the shining light of Liberalism.

Kot's departure coincided with a tangle of misunderstandings between Joseph and Rosenstock. It reached a crisis when important alterations in the Koszylowce house, and the installation of replacements in its distillery, required the owner's immediate attention and presence. Rather pompously Joseph delegated to L the task of going south and looking into the dilemma. His decisions would be made on the force of L's report. The train journey was circuitous, with many connections. But it was L's first unaccompanied journey of such length, and he was heading for land which would be his some day. An exhilaration felt once before—when moving about the Pantalicha beside Theodor eyeing his flocks and herds—kept L happy as he mused on his future. At the station he was met by the new Koszylowce factor and the Koszylowce sledge. The long monochrome miles, which stretched out under a low grey sky, were swiftly covered. Cold wind prevented speech, upturned collars hid faces, hunched shoulders made all men look pretty well alike. Drifts of deep snow disguised the land's true configuration. All diversities were smothered. But in the two rooms made snug for him L confronted the factor, later defined by him as the personification of all he was to dislike in those Jews he was not prepared to tolerate. Yet Koszylowce drew him to itself at once, and he eagerly looked forward to seeing it unblanketed. His return journey was devoted to planning and phrasing the report for Joseph. Absorbed, he had completed it in essentials when, not long before Skalat, some boisterous men entered his carriage. Seeing that they were unknown to him, he settled down again to give his work its last touches. But when the strangers mentioned his father, he began to listen. Joseph's farming of the land that the train was jogging through they praised. His good luck they envied, but they mocked him as a Jew more Polish than the Poles—a scion of the northern gentry, if you please. One of the men drew a word picture—of the noisome Koszylowce factor to the life. Another tacked on to it Joseph's name. A third summed up—Yids were Yids, no people to mix with, whatever their virtues. Vociferating, the men bundled themselves out into the corridor to alight. Struck dumb— having heard for the first time 'the peculiarities with which the Jew is taunted (and sometimes tainted)', as he put it—L sat on till the anxious face of a servant peered in at the carriage window. He rose as the man came in to take down his bag.

In the following weeks father and son drew closer together. Of one accord they sought to establish a partnership that could work. The quality of L's report on Koszylowce had astonished Joseph. He foresaw a brilliant future for 'this young life' if only L would buttress his business acumen with a thorough knowledge of Polish and Austrian law. Science was no good. Palpably sincere, Joseph's eloquence was moving, and L succumbed, for once, to his father's charm and grand manner which hitherto had irritated him as put-on acts. Deeply stirred, he understood something of Theodora's devotion to Joseph, whom L suddenly saw as old. But concerned not to hurt the frail, distinguished looking old man, he found no opportunity for a heart-to-heart talk about the Koszylowce factor or the gibes overheard on the train. Held as a secret, both experiences sank into his memory to rankle there.

L's marksmanship astonished Joseph even more than had his intellectual achievement. From whom could this ability have descended to the boy? No ancestor would have touched a lethal weapon since the sack of Jerusalem. Yet here he was, in next to no time handling his gun with ease and hardly ever missing his target. What a throw-back! L, then in a relatively mute phase, was perturbed, but hid it under flippant loquacity. Towards the end of the winter father and son were invited to shoot wild boars some miles away. Joseph decided not to go: he was a poor shot and felt far from well. But he accepted for L, stressing this to be an excellent chance for a beginner. The very best sport was to be had in the weeks which some described as the tail-end of winter, others as the first glance of spring.

There are two ways of shooting wild boars in Poland. In the densely wooded north-east, where a boar can weigh over 300 lb., huntsmen go out to follow spoor with a brace of gundogs—a local breed, tan and flat-coated. The dogs raise the quarry, shot by the men. In the sparsely wooded south, beaters drive the somewhat smaller boars to where the guns are posted. Opinions vary on the method prevalent in regions neither truly of the north nor of the south. But on the whole, it is more likely that beaters were used at L's first shoot. Either way, he set out by sledge early enough to reach the rendezvous before eleven o'clock. The morning air was still crisp, the sun already warm. He wondered if the offensive strangers would be there. They might be. What should he do if confronted by one of them? Punch him in the face? But no one, least of all perhaps the man himself, could possibly guess why L was attacking him. And to explain was unthinkable. At a loss what to do in the feared contingency, he decided to take up boxing in the next few weeks. A man's fist should be his ever-ready weapon.

To L's joy none of the obnoxious strangers was there. In next to no time his interest increased to excitement. He felt very hot without immediately realizing that the wind had changed its quarter and a thaw was setting in. The day was an outstanding success. The boars that had been hoped for were all put up and killed. And not until the elated guns were regaining their sledges, at about three in the afternoon, did anyone notice how wet he was about the feet, legs, and shoulders. As L drove away, his horse's hooves chucked back at him lumps of melting snow, and the runners of his sledge sprayed him with icy slush. When the sun slipped into a wide band of haze, the wind swung back to the east. His clothes began to freeze on him. He reached home stiff with cold and running a temperature.

L was in bed with pleurisy for some weeks. As soon as possible, perhaps too soon, he returned to his lessons: the date of the gymnasium finals, once fixed, was immovable. He worked hard, but failed to throw off a languor interspersed with bouts of animation that flushed his cheeks a deep red. Joseph, alarmed, called a concilium of doctors. They located a patch on one lung and pressed L to take things easy. They also insisted that he should dismiss all thoughts of science. Laboratories were smelly, stuffy, poky places while his primary need was for clean, fresh air.

L submitted without fuss or flurry. He had been thinking matters over. The Nowosiolka phase of his life was closing. It had been a period of hesitant preparation. Prodigious urges drove him on: to absorb vast amounts of significant knowledge while keeping his mind alert to the world around him; and to strengthen his arms and his fists while keeping his body agile but robust.

CHAPTER FOUR

False Starts
1906–1908

L and Theodora again passed their examinations with distinction. And this was no mere milestone, but a bourne marking the end of eight years seen by L as a single sequence, a chunk of life happily done with. Because the move to Koszylowce closely followed the examinations, there was little leave-taking. Yet two farewells L prolonged to the verges of a sweet heartache. Ella he saw for the last time in her garden. They sat on a bench in the shade. His arm was round her shoulders and, as she fought back the tears that would come while she joked about his always having preferred to sit and walk in the sun, he shyly comforted her by alternately increasing and easing the pressure of his hand on her shoulder—a habit he retained for life. With the bee-keeper he strolled between the orchard gate and the hives till the old man stopped, to ascertain how much the boy had outgrown him. They embraced, and L wished his friend (now seen to be tiny) the solace of many fruitful autumns and many winters not too isolated by deep drifts of snow.

In the first weeks at Koszylowce, L and Theodora drew closer together than of late. The parents were preoccupied. The servants bustled about, obeying orders or failing to do so in sheer perplexity. At a loose end, brother and sister rode out to explore the setting of their new life. In the course of one ride L, having taken a jump ahead of his sister, sensed something was wrong, looked over his shoulder, and was jolted into a state he never forgot. He called it his first cleavage—a state of mind in which he simultaneously saw an event in two ways. Theodora, her skirt caught on a post or branch, dangled head down. Her back was to him. He thought her dead. But she stiffened, with a feline twist arched her back, shoulders and neck, and from an unusual angle looked at him severely. Her bowler hat was rakishly cocked over one eye, and a cheek was slashed by a coil of chestnut hair that he mistook, in the sun, for blood. The carefully groomed Theodora, decorous to the point of seeming to him pompous more often than not, was hooked in a ludicrous position. He went limp with helpless laughter. Yet he thought in anguish: her back's broken, she'll never walk or ride again, what do I do, how do I get her home, how do I tell the parents? In a robust voice she bade him not to be a fool and told him to bring her capering horse back to her immediately. The cleavage closed. He rode up, disengaged her skirt, caught her horse, helped her to mount, and tried to explain the interesting state he had been in. She begged him not to make excuses or talk rot—she was a bit shaken. He forgave the snub and the misinterpretation because of her courage. She forgave his silliness because of his being, she thought, docile for once. Riding home they pledged themselves to secrecy—the parents must never know. Nor did L speak again of the cleavage. But unforgettable, it gave an edge to his emerging love for Koszylowce, a plot of land where he seemed to be discovering some ancient root rather than striking a new one.

Swift rivers flowing through canyons were the region's dominant feature. The greatest, the Dniester, having long pushed to the east, here swung its course to the south before turning more resolutely and wriggling its way to the Black Sea. The resistant rock of the region had imposed contortions so fantastical upon its rivers that they sometimes even doubled back—the Dniester flowing west for a while, the Dzurin north. Between the canyons, vast cornfields of superb wheat ripened to a deep gold; sturdy beeches rose singly here and there out of well-watered flax fields or gently undulating fallows; willow-trees leant over streams— narrow, slow, and shallow compared with the rivers, yet fast enough. The canyons, though of no great depth, gave L the illusion that he rode high, above forceful life-giving waters. The woods and copses, sparsely scattered about, could not hush his sense of buoyant freedom as he surveyed *his* promised land— Joseph's only for a matter of years soon to pass. All things, all creatures found joy here in an airiness that imparted energy to them. Wherever he went, wherever he looked, he neither sensed nor saw any obstacle that might waken, let alone exasperate, his dormant malaise. He was abundantly happy.

Yellowing pages of typescript entitled 'historical geography' which I found after L's death, say:

The Dniester's more pronounced loops can be swum and waded across in half an hour; yet to follow on foot the contour of a loop would take very long. There is no point in doing so, but should you set yourself this task and steadily advance along the great river's course, you would be going down time and again, into the canyons of its many tributaries, and next coming out of them. For many months of the year the country, some 40 or 50 miles north of the Dniester, is a wide open road—a vastness of snow and ice sped-over in a sleigh. For an equal number of months in the summer, this wide-flung road is dense with grasses. I speak, of course, of the steppes, where the summer rains are too rare and light ever seriously to impede movement.

Content in the new surroundings Ann had turned her attention to the gardens. Flowers, hard fruit, soft fruit, vines were to be concentrated in the places best suited to them. The vegetable garden would be enlarged, and new varieties introduced into the melonery. Work on an up-to-date greenhouse would have to be started at once. The details of her plans she discussed with Joseph in front of the children who, affected by her enthusiasm, made a point of passing several times a day wherever work was in progress.

Late one afternoon, with the sunlight striking the soil at a revealing angle, L spotted in the rectangle that was being dug for the greenhouse foundations a deliberately shaped object. He bent down and picked it up. As an old man he still remembered the immediate combined effect on him of visual and tactile conviction. The clay figurine in the palm of his hand was archaic: a small, crudely-shaped woman crouching or clumsily seated, with a perforated transversal crest on her head (for looping in hair no doubt) and huge pendulous breasts, not fully formed but clearly indicated. L's hands and eyes simultaneously registered her indubitable antiquity. The expert knowledge of older men was presently to prove his pronouncement correct. His own lightning-quick conviction came unlaboured, through other channels. By his side Theodora, a shade sceptical, showed interest while the young diggers from the village looked on, uncomprehending and amused. One of them said that many such dollies lay about, with heaps of broken pots, not far below ground, near a wood. You would want a dray to carry them. Brother and sister hurried to the spot.

In the following weeks L spent long hours digging. Since the age when he first began to dress unaided he had never been spruce enough to satisfy his father or sister. But now his baggy, smeared trousers, sweaty shirt, and soiled shoes exasperated even Ann. Immediately chagrined by this, he quickly came to resent it as an infringement of his freedom. Did no one there understand that he had to press on and find enough material for its quality and bulk to prove his flash of insight true? How could they want him to waste time on appearances! Early in September he would be leaving for Lwow University. For years he would be studying law. An hour lost now was lost forever. What he failed to prove now, he would never prove, and not one of them cared. In a rebellious mood he wrote to a friend of Heilpern's, a student of primitive cultures who lived and worked at Czernowice. A stimulating exchange of letters followed.

In next to no time September was upon L and, for once, he was reluctant to leave home. He was even reluctant to launch out into the study of a subject in which he was never to lose interest. At Lwow his experiences proved to be so disagreeable that in his later years he must have forgotten them, perhaps deliberately. To me he never spoke of the Lwow incident, and of all the friends of his youth whom I saw or corresponded with after his death, only President August Zaleski knew of it. By a stroke of good luck his recollection of the set-up and its implications was precise.

Apparently, at the Faculty of Law L at once came up against nationalist students of the extreme type—resembling the Nazis of later days. They took their ideas and inspiration from Roman Dmowski—an aggressively anti-Semitic politician of considerable stature who during World War I became L's personal enemy and proved himself a most unscrupulous intriguer. In 1906 Dmowski had already drawn round him a small but vociferous group of Poles mostly resident in Warsaw, and had gained sympathizers in

Austrian Poland too. At Lwow University L was confronted by
a closely-knit anti-Semitic gang of fierce young Dmowski-ites—
the only politically organized group of students. Appalled by their
crude methods of argument and the type of mind these methods
revealed, and finding no group to join or any congenial men to
consort with, L made his first important decision. He wrote to
his father and returned home, where the Lwow unpleasantness
was at once lost, as it were, in the satisfaction of two developments.

Heilpern's friend, the Czernowice ethnologist with whom L had
corresponded, was eager to come and stay. His response to L's
descriptions of the figurine and dug-up pots and sherds was
rapturous. Koszylowce was only just outside the Transylvanian
'painted pottery' region. L could be fumbling at the remains of a
neolithic settlement three to five thousand years old. It might well
be worth organizing a try-out dig to the south of the plateau
where the house stood. In fact the whole of Koszylowce should
be inspected for neolithic remains. The scholar wondered if he
himself should not immediately undertake the task, and then
insisted that he must. Joseph was appalled. L, curbing an upsurge
of filial exasperation, used every argument in favour of the man,
the visit, the dig. With Theodora's support he even threw himself
into the preliminary arrangements. The household grumbled. The
parents thought him an eccentric bore but, whatever their displeasure, they gave in under sustained pressure. The man was
invited. And from then on, whenever L took a couple of the more
alert village boys off their immediate tasks in field or garden, the
tension between father and son was heightened. Resentments
increased.

To placate his father, L accepted without a murmur the plan
for his university education thought up by Joseph and his new
doctor—infallible for a while like his predecessors. The boy was
to be put under the medical care of the world-famous lung
specialist, Demieville, who practised in Lausanne, and many of
whose young patients attended the university there. L himself, his
initial astonishment subsiding, realized that he would be nearer
the hub of the world, and at a pleasing distance from narrow-
minded, self-engrossed provincials, indifferent to all but their
immediate present, indifferent even to the vestiges of prehistoric

squatters on their land. With no hitch or opposition from any quarter, it was smoothly decided that father and son would go to Switzerland as soon as Koszylowce allowed. In Lausanne Joseph would discuss relevant matters with the university authorities, and he would vet the people his son was most likely to mix with, as well as examine his future quarters.

The Czernowice scholar—in the field of archaeology a conscientious amateur immersed in fanciful interpretations of a wide variety of finds—had roughed it often enough to appreciate comfortable lodgings. His day's work done, he listened in somnolent well-being to Joseph's flights of imagination in a variety of spheres, and admired his host's ability to pull out of the coffers of his memory facts which proved or disproved whatever was under discussion. L, quick to read auspicious signs and bent on making the most of every lucky chance, organized an excursion to some distant acres planted with young trees. Among the tidy rows of saplings was a spatter of bald patches, a phenomenon to which the forester in the nearby lodge had no clue. Sure enough, at no great depth, L and his jubilant diggers unearthed arrowheads of flint and tools of bone. But to their annoyance the expert moved the boys to a loop of the river—where, in the loess below the black earth, near a heap of broken figurines and sherds, they struck a handsome, hardly damaged, painted pot of well levigated clay. The scholar had proved his point. Another interesting yield was drawn from a mound on a home farm called Biala. With three lucky dips to his credit the ethnologist had enough material for a short report to the society of primitive cultures of which he was a member. Impatient to spread the good news he returned to Czernowice.

In the remaining few days before the departure for Lausanne L entirely rearranged his room. To Ann's consternation its chief feature was to be a cabinet filled with dingy bits and pieces of many shapes and sizes, all correctly and neatly labelled and entered in a book. This was L's Koszylowce collection later admired by Kot. Spurned by the family, it was his very own—a cupboardful of the first inanimate objects to evoke in him an aesthetic response. By the time he had completed his job, the response had matured to an attachment.

In Lausanne father and son agreed on the excellence of Dr. Demieville. Gracious to the verbose and reassuring to the anxious, he had stilled Joseph's fears. Clever at fixing on each consecutive patient his first-rate mind tensed to give of its best, he had turned L's questing hostility into a happy foretaste of future visits. At once arrangements were made for the new patient to occupy a large sunny room at the Hotel Eden in Montreux, a quieter town. Communications between Montreux and Lausanne were easy, and at the Eden lived a French lady whose little daughter had recently been placed by Dr. Demieville in a sanatorium high up in the hills. The child's brother—attending a university course on the moral and political sciences—was also under medical supervision. The father had died of T.B.

Swiss universities differed much from the English. For one thing, an undergraduate drew up his own syllabus; for another, most men moved about a great deal, attending a university only for one term perhaps, before moving on to another. In such perambulations language alone seems to have been a limiting factor: German-speaking undergraduates went as far afield as Germany, the French-speaking as far as France (notably to the Sorbonne). But between the universities of the French- and German-speaking regions of Switzerland itself there was hardly any such movement.

On 6 November 1906 L was entered on the list of winter-term undergraduates at the Faculty of Law. At once he began to attend Professor Vilfredo Pareto's lectures on sociology, Professor Boninsegni's on statistics and finance, Professor Roguin's on law, Professor Edmond Rossier's on the history of the French Revolution; and also lectures on general philosophy, and some Russian courses. When disgruntled, he, like the men about him, tended to hanker after the matchless Sorbonne. On train or tram journeys to and from the university L and Guy (the young Frenchman) soon became friends and at the Eden L was introduced to Guy's mother. He often spoke to me of her, and mentioned a couple of times her full name and title; but it was not a name I knew and I have remembered both only approximately. I shall call her Mme de X. Much of L's life was managed by her in the following four months, during which she founded his lifelong admiration for

France: a regard touched with gratitude for the civilizing influence France has had on the rest of Europe, and through Europe on the world.

Mme de X and her husband were descended from families that had emigrated early in the French Revolution, had returned to France at the first opportunity, and withdrawn—disappointed—to swell the ranks of the *émigrés à l'intérieur*. Her attitude to the situation, which still dominated her, was one of amused regret. Too intelligent, wise, and kind to have banal prejudices, she was too widely read, too well versed in the vagaries of human relations, too perspicacious, and too shrewd, to imagine she could dispel those of others, however foolish. Her appraisal of Guy was based on the same kind of clear understanding. She knew his mind was inferior, and felt relieved that his poor brain should be well camouflaged by facile brilliance, light-hearted courtesy, a rare elegance, and striking good looks. She must have liked L from the start since she undertook expertly to polish him up. They spent many quiet evenings together in elevated discourse spattered with wit and, when Christmas came, she wrote to Joseph suggesting that L should accompany herself and Guy up the mountainside to where her daughter was being treated. L's parents readily agreed.

In the high snows and keen air Mme de X's party was presently enlarged by a couple of whom she would hardly have seen much, if anything, in France. The elderly husband, recovering from an internal complaint, was a vastly rich industrialist. His very young wife, bored stiff, was a little actress, more pretty than talented. She and Guy threw themselves with passion into such mid-winter frolics as were provided, while the ailing husband and L entertained Mme de X when she was not with her daughter, and each other when she was. By the end of the Christmas vacation Mme de X had decided against returning to Montreux, and had taken a villa in Lausanne (Ouchy) near the Hotel Beau-Rivage where the rich husband and pretty wife intended to stay for a while. At the villa and in the hotel gardens L spent many agreeable and instructive hours, coming to see—under the influence of his two mature friends—that the Sorbonne definitely was the only university for him.

But spring was in the air. Mme de X, grown restless, dreamed up a journey for L—to Italy, and as simple as could be: on foot, with Burckhardt's classic in a pocket and a few essentials thrown into a little canvas bag. Helped by L she worked out an entrancing route: east along the rim of Lake Leman to the valley of the Rhône; up the valley to the Simplon; over the Simplon—exhilarating views, romantic scenery—down into Italy; on to Tuscany; a few days in Florence, for a brush-down and to pick up letters; and on the move again to San Giminiano, Siena, Sinalunga, Montepulciano. . . . After the end of term Mme de X and Guy returned to Paris on family business. L stuffed Burckhardt into a capacious pocket, threw into a rucksack a few essentials, and walked away from Montreux into Italy.

The brilliant weather broke as he reached the valley of the Arno, and he entered Florence in a downpour. Short of cash he hesitated to hire a cab, did so, and went the round of inexpensive hotels. With Easter near, not a bed was to be had. And on that drive in sloshing rain through his first Renaissance city, L acquired two Italianisms often used by him with amusing relevance: on a sigh of resignation like the cabman's, '*Piove, ladro governo*' (It rains. We're governed by rascals); and from the same source—when L was once again eyed with suspicion for being without luggage—'*Sono troppo, troppo stupidi*' (A wretchedly stupid lot). In the end the cabman, warming to his passenger's predicament, took him up the hill on the way to Fiesole to a house he declared suitable. There the bedraggled foreigner—with next to no Italian—was put up in an isolated room at the top. It had small windows in all four walls. From one of them L caught sight of the proud tower of the Signoria and of Bruneleschi's brown cupola veined with white. They jutted forth from a sprawl of buildings, by comparison indistinguishably squat, into a sky that cleared as it darkened. Flinging open a window L lent out and, regardless of expostulations and gesticulations, stayed there till every trace of daylight had gone.

Having written home to explain his circumstances, L began to explore the city. He could remember no time when he had not known of his parents' impressions of Italy, and he had long been chanting Goethe's verses on the land where the lemons grow. But this Italy, this Florence, was far beyond even what Mme de X and Burckhardt had led him to expect. Wandering round, he felt his pulse beat in unison with the heart of an intimately understood entity, a political city as corrupt as it was beautiful and glorious; delightfully old, too. By return of post he received from Ann money and a letter bidding him go to Rome, there to join her and Theodora at the Hotel Lucerne; after a fortnight or so together abroad they would be returning to Koszylowce.

Since there was no great hurry L soon left Florence for San Giminiano on its rugged hill. Full of zest, he precipitated himself from the Piazza della Cisterna down steep, flagged alley-ways; bounded up flights of honey-coloured steps to terraces, tiny or spacious; glimpsed from one angle and another, on every side and at all levels, towers without number, all of the same pale or tawny stone. After Siena he stayed for a matter of hours at Sinalunga and Montepulciano, losing his heart to restive, hardworking communities of men both proud and wily. In Rome Ann was delighted to see him robust and forthcoming. Theodora relentlessly organized a round of all the sights to be enjoyed on a first visit. And, having stretched their absence from home to its utmost, Ann took back to Koszylowce her tall, bouncing children in an expansive mood. But Joseph, the first greetings over, silently handed his son a batch of letters with a Paris postmark. His questioning look was reproachful: the nervous handwriting was clearly a woman's. And indeed, the pretty little actress incontinently wrote about waves of unreasonableness that were sweeping off balance the volatile Guy and her ponderous husband. She was distressed, lonely, with no one but Ludwik to confide in, why did he not answer? She needed advice, help, consolation. L mustered all the tact he could on the spur of the moment, and innocently explained as much as he thought fair. His reticence Joseph misinterpreted as lame excuses which he let pass with no more than a raised eyebrow. But when, some time later, the matter of L's university education was broached, Joseph flatly refused even to consider the Sorbonne. For L, Paris was out.

From his grandfather L had inherited, or absorbed, a steely firmness of purpose and he mimicked his father's unrelenting, grim tenacity. That summer two preoccupations kept him and Joseph hammering away at each other. There were the neolithic remains. In the museums of Florence, Siena, and Rome, L had contrived to meet keepers and curators, and was now convinced that no amateur, however conscientious, could serve his purpose. He wished to organize a dig backed by an archaeological museum, or the archaeological department of a great national museum. He began a wideflung yet selective and carefully worded correspondence, took up again his almost solitary digging, and sat for hours in the seclusion of his room piecing together, with remarkable flashes of insight and the greatest delicacy, old pots which had disintegrated into smithereens.

Joseph was thoroughly alarmed. What would become of Koszylowce after his death? Was it to be inherited by a wastrel? From whom could this associate of Parisian actresses, this digger-up of rubbish, have inherited his disastrous inclinations? Acrimoniously he subjected L to tirades on the responsibilities that go with the possession of good land—Koszylowce was worth the sacrifice of any whim; and at every opportunity he preached the importance of an impeccable knowledge of the law. In a world increasingly open to catastrophe, yet rich in opportunities, two codes of the law were an obligatory equipment for L: the Polish and the Austrian. The heir to Koszylowce must excel in the ability to use both to its advantage—to the ultimate increase of its acres. Yet on the rare days when Joseph was free of depression or febrile euphoria, he dreamily boosted Lausanne: Demieville was a gem of a doctor; for the privilege of being in his care much could for a while be sacrificed, though for a while only.

The greater Joseph's eloquence, the more reluctant was L to continue at Lausanne. Soon, under constant pressure, his opposition hardened to a resolution; come what may, he would go elsewhere. An escape route out of the impasse was fortuitously opened by an Anglophile cousin who had spent most of 1905 in England writing a doctoral thesis on Common Law. Breaking at Koszylowce a journey to Vienna, he praised sky-high a new, forward-looking venture in education, the London School of Economics. L turned to his father: since Paris was out, what of London?—Vilfredo Pareto had spoken well of this 'School'; he held in high esteem some of the men who taught there and expected much of their pupils. Joseph, still haunted by Paris, consented with a shudder of relief. The methodical cousin settled down to instruct his junior on the best way to travel, where and how to live in London, and whom to approach when there.

Bloomsbury and Holborn in 1907 amazed L. Their sombre vitality galvanized his thinking, but his senses were offended by their uglier manifestations, and his feelings were outraged when he grasped the historical context of what he saw, heard, and smelt. At first he lodged at 36 Bedford Place, and on his daily walks to and from the School followed a network of mean tortuous streets, immediately to the west of the line later drawn from north to south by Kingsway. Perplexing culinary stenches, spiced with the smell of coal-dust, turned his stomach. The bloated bleary faces and misshapen bodies of nondescript women hovering about areas to exchange raucous guffaws with labourers or carriers wizened but full of swagger seemed gruesome inventions of a diseased mind. But they were there, day after day. Peasant poverty L had been aware of in Galicia. Sympathy for its victims had made him a socialist after the Polish manner. But the English urban wretchedness that now horrified yet fascinated him, revealed a degradation hitherto unsuspected. The answer to its challenge had to be as English as the phenomenon. The Fabian Society in its 'second blooming' seemed to offer one, and L hastened to enter an intellectual pasture so distinctively English.

In the November issue of *Fabian News* his name appeared in a long list of candidates for election. At once availing himself of the privilege to join gatherings 'for members only', he still continued to attend a variety of others at the School and elsewhere. Time and again he met Sidney and Beatrice Webb, intent on 'permeation'. And they, as often as not, had Bernard Shaw in tow. L was reading Shaw's plays as they appeared, in English or in translation. Some he had seen on the stage. But to hear the prodigious dramatist, and see him—tall and bearded—putting on an act the better to impress while speaking, was a revelation. Shaw's vocal skills and puckish verve suggested a new, up-to-date and idiosyncratic form of oratory. And presently, close-ups of H. G. Wells—bland pink face, sandy hair, round china blue eyes—sharpened the dowdy outline of Wellsian characters. Despite the unfortunate high-pitched, barely audible voice, Wells's grasp of detail was—to L's mind—most effective in swift acrimonious exchanges: it helped memorably to point the sweeping Wellsian presentation of problems and circumstances. The stimulating edge to his talks was, at that time, more likely than not, due to his beginning to feel cantankerous in the Fabian set-up. L enjoyed witty sarcasms. And it was some ill-humoured well-timed remark of Wells that focused his attention on the English way of managing a nation's life through parliamentary debate. Curiosity about Parliament's subtler, cannier life behind the scenes had been aroused. To learn more he engaged any willing teacher in long informative talks, and flung himself into arguments with undergraduates. Yet only two enduring friendships struck root that winter. August Zaleski (later Minister for Foreign Affairs), a Polish fellow student, suitably endowed for a brilliant career in diplomacy and statesmanship—very tall, handsome, and with a powerful melodious voice—was so immediately congenial that they became inseparable. And in the Junior Common Room L's 'singularly bright eyes, extraordinary vitality and striking manner in discussion' were noticed early on by Tegan Harris. Recently married to Frank Reginald Harris (of the Foreign Office but given leave of absence to write a life of the Fourth Earl of Sandwich) Tegan, living in Doughty Street near the Foundling Hospital, had given up her intention of reading literature at one of the older universities. Good-humouredly she had resigned herself to attending courses at the L.S.E. Contemporaries have described her as a vivacious listener, good to look at and well turned out, a dark girl with masses of hair coiled round her head. She and L, having singled each other out, were much together and Tegan insists that he already knew English perfectly, 'did not make grammatical mistakes nor fumble for words as a beginner does, spoke fluently enough and could get across anything he wanted to. But his manner of speaking was rather quiet, demanding heightened attention.' This was seldom denied him; and she adds, 'despite a very heavy accent he was never difficult to understand. It was not the well-known German accent. I often wondered who taught him.' The answer comes from L: a Polish teacher, of French in the first place but also of English, with a

Vienna diploma. But let this be said: L was unable to distinguish between some of the more elusive sounds in which the English language abounds and, not yet aware of it, remained baffled when corrected. Only his Polish and his Viennese German were perfect. Those he had learnt in early childhood. Any language picked up or studied after his shooting practice at the bee-keeper's, was a hit or miss affair as far as speech went. By the time we met, he was never sure if he correctly articulated, pronounced, or stressed an English word or sequence of words. A grave handicap for one whose mind needed vigorous, quick, tit-for-tat exchanges to spark off its own excellence.

At the L.S.E. his manner in discussion attracted Rachel Barrett—socialist, suffragette, and first-rate orator later prominent in the Women's Social and Political Union. One day, with Tegan by her side, Rachel Barrett engaged L in a spirited argument that she almost at once turned into a soliloquy. L, not easily obliterated, was firmly edging in a quiet, unrelenting little piece when she suddenly slapped him on the arm, shouting, 'You listen to me and be quiet.' He was dumbfounded. Any disputations with his father or tutors, however eloquent, had been formal to a degree. But he liked this Welshwoman of fierce brilliance enough to sit amiably silent through the explosion of general laughter and the rest of her harangue. They became good friends. Yet the winter's outstanding event, of immediate and far-reaching importance, came of L's friendship with Tegan. They met most days; she spoke of him to her husband; and Harris—an older man devoted to the young and anxious that the best of them be 'given a chance'—suggested that she ask L to their house. Soon Harris found himself explaining to the eager youth his method of research into the personality and activities of the fascinating eighteenth-century statesman, Lord Sandwich. In a flash L's grasp of problem and method crystallized into counter-suggestions for a different approach to the task. As their liking of each other was enhanced by mutual regard, Harris—a graduate of New College—wrote to Oxford dons about his outlandish protégé whose abilities were being wasted on economics at the L.S.E. Nothing came of it. Undeterred, he wrote to the future Warden of New College, H. A. L. Fisher, who advised a tactful approach to A. L. Smith, another old friend, then Senior History Tutor at Balliol. A. L. Smith answered evasively. Harris wrote again. An even more evasive answer was slow to come. Harris pressed his point, and there was no answer.

For Christmas L had gone home. On his return from the snow-covered, sparkling plateau of Koszylowce, Bloomsbury's tightly-packed smoke-stained houses depressed him. Overcome by sleeplessness, he rushed about in mounting anxiety determined to find more congenial lodgings; saw nothing he really liked; yet moved to 40 Prince's Square, north of Kensington Gardens. Unable to afford riding in the park he spent his weekends, a little sadly, with a book, on the sunniest bench he could see. Between chapters he sauntered round looking at children and dogs. His daily walks, too, were now over grass under trees, to or from one of the east gates where he mounted, or left, a bus.

English people and their ways increasingly puzzled L. To learn more of them and completely to dispel his fit of claustrophobia he made arrangements to join the Second Fabian Summer School at Llanbedr by the 'ocean'. 'The sea' still meant to him one of three seas: The Black, the Mediterranean, or the Baltic.

Suddenly out of the April blue came a summons to Oxford. A. L. Smith wished to see him. Harris, much gratified but anxious lest L disgrace himself by some continental over-elaboration which would register as an awkwardness unheard of in public-school circles, brought about a change of the summons into an invitation to lunch for them both. He need not have worried. With a speed and certainty like that which has been exalted in literary descriptions of love at first sight, the middle-aged Senior Tutor and the aspiring pupil recognized they were cut out for each other. The noontide pangs of hunger barely stilled, A. L. Smith elicited from his young guest brilliant yet pre-eminently sensible remarks and observations on Europe's actual predicaments and past history. L's grasp of relevant and precise data ranging over much of the continent, and his compact summing-up of arguments, delighted A. L. Smith. When the twice delayed leave-taking did come, he murmured in an off-hand manner that yet had the quality of a gladly given command, 'For Michaelmas Term we'll see you here then.'

L's attendance at the L.S.E. had been good, but after the momentous luncheon it became less frequent. He remained enthusiastic only for lectures by Professor Mackinder, to whose teaching he later ascribed his own appreciation of geographical factors in the shaping of history. His interest in the seminars also flagged after Easter. For Michaelmas term he had sent in five essays, for Lent term nine; but during the Summer term he wrote one only, on the theory of statistics for Mr. Bowley, whose mathematical subjects were among L's best. Dr. Lilian Knowles (French and German translations and the History of Economics) had indeed given him the full hundred marks on one occasion: but that was before Easter. His summer-term essay was handed in on 6 May and received back on 14 May marked ninety-five out of a hundred. L's current absorbing anxiety was how to make Joseph accept his change-over from the L.S.E. to Balliol as a fantastic stroke of luck, not as yet another sign of his instability. L's mind was working on this problem as he packed for home.

He found Joseph tormented by dejection and flurry: a state of mind and nerves which Theodora alone knew how to ease. It scared L off. Dimly conscious of much the same gloomy agitation latent in himself, he tried to shut it out, to put up barriers against it. Withdrawn, he made minute, implacable observations of his father's demeanour. Once again, as years before, the family divided. The good-looking, carefully groomed father and daughter dismissed the mother and son as obstinately inelegant, a lesser breed. Ann, by now roly-poly, was still impeccably neat but had never attempted to be anything more. And L, though tall and upright, had inherited her features, heavy by comparison with theirs, and her altogether clumsier build. Angered by their attitude to Ann, L dubbed the superior pair 'haughty camels'. Tall, slim, with long necks bearing aloft narrow faces, finely-featured, and with chins held up, moreover glorying inordinately in the gloss of things, they represented to him a type of which he noted all the ridicule but missed the pathos.

He was lonely. Not even Ann could give him the time and attention they both wished she might. Up and about very early she was held captive till nightfall by the rhythms and needs of the house and household. The cellars were being made ready for storing enough meat and vegetables to last through the winter, too harsh for transport to be relied on. Outside—in a cluster of sheds—small cucumbers, large beetroots and cabbage heads of all sizes, both chopped and whole, were being pickled; meats were being smoked or preserved in salt. At the bottom of the garden peasant women might be standing mid-stream, washing the seed out of enormous cucumbers, and then rinsing them in quick-flowing eddies or still pools captured in tubs. Thoroughly washed, the seed was strewn on large trays and exposed to the hot sun till properly dry for packing. Ann was an infallible judge of the perfect moment to pick the cucumbers so as to obtain the best seed. Elsewhere, in another reach or a different stream, men might be thumping hemp with implements cunningly devised for this job. The proceeds from top grade cord and matting were good. The orchards had to be inspected also, with Ann's attention divided between fruit trees and waddling geese. And every activity involved its own paperwork. Besides, all day she was judging the working men and women, eager to spot at least one to whom she might presently pass on some of her strenuous tasks.

With greater awareness than before L was growing apart from the family—a situation curiously general in that part of Galicia. Soon after his death I was sent a cutting from a Polish journal, a moving appraisal of L, which stated, 'Our families were close neighbours in the Galician province of Podolye.' The author (Count Kajetan Czarkowski-Golejewski), then living in Munich, was a service pilot till he lost an eye in a rashly valiant exploit at the close of World War I. After the Polish tragedy of World War II, he came to see us in London; and I knew that his elder brother, Victor—murdered during a communist raid into Podolye—was at one time a close friend of L. I wrote to Count Kajetan and I learnt that he was eight years younger than L—too vast a gulf in adolescence for the younger brother to know much of the elder boys' friendship. But carried away by reminiscences, he described to me 'the life of youngsters of good families in our neighbourhood'. It was

the dullest possible. . . . Solitude surrounded by an army of private tutors, governesses, music teachers and similar individuals. [The yearly school examinations] imposed at home a daily routine consisting of some five hours schoolwork in the mornings, preparatory work in the evenings and innumerable language and music lessons in between. Of sports only three were thought right for gentlemen: riding, shooting and tennis. . . . The great thrill was coursing, with greyhounds. . . . You can well imagine that a boy . . . used all his energy and [many] ruses to escape the boring and sometimes tyrannical tutors, and found more pleasant the company of horses and dogs. . . . There was no other. . . . The distances between [the houses of] neighbouring estates was great. No cars in those days, and every visit to neighbours in that country was an expedition, often a ceremonial one. The life of the youth of those days was not gay. A certain melancholy due to national disasters permeated the whole history, literature, and life. The strict classical lines of the social system (rigorously hierarchical) didn't leave much room for a healthy *joie de vivre*. . . . My brother Victor was very taciturn and intro-spective. We never discussed personal experiences, feelings or people.

Lyrically taking wing, the description continued,

I remember from those pre-1914 days, the face and voice of every servant, game-keeper, groom; of every pedlar or small trader; every horse and dog; and every road—on the estate of my father. Maybe one day I shall write my memoirs as a kind of sentimental journey into the past . . . of the land where your husband grew.

Victor's brother—as L mostly called him—was a somewhat reckless man of action. Yet his lonely formative years in a crowded, isolated household had sharpened his senses much as Nowosiolka and Koszylowce had L's. The childhood impressions he shared with L remained permanently and deeply incised on the memory of both. If they embraced at a chance encounter, the spontaneous gesture was their salute to a largely similar past. Yet L's background was the less frustrating. His tutors had been unusual men, and for him the Nowosiolka library had always been to hand. At Koszylowce it still was, Theodora having taken charge of it. On her visits to Vienna she carefully selected books on art for her own shelves and picked up important or rare volumes on archaeology for her brother's. Besides, by the summer of 1908 the L.S.E. had awakened in L interests which led him, when out riding alone, to dismount at the houses of peasants designated as 'Americans' or 'Canadians'.

The pervasive regional melancholy played its part in prompting the more audacious among the disgruntled breadwinners to venture across the Atlantic. They could be heads of families or able-bodied sons. All believed that hard work and well deserved, well utilized strokes of luck must result in the accumulation of a tidy capital. Successful survivors did return enriched: fathers to their families, sons to found new ones. In the intervening years they would have been sending home letters full of wondrous tales, and enough money to help the family eke out an existence not below the prevalent standard. L found stimulating his step by step detection of a family's economic involvements, and went on systematically to trace the blind urges, flashes of insight, day-dreams, tantalizing alternatives (risks and possibilities) that drew living creatures into well or loosely organized corporate move-ments across vast spaces. He groped for regularities in the tangle; and as he groped he availed himself of many occasions to collect evidence. Riding away from homesteads financially and emotion-ally linked to the New World he pondered the migrations of men fed up with the humdrum, the movements of birds seasonally heading away from a climate become uncongenial, and the remem-bered—never cancelled—urges of lemmings persistently racing to their doom. The word 'lemmings' never failed to evoke for him the smell of hemp in strong sunlight. Many rides skirted or cut across Joseph's hemp plantations and L, able to judge at sight the quality of stalk or stem, rejoiced at the abundant signs of good management. It made him feel prosperous. But his mind was restive and, far away in Wales, the Fabians offered him much of what he longed for: stimulating verbal exchanges on a variety of topics intensely important to him; debates with men and women of his own age whose minds he enjoyed; discussions with a string of somewhat older men and women who knew more than he did, were eager to communicate what they knew, and glad to find him eager. Some of this had delighted L in gloomy London. Six weeks of it in a still unknown rugged country by the sea was a prospect his mind dwelt on with pleasure.

The first four Fabian Summer Schools (1907–10) were held in North Wales at Pen-yr-Allt, a fine house standing in its grounds on a wooded spur of a hill, one mile and a half from the sea and seven miles north of Barmouth. The situation pleased L. Harlech Castle was a rewarding if obvious goal for short walks, the slopes of Cadr Idris enticed aspiring climbers whenever time allowed, while paths good for strolling, and even bicycling, ran along stretches of undulating grassland. The organized lectures of 1908 were to start at the end of July and cease in mid-September. L, arriving some days before most participants, was welcomed by a skeleton staff and befriended by Henry Allsopp, the year's Resident Secretary. A Balliol man, and another protégé of A. L. Smith, Allsopp at once advised L to hire a bicycle and learn to ride. The advice was accepted, but L never took to his 'inanimate mount', and even at Oxford, where he bicycled as a matter of course, he still found it uncongenial. In every other respect the Summer School was a great success with him, owing partly to his securing a room to himself; which perplexed his gregarious companions. Of the older people whom L met during his six weeks at Llanbedr the most important to him in later years were R. H. Tawney—who arrived early to give three lectures—and Graham Wallas—who generously stepped in when G.B.S. failed to turn up. L also remembered special addresses on foreign and colonial policy—one of them in moonlight on the lawn of Tynmawr, yet another house taken by the society for the heavily over-subscribed six weeks. Some evenings were devoted to entertainment: the jolliest being on the last Saturday when a one-act play was produced by Miss Gladys Jones—probably a link for L (besides Rachel Barrett) with her brother Thomas Jones (later Deputy Secretary to the Cabinet). Both he and L remembered first meeting at a Fabian Summer School, but, by the time we spoke of it, neither could be sure of the year. Towards the end of L's first Summer School some younger members asked for permission to use the fast-emptying Pen-yr-Allt as a base from which to undertake a round of excursions. Of all places then visited, L retained the most vivid impression of Dolgelly. And when, after World War II, his work took him through Merioneth and Montgomeryshire the fine new roads of the region and other signs of our mechanized and mechanizing post-war age astonished him without blotting out the more vivid impressions retained for over forty years. Here and there he would ask me to slow down or even stop the car, that he might better describe, and I take in, how things were when first seen by him.

At the final dispersal a few boys and girls with time on their hands decided to walk back into England. Their direction—to the south-east—suited L, and he joined them. Meals were now snatched anywhere and a good night's sleep was chancy. But he did not mind. The varying landscape delighted him, and he was sorry to see the jolly, friendly band dwindle at the bigger cross-roads. When left alone, he boarded a train to Oxford. In exuberant health and his mind surging with ideas, he walked round the Balliol quad admiring its mulberry trees, and then crossed over to the Westminster Bank to open an account with the money waiting for him. The few days till beginning of term he largely spent in the Bodleian following up the new flights of thought that haunted, virtually pursued, him. Bewitched by the country he had been walking through and the endearing oddities of his English companions, he was losing his heart to England.

PART II

COLLISIONS

CHAPTER FIVE

Learning to Think
1908–1912

Throughout his adult life, Balliol remained a constant object of devotion for L. In his last years I had occasion to ask him why. He answered with lapidary emphasis, 'They taught me to think.' At Nowosiolka under guidance from Weissberg and Heilpern he had recognized, and had come to enjoy, the vigour of his own mind. At Balliol he was trained to use it properly, and because of his early maturity he found that his tutors meant more to him than did his contemporaries.

Even before L arrived in Balliol on 17 October 1908, he was being talked of; and when he did arrive he became one of Balliol's memorable figures—a man unattractively different from the rest but captivating because, in an absurd way, indisputably remarkable. 'His personality,' states a relevant letter, 'was exuberant and, to our insular eyes, exotic.' He caught his contemporaries' imagination and without knowing it or meaning to, teased the more inventive undergraduates into concocting about him stories tenuously based on some isolated and slightly distorted fact. A college wit would enliven with uproarious detail one such story after another; and in next to no time a cycle of 'Berners' legends had formed, taken wing, and started on a prolific life of its own.

Paradoxically, his unwanted solitariness marked him out for singular success. Belonging to no group he became uniquely acceptable throughout Balliol.

You ask about other possible Balliol men who knew him—I dare not mention more names, the men may be dead—but indeed, anyone who was up with him knew and will remember Lewis.

I think that between 1908 and '12 (or is it '11?) all Balliol knew him. He was that sort of a man.

He rode roughshod over normal barriers which then made Balliol little more than a collection of small social circles which had little to do with each other. All his life he stood outside the English social system. No man was less selective in his friendships, he was socially omnivorous.

As a result, the undergraduates 'after being half amused and half enraged at his oddities, decided to adopt him as one of [their] Balliol institutions'.

The wish to learn is not very strong in England and even in the universities was then not widespread. But L's sense of urgency was compulsive: he had to know, or at once set about getting to know. Concentrated reading could of course serve up to a point; and he had a weird ability for memorizing printed pages in their entirety while staring at them with knitted brow for a minute or two. Yet in order to know with the quality of knowledge he hankered after, he needed lively talk—an exchange that simultaneously served two ends: an easy assimilation of knowledge different from his own because even the same facts were being seen and presented differently, and an enthralling clarification of his own thoughts. For this twofold joy his desire was relentless—a blind determination that drove him to commit actions natural only to him, unthinkable outside the context of his personality. In the cycle of Berners-Namier legends are several variants of an episode which is said to have infuriated and then disarmed his chosen victim. Placed during L's first term, it tells of his gate-crashing on the morose delights of an Englishman's breakfast. One variant declares it was the victim's first intimation that L was in Balliol at all. Be that as it may, this much the legend does prove: the nocturnal miseries of childhood had been overcome and L already was a sociable waker, full of zest. Even when old and ill, he still felt as Walt Whitman had written, 'Stranger, if you passing meet me and desire to speak to me, why should you not speak to me, and [in L's case above all] why should I not speak to you?' Simplicity and directness in going forth to learn about mankind from men remained with him to the end.

Inventions about L were made even easier because he seldom took part in games: a little tennis which he had played at home, a little soccer, and lacrosse at which he was clumsy but good; that was all. His interest in the river was wholly vicarious. And hardly anyone knew that for all his lumbering clumsiness on foot, he was a first-rate horseman. As a matter of fact, Balliol in its earlier, pre-athletic days, when Jowett was buying Shotover Hill because its top gave the Master and Scholars somewhere agreeable to ride, might well have suited his taste in recreation better, and he might then have been accepted less ambiguously. As things were, games with older men—from overseas—were more to his liking and drew him to a number of Rhodes Scholars. On the whole, he took in good part the ragging meted out to him. Yet 'with almost every one of us,' writes a contemporary, 'he was at one time or another not on speaking terms'. 'Warm-hearted yet sensitive, quick to take offence and loath to give up his resentments,' wrote L in 1958-60 of George Townshend (brother of Charles)—a flash of insight not only into Townshend but also into himself.

However, comical flourishes were not L's only contribution to Balliol. A letter written immediately after the announcement of his death says,

When he turned up at Balliol—a year later than I had—he at once made an enormous impression on one, a lasting impression. His intellectual life was full of excitement for him, and his excitement was infectious, so one's talks with him were an important part of one's education, and a very lively and thrilling part. I will not venture to speak about the endearing qualities in his character.

Another letter elaborates,

Though pre-first-war Balliol was full of remarkable and highly individual people, his arrival made a considerable stir in College. He came out of a world that, before 1914, was practically unknown to most of us in Britain. He was bursting with first-hand information about Eastern Europe and was eager to communicate it to us.

Yet another Balliol man says,

It was, probably late in 1908, in a forgotten undergraduate's room, that some nine or ten of us assembled and Berners was holding forth—on the hatred of the Germans in Eastern Europe, of the *tedeschi* in Italy; on the ambitions of the German militarists and the inevitability of war. War?! I had lived in a world which had no conception of war except as a regrettable colonial adventure for professional soldiers. I thought the fellow was talking rot.

Quite so. But throughout the Bosnian crisis, war was a grim likelihood at Koszylowce. Uncomfortably near the frontiers of Russia and Romania, it was to be outraged twice in L's lifetime by armies bringing carnage to its cosy villages and devastation to its placid fields and rich orchards. Being forced to envisage such a likelihood can speed up the maturing of a young man; it may also affect his scale of values. Small wonder that L struck most contemporaries at Balliol as being 'an older man', even 'a droll savant among boys'.

Undergraduates' friendships were starting up and falling into patterns—flexible, transient, and none the worse for that. G. N. Clark and L happened to sign the Fabians' Oxford University list at the same time, and continued to go together to Fabian gatherings. With Arnold Toynbee L shared a curiosity about far-flung journeys of historical personages venturing over land and sea; together they traced routes on maps, discussing the while similarities and diversities of situations and occurrences scattered about the records of mankind. Philip Plowden also speaks of 1908 as 'a very distinguished year' and goes on to say,

[L] was one of the most remarkable men in it. I knew him through the Balliol Historical Society of which I was secretary for two or three terms from October 1908. In spite of the fact that we usually had a distinguished audience and contributors, he stood out through his knowledge, keen analytical brain, experience of life and strong character. I remember he made a great impression on H. W. C. Davis who was a very shrewd judge of character. I went into lodgings in 1909 till my finals, and left Oxford in 1910. It is something that I remember him so vividly as an outstanding man after fifty-five years and a few meetings at a historical society. I never had the opportunity of meeting him again, which I regret. He was one of the most dynamic men I have ever known.

Attempts to fix the exact dates of L's visits to Koszylowce, while he was up at Oxford, have failed. But from him I know that he spent there the better part of his long vacations, was always with his parents for Christmas, and usually for Easter. In 1909 he brought back with him to Oxford the bulk of his neolithic collection, packed in a huge unwieldy chest which remained for years his most cumbersome possession and gave yet another comic twist to his singularity. Of his Balliol friends only G. D. H. Cole shared for a while L's concern with the contents of this monstrous chest, but many knew of it. The incentive for the collection's removal had been complex. Earlier efforts to draw proper attention to the Koszylowce finds were at last being rewarded with success. An eminent archaeologist, Professor K. Hadaczek of Lwow University, had undertaken to carry out the intentions of a deceased colleague to visit the site. He was organizing an expedition planned to include several regional commissioners for the preservation of antiquities, and was making preliminary arrangements to divide the best items fairly between suitable museums in Lwow and Vienna. But psychological and political factors had played their part, and a grave one, in prompting L to remove his collection. After the annexation of Bosnia and Hercegovina, Eastern Galicians were haunted by forebodings of a general war. Their dread of occupation by armies, defensive or offensive, was mounting. And Joseph—prone to react rashly to a pervasive mood—had responded to the widespread anxiety by giving his ineradicable passion its head. During the long vacation that year Ann revealed to her son his father's disastrous addiction to gambling. L, with the images of his Oxford tutors already stamped on his mind, and with their urbanity, tempered by Spartan rigour, already rubbing off on to him, took it badly. Only the dryness of Ann's statement—coupled with the warm affection shown by her without reserve as she deliberately raised her son to the status of a fully-informed fellow-sufferer—prevented his rage from exploding. Had it exploded, the household could well have broken up. But Ann's calm analysis of her early married life, when she realized how much she would have preferred Joseph to stray—since stray he did—to another's bed rather than to the gaming tables, was to L heart-rending. Her summing-up: 'affairs (politely called "of the heart") pass, vices don't; recurring they ruin the family', rang inexorably true. Appalled, he wished to obliterate his father, or at least to break with him. Restrained by Ann's implacable dignity, he carried through the only demonstrative action open to him, and took his most treasured possession from under his father's roof.

Later that year, L sold to the Ashmolean Museum two lots of

neolithic remains: Nos. 932 to 940 for £10, and Nos. 1187 to 1211 for £14. In the following year he sold for the price of £5 a third lot, consisting of two figurines remarkably unlike the crouching, heavy old woman who had sparked off his enthusiasm. These svelte figurines carry no elaborate transversal crest; theirs is a simplified version, turned half-circle so that each small head is adorned with a single graceful loop that begins at the nape and continues with a fine curving sweep to the tip of the nose, emphasized by it to a beak. And the elongated, frontally positioned bodies are thin-legged, narrow, with small breasts set wide apart at shoulder level. Rigid yet daring, they have a surprisingly modern air, not in the least suggestive of fertility. Yet Professor Tadeusz Sulimirski tells me that their clay—mixed with grain while moist—proves their having been intended for ceremonial use in fertility rites. And he knows the collection well: accompanied by Mme Sulimirska, he often stayed at Koszylowce in the late 1920s and early 1930s. Whether L was hard-pressed for cash at the moment of the sales or, on a wave of heightened anxiety, wanted his favourite pieces more securely housed, he never said. But the loving care he put into the transaction is reflected in his delicately precise sketch-plan of the site where they were found. The sketch, reproduced below, is also at the Ashmolean.

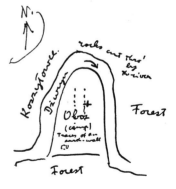

Almost any event that came along added to L's reputation for oddity. And since, even with the retarded young, interest in sex can lead to indiscretion at some time on the way to maturity, an undergraduate would occasionally be involved in a more or less scandalous scrape. Whether the offender was rusticated or sent down, such events were immediately localized and hushed up, but talked over for a while in little groups. And again L startled his friends. Having grown up in the country among Slavs, he viewed the sexual act with light-hearted frankness—in the farm-yards mating and procreation were part of a seasonal routine; analogies between man and beast, when obtrusive, seemed comic, rather than shaming. Yet L's approach to human relations in their elusive but rich variety was tender, basically Christian, with quaint romantic embellishments which, too, was typically Slav. But at Balliol this alien medley appeared to be equivocal and caused dismay. His contemporaries' views on sex were at best gothick-puritanical (Victorianism lingering on) while their appraisal of human relations was being cast into a proconsular mould reinforced with stoical athleticism and decked out with idealistic sentimentality. Here L delightedly went with his friends a long way, stopping short only of the heartiest athleticisms and the most naïve sentimentalities. All the more puzzling to them was his levity over regrettable scrapes. Misinterpretations were unavoidable; and the encircling aura of puzzlement thickened round him while he lumbered on, blandly unaware that no one could make him out.

Among L's friendships dating back to Oxford was one which—free on both sides of ambivalences or reservations—casts a brighter beam on to his maturing personality than any other single testimony I know of. Cuthbert Holmes writes:

I must have met Berners very shortly after I went up to Balliol, which was a whole year after he went up. And from 1909 to 1913 we met often. I had seen enough of the world (three continents by then) to realize that he was a strong man. He looked it, he spoke like it, he acted like it. By then, I had lived in France, Switzerland and Germany for two years each, with a bit of Italy thrown in. I was partly Spanish myself and partly Irish. Perhaps because I knew and spoke French and German like a native, we usually spoke French. We both rather disliked the Germans and feared they would, at best, not avoid war. From him I learnt to be very wary of official Austrian aims. One of the things that hurt me most when wounded and out of Europe—in fact out of every-thing for a long time—was that I could not continue my warm friend-ship with him.

Starting in the Balliol buttery, where the two discussed at length a variety of topics, their friendship was stabilized for good during the Easter Vacation of 1910, in Brighton. There they read together French books on pre-revolutionary France; and between times went for walks along the seashore or over the downs. And there Holmes discovered 'how charming a companion' L was, and remembered in particular that 'he laughed readily, spontaneously, with infectious sincerity'. Most clearly Holmes remembered the 'power' which at that time emanated from L. And next his original thought, expressed in striking comment and lightly offered in a mood of sparkling, warm tranquillity. Thirty years later, I, too, was confronted by this force—a stolidity transfused with active vigour. Intellectually stimulating it enthralled and could enslave. And I, too, was disturbed by the isolation that encircled L; of which Holmes remarks, 'in 1909 he seemed to me a rather lonely man'.

The 1910 visit to Brighton was unique. But some part of his summer vacation L regularly spent among Fabians at Pen-yr-Allt, associating chiefly with older men glad of opportunities to converse on contemporary English politics with young people ready to listen. To his assiduity and volubility at these gatherings L owed—besides his friendship with Thomas Jones—acquaintance with R. H. Tawney, A. D. Lindsay, Lawson Dodd, and Josiah Wedgwood. On his political thinking their influence was greater than they knew, though hardly what they would have wished. Defining where and why he differed from Fabians in general, and from this or that speaker in particular, L was imperceptibly plotting his future political course, with the help of a well-informed, wittily garrulous contemporary, Hugh Dalton. Rex Leeper remembered L sharing his own Liberal views. But this could only have been in the widest sense of the word 'liberal'. During his Oxford years L remained politically malleable, and receptive to a high degree. To the shaping of his views on wider issues personal influences continued important. His persistent analysis of why, how, and where his views collided with or diverged from those of men whom he liked and esteemed, was passionate. His tutors contributed much to this process of refinement. The dominant influence was that of his senior tutor, A. L.

Smith, admired by L for his intellect, learning, basic seriousness, ready wit, and genuine distress over the dispossessed which drove him to do all he could to better their lot. Kind by nature but austere by inclination, A. L. Smith helped L to discover in himself the same characteristics and to affirm them. They were much in each other's company: with others at tutorials or on walks out of Oxford; alone at his house, the King's Mound, under the apple trees by preference, with Mrs. A. L. Smith and their younger children somewhere in the background. Most subjects of interest to either were discussed at some time. And A. L. Smith's dicta and mannerisms unforgettably 'engraved' themselves on what L came to call the 'tablets' of his memory.

His other tutors also left their mark on L. Francis Fortescue Urquhart (even now 'Sligger' in Balliol) was a European with a great love of France where he had lived as a boy and where he later inherited a chalet with some land (at S. Gervais in the Haute Savoie). As early as 1905 he had advocated introducing into Balliol 'men who can be gentlemanly companions . . . to the young fellows'; 'men who will really take interest in *them* and not merely in their work'. His study overlooking the Martyrs' Memorial was, during term, a centre of education well into the night. After 10.30 p.m. undergraduates were free to assemble there and talk lightly on any subject they pleased. No one was barred, but the choice and manner of presentation were meticulously observed by the alert, polished—on those occasions rather silent—host, whose appreciation of nonsense had been finely developed by Edward Lear, a family friend. At such gatherings Sligger encouraged L to probe carefully what topics a roomful of young Englishmen could bear to broach at the end of a long day, and the manner of discussion or banter best suited to their sensibilities of the hour. To his tutorials in the same room L went, for a considerable time, with Cuthbert Holmes, their knowledge of French history and literature being equally in advance of their contemporaries'. Sligger kindled in both of them a keen delight in the great memoir-writers, but in L he also planted an enduring appreciation of Sainte-Beuve—the master of '*ce que je fais là d'étrange en critique littéraire*'. Sainte-Beuve was the earliest formative influence on L as a future reviewer of memoirs, diaries, and historical works in general. L's third tutor, Henry William Carless Davis ('Fluffy' in Balliol), gave him the first significant nudge to go ferreting for facts and details, and taught him how best to set about it. L found the exercise to his taste, soon diverged, and then turned his tutor's advice topsy-turvy, adapting it in his own way to his own use. They ended by disagreeing on the aims and the method of historical research. Still, the nudge had been, and was recognized by L to have been, important. He was to remain affected directly or contrariwise by many. While taking over no man's stream of thought, L found the detection of the effects a man's experiences had on his personality both thrilling and enriching.

In L's second year, a variety of influences—seemingly thrown together by chance—were enticing him on to paths trodden by few. The pursuit of Calvinism was the most bizarre. It has proved impossible to discover whose influence prompted him to steep himself in Calvin's writings. For interpreters he had, of course, no use; but even thirty years later he would quote to me in Latin (when clinching a theological argument of which we had many) entire clauses from the *Institutions,* and would praise Calvin's intellectual integrity. Calvin's basic apprehension of Predestination satisfied L who had, by then, perceived every person as living in a double cage of neither his choosing nor his making. Parents and family, home and background, nationality and time of birth formed the bars of a man's personal cage. And at the confines of his universe another, universal, cage circumscribed him. Constant challenges to his drive and ingenuity came from both, for both were amenable to slight alterations. Some bars could be bent, others broken. But no man could shake off his double cage nor slip through its bars. Definitely not a fatalist since he put great store by 'chance' or 'luck', and 'choice', L rejected double pre-destination outright: living irrevocably inside his two ineluctable cages, man was within those confines remarkably free.

Another of L's new and equally abiding interests was in current English politics. He avidly read the daily papers, fortnightlies, and monthlies, following the realignments of parliamentary parties and of groups representing this interest or that view, and watching the 'pirouettes' of individual members committed to one or other contingent but momentarily stirring issue. His interest in Parliament was growing as deep as it was wide. He took to reading Hansard. And out of these pursuits emerged, between the two General Elections of 1910, an obsessive delight in seeing the flexible British Empire affected by incidents at home or abroad. All was grist to his mills. But here, too, three personal influences were formative.

Since the Mastership of Jowett, Balliol no longer produced only scholars and teachers. Its importance in providing men for the Civil Service, at home and in India, reached a peak between 1908 and 1912. In that setting the British Empire's world-wide significance was defined for L by Lionel George Curtis, Ronald Wingate, and Ronald's father, Sir Reginald. Curtis had served in the Boer War and was a dedicated, theorizing, voluble Empire-builder. His anxious face and persuasive words had become a feature of Oxford where he went about, drawing undergraduates (and occasionally a tutor) into the slipstream of his enthusiasm. His ideal he preferred to call 'Commonwealth', and to its realization he was devoting his life. Ronald Wingate, who went up to Oxford in 1906, was preparing to enter the Indian Civil Service. A slightly senior contemporary of L's, he deplored Curtis's use of a clumsy long word lacking all splendour of overtones where the customary, resonant, short, vastly evocative word 'Empire' was also more correct. Sure of ear and delicate of touch, Ronald Wingate already was an exquisite pianist. L was to follow his career with warm concern; and when in the late 1950s Ronald published a book on his father followed by one on himself, L enjoyed reading both. In his son's Oxford days Sir Reginald was Governor-General of the Sudan and Sirdar of the Egyptian Army. The entity he had served 'was not imperialism. It was the Empire at its very best. Paternalism if you wish, but paternalism with co-operation and friendship at all levels.' His son goes on to say that he himself had occasion to observe how in the Sudan and Egypt such beneficent paternalism came easily to soldier-adminis-trators—initiated into the mystery of human relations through the dangers, rigours, and camaraderie of the battle-field; but in India it came only seldom to civilian administrators, inclined to feel remote at all times from those they ruled. L, invited to stay at Knockenhair (the Wingates' home on a wind-tormented hill outside Dunbar), was equally impressed by the Sirdar's character and his vision. The young scholar had some memorable talks with the mature administrator and L soon introduced 'the maker of the Anglo-Egyptian Sudan' into his portrait-gallery of outstanding people which he had been building up, in the vast museum of his mind, since Lausanne (because of the impression left by Pareto and Mme de X). In that gallery the Sirdar remained, for as long as L lived, the tutelary spirit of a great and good Empire. On subsequent visits to Koszylowce L drew frequent comparisons between the Empire served by the Sirdar and the Austro-Hungarian hugger-mugger of which his dislike was increasingly purposeful.

Early in the long vacation of 1910 the family at Koszylowce showed signs of being in turmoil. Almost a year had passed since Joseph had sent a petition to Vienna, asking that the imposed name, Bernsztajn, be revoked and the old name, Niemirowski, be fully restored to him. Fortunate in being able to pull certain strings while the mood in relevant circles was propitious, he professed to have no doubts about the result; but the long drawn out delay had got him hopping-mad and he went about the place ravelling cat's-cradles of tension. The effect on Ann was to set her thinking, almost obsessively, about the past. L, looking a stranger in his clothes of foreign cut yet still her most intimate preoccupation, was her chosen and fascinated listener. A natural story-teller, she brought into her narrative comments forcefully expressive of her earthy wisdom, which delighted him. In a few weeks of heart-to-heart communication, the two came to know, love, and admire each other as never before, and he learnt details about himself that he never forgot. But Theodora, for once morose, sought nobody's company. She had been much in Vienna perfecting her art and also sitting for her portrait by a fashionable painter. On the crest of a tempestuous infatuation they became engaged to be married, but only then did Theodora discover, rather crudely, that he—well known among his cronies for a boisterous amorist—had no patience with any bourgeois taboos.

She, proud and fastidious, did not find endearing his wide-flung, unabated, and much twittered-about exuberances, refused all compromise or accommodation and broke off the engagement, forbidding him ever again to enter her parents' house where she withdrew in haughty gloom.

The long-awaited documents came from Vienna towards the end of L's holiday. In the dignified jubilation that followed, Theodora identified herself with Joseph. Again inseparable, they decided it was time the family officially joined the Catholic Church, and that it would be done when they next went to Vienna. For years they had patronized the local churches and contributed to church charities, getting by as supporters and well-wishers. But many straws were astir in a wind of change: the years of liberalism and laxity were running out, public opinion was veering to intolerance, and the desire that unclear situations be tidied up was widespread. L, who was expected as a matter of course to do as the family did, resolutely dug in his heels and declared against the project, for himself—because he was a Calvinist. Joseph blew up: what idiocy was this? Theodora laughed. Ann was nonplussed. And they were further angered or puzzled in the next few days when L said that he—known even outside his college, through speaking at debates and writing in Oxford magazines—could not possibly switch over from being Ludwik Bernstein (and Berners) to Niemirowski, with no more ado. His name would have to be changed according to the English custom, by deed poll; and he proposed, at one go, to have his name Anglicized—that it should look less cumbersome, less ungainly on the title-page of the English books he would one day write. Undeterred by reasoning or ridicule, yet resenting both and hurt by Ann's lack of understanding, he further explained that it might be best for him to spell the first syllable NAY (to guide the English pronunciation) and lop off the last two—a puzzling, spluttering redundancy to the English ear. Displeasure thickened round him. It had not thinned when he left for England to do before the year was out exactly as he had said. On 21 December 1910, at a solicitor's office in Gresham Street, London, E.C., he signed the deed poll 'declaring change of name from Ludwik Bernstein to Lewis Bernstein Naymier'. And almost at once he regretted that, of his own free choice, he had introduced into his new name—which in its English form he felt to be exclusively his—a redundant 'y'. He could have kicked himself.

In the Michaelmas term L had enjoyed the Oxford whirl as never before. He studied with his usual enthusiasm, but little of what he read was directly profitable to his final examinations, and in next to no time he again found himself in Koszylowce. There Theodora on her better days wittily scoffed at her brother, on her bad days mocked him. Joseph brooded on Koszylowce's need for more money. Ann grieved over the accumulation of Joseph's debts, and reverted to lulling herself and her son into the security of time past where, to her at any rate, the worst was known and nothing unexpected by her (indeed nothing well-forgotten by her) could pounce on them. And as she added fresh touches to her reminiscences of their common life, they dallied where they chose. But Joseph presently jerked L out of this some-what torpid state of happiness by speaking in confidence of a new financial venture full of rosy possibilities for all of them. The son of a small employee on the Darachow estate in Theodor's day, who had himself been, in L's words, 'some kind of bottle-washer in the alcohol distillery' before he emigrated to avoid conscription in the Austro-Hungarian army, had made good. Writing from New York all aquiver with lucrative schemes he had also been buying up Joseph's promissory notes. The lot would be cancelled with no more ado if, in due course, L went out to help increase the dashing little bottle-washer's fortune while building up his own and his family's. How serious any of this was L could not judge. His final examinations were on his mind.

Well over two years had passed since L had taken his First Public Examination ('Prelims') in Law, under the tuition of Edward Hilliard. During this time his enthusiasm for 'Divvers' (an examination in Divinity, abolished after the war) was thought very funny. None but Sligger and A. L. Smith (who consecutively tutored him) could have said why L was to remember with high relish this unusually long period. At the time only they knew that he had asked to do twice as much as required and had enthusiastically worked through two Gospels, John and Luke. Curiosity about languages and a new experience had led to it. Plato's Greek adjusting itself to a Christian ethos aroused his detective zeal; and his own glad submission to the forceful cadences of the Authorized Version gave him undreamt-of pleasure. Resounding through him the cadences helped to form his distinctive, very personal prose-style. His Second Public Examination (the 'Finals') was for him a special wrestling match with the language he wished to master. Scrutinizing the new experiences that dominated him, he observed that he was thinking in English. The result—a First in Modern History and the degree of B.A. (from which the M.A. followed after three years without further examination) greatly satisfied him; his tussle with the tongue he wished to make his had steadied for him an ambition that was to endure.

In their last year at Oxford, L and Ronald Wingate saw much more of each other than before, when Lewis had still lived in college. And as soon as circumstances allowed they travelled together north, for what was to be L's last visit to Knockenhair. Ronald never forgot how hopeless a pupil L was at golf; L remembered Lady Wingate's approval of him as an agreeably sagacious partner at bridge. And the Sirdar proved himself a man of stern independence of mind transfused with a sensitive social conscience. But while Empire was establishing itself in L's scheme of human affairs, a new anxiety was beginning to well up and the two became blended. He still knew next to nothing of Jewish life. A blank so unexpected, indeed incongruous, in a man with features unmistakably Semitic and an avowed pride in his ancestors, led to many awkward situations. At Oxford, English-Jewish undergraduates, who knew only their own kind and impoverished small-town immigrants from the Eastern Pale, could not make him out at all. Aware of it, he was intrigued by his singularity among them; and soon developed a curiosity about Jews in general. Scanning the press with his usual care, he read of the uneasy political situation in Russia, Turkey, and countries bordering on them, which was setting in motion increasing waves of apprehension. A crag on which the waves broke, to swell with renewed vigour, was a timely re-publication of the *Protocols of the Elders of Zion*; and related to it was a recurring, tedious, yet heated correspondence in *The Times*. Dr. M. Gaster there passionately refuted allegations against his coreligionists accused of running the Young Turks Committees in Salonica and elsewhere. Gaster's opponents, renewing their attack, affirmed that Jews should be held responsible for some of the worst misdemeanours of the Committee of Union and Progress throughout Turkey. L, disposed to grope for solid facts in obscure situations, was alerted, poised for action. Thus, when in the industrial valleys of South Wales riots broke out, involving attacks on Jewish shops, he set out for Tredegar—reputed the worst trouble spot.

The summer of 1911 was unusually hot. From June to the end of August the temperature repeatedly rose above eighty. Drought was wide-spread. Nerves were frayed, tempers short. Industrial unrest simmered at home and on the continent. Here and there ugly situations boiled up. On 16 August the long-threatened national railway strike affected services for three days. But it did not prevent L from reaching his destination, though it led to his taking a roundabout route and making the journey in several parts (whereby a pattern of voyaging was set, perfected in the last ten years of his life). Urgent need for specific information suggested that he should break his course to Tredegar at Coldeast, Claud Montefiore's house in Hampshire. Availability of transport enabled L's wish to become a plan, and the route proved no less significant than the goal.

At Coldeast L was implacably stone-walled by his learned host whose son, a good friend, had been at Oxford with L. Well aware that the recurrent ill-humour between him and other young Jews at Oxford was largely due to his ignorance of their internecine preoccupations and collisions, L had remained uninterested until this juncture. Eager now to spare himself and his Jewish hosts at Tredegar any avoidable embarrassment he had decided to learn, in the easy give-and-take of conversation, some essential facts of the current conflicts among English Jews. Nothing came of it. Claud Montefiore, firmly uncommunicative throughout L's short stay, finished by being pointedly rude. L was unable to understand how a serious theologian of world renown could refuse—in hostile silence—to help him, when all he wanted was to avoid giving offence to humble co-religionists whom he, an outsider, was about to see in their plundered homes. He dismissed Claud Montefiore as a learned old humbug. In time, he spread this personal aversion in a general way to rich Jews specializing in Biblical studies; and for the rest of his life detested learned men of caustic vanity. Yet about Tredegar his apprehensions proved to be unfounded. Having been refused all help at Coldeast, he lapsed into a state of puzzled sincerity typical of him when impelled to act in the dark but afraid to give pain. From an ultra-orthodox small-town rabbi (whom he affectionately depicted some years later, see *Conflicts*, p. 172), L reaped the benefit of a spontaneous, warm response. This, too, he never forgot. The contrast between his rich and pompous host and the poorly-educated man full of understanding, left an indelible impression on L: its harshness aggravated many future hostilities, its tenderness enhanced some devotions.

The excitement of Tredegar was heightened by the pace at which L was obliged to carry out his inquiries. That year's Fabian Summer School—L's last—was held abroad, in Switzerland at Saas-Grund in the Valais. All available rooms, including the whole of the Monte Moro Hotel and a large chalet belonging to the Commune, had been booked by the committee from 29 July to 8 September. Subscribers were many, and had to be divided into three groups, each assigned a fortnight only. L, whose name was down for the last week in August through the first in September, was rather pressed to reach in time the small village isolated in the High Alps. Yet so great was his zeal to gather in the facts of the Tredegar pogrom and so exhilarating was the mere expectation of mountaineering that even in retrospect the pressure of those days increased his sense of enjoyment. On the two occasions when, in the late 1950s, we stayed together at Montana, L often paused on our walks to look across the Rhône valley towards Italy. He talked much of his last Fabian Summer School—among bare rocks, hemmed in by snow-peaks and glaciers. Some reminiscences were tinged with amusement at the surprised delight of the leading feminists of the party when they grasped that their group, the only one led by a woman (Miss Mabel

Atkinson) was the most adventurous in its expeditions and would be noted as such in the log-book. From childhood L and Theodora had ridden out for adventure neck and neck; of the two she was, if anything, the more adventurous; and, as children, they had picked up the oral family tradition of their mother's and their paternal grandmother's administrative abilities and fearless decisions when the family was in a fix. The prowess of women often delighted but never astonished L.

The brief Saas-Grund holiday was followed by agitated weeks at home. Political tensions—originating in traditionally Slav lands occupied by Turkey—threatened to involve the neighbouring Great Powers. Young Austrian Poles, eager to accept nascent challenges, analysed positions, debated issues, and speculated on the future. L, scornful of his father's prolix liberalism, drew closer to his one congenial neighbour, Victor Czarkowski-Golejewski. They went about a great deal together and, shoulder to shoulder, opposed Theodora and Joseph. On one point only were the four agreed: whatever the solution, an emergent Poland would have a vital part to play in establishing a more just world so organized that mankind's inherent rapacity would never again be allowed to dominate its affairs.

Intellectually seminal arguments, resembling hot quarrels, were cut short by a curious bout of ill-health which, on Joseph's insistence, took L to Vienna. The diagnosis was prompt: headaches, lassitude, inordinate irritability, were all due to an ulceration of the gums—like Joseph's at the time of his son's birth. A peculiar distrust of himself gripped L. Had he not inherited—together with something of Joseph's brilliant intellect—a subtle rottenness of body and character? Was this the message transmitted by the hand of destiny when it weighed heavy on his shoulder? Yet he responded well to the treatments and returned home ready for new disputes. But Joseph had been corresponding with the former bottle-washer—Louis N. Hammerling of New York—and it had been agreed that L should go out to take up a well paid administrative position in the Foreign Languages Press. At first flush he was obstreperous, having planned to work hard in Oxford and London on unpublished material for a book on the Empire. If this now seemed too self-indulgent, a plan put forward by A. L. Smith and Sligger could perhaps be brought forward by a year. After L's finals both tutors had thought he might try for a fellowship at All Souls in November 1912. Why not in November 1911? Braced by the ease of his recent successes, L saw no serious objection. Joseph demurred. But Ann, above all a peacemaker in those days, suggested a compromise: should events prove their son to have been foolhardy, he could go to the U.S. in the new year; should he succeed, another academic distinction would do no harm whatever turn his life took. Of the details they could talk later.

On the journey to England L's new malaise increased. His jaws and head ached till he thought he must be disintegrating. Haunted by his past observations of Joseph's defects, he foresaw a menacing future. With his mind swinging backward and forward, his grip on the present loosened. As occurs in families well informed on their long lineage yet unafraid to face reality, L knew of distant and more spectacular, and of recent and more tawdry, cases of insanity among ancestors and kin. He began to fear observing himself, yet did so the more meticulously.

In Oxford L took rooms at 44 New Inn Hall Street and called on A. L. Smith, tentatively to disclose his plan which was at once approved by this, his highest, authority. A. L. Smith's remark, 'a devilishly clever fellow, Namier', probably belongs to those days. It is remembered by A. L. Smith's daughter, Rosalind, to whom L at some time confided his delight in having heard of it. Soon came a day when he was asked to dine at All Souls. Sligger, the kindest of mentors, took him in hand. On no account was L to speak unless spoken to. And he was to be attentive to whatever others said—small talk, of course, but wise, and beautifully put. Subdued yet eager, L found himself sitting beside one great luminary in the firmament of history and opposite another. Over the soup there was no talking. Next came a pie. 'Dicey,' called L's neighbour somewhat querulously to the man opposite, 'is this what they describe as pigeon pie?' The man opposite mumbled an affirmative. Silence. 'Dicey,' softly wailed L's neighbour, 'why do they call it pigeon pie when there is no pigeon in this pie?' The mumble from across the table was noncommittal. But over coffee there finally was some conversation and several

Fellows spoke to L. What they said was too trivial to remember.

By the end of October frequent pain was affecting his powers of concentration. Some nights he lay half-awake, feverishly imagining a quarrel with his Viennese doctor. L wanted all his teeth out, and the useless drugs that had been pressed on him he wanted flushed down the drain; the doctor was furious—extractions might pump the poison into the bloodstream and weaken the patient's heart; drugs were safer; he knew what he was doing. On 3 November L went to the college hall. He later described the exam in vivid terms: sitting down and looking at the white sheets of paper before him, he realized that the pain had lifted, his mind had cleared, the ideas he had been gathering for the occasion were moving in. To make them communicable, he only had to encase them in words. And away they sped. Past the numinous void's narrow rim where L waited and looked on aghast, the stream of time, grown visible, carried away his store of ideas. Streaming time annihilated ticking time. Words failed him. Near panic, he snatched at this or that, here and there, putting down on paper whatever it was, with little regard for coherence.

Unsuccessful papers are always burnt at All Souls; the verdict passed on them is never disclosed—the electors remain pledged to silence; and rumours together with interpretations of rumours go the round of Oxford. When it became clear that L had failed, three explanations began to circulate. The first theory was that his paper had shocked the adjudicators by its unconventional brilliance even more than by its lack of any conventional presentation—no Englishman could have shown such disregard for the rules. The second interpretation went as follows: a Jew and (as some imagined) recently sent by fabulously rich Jews to Tredegar, he was thought dangerous by secret yet rabid anti-Semites who had cast their vote against him. The third rumour claimed that a most important person, who was also a highly prized Fellow but had not been at All Souls when L dined there, found himself shuddering to think how L would behave 'aftah dinnah'. L himself thought that in the first rumour there definitely were, and in the third there might be, shreds of truth. The second rumour he rejected outright as pure fabrication. The Oxford he knew was not anti-Semitic, and there was no such caucus at All Souls. Yet A. F. Pollard, in a letter to his parents dated 5 November 1911, wrote,

The meeting on Friday morning for the election of Fellows was lively, and I was told the debate was the best on record, which perhaps I should not repeat as I had to take a considerable part in it. The lawyers could not conscientiously run a law candidate, so we had two for history. The best man by far in sheer intellect was a Balliol man of Polish-Jewish origin and I did my best for him, but the Warden and majority of Fellows shied at his race, and eventually we elected the two next best.

Alongside the phrase 'a Balliol man of Polish-Jewish origin' is a marginal note by Pollard added later: 'Namier'.

L (who never knew about Pollard's letter) would often remark, when speaking of the incident in years to come, that by no means every Jew is disliked, by all those who dislike him, just because he is a Jew; and that he himself had detested some Englishmen though he loved the English who were on the whole a delightful lot. The good guess (the first theory) he explained as correct deduction supported by touches of telepathy. In 1953, speaking on the wireless on 'Human Nature in Politics', he was to say, 'We do not even know some of the means whereby men communicate thoughts and emotions to each other.' And to me he remarked that, morally lazy, we ignore the promptings of empathy if it increases our responsibility for others.

Such of L's contemporaries as are now well placed to analyse the 1911 All Souls event, tend to think the conditions of the test—three hours of hurried, tense writing on a general subject as vast as the contestant chose to make it—were a snare for him; and that a thesis written at leisure in an ambience of his own choosing would have been unanimously acclaimed a work of impressive merit. In 1912 another Fellow, Geoffrey Robinson, who was present at the crucial meeting, mentioned in passing, 'I think we were all impressed with his brilliance'. But L, the brilliant failure, had travelled home despondent immediately after the fiasco—uncertain how best to tackle his doctor and his father. Vain apprehensions. In Vienna a couple of L's teeth were extracted, and at Koszylowce Joseph was impressed by his son's unifying theme now beautifully put across in Polish. With Ann's support,

L was not prevented from returning to Oxford, nor from moving about Europe a good deal. During 1912 L followed an original and intensive postgraduate course of his own planning, financed largely by Joseph and supplemented by L's free-lance journalism. With eagerness he snatched every occasion to study books and burrow in manuscripts; but books and manuscripts could never block the wider field of vision which was typical of him. As a squirrel lays in nuts, wherever L went in this season of his life he amassed hot news and vivid impressions, only some of which were for immediate use. He was intellectually and emotionally retentive beyond our general scope.

CHAPTER SIX

Scholar in Bondage
1912–1915

A contribution of L's to the *Blue Book*—an Oxford under-graduates' bi-monthly magazine—marks an important stage in his adjustment to his environment. 'The very first article' (in the May 1912 issue, its first number) 'was by him,' writes the then editor, William C. Greene who remembers L 'with pleasure' as 'some-what detached but friendly and a very good talker'. Entitled '*C'est l'amour du vieux monde*', the article shows L's love of Europe exacerbated by his own censure of it. He had observed how 'dense masses, lifted up or depressed by forces which are not of their own making' were being turned into arbiters of taste. Since none of them had passed 'through the purifying moments through which the lonely wanderer' must go, the quality of their preferences spread a subtle corruption. Pandered to, they remained 'dull and nerveless as before'. Their minds continued drab, their interest petty. George Bernard Shaw, too, had seen this writing on the wall; and L did not doubt that his own judgement of the observed facts was correct. The loved Old World was drifting into despic-able vulgarity. Even valiant men of action serving their country with pure devotion were induced to appear on the pages of 'illus-trated society papers' alongside prize-fighters and ostentatious dancers, all decked with the same tinsel. The group L tilted at was reaching out 'for the unbought graciousness of life' unaware that borrowed forms have no 'circulatory energy'. But there was still hope. The creative abilities and drive, absent among petty townsfolk intent on aping an opulent Upper Crust, were vigor-ously surging through groups of 'working-men' in whose instruc-tion L, under guidance from A. L. Smith, was taking part. If more men with well-trained first-rate minds dedicated themselves to supporting the Workers' Educational Association, a new flowering

of creative energies might well stamp out the pervasive rot. In
his audiences of working men L had sensed an austere passion
for knowledge resembling his own. He thought they realized as
he had—and as Sir William Anson had said in the House of
Commons on 7 May 1902—that 'education cannot secure success
in life but may go a long way to make life interesting'. L took it
that the English working man was ravenous for advanced learning
capable of radically transforming even his 'dreary surroundings
and monotonous life'. In the Galician doldrums L had felt equally
depressed and deprived.

Apace with his mounting criticism of the vulgarity creeping
through the Old World, L's interest in the New World advanced.
He was gathering in the Bodleian, the British Museum Reading
Room, and the Royal Colonial Institute a multitude of facts for a
book on 'The Imperial Problem during the American Revolution'. A. L. Smith and Sligger knew of the collection and were
intrigued by L's ideas based on it. As the year advanced, they
pressed him to infuse cohesion into the heap by writing the 1912
Beit Prize Essay on 'Proposals in the direction of a closer union
of the Empire before the opening of the Colonial Conference of
1887'. Because he had resisted—with spontaneous vehemence—
their advice to try a second time for the All Souls Fellowship, L
was reluctant to turn down their new suggestion. But he agreed
only half-heartedly, and settled down to write the essay absurdly
near the final date for sending it in. He liked to recall later some
comic details of the situation he had thoughtlessly built up.
Through two nights and a day he wrote his essay in longhand
while friends stood by—to renew cooling compresses on his overworked head, press on him cups of strong coffee, and carry the
accumulating pages from his lodgings to the typists' office and
back.

L opened his essay with: 'It would be easy to pick out a number
of plans scattered over the two-and-a-half centuries which this
essay covers.' But it would be pointless: 'Plans for a closer union
of the Empire' were 'of two types', or some combination of the
two. Type one was colonial representation in the existing Parliament at Westminster, complicated by various suggestions of
inter-colonial federation—tentative efforts to overcome the

awkwardness of some political units being too small, too poor, or insufficiently populous for just representation along with others. Type two amounted to union in a new National Parliament, in the sense of different 'nations' (self-aware communities) being represented in it as 'national' equals. Already he had perceived a tension between nationality and constitutional development. In 1948, writing of the European revolution of the intellectuals, he was to linger on it, but in the Beit Essay he had already noted the strain—on the way to concluding his introductory section with: 'the only real study of proposals for a closer union of Empire . . . is the study of the Imperial Idea or the Imperial Spirit'; which he thought best done by examining one 'crowded moment'—in his essay's context, the eve of the American Revolution.

'The first crisis in the history of the British Empire . . . [was] . . . the Civil War in England'—L ran through those years and the following decades substantiating each statement so well yet so crisply that the pace is immediately breathless. As he approached the American Revolution, a close study of his massive documentation would clearly have made the essay lop-sided and gigantic. Dropping narrative, he had recourse to appendices where he listed and snappily analysed his sources, including a great many contemporary pamphlets. The imperial idea or spirit was not defined or dealt with. Yet the essay is impressive owing to the author's ability to communicate his sense of the inexorable drift of time. From this emanates a coherence that gives the essay an unexpected shapeliness. Moreover, the receptive reader is made aware that solutions possible or even excellent at one historical moment (call it T) are either not possible or no longer good at another (call it F); but unfortunately the tradition of T's desirability, more often than not, persists even beyond F. The overall message is that many political incongruities derive from this elusive tendency in human affairs; that from the second half of the eighteenth century it coloured the accounts, and in some respects affected the manner, of the first British Empire's disruption; and that much historical reality rests hidden from the mind's eye by outworn figures of speech, or rhetoric become food for fancy. L's brilliant near-failure was awarded a half-prize; the other half going to Alfred le Roy Burt, a Canadian Rhodes

Scholar at Corpus Christi College, afterwards Professor of History at Minnesota, 1930–57. L's view of his own essay is stated on one of its carbon copies—a mere 'skeleton'.

Following on his Beit Essay L brought some order into his collection of material on little known trends at work in the Austro-Hungarian Empire. I hold twenty-two typed pages marked by him in 1946 as 'written early in 1913 for *The Times*'. It is a closely reasoned forecast of the likely attitude among Austrian, German, and Russian Poles in case of war in east-central Europe. Amplified with on-the-spot observations and facts dug up in local or not too distant (Continental) libraries, it amounts to an analysis of particular multi-racial problems, with stress on Galicia since public opinion was allowed considerable freedom of expression in Austrian Poland. The contradictions that held the scattered nationalities of the Dual Monarchy rigidly interlocked were here first exposed by L. He was to expound them throughout two world wars. During the same period, 1912–13, L was, by his own account, sending information on imperial affairs and on east-central Europe to H. W. Massingham. Yet his name does not appear in the issues of *The Nation* for that year and since the journal's pre-1914 account-books perished in World War II during the air-raids on London, one cannot even know what L was paid for whatever contributions he sent in. Most likely, as with *The Times* report, that material was used by others at an opportune political moment. He must have had in mind such extracts from his amassed knowledge when he wrote in 1930, in his Introduction to *Skyscrapers,* of his eighteen-year-old association with the press. From his collection of material, largely incorporated in the Beit Essay and *The Times* report, disparate notes have survived. The small, firm, clear, well-spaced and rather heavy handwriting that covers the yellowing pages indicates the period. There are long quotations and short ones from rare, important, or ephemeral yet significant works on economics as well as history; and there are many statistical tables—movements of populations and the like.

Invigorated by congenial work L was also enjoying his social life, still largely based on Oxford. At the King's Mound A. L. Smith's gifted, amusing, and remarkably good-looking daughters—four of whom were still at home—composed, with their father's help, some illuminating lines of verse,

> There was a young person called Namier
> Who came here and came here and came 'ere.
> Is it Pa, you or me, whom he comes here to see?
> Oh, which of us all is his flame 'ere!

None the less the main tributary of L's life continued at Koszy-lowce, and Joseph pressed him to leave for New York. There was much to be said for his taking up a responsible position in the Foreign Languages Press; and the Bancroft Transcripts that he wished to study for his book on 'The Imperial Problem' were at the New York Public Library; also, like most young people, he wanted to see the world and travel far. Yet his father's transaction with Hammerling deeply offended L's sense of proper human relations. In time his favourite summing up of the deal was 'They [his family] sold me as bondsman for my father's debts'; while at once two combined acts rejecting his background expressed the intensity of his distaste. On 25 March 1913 he was granted by 'one of His Majesty's Principal Secretaries of State' a Certificate of Naturalization and was declared a British subject which, as a matter of course, was followed, on 31 March, by his swearing and subscribing his Oath of Allegiance to King George V; and on 17 April he changed—once more by deed poll—the spelling of his name, omitting the 'y' after the 'a'. Having for a second time enacted and registered his independence—and having deposited his chest of neolithic sherds in G. D. H. Cole's rooms—L sailed for New York early in May on a Cunarder (R.M.S. *Carmania*) to do his father's bidding.

By arrangement or chance Lord Eustace Percy, travelling to Washington as honorary attaché, was on the same boat. In 1952 they talked of it in my hearing. Neither could remember when or how they first met, only that they already knew each other well. Whether Sir Cecil Spring Rice (the new ambassador) was on board or not they disagreed. L felt sure he had been on board, and that Lord Eustace had there introduced them; and it was to this introduction that L ascribed Sir Cecil's marked kindness to him in America. But Lord Eustace remembered nothing of it.

About the arrival in New York, L sought no such corroborative evidence. An exasperating disappointment that struck him at once and an enchantment that never paled both stamped their details boldly on his mind. In his notes on 'Zionism and Jews' he says of Louis N. Hammerling,

> He got me to come over to America as his understudy for President of the Foreign Languages Press; but about the time I arrived, he had a new idea. He was about to start a mail order house for the foreign-language population, in order to capitalise his influence in a new direction. It was essential for him to put in someone whose honesty he could absolutely trust, and I spent in the mail order house most of my year in America. . . .

The articles that appeared in the Foreign Languages Press over Hammerling's name

> must have been written by some fifth secretary of his, but they brought the great man (fluent only in Yiddish) a comfortable side income of 12,000 dollars a year. . . .

A confused paragraph about the way in which payments for articles were interlocked with advertisements ends,

> The charge for the advertisements was very high. But one of the great secrets of H's enterprises was how much he received and how much he disbursed. This I could not gauge since I never worked in that office. But watching from a distance with real amazement his system of corruption, I learnt a certain amount of worldly wisdom from the pragmatic genius of the man.

To have been lured across the Atlantic because 'the boss' had doubts about any other available man's honesty, deeply riled L. Administrative work in a mail order house was such a sorry waste of time that even the aim of wiping out Joseph's debts did not always seem to justify it. But L found compensation, indeed comfort, even during the first weeks of resentful rage, in the impression made on him by New York's visually and intellectually stimulating skyscrapers. That the human race, faced by the need to house many of its kind in a small space blessed with a solid rock foundation, should have had the ingenuity to join into long units the small separate houses of the straight horizontally-planned streets and, hoisting the units into a vertical position, send them soaring to scrape the sky, did more than amuse or even delight him. It sparked his own inventiveness. Soon he was using the skyscraper as an ideograph for the interplay of man's independence and interdependence. An example of such interplay is the economic solidarity of nations which curb their political self-assertiveness in order to form part of a viable cluster and yet, if sagacious, continue to affirm each man's inalienable right to his political passions by insisting on the secrecy of his vote. In short, the skyscraper remained in L's private script the ideograph for man's creative adaptability. Yet in due course it became also a code word in his universe of expanding symbols, each of which acquired variants and dilations according to its own laws, and to which he but seldom added a deliberate touch. It had also introduced into L's mind an ever-green 'American' strand. Thus counterbalanced, L's hostility to his employer never developed into rancour. Besides, being honest in a drab set-up left him with an overflow of energy he was free to use as he chose.

When the hot weather began, Hammerling encouraged L to wander where he wished and to indulge any whim. The first 'whim' to assert itself was contemporary history. Unrest, involving local murder and widespread economic dislocation, had been tormenting Mexico. When President Francisco Madero was assassinated and General Huerta (said by some to have engineered the plot) affirmed himself head of state, the dovecots of the European press went a-twittering and a-fluttering. In July *The Times* spoke of U.S. intervention, and on 25 July Sir Cecil Spring Rice wrote to L,

What do people think about Mexico? Grey did not make any official communication but merely asked Page privately whether the U.S. government could do what the other powers had done and recognize Huerta provisionally, until the elections are held in October; and if they had other information different from that which had led the other powers to recognize. There is very great pressure in Europe on behalf of the banks. I presume the U.S. Government don't want to 'grasp the bloodstained hand' especially when the owner appears to be going down the precipice. I have made no official representation whatever. I think personally the U.S. are the best judges of the situation and are certainly most nearly interested. What do you hear?

A few days later Sir Cecil again wrote,

Of course tell what you know. What happened is that the representatives in Mexico (not without the knowledge of Ambassador Wilson) met together and sent a telegram to the European governments asking them to suggest to the U.S. government that the best way to secure peace was to recognize Huerta. The governments did not want to make a joint or separate communication in this sense to the U.S. government as such joint communications give rise to trouble, but Grey told Page privately what had occurred and asked him if the U.S. government could not join in a temporary and provisional recognition of Huerta till the legal elections; and he also asked, if the U.S. government did not see its way to doing this, what other steps they proposed taking. I don't think the U.S. government has yet sent its answer—at least I have not heard of any. Since then the British government has asked that early notice should be given them if the U.S. government intended using force, in order that ships might be sent to protect British subjects, if protection was required. We have no ships in the neighbourhood at present (as far as I know).

You are perfectly right that our government has no intention of intervening itself but the interests concerned are very large indeed and there is a great deal of pressure. . . .

Of dictators—a major plague in L's lifetime—he wrote most significantly during World War II—for example, 'The First Mountebank Dictator'.[1] But Huerta was the first of the evanescent breed whose wild yet calculated course he followed in the local press, through private correspondence, and in wide discussions.

In Yale where L had gone to work on the Ezra Styles MSS. his analysis of the position and its possibilities seems to have pleased. He was voted into a select undergraduates' club because, as one enthusiastic and outspoken voter explained, although a declared Jew he carried a clean hull, with no Jewish barnacles attached to it. His solitariness had again been noticed. On it he commented twenty years later: 'We [Jews] are safest where . . . we receive individual treatment.' Meantime Sir Cecil Spring Rice wrote,

It is very interesting what you say about New Haven and Yale. I am very glad people have been so friendly. I should love to go round their universities if it did not imply, as it seems to, formal ceremonies. But I dare say I shall soon have more acquaintances and be able to do what you are doing.

[1] Reprinted in *Facing East*, 1947.

The circle of L's friends was widening fast. Soon he went deeper into Connecticut; and then beyond the Hudson into rural Pennsylvania. These expeditions he described as spells of relaxation in highly congenial company. Some of his hosts were linked with Balliol personally or through relatives; and he managed to put in a good deal of riding, still his favourite recreation. Alfred A. Biddle remembers L best as 'a teller of jokes and discoveries; jokes and discoveries about the Puritans and, the less attractive, Cavaliers'. L's second 'whim', the eighteenth century whose imperial crisis started in the seventeenth, had begun to absorb him. Of it, too, he spoke much in Yale. On what business, wild-goose chase, or spree he had also been to Canada, there is no telling. But the ever helpful Sir Cecil wrote,

I . . . have . . . written to Canada to ask for facilities. As everyone is away I think it may be a long time before I get an answer. Perhaps therefore it would be safer if I were to send you this letter direct. I received from Balliol College the strongest letters of recommendation in your favour and was informed that you had gained a very high position in Balliol where you were known as a man of great zeal and intelligence. I was also told (and have since had ocular demonstration of the same) that your business in America was connected with the non-English press, and that you are inspired by the most patriotic feelings with regard to the Empire. I hope that everyone you meet in Canada will afford you every assistance of which you may stand in need.

But even the most delightful seasons end. And Alfred A. Biddle's note on L to me concludes with a flourish checked by consternation, 'A master of encapsulating vast subjects, what a cheerful soul he was. But he would go to New York!'

Back on tedious mail-order work, L organized his life differently. He had made an observation while away: there definitely was something odd about his speech. New York abounded in elocution classes. He found a well-established teacher and arranged to follow privately with her a full course remembered chiefly for being punctuated by admonitions to, 'Energize your lips, Mr. Er-r, energize your lips'. His evenings and Sundays he spent in the New York Public Library, indulging to the full his second 'whim'. Before mid-winter the assiduous perusal of eighteenth-century Anglo-American activities took him to New

Haven again. There he completed his notes on the Ezra Styles MSS. and sought an interview with Professor Charles MacAndrew of Yale. For the wisdom of this 'straightforward, punctilious, and dignified elder in history' L retained the highest regard. 'He put it to me that while a great deal of work on the condition of the Empire in the eighteenth century is being done in America, they received but little help from our side.' In short, told to go home and work from there, he accepted the advice without demur.

By mid-winter L's prejudice against his employer had lifted. He was observing Hammerling with an empathy combined with the 'sadistic' joy of dissection; and presently classified him as a rare specimen—a brilliant ruffian resembling the *condottieri* of the Italian Renaissance but freakishly reared in a Galician backwater and transported to a brash new world while still malleable. L summed up his analysis, 'The story of Louis N. Hammerling will never be written. Not even his children could tell it; and I know too little never having been properly in his business. . . .' But three characteristic episodes stuck in L's mind,

The first concerned a silly little girl, a typist, and the efficient chief of the typing room. After the rumpus between them was over, H said to me, 'What did he want of her?—she works here for ten dollars a week'. I never forgot the moral: if you throw on people responsibility beyond the range of their knowledge or ability to think, or out of proportion to the pay they receive, and things go wrong—don't blame them, blame yourself.

The second story starts with H coming one day into my room and finding me writing in long hand. Asked what I was doing, I explained that, having nothing to do, I was writing letters. To which he remarked that if I had nothing to do I ought to go for a walk; letters should be dictated, to people worth 40 dollars a month—I was even then getting 200. From that day I took to dictating whenever I could. And the habit served me well when my right hand gave out.

The last story I remember was more complicated. Yiddish was probably the only language H knew well. Yet in America he denied being a Jew which everybody knew he was, though he did not look it. One day I asked him the point of denying a fact so widely known. He answered: 'Among my 500 editors there are more than 200 Roman Catholic priests. They may all know that I am a Jew, but that's nothing. So long as I don't go on record with it, they can vote for me as President of the Association; and they will because it suits their interest. But if only once

I openly admit to being a Jew, they could no longer vote for me—and both sides would suffer a loss.' Though I despised his action, he taught me a lesson here too. I never forgot: '. . . so long as I don't go on record . . .'

By the time I was leaving, we both knew that we did not suit each other, and that I would never suit the job. Yet for various reasons he wanted me back; and before I sailed for home, in the spring of 1914, it was settled that, after my holiday, I would return not to Hammerling, but instead would enter the law office of Charles Nagel, former Minister for Commerce and leader of the Taft Administration.

After L's first book on the eighteenth century had appeared, Charles Nagel wrote to express his pleasure 'at seeing your name as the author of so important a publication'; and spoke of a time when 'we saw more or less of each other, and . . . were in a fashion co-operating'.

L continued to approve of Hammerling for talking often 'when a very rich man . . . about his distant days' in Darachow 'with no embarrassment but much gratitude and admiration for the family that had helped him [to emigrate]'. Yet L was appalled by the man's defects when he induced L—again because his honesty and discretion were obvious—to try to push through a divorce on which the *condottiere* had set his heart. A certain amount of correspondence in English, German, Yiddish, and Hebrew—relating to this most distasteful of all L's American chores—long survived in a large envelope inscribed by him 'To be destroyed after my death'. When I agreed (in 1959) to write L's biography, he instructed me to read as much of it as I could before throwing away the lot. It showed that he had been prevailed on to help disentangle niceties of American laws, Austrian laws, and the laws of Jewish traditional courts, which in aggregate exposed the stupid futility of starting divorce proceedings at all; nevertheless L had to spend much time and even ingenuity on this task. Finally, on 16 January 1914 L wrote, at considerable length, to Mr. Marshall of Guggenheimer, Untermeyer and Marshall,

I hope you will forgive my troubling you once more with the matter on which you had kindly given your legal opinion on September 3rd, 1913, and then in an additional letter on September 9th, i.e. in the matter of my friend, the Austrian Jew (now an American citizen) who having first contracted a void, 'Jewish religious' marriage in Austria, subsequently contracted a valid common law marriage under the laws of the State of Pa. and now seeks a legal dissolution [of the Austrian marriage].

On 17 January Marshall clinched the silly business, 'Your friend had apparently concluded to maintain his American citizenship and residence, and was seeking to obtain a decree in the court whose jurisdiction might at some future time have been questioned.' They would not touch it.

While L's mixed impressions of the boss were crystallizing, he devoted some time also to his third 'whim', journalism—in his employer's view the least whimsical of them. Among A. L. Smith's invariably undated letters, one says, 'I have been tremendously interested by your articles in the *American Leader* and love to receive it [a New York weekly, later a monthly publication, now extinct]. You always have something keen and original to say, and say it so well too.' On another occasion A. L. Smith inquired, 'Have you made friends enough?' And in a mood of gentle raillery, 'Do you want any introductions? I should like to give you one. . . . But [the delightful couple whom he had in mind] though in touch with everyone are not wealthy people or financiers, and perhaps you only go for such, now, on your rapid road to bossdom.' It was on R.M.S. *Lusitania* (sunk by a German submarine on 7 May 1915) that L sailed home. Among his American papers was inserted a menu stamped with the ship's name, dated 25 April 1914, and inscribed with ten signatures of which his alone is in a firm bold hand.

Thinking back in 1931 L wrote of 1914 'in May I set out for a short tour through Central and Eastern Europe'. He had a good reason for doing more than visit his family—the *American Leader* wanted an article on the European situation.[1] In the lands he visited L found momentous changes. Till about 1911 'the Balkan Peninsula was, owing to divergent interests of the different states, balanced within itself'; now it presented 'a definitely anti-Austrian array'. In 1912–13 German hostility was chiefly directed against the West—the British Navy was the bug-bear. With Russia, Germany then had no quarrel. Both aimed at keeping Poland dis-

[1] 'The European Situation' was reprinted in *Skyscrapers*, 1931.

membered and depressed. Their basic interests collided nowhere. Berlin and St. Petersburg approved of each other's autocratic government. But the recent Balkan wars had radically changed the significance of Austria-Hungary. She had backed the wrong horse, Bulgaria; had lost an ally, Turkey; had witnessed the elevation of an enemy, Serbia; and had suffered the estrangement of Romania. Having long been 'a dead body, with no inherent force or initiative of its own' the Austro-Hungarian Empire—moribund yet still cohering—had tempted Berlin to infiltrate its body and reach far down to the south and east of Europe. The point had been reached when 'through the disruption of Austria, Germany would be practically changed from a central-European into a merely north-European power'. Yet Russia now aimed 'in no ambiguous way' at acquiring Galicia, was favouring the Great Serbian movement in the south, and seething with political discussion about the 'coming dissolution of Austria'. A fortnight before the Sarajevo murder, L announced that the storm-centre of Europe had shifted to the Balkans.

On his return to London early in June, L called on his friend Eric Forbes Adam at the Foreign Office. More outspoken with a friend than in writing for a journal, he alarmed Eric who reported the conversation to his immediate chief. But the circles where the young men moved continued firmly optimistic. The Liberal Government's fixed idea of calming down Germany by a display of genuine kindness continued highly popular. After a short and fruitless stay in London L organized himself for writing in Oxford his book on 'The Imperial Problem', found comfortable rooms, and engaged a secretary who agreed to take her summer holiday early. Waiting for her return, he resumed lecturing for the Workers' Educational Association, visiting the King's Mound, and reading in the Bodleian.

The weeks of political indecision in high places witnessed the establishment at Oxford of two friendships that L prized greatly. C. G. Stone had been at Balliol some years before, had taught medieval history for several terms in Manchester University, and had then returned to Balliol. Though his teaching subject was history, his passion was for Moral Philosophy, on which he was writing a book, *The Social Contract of the Universe*—the only contemporary philosophical work that L cherished and claimed to understand. Its first chapter starts, 'Of one thing at least we may be certain, that there is something and not only nothing.' For L the operative words were 'not only'—another's recognition of the numinous void that had haunted him since his tenth birthday. Moreover, discussing Stone's sixth chapter, 'The Finite Enterprise of the Universe', they probed the limits drawn by man's two ineluctable cages whose decisive significance Calvin had reaffirmed for L some years before (man's immediate, personal limits; and his remote, universal ones). In such arguments the two men delighted. But when A. L. Smith and his family went north, to Bramber, despite proliferating ultimata and the dates of their expiry being inexorably reached, L's recently returned secretary wished to rejoin her mother. Restless, he felt unable to concentrate on the eighteenth century; and walking aimlessly around fell in with T. E. Lawrence.

Exactly when L met Lawrence is unknown. But his youngest brother, Arnold, speaks of a visual impression that he dates about 1909. Sliding down the stairway on a folded carpet, he made a false movement and was swiftly carried to the front door where a pair of trousered legs stopped him. Looking up, the nine-year-old Arnold saw an amused, large pink face coming down to him from far above. He had become aware of Lewis, from then on remembered as an immovable factor in his own and his brother's life. In the general disarray that preceded the outbreak of war, L's coming and going left no impression on Arnold. But L remembered being taken by T. E. Lawrence to a disused claypit to practise shooting with a rifle that Lawrence had got hold of; and he recalled seeing a good deal of the Lawrences while throughout the country men were enlisting.

L first thought of joining the Royal Flying Corps. Rejected as too heavy for the aircraft of that year—better suited for men of jockey weight—he tried for the army, and was failed on his eyesight. It had been in the States, after a deplorable game of tennis during which he had missed too many balls, that he went to an oculist, was diagnosed as very short-sighted, and told to wear spectacles. But since in his opinion bad eyesight was irrelevant when a man wished to fight alongside his friends, he now memorized the sight-card with his spectacles on, went for a walk, returned without spectacles, was passed and, on 5 September, was drafted into 'C' Company of the 20th (public schools and universities) Service Battalion, the Royal Fusiliers, stationed at Epsom.

The army authorities had taken for granted that the well-educated contingent of the 20th Battalion would soon reach officers' rank and be dispatched en route for the front. The presence in the battalion of a private like L was not foreseen. As the spy-scare increased and the horrified recoil from anything even remotely German became hysterical, L—with his odd way of speaking English and his middle name that sounded German— stood out, for all his ardour, as a conspicuous square peg. The fear established itself that men entrusted to his command might well refuse to obey an unpopular order coming from him, even if they did immediately understand it; and that a muddled senior officer in a flurry might have him peremptorily shot as a suspect. To give L a commission was to foredoom him, apparently, to an igno-minious death. Yet his popularity in the platoon—and the whole of 'C' Company—was such that his predicament became a major topic of conversation, to which he contributed amusing titbits. When asked by a friendly N.C.O. what he really would do if closely questioned in a queer spot about his accent, L answered to the enjoyment of everyone including the N.C.O., a Man-cunian, 'I'll say I cum from Mahnchester'. His comrades' per-plexity reached a peak when on another occasion he closed a similar discussion by coining his epitaph (for a lonely rogue's grave somewhere in the mud of France or Flanders)—'He gave his life for his adopted country and died for a shibboleth.' What were they to do with him?

The gloomy season, with its shortening wet days, had driven L's Company out of the pretty, wooded countryside and the men were billeted, in twos and threes, on the townsfolk of Epsom. L was lucky in the quarters allotted him; the landlady was tolerant and he had liked from the start the benign sense of fun typical of 'Stottie', his room-mate. Whether Stott was the man's full name or a stressed syllable of it I no longer remember; anyway, to his friends he was always 'Stottie'—an irrepressibly cheerful man, with mild blue eyes fixed on the silver lining of whatever cloud drifted in—a true Englishman of his day and class: conditioned never to grow up and glad not to. L, who in the ordinary course of events loathed sharing a room, felt that this was more like having by his side at any hour a well-domesticated, useful pet, as different from himself as a pet should be. Of the anecdotal situations which arose from their being together at such close quarters, two can be retold. The platoon was being vaccinated against a variety of bugs. Last came a tricky injection accompanied by a warning to keep off spirits for a certain length of time: even if absolutely sober most of the men would be feeling ill enough sometime during the next twenty-four hours. Forewarned, L thought he felt strangely groggy and had better go to bed earlier than usual. As he opened the door of their room, he saw Stott dishevelled and disconsolate, rummaging among his belongings spread out on the bed before him. Looking up he whimpered, mumbling something like, 'Can't find it, Namie, can't find it. Thish vacshine ish 'orrible.' Gently L wormed out of him the cause of his plight. Dared to have a drink, Stott had indulged in several. Having staggered back to their room he had vomited into their wash-stand bucket and, before putting it out into the passage, was determined to place his visiting card on it—so that the landlady should on no account mistake the vomit for his friend's, which would be so unfair. L strove to persuade the poor boy that the trivial matter was not worth worrying about; but it was a long time before Stott gave up searching for his visiting cards (most likely never there) and settled down for the night. The ludicrous incident was a further milestone along the way of their friendship and very likely made possible a rather more unusual talk. Already some men were being given commissions, and the thoughts of most dwelt on the probabilities of survival. One evening, sitting each on his bed too tired to undress immediately, L and Stott drifted lazily into enumerating the men who would come through and those who would die. Stott began the roll-call without their realizing it was in any way out of the ordinary. Of one man, whom both liked very much, he said blood was trickling down his face from a lethal head-wound. L agreed, he saw him that way too; and added that another was being blown to

118

bits, with which Stott agreed. They went over the whole Company, still unaware that such matter-of-fact certainty was not usual; and they finally agreed that they would both survive; to which Stott added, as L remembered it: 'Yes, I shall survive but then—I don't know.' He was actually drowned in the 1920s, some years after he and L had met again, checked their list of survivors, and found it correct. Then only—at Scott's in Piccadilly—did they realize how unusual a performance their roll-call had been.

The imminence of death, his own above all, did not worry L. Lack of cash was a different matter. His father, satisfied with the successes in New York, had undertaken to support L handsomely while the book was being written. The one condition was that L should return to the States in the following year. But England's entry into the war against Germany had automatically stopped all financial transactions between her and Austria-Hungary. Probably alone of his battalion L was faced with the impossible task of actually living on the Queen's shilling. Fortunately Stone had grasped the situation in next to no time, and was sending him small but regular 'secret contributions to the war effort'. As the first flush of belligerency—with its expectation of decisive battles to be fought at once and a dictated peace to follow—merged into the frustrating perplexities of siege warfare with its line of trenches running from Switzerland to the sea, Stone did more. The wheels of diplomacy had again begun to turn; many auxiliary wartime offices were being set up in Whitehall and Westminster. They were staffed by gifted men unsuited, for whatever reason, to active service; and L—Stone thought—had to be got out of the army and enrolled in some such office. Having spoken of it to A. L. Smith and Sligger, both of whom had useful connections in high places, he was confident that their joint efforts would not flag, though results might be slow to come. But at a crucial moment of some wire-pulling, Lord Eustace Percy, now at the Foreign Office, invited L to dinner at his club, ostensibly to discuss certain implications of L's articles in the *American Leader,* and a pamphlet, 'Germany and Eastern Europe', that L wrote while serving as a private.

Both talked volubly. There was much to communicate, discuss, analyse, and forecast. When either touched on Eastern Europe, L visualized his homeland. Having the gift to transmit his unexpressed emotions to an attentive listener, he had soon increased Lord Eustace's interest in Koszylowce to a concern for it. L thought the invasion of Galicia by the Russians was not likely to have endangered the lives of his family; but who could say what havoc the shelling might have done to the house and farmsteads, the peasants' holdings, the land? Lord Eustace was thinking up the best way to find out, through the International Red Cross, when L suddenly realized he had barely time to catch the last train even if he started at once and walked the distance from the Athenaeum to Victoria Station as fast as a private dared to. Lord Eustace demurred—there was plenty of time, he would have a taxi-cab called. L began to explain how difficult it was to reach the station by public transport from Waterloo Place; and as he spoke, his host measured the extent of L's plight—cut off from his captured home and with nothing to live on. At once Lord Eustace thought up an engagement, vaguely beyond Victoria, and ordered a cab for himself: he would drop L at the station and go on; which gave them a little longer together. In the cab Lord Eustace devised a plan for mustering relations and close friends to effect and speed up L's release from the army. At the station, scrambling out, L asked what address to give the driver, and was surprised to hear Lord Eustace say, irritably, something like, 'Oh, don't bother, you fool, get along to your train, do!' And as L hovered, peering into the cab, his host muttered crossly that having forgotten something at the club he would have to go back.

The little comedy's spontaneous and naïve delicacy unforgettably engraved itself on L's memory. In years to come he was often to cross swords on Lord Eustace's behalf with some members of that vast kinship who had become his own devoted friends. They, in a disparaging mood, would declare that this cousin's brilliant intellect was marred, indeed rendered largely ineffective, by an ineradicable flaw in his character—an insensitivity, amounting to blindness, whenever lives or circumstances unlike his own were involved. L would protest with such vehemence that they would laugh it off, dismissing him as not knowing, for once, what he was talking about. Their sarcasm against himself L took in good part; but he would doggedly repeat that Eustace was a man of rare insight, blessed with a remarkable delicacy of touch; and that he, for one, had irrefutable proof of it.

Much pressure, exerted with finesse, achieved the wellnigh impossible. On 1 February 1914 Lord Eustace wrote to L, 'Could you get leave to come up to town tomorrow to see me at the F.O. ?' Twelve days later, Claud Schuster, a high official in an intelligence bureau known as Wellington House, was writing twice about L's affairs: to Lord Eustace, 'The War Office are writing today to Namier's C.O. directing him to discharge him. I had not expected that they would move so expeditiously'; and to L,

I hear from the War Office today that they are writing to your Commanding Officer to discharge you. I had supposed that they would have given me some warning before taking this step. They are seldom so prompt in action.

Will you be so good as to come here on whatever day next week suits you to begin operations. I myself will be away during the early part of the week; ask for Mr. Gowers [later Sir Ernest] and arrange matters with him. I think the first thing to do will be to consider what foreign language papers you want and how to get them. There are, however, other jobs which will occupy, I think, as much of your time as you can spare for us.

On the following day, 14 February, Private Lewis B. Namier was given his certificate of discharge, 'in consequence of War Office letter 1352/A.G. 2B'. He had served five months with the Colours and five days in the Army Reserve. Described officially on 19 February as aged twenty-six years eight months, six feet tall, with fresh complexion, blue-grey eyes, dark brown hair, and no scars or marks, the discharged private left Epsom promising himself to serve his adopted country no less efficiently, and much more imaginatively, than any private could do at any sector of the front.

CHAPTER SEVEN

Snags and Snares
February 1915–November 1918

From the second year of World War I a multitude of interweaving streams or currents was established in L's life, making
of it a turbulent torrent. Pressing the metaphor, they can be said
to have differed from each other in temperature, salinity, and
speed. Some turned sluggish and sank out of sight. But none was
lost. Each reappeared near the surface at some time, to break in
its own way the reflected shapes of the new landscape he was
moving through and the colours of the new season that canopied
him. During the remaining three war years and the Paris Peace
Conference three currents kept near the surface. The first of them
was his intense sympathy for down-trodden or defaced nations,
which coincided with the widespread mood that was to give rise
to the League of Nations; yet he came to despise the legalistically-
minded international body as being ineffective when not perverse.
The second current was his poignant concern for individuals set
adrift by overwhelming circumstances, a concern which can be
traced in part to the influence of his home background. The
third was a fierce enjoyment of standing up for himself when
under attack by unscrupulous opponents; and this current intensified his determination not to act as they did, despite the flashy
successes of their snide methods. Whatever the odds, he would
survive uncontaminated by them, the very force of his retaliation
keeping him clean.

Released from the army, he was put to work in one of the many
information bureaus which had sprung up, each as a propaganda
section of some ministry. His, Wellington House in Buckingham
Gate, was affiliated—rather than subordinated—to the Foreign
Office. At once he was allotted the press of the Austro-Hungarian
Empire as far south and south-east as the borders of Serbia and

Romania, and he found incorporated in his province Galicia—
his homeground become a contentious part of re-emerging
Poland. Naturally enough, devotion to his old, nationally fair-
minded, Polish friends (intensified by a daily scrutiny of the
internecine and international intrigues of their rabidly nationalistic
Polish opponents) on occasion outstripped his concern for some
of the crumbling empire's less ill-starred bits and pieces. But his
zest, and his grasp of local and general problems, at once attracted
attention to all his comments; and years later he wrote that he had
agreed in 1915, as a matter of course, to supply the Leepers
(Allen or A.W.A.L., and Rex later Sir Reginald) 'of Mair's office,
with interesting paragraphs for their much more regular and frequent reports'. Temporary clerks spent many out-of-office hours
in each other's company. And even when the chiefs of some
bureaux indulged in rivalries, secret or open, their Balliol under-
lings tended to seek out and help each other.

At first L wrote pieces resembling essays: on ancient Cracow—a
monumental expression of Poland's most powerful period; on
Golden Prague (Zlata Praha) with its Slav acropolis—Hradčany;
and other distinctive cities and places. But his weekly and monthly
reports reached the Foreign Office, and within a year he was
through with evocative descriptions. Even when marred by signs
of hurried translation his reports were now uncluttered, matter
of fact, and often marked 'Printed for the Use of the Cabinet'.

Meantime the Polish nation was being spoken of more often
as a likely presence on the international post-war scene. Rivalry
among Polish politicians increased and merged with the still
vague intentions of the Great Powers for reconstructing a viable
Poland. Each of the chief belligerents was adumbrating plans of
its own. Some German-Austrian plans that it was L's business to
uncover and piece together, he saw as potentially destructive of
the Allies' declared aims. He analysed them for his chiefs, and
found himself involved in an imbroglio harmful to his career in
England, and to his image abroad. Though the exact reasons for
the vicious attacks presently launched against L in print, and
spread about in private, cannot be thoroughly understood without detailed knowledge of the history of dismembered Poland, a
few cardinal facts can explain, up to a point, the persistent attempts

to discredit him by one group of Poles, the Social Democrats led
by Roman Dmowski who had climbed to the top rungs of politics
by devising a nationalist ideology consonant with the 'black'
Russian monarchism of the day.

Generations earlier, most Polish families of good standing had
resolved to survive as sons of a dormant Poland and not as
Germans, Austrians, or Russians, of Polish descent. To carry out
their resolution in reasonable security and prosperity, they had
evolved the doctrine of 'triple loyalty' which prescribed that each
group accept with good grace temporary subordination to the
partitioning power that was master in its particular region. But
after Germany and Austria went to war with Russia, and Eastern
Europe drifted into chaos, Dmowski was tempted to enlarge his
own following and consolidate his people's post-war advantages
through initiating secret negotiations athwart the principle of
triple loyalty. Having been a Polish member in two Russian
dumas (from 20 February to 2 June 1907, and 1 November 1907
to 9 June 1912), and having continued on friendly terms with
Russian reactionaries after his defeat as member for Warsaw late
in 1912, he had become, on the outbreak of war, president of the
Polish National Committee formed in Warsaw with tsarist support, and in 1915 came to London with Russian approval. At once
he and L began suspiciously to eye each other and to note any
relevant gossip that floated around.

Many Poles were flitting between Paris, Scandinavia, and
London. Whatever their hopes, plans, rivalries, or even hatreds,
they remained members of the same Church and the same nation.
Some were kinsmen, most knew of each other anything they
wished to know and had no scruples in transmitting, to friends
in useful places, whatever they thought good in the long run for
emergent Poland. L had many old friends among the itinerants.
Rumours thickened round his name; friendships grew warmer,
enmities sharper; and Arnold Toynbee observed a revealing
comical detail. When L and Dmowski sat listening to each other's
public lectures on Eastern Europe in King's College, London,
neither questioned any statement made by the other but both
listened attentively and glared. Yet this hardening enmity did not
leap into the open till L found proof of Dmowski's secret dis-

cussions in Lausanne with a group of Austrian (or 'Habsburg') Poles, and Dmowski's friends or agents somehow got wind of L's official reports on the matter. The first defamatory attack against L was typical of Dmowski's circuitous ways and was in keeping with the usages of Polish émigrés scattered wide, hence free of any one of the three loyalties.

On 30 July 1916 the Moscow newspaper *Russkoe Slovo* followed up some recent articles on the Polish question with a long and impassioned letter signed by the chairman of the Moscow Polish Committee, Aleksander Lednicki, a former member of the duma and, in 1916, still an associate of Dmowski. Having vigorously denied that any German-Austrian approaches had been seriously considered by the Poles in Russia, or discussed by them, Lednicki further denied that any subversive Austrophile meeting was held at all, let alone in secret; he then emphatically declared that Dmowski had never and nowhere undertaken to bring about the conversion of Russian Poles to the Austro-German point of view; and forcefully stated that no letter urging the Austrian solution was ever written by Dmowski. Next came this,

The absolutely false rumours must have come from abroad, where they are being spread about by Austro-German agents intent on fostering discord between Russia and the Poles. The originator of such accusations against Roman Dmowski, a certain Namier, has been recently unmasked by the English authorities. [My translation.]

In Foreign Office circles, far greater concern was aroused by the initial pretext for the *Russkoe Slovo* articles—a memorandum of the Russian Minister for Home Affairs on the Polish question— than by the letter which stuck in L's throat. Some of his best friends in important posts persuaded him to recognize that so absurd a lie was best dropped altogether, and that a minor incident in a highly complex and largely secret operation should never be singled out for immediate denial. He accepted the view. But, deprived as a civil servant of the gratification of suing Lednicki for libel, L continued to smart under the restraint. Not that the lingering rancour over the libel ever made him swerve from the political course consistently seen by him as the best for emergent Poland and the truest to the Allies' proclaimed ideals. But on

2 April 1917 he still tried to explain the basis of his own views and feelings to the Prime Minister's Private Secretary (Philip Kerr).

You know me well enough to believe me that I am not actuated here by personal resentment against . . . [that] Polish Black-Hundred crew. After all, from the very beginning it was not a personal question. I have never known any of their leaders personally and merely distrusted them as one disliked and distrusted their Russian reactionary confrères.

He offered a clue to his unabated concern, 'Should our Government continue relations with them and let itself be in any way directed by them in Polish affairs, the impression both in Russia [a few weeks after the February Revolution] and in Poland itself would be disastrous'; and he further explained, 'as all Poles have the appearance of having been "persecuted", Englishmen have often gone wrong, and may yet easily go wrong, with regard to the Polish reactionaries'. Ten years later, describing how Dmowski had moved heaven and earth to have him dismissed from Wellington House, L admitted that his enemies' sole achievement had been 'that Ernest Gowers requested me to send in future any such material to the F.O. in typescript—when printed, it reached too many people and was likely to leak out'. Actually the director of L's propaganda section had seen and had strongly advised L's account of the Lausanne report to be printed, removing from his subordinate all responsibility before the 'rumpus' ever started. But there was a sequel, of which L wrote, 'More significant was Dmowski's success in getting his great friend Rothey Reynolds into a leading Press Department to counteract my "undesirable influence".' The persecution continued with the help of several similarly well placed friends of Dmowski, most of them, curiously enough, recent converts to Roman Catholicism. Dmowski and these people continued to observe, listen, and collect evidence for fresh attacks. But L was no shorn lamb. His mind was being strictly disciplined; his spirit remained indomitable, and he too had devoted friends. Many were Poles destined to make brilliant careers during World War II. And the creator of Czechoslovakia, Thomas Masaryk, offered substantial support. In the note quoted above, L goes on to say, 'President Masaryk considered my suppositions, as well as my

5. Marie Beer

6. L shortly before World War I

information, correct'; 'he handed over to me a confidential report on the Lausanne conference'. 'It bore out my contentions but, since it had been obtained through secret channels, he asked me not to use it unless I were in real danger and absolutely had to. . . . The need never arose.'

Despite L's continuing to be spotlighted in Dmowski's field of observation, his position solidified as an expert on the Allies' uneasy balance of friendship with Russia as well as Poland. He was even asked at one stage to 'handle current business' though the task of his department remained throughout the war to 'supply information, write surveys' and the like. Grown aware of multiple snags and snares, he yet held a steady course even when contributing, to dailies and weeklies, articles written less explicitly and in a lighter vein than were his official reports, and when publishing sundry pamphlets and booklets on topical questions. On 10 October 1917 Professor Vinogradoff congratulating L for having been entrusted *ex officio* with the criticism of a secret memoir by Dmowski, dismissed it as a mixture of political sophistry, historical perversion, and fantastic dreams doomed to failure by the already obvious course of events; yet Vinogradoff stressed that it was not the time to start polemics between Russians and Poles; and cautioned contributors to *New Europe* against refuting any such fancies; even in short, matter-of-fact notices.

By then the editor of *New Europe* had implied that L was their brilliant and frequent contributor 'N'. Having taken heed of Vinogradoff's counsel 'N' lay low for a while; but threw away all caution on 18 April 1918 with a long note on *The Revolutionary Forces in Austria*. Much that Dmowski wished above all to keep from the Allies, was here stated and explained. No one could miss the message: Polish demands recently submitted to the Emperor Charles were imperialistic, damaging to the Ukrainians, incompatible with the Allies' avowed ideals. L's arch-enemy pounced again. Of this attempt to destroy L a short, misdated, and garbled account appeared in Dmowski's reminiscences (*Polityka Polska i Odbudowanie Panstwa,* 1925). In these reminiscences Dmowski claimed that in 1917 L had at last been 'properly dealt with' in 'an English paper' by his, Dmowski's, friend Robert Ussher; and he stated that 'Namier promised not to write any more in news-papers'. L made of this claim an occasion to get the whole matter off his chest, using personal experience supplemented or supported by talks with the deputy chief of the Political Intelli-gence Department of the Foreign Office (James Headlam-Morley) and by remarks made to L himself by the chief of the Political Intelligence Department (Sir William Tyrrell). L proved that Dmowski's last lie was told 'in ignorance of the rules under which we worked'. Even in Gleichen's office—formerly Welling-ton House combined with Mair's office and others before being incorporated into the P.I.D. with more bureaux—every article and every paragraph written by a temporary clerk for the press had to be submitted first to the chief of the office, then to the head of the department. Anything L printed, as he later explained,

including the articles that so much angered Dmowski, had received official approval. Besides, had my chiefs wished me not to write, no promise would have been extracted from me and no change in our regulations would have been needed. Tyrrell would merely have refused approval of further articles. But he did not.

Headlam-Morley related that when Dmowski learned of L's appointment to the P.I.D. (in March 1918, not in 1917) he came to London with a dossier against L to prove that he was a German or Austrian agent. Dmowski gave the dossier to friends of his in a department of the Military Intelligence and managed to make such an impression that they wrote about L to the F.O. But very soon Sir Eric Drummond was, in L's words,

instructed to protest against F.O. officials being attacked by Dmowski in the British press (his Committee was then receiving a subsidy of £3,000 from the F.O.). Drummond was to say, simply but firmly, that the attacks must stop. Dmowski countered by giving his word of honour that he had nothing to do with the campaign against me and was quite unable to influence it. [On 12 July] another such article appeared in the *New Witness* with some names spelt phonetically—in the Polish manner: e.g. Stemberg was spelt Sztemberg. I took it myself to Tyrrell and asked what source he thought this could have come from. Tyrrell was furious, and took the article straight away to Hardinge.

Tyrrell was at this time investigating the Military Intelligence scare started by Dmowski's friends; and had been so incensed at anyone taking 'such rubbish' seriously that he demanded an apology. L was also told that Dmowski came to see Tyrrell personally on 20 April 1918, the Saturday before an attack against L, headed 'Potash and Perlmutter', appeared in the *New Witness*. Soon after, L wrote:

I have it from an absolutely authoritative source that when Dmowski entered the room, Tyrrell stopped him near the door, saying he refused to discuss anything unless Dmowski first withdrew all his accusations. Dmowski did so. And five days later appeared the article which, in his *Memoirs* he admits to having inspired.

Incidentally in the first article by R. Ussher [26 April 1918] one of mine was quoted which clearly worked against the thesis that I was an Austrian or German agent: my *Austria, Germany's Vassal* was most damaging to the Central Powers since it explained the need and inevitability of the Austrian Empire's break-up largely because of Germany's role there. What was the purpose of quoting the article? Close to it my father's name and address were given in full—an attempt (I don't know who planned it or if Ussher ever understood what was being done) to supply information or material against my father to the Austrian police.

By now Dmowski's aim was to convey, in Central Europe, that both father and son were involved in all-round betrayals. L pointed this out to Tyrrell who 'immediately telephoned to Scotland Yard and asked them to prevent any copy of that number of the *New Witness* going abroad'. Yet Dmowski's endeavours did not fail completely; he had contributed to the final break between L and his father.

But to return to the 'rumpus'. L was told by Headlam-Morley that after the article on 12 July (with some names spelt in the Polish way) Dmowski's representative was warned that if another attack appeared in any English paper, 'their subsidy would be automatically stopped without further enquiries. Immediately the attacks ceased. So much for Mr. Dmowski's word of honour.' How much Dmowski could be detested by a compatriot I saw shortly after L's death when having tea with President Zaleski, by then a most benign elder statesman. The mellowing of years had not extinguished his fury against a 'wily framer' whom he thought a disgrace to his nation; and he made clear to me how much this unscrupulous politician was detested.

Placed between the belligerents even more awkwardly in civilian life than he had been in the army, L found relief in daily association with people who knew him from Oxford. And any approaches made by old friends, employed further afield, he invariably took up. For G. D. H. Cole he produced a memo: about a thousand words on the Austro-Hungarian situation, to be presented as a basis for discussion by the small International Advisory Committee of the Labour Party. And on the suggestion of Arnold Toynbee L gave at King's College, London, a series of lectures on the English Puritan Writers. Rosalind Toynbee remembered wondering—on an occasion when L dined at their house—how he could make the English puritans whom she 'had not connected with him at all . . . so fascinatingly interesting' that she 'listened enthralled' despite the subject being 'profoundly unsympathetic' to her. Restless, brimming over with vigour, L was before long following a trend become general among temporary clerks working for Intelligence or Propaganda. Many were studying languages in order to converse easily, idiomatically with interesting and voluble foreigners. L, better equipped than most of his colleagues, was aware of his imperfect Russian often toppling into Ukrainian. (Besides Vinogradoff he was seeing much of Miliukoff and others.) The Leepers—outstanding among learners—warmly recommended to him 'Pony', their own teacher, a diminutive young woman trapped by the war while sightseeing in Wales, and whose full name was Clara Sophia Poniatowska. Timid, she had refused to return home through Scandinavia with her elder sister and, left alone in London, had obtained work as a clerk and interpreter in a Russian war-time office in Holborn. Her Russian was even better than her Polish and her English was good though occasionally quaint. She had a Russian passport, a Polish name, and some endearing Mongolian characteristics. The Leepers found her congenial, and both had made good progress.

At L's suggestion he began by reading to Pony the Russian classics. But when he found that she had a pretty singing voice, was a talented *diseuse,* knew Polish, Ukrainian, and Russian songs by the dozen, and could recite with charm many well-known Russian poems and verses of the nineteenth and early twentieth centuries, he spent most of his lessons listening and relaxing. Very soon she was teaching him the text of his favourite songs and, for good measure, snippets of idiomatic dialogue, some of it amusingly vulgar. Delighted, he even let himself be drilled into singing, with excellent results for his pronunciation and intonation despite his damaged ear-drums. In next to no time they had drifted into an affair. L had come to think of her as a heart-rending waif, lost and uncared for. Right up to her death, and even after, he insisted that, though forthcoming enough, she was never promiscuous. His own position was more complex. Definitely a European—however devoted or adapted to England —he had grown up in a world where sex, while no topic for conversation (least of all in families, except among male adolescents perhaps), was accepted as an inevitable and ever present factor in everybody's life. Usually by his thirties a man was married or kept a mistress. Before settling down to either state, he had easy, friendly, more or less fleeting relations with women who met him half-way. Up to the outbreak of war L, with frequent visits abroad, managed well. After the autumn of 1914 things were more difficult. Though not yet the hypochondriac he was to become, he had picked up from his father a certain apprehensiveness, which he had concentrated into a great dread of venereal diseases. Tarts and brothels were not for him. He even avoided public lavatories when possible. Naturally he turned his attention to amiable amateurs; but was singularly unlucky, his companions proving to be either frigid, which chilled him; or so brash that on closer acquaintance he found them off-putting. Clara, in whom he was presently to find a multiplicity of defects, belonged to a civilized erotic tradition. L's agitation, which had been mounting as the Dmowski rumpus developed, lifted. Like others, who have complained of it in print, he had been tormented by the major plague of sleeplessness; in next to no time he regained the knack of sleeping. Things went well between them till Clara, feeling edgy—possibly because she dreaded air-raids over London— shattered L by saying it was time they got married. He had assumed from the start that she was an estranged but definitely married woman. She insisted that she could never have said so, since in the summer of 1914 she went abroad to try and get over the shock of her husband's sudden death. L, in all honesty, did not remember if he had heard from her or assumed that she was actually married. Appalled, he sought advice from a new but true friend, a future leading authority on the Hellenistic age, doing his war work in the German office of the Political Intelligence Department.

Edwyn R. Bevan was an older man of rare distinction in appearance, manner, feelings, and mind—a just man of the Anglo-Saxon stamp. At the time of the Lednicki business L had turned to him for moral refreshment even more than for counsel, and he now approached him absolutely certain that Bevan's advice would be good and wise. More than once L described the scene to me. Very tall, very thin, slightly angular, Edwyn Bevan sat folded in an arm-chair; chin on chest, hands lightly clasped. L, intent on being objective, stated his problem with meticulous care and waited. His host straightened up, looked L in the face with limpid eyes and quietly, firmly said he saw no problem. L was having sexual relations with a lonely young woman and intended to continue having them. She wanted him to marry her and they were both free. Clearly he must. In the following weeks L comforted himself with the borrowed conviction that he was doing the right thing and the undeniable fact that he was sleeping well. A twinge of doubt flustered him only when Clara, in pensive mood, said she hoped to goodness she was not again heading for divorce. Was Poniatowski alive then? No, they had divorced shortly before he died. L impressed upon her the dire consequences of bigamy. She scoffed the matter away: nothing could be safer than her being both divorced and a widow, and surely not even the English could fuss over a divorce grown so obsolete. L dragged his feet. And for the second time Clara took the initiative, going herself to St. Giles's Registry Office.

They were married there on 6 January 1917; the witnesses being Allen Leeper, and Edwyn Bevan who gave L a pair of ivory-backed hair brushes engraved with his monogram. Not long after, searching high and low for some important notes which had disappeared during the move to a Bloomsbury boarding-house, L came across their marriage certificate, paused to read it, and saw that his wife's former name was entered as Clara Sophia Edeleff otherwise Poniatowska. The widow of an Edeleff?—a

Tartar name by the way. Her explanations were a plausible tangle of cousinages tied up with parental second marriages. And the confusion was to increase. After Clara's death in 1945, L sought my help in reading a batch of letters written in Russian characters grown very faint. All we found out for sure was that Clara's mother's name was Edeleff during a matter of years after World War I. With a helpless, self-denigrating smile he resigned himself to the irony of his position: he who by then knew everything worth knowing about Thomas, Duke of Newcastle, and a string of other eighteenth-century notables, knew nothing definite about the origins of the woman who for twenty-eight years had been his wife. He had also realized how wearisome Clara must have found his insistence on the hardness of facts, and how much quiet pleasure she must have derived from spinning yarns about herself. He had even recognized by then that his passion for ferreting out irrefutable evidence might have intensified her allergy to truth. The marriage was anyhow doomed to failure. Yet short spells of almost unclouded happiness they did have. And that summer one spell was witnessed by Agnes Headlam-Morley, who in 1917 was an impressionable schoolgirl. L and Clara, who often went to the seaside at weekends, were in Eastbourne on a longer visit. After a while Agnes and her parents arrived. Though not staying in the same house, the two families saw much of each other. But Agnes remembered best her first glimpse of the young couple who had come to meet the train. As it pulled in, they stood far down the platform. Having caught sight of the Headlam-Morleys, L grasped Clara by the hand and they ran forward, keeping step, laughing and waving. To Agnes they looked like bouncing, carefree children, and she labelled their marriage a radiantly happy one.

The fair spell did not last. Unreasonable anxieties and the constant niggling privations of the war wore Clara down: she gave up her work at the Russian office and turned down all requests for lessons. A prey to premonitions, grown reluctant even to look after herself and her clothes, she was bored to tears yet hardly ever left her room. L suggested they should move to a flat; she refused outright. Then in late January 1918 came the first night air-raid over Holborn. In a panic she lay awake till dawn forming the resolution never again to sleep at night while raids were likely. For weeks she dozed all day instead, and when awake nagged at L till he agreed that they should move to Oxford. In a renewed bout of energy she found—with help from L's Oxford friends—quiet, reasonably spacious rooms and before spring they settled in. But the move benefited neither. Inertia again beset Clara who had a horror of pregnancy yet longed for the hum of family life: not the bustle of children to rear but a vast hum of active interrelated adults, with herself at the tranquil centre—a child free from any obligation, spoilt by all. In fact, while never wanting a family of her own she craved for life in a tribal setting. As for L's Balliol friends, Clara blocked all their attempts to establish any contact with her, and to L dismissed them as a narrow-minded, pompous lot. Even when staying at Rottingdean, with the Bevans of whom she approved, she was pointedly farouche. A remembered visit occurred at a time when the German guns were often heard from across the Channel. Despite the ominous implications, L and his hosts greatly enjoyed themselves out of doors. But Clara withdrew to a well-upholstered room, refusing to join the others on the tennis court or in the garden. Travelling back to Oxford, she was dejected and morose. L on his way to London was harassed by the political situation.

With the Bolsheviks' advent and the melting away of the eastern front, demands on his time and energy had risen steeply. His prime speciality, Austria-Hungary, continued to crumble; and with its limits blurred the region's problems piled up prodigiously. Not even he had foreseen—though he had feared—that the methods of discussion used at Brest-Litovsk by the German High Command, or its spokesmen, and the immediately rewarding German treachery cleverly and glibly carried out beyond the eastern front would set for some of the emerging nations a pattern of behaviour destined to exacerbate, not restrain, the turbulence unleashed by Lenin's men. The by now blindly resentful, unyoked nationalities of east-central Europe, seething with generalized hate, were already goring each other. L needed and wished to be near his sources of information. He was in London every weekday and returned to Oxford by the last train or not at all if he was lecturing or had meetings to attend, and could find a bed. Between him and Clara communications almost stopped till luck in the battlefield swung over to the Allies and the German armies retreated too far back for air-raids over England to be at all possible. Rooms were found in Earls Court; and on 11 November L danced as a Londoner through Horse Guards Parade to Trafalgar Square with a throng of men and women he never saw before or after. For him as for everyone, a great constricting vice seemed to have been miraculously unclamped. One could again breathe deep, breathe fully. L even allowed himself to forget that the war, far from being over in the sphere of his concern, had long since got out of hand there. A few days later Political Intelligence Department officials were switched over to work for the Peace Conference; and L was next set the task of preparing the British case for the Polish settlement. Peace was now his and his colleagues' declared business. But the same circumstances that prevented the 'case' ever being completed drew L into the most bloody events of the P.I.D.'s Paris year.

CHAPTER EIGHT

Culpability

1919–1920

The full blast of embattled man's misrule hit L in 1919. Clusters of humanity (men, women, adolescents, shorn of possessions, regular means of livelihood, self-respect, and security) swirled about lands he knew and among people he understood as only a local boy can. His forcefully expressed rage at their worsening plight survives in the year's correspondence and a pile of folders, bursting with contemporary records of little known but significant events. The records are interleaved with L's contemporary comments on the events' origins and likely outcome. The correspondence together with the folders he called his 'reservoir' because they served as a reliable source for explaining, whenever the need arose, that year's East-European tragedies. For seven months L had closely studied the development of a mismanaged regional pacification which became a morass of iniquities puzzling to everyone. To him the experience was unforgettable; but what he had found significant was the exact sequence of events which got 'telescoped' in his mind as time passed. And yet the idea of building up the reservoir had come from outside. Headlam-Morley, having left for Paris in January, at once wrote home for 'as much information on current events in different countries as the P.I.D. are able to send us'. L responded at length and his first letter crossed Headlam-Morley's to him: 'If not officially, write to me at any rate quite freely.' L having already done so, they continued in the same vein with unabated zest till late in the autumn.

Boundaries had to be established, defined and traced between nations with long memories, re-emerging on lands which had been dominated by Austria or Russia for a long stretch of time. But inherent in the jumbled-up national situation were perplexities that were already getting tangled and more complex. Which of the clamant nations was to qualify as a state? Which was only to be allowed rudimentary rebirth—as a respectable parasite living in, rather than on, an alien body accorded full international status by its peers? Were the national cravings of a separatist group to be given precedence over a 'mixed' region's economic advantages, or subordinated to it? Would (indeed could) the League of Nations exercise sufficient power; and would its ardently propagated views—congealed into public opinion—muster the authority needed to protect racial minorities from harassment or obliteration by new but already fully established nations? And how to apportion, as among equals, territories coveted or claimed by several because of historic rights that conflicted owing to the ineradicable time factor? (Which of several conquests of B over A and A over B was to count as decisive in 1919?) Opinions on the best solution for particular cases varied from region to region and group to group, almost from one informed Englishman to another; and opinions differed strongly between statesmen of the two major European powers whose task was to stimulate the birth-pangs of the Peace Conference.

L's stand among the Polish factions had also changed, up to a point. It could hardly have done otherwise. Tsardom had collapsed, the Kerensky government had acknowledged Poland's independence in principle, and Dmowski was chairman of the highly active Polish National Committee formed in Paris. Backed by this officially recognized body—very influential with the French—Dmowski opposed Joseph Pilsudski, the heroic leader of L's boyhood, who had been appointed Commander of Polish Legions in the Central powers' armies but whose views on nationhood continued reasonable. Dmowski's views continued extreme. In accord with his political party's aspirations he strove to extend the new Poland's frontiers in complete disregard (indeed even to the contrived extinction) of smaller, weaker, less articulate nations also anxious to live free at last. The Ruthenians of Galicia, loved by L since boyhood, formed one such ethnic group; and his attention seldom left them till Dmowski had irrevocably achieved a settlement (which proved disastrous to them), and Pilsudski, coerced to play Dmowski's game, had become for L a shattered idol.

While the two Polish leaders continued in bitter enmity L had praised to Headlam-Morley Pilsudski's policy of social reform which alone could save Poland from Bolshevism. But very shortly after, L was deploring that 'the campaign of lies and intrigues' had achieved its aim: Pilsudski had abandoned his benign policy, and 'the bridge between the Right and the Left' was broken—a disaster for Poland and all east-central Europe. Pilsudski's prestige would now make respectable Dmowski's 'policy of aggression'. Drawing a firm distinction between the past and the present, L declared to Headlam-Morley,

The Poland I am now concerned with is the Poland of international affairs. We should now work to prevent the present generation of Polish politicians from building up a Poland that would make another war inevitable. And should she with the help of her devoted friends obtain any part of Belorussia or Eastern Galicia (Western Ukraine), that war will come, and Poland will again be destroyed.

In sorrow and anger L had 'written off' Pilsudski 'as a lost leader'. Yet, loath to despise a man so much revered in the past, he found explanations, if not justifications, for so abject a submission to a nimbler politician. In 1917—with the German forces in occupation in Warsaw—Pilsudski had felt incensed that Germany should still refuse to emulate the Russians' recognition of Polish independence. In a rage, he had plotted a 'mad *coup*', was arrested by the Germans and imprisoned in Magdeburg till the armistice when, according to L, he came out of prison 'a broken man'. Ruminating on the tragedy—personal, national, and international—L found comfort in writing to Headlam-Morley that the course of political events does not depend much on the quality of individuals:

Men matter little in politics, systems and ideas are everything. As applied to politics one might almost begin to believe in Plato's ideas and those of the medieval realists; or, with the Calvinists, that 'non est in potestate uniuscujusque hominis salvari'. [Salvation comes through God alone.] In the realm of politics a man cannot act efficiently except through one faith—in a leading idea. He who simultaneously harbours two conflicting ideas is like a photographic plate with two photographs, the one superimposed on the other. That is what Pilsudski turned out to be. And now he is a political wreck. He had to make a choice, and made a mess of it. Had he come to decent arrangements with Poland's neighbours, he would hardly have needed help from the Entente—

which won't amount to much and is being paid for too dearly. But he was out for unclean gains.

The once great man had sunk to his opponent's level: 'Now for a policy of aggression hand in hand with Dmowski!'

Though the Polish leaders' reconciliation had increased the likelihood of incalculable dangers attacking Europe from the unstable and totally unpredictable new Russia, it had been widely applauded. Only L clearly saw the likely consequences and detailed to Headlam-Morley a course of protective non-involvement:

Our purpose should be to rally round us all moderate socialist elements. The Poles in Lithuania stand for the big landed interests and for the most reactionary policy, opposed to any land reform on social as well as national grounds. Our intervention there on the side of, and in common with, the Poles would drive practically the whole of the Lithuanians and Belorussians—both peasant nations—into the Bolshevik camp. And we would next be wasting ourselves fighting for aims we fundamentally disapprove of. Why bother to draw up fine proposals on paper if we are to let ourselves be manoeuvred into actions which by the logic of facts are bound inexorably to drag us in the opposite direction?

Summing up, he formulated two precepts:

1. If we are to do battle against Bolshevism, this, like fighting a flood, has to be conceived on a grand scale and based on a survey of the widest. It must not be entered into casually.
2. Poland, owing to its geographical position, social stratification, and imperialist claims against the neighbouring peasant nations (including the Ukrainians of Galicia) will, unless restrained, drive these nations—and even their most moderate socialists—into the Bolshevik camp. The Polish so-called 'National' committee must not be allowed to trick the Allies into participating in outmoded imperialist designs. What an augury for the League of Nations if they do!

A month later, after the reconciliation, L asked Headlam-Morley to take good note of a wire from Lord Kilmarnock, dated 10 February. It stated that fear of the Polish Legionaries and the actual Polish government was largely responsible for the spread in Lithuania of a movement which called itself Communistic not Bolshevik. 'Are we determined to drive everybody into the

Bolshevik camp?' asked L dramatically. A short note from the Foreign Office Section in Paris, housed in the Hotel Astoria, quickly confirmed his 'prognostication'. The reunion of the entire Left was now inevitable; and in the united Left the stepped-up struggle against the Right was certain to increase the Bolshevik influence; the passing of power to the Right was also bound to intensify unrest among the peasantry. The insincerity of Dmowski's cry for a fair coalition with Pilsudski was fully exposed and Headlam-Morley resignedly remarked that Polish imperialism was a 'disease by now well known to all'. And the clock could not be put back. The deplorable retarding of Europe's reconstruction by Polish territorial greed had been aggravated by less daring and spectacular but similar exploits by other national groups. Conniving or vying with each other, all recklessly tried to forestall events. Some wished to pull off a *fait-accompli* before a carefully selected inter-allied commission arrived to finalize on the spot the tracing of a boundary, others before a blueprint, deemed best by the Allies for the fair assessment of a population's political aspirations or allegiances, could be drawn up. The 'Hungarian mess' had tempted Romanian, Yugoslav, and Czechoslovak forces to occupy indisputably Magyar territory; the Czecho-Polish dispute on the Oderberg-Teschen line had disclosed irreconcilable conflicts inherent between the pursuit of general economic advantages and a population's right to self-determination, simultaneously affirmed. Yet in Vienna, where a mood of torpid resignation prevailed, things were no better. The majority of citizens gladly accepted the French lead, and opposed the reunion of German Austria with Germany. Their easy acquiescence with France seemed a good way to 'shrug off the German stigma' together with all 'joint financial and economic responsibilities'. The long-term consideration that so small an Austrian rump could have no future was ignored.

Throughout the ominous late winter L grappled mentally with deep-rooted international enmities and their ramifications. Doing so he reassessed the defeated nations, and wrote on 13 February to Headlam-Morley:

Much of the praise given [in a particular report] to German Austria and especially to Vienna, is well deserved. I am struck by the outstanding common-sense of the Vienna leaders. Of the masses I am unable to say if their restraint comes from sanity or listless exhaustion. And since you know my sincere hostility to Germany, to you I wish to say how impressed I am by the Germans themselves. Much of what the French papers, and ours, describe as arrogance, I see as indomitable self-respect and a proper sense of human dignity, good to see in a great nation when down. Their attitude to the coming peace has a touch of the Promethean lines: 'Musst mir meine Erde//Doch lassen stehn//Und meine Hütte die du nicht gebaut//Und meinen Herd//Und dessen Glut//Du mich beneidest'.[1] [You still must leave me my earth standing, and my hut which you did not build, and my hearth for whose warm glow you envy me.] Of course Frenchmen and Belgians whose homes and hearths have not been left standing can't be expected to share this view. But what I really dread—in this world of ours that hums with feuds, rancours, and petty quarrels of small nations—is *der stille Groll* of the great.

With fierce irruptions of hostility continuing unabated between the embattled Poles and the grimly resisting Ukrainians (who included the Ruthenians)[2] L dreaded above all the cumulative anger of Russia, bound to explode one day; all the more perilously the longer her neighbours baited her during her impotence.

Headlam-Morley was not the only official to whom L communicated his views on current affairs clearly and cogently. Though to others he wrote with greater restraint, he spoke to all with equal abandon, insisting that Poland's internal affairs should no longer be interfered with or managed, and that the popular but wrong-headed leaders should be refused arms or ammunition 'whether for invasions (of Lithuania, Russia, or the Ukraine) or for pogroms'. Many thought L's views perverse. His trenchant manner irritated some. Following the Dmowski unpleasantness of the previous years the new, widespread disapproval prompted L's latent enemies—in the press, the Foreign Office, and other departments—to make things difficult for him. One of his important memoranda was even suppressed. Yet his immediate superiors continued to prize highly his unique knowledge; and they relied increasingly on his insight and advice. Early on, Headlam-Morley spoke of the need to have by his side 'someone with actual

[1] From Goethe's 'Prometheus'.
[2] For an explanation of the terms 'Ukrainian' and 'Ruthenian' see Appendix.

knowledge of the Galician question', in other words L, who himself felt he would be more immediately efficient in Paris. When a man was being 'chosen specially to look after the boundaries of Poland', all expected L to get the appointment. But London sent out in this capacity J. H. Paton, L's contemporary in Balliol, of whom he had written shortly before, 'poor Paton is very depressed'. Resigned as always to an accomplished fact yet clear-sighted, L told Headlam-Morley, 'Paton's being summoned and my having been passed over will be exploited by my enemies'. It was. But he continued carefully and minutely to prime Paton (as he had by word of mouth in London) with facts about the whole of new Poland's past and present entanglements; and while Polish-Galician affairs were being tacitly withdrawn from L's sphere of advice or influence, Headlam-Morley had his way, in an attenuated form.

Late in April L went to Paris for about ten days. Unexpected help for the small triumph came from Ignacy Paderewski, the brilliant pianist. Dmowski had brought him over from America, as the only Pole of world renown, to be elected the first president of the Polish republic; and Paderewski wished to talk over with L the Jews' position as a racial minority within Poland's borders. During L's stay in Paris Headlam-Morley wrote to a senior official in the Foreign Office about L's giving 'lots of useful information' and his 'buzzing around' most helpfully. He was meeting old friends, making new ones, bringing people together, thinking up lines of approach to Polish notables turned politicians and come to Paris on international business. This first post-war visit to Paris also marked for L the beginning of a new interest— Zionism, which he discussed with Dr. Chaim Weizmann and some senior American Jews. But Zionism was to remain dormant at the back of his mind for some years yet. Matters of more immediate urgency claimed him.

So far, even L's most ingenious efforts to get in touch with his mother had entirely failed. But on 4 July 'a man called Frazer' sought him out in the London office. Having been confined in Austria during the war, Frazer had known some friends of L's family, had been entrusted with a letter, and was volubly communicative. The manor house of Koszylowce had been looted

7. L with his mother and sister at Koszylowce during one of his vacations from Oxford

8b. Clara

8a. L's sister while a nurse in World War I

and set on fire by Ukrainians. His mother and sister had been driven away; his father, seriously ill, had been left behind. One detail in the list of woes was most revealing to L: Joseph had been stressing the detested name of Bernsztajn. The implications were clear. Ukrainians, no less enthusiastic Jew-baiters than were the Poles, confined their pogroms chiefly to small towns and particular villages where Jews clustered. But owners of manor houses were being beaten up, tortured, and killed because they were Poles. A Jewish owner of a manor was a white crow less likely to be hurt; and the re-emphasized Bernsztajn was Joseph's protective colouring against stray Ukrainians from other districts, who happened to be milling around the district of Zaleszcziki in those fatal weeks. The political implications L had grasped at once. The calamitous human factor—Joseph's bitter humiliation that he later claimed to be the worst in his life—was grievously to affect L some years hence. As a result of Frazer's visit, the Foreign Office and L's friends elsewhere rallied round. Three weeks later a reassuring wire reached him from an English official in Vienna, Sir Percy Wyndham, and L at once shared the news with Headlam-Morley, 'My best thanks to you and Kisch for the trouble you have taken. My family were all found at Koszylowce. Only our manager was killed. Details I hope to get by bag.' But most of these trickled in by word of mouth, from friends who, trapped in France by the war, were starting to move about Europe again in the hope of re-twining snipped threads. All accounts were greatly to Theodora's credit. Her wellnigh congenital hubris and absurdly regal manner—which remained striking even when, old and crippled but unbroken in spirit, she weathered the vicissitudes and indignities of World War II—worked like magic while she was young and of outstanding good looks. After a day or two she had her captors vying with each other to placate, then please, and finally escort her and her mother back home. They found Joseph put up in the dead manager's house, cosseted but alarmingly irate. To break his vile temper Theodora produced, with the meagre resources to hand, amusing charades where nostalgia emphasized apposite contemporary allusions. Her success smoothed over many local grievances; and so well broke Joseph's ill-humour that he consented to rebuild, which in time led to Theodora's feeling possessive about the new house as she never had about the old one.

Before L knew his family had survived, he was already veering away from the personal tragedy and, far from inveighing against the Ukrainians was praising them for having maintained order so long.

They strove hard to be a proper government. But a peasant nation exasperated by centuries of oppression and fighting for its life against landowners—and the foreign dominion for which these stand—cannot be expected to show superhuman self-control. My father was always on the Polish side and known to be closely involved with the Polish nobility. The wave of cruel reprisals could hardly by-pass him. But the responsibility rests with the Polish jingoes and those Allied statesmen who, lacking adequate energy, bungled. The last decision of the Peace Congress foredooms worse to come. All the massacres in Macedonia will seem as nothing compared with those coming to Eastern Galicia.

For all my personal loss and anxieties I do insist that grievous wrong has been done to the Ukrainians. Left in peace to establish a strongly radical but decent government, they might well have organized themselves. Driven to despair, insidiously pushed daily toward bolshevism and into committing atrocious crimes, they know—and we shall see—that a Polish military occupation, as foreshadowed in the Foreign Minister's decision of 25 June, means disaster without end. And I insist that no number of atrocities however horrible can deprive a nation of its right to independence, nor justify its being put under the heel of its worst enemies and persecutors. If the horrifying excesses reported by the Poles are true, they only prove the intensity of the Ukrainians' detestation of them. The instigators, the Poles, will now retaliate in kind with Allied open support. Where can such folly lead?

If the League of Nations is to be anything better than a storehouse of hypocritical cant or an organization for the aid of international finance, it must act now. The solution supported by us for months, of a High Commissioner of the League in a neutralized Eastern Galicia, is the only workable solution.

The date L had mentioned (25 June) was of paramount importance. The Supreme Council were occupied with the imminent signing of the Versailles Treaty. In a flurry, and humouring Balfour, the council at long last accepted his advocacy of a plebiscite at some future date. In response (some said, in a spell of abstraction) he acceded to the Polish mandate; and sold the

Ruthenians down the river. Headlam-Morley, coming to after the Versailles toils and celebrations, wrote: 'that Eastern Galicia be given over to Poland seems to me quite incomprehensible'. 'Worse than incomprehensible,' retorted L, 'it is a scandalous letting down of the Ukrainians.' And his shortest printable comment to a younger correspondent was, 'I am flabbergasted. The political system has broken down completely.'

Because the plebiscite still stood, the final phase of the Ruthenians' attrition involved the Allied and Associated Powers in Polish administration of Eastern Galicia, and required their countenancing the application there of Poland's agrarian reforms. Of the agrarian question L had abundant knowledge. And since the enforcing of alien administration called for decisions on the rights of the Ruthenian Diet, Ruthenian representation in the Polish Diet, and the conscription of Ruthenians into the Polish army—all matters long pondered by L—he had precise and coherent views on them also. But when, late in July, the Polish Commission's sub-committee of experts was set, among other tasks, to find solutions to the four vexedly urgent problems, he was not consulted on any one of them. Some two weeks earlier though, intent on helping the Ukrainians survive their 'miserable days of occupation', and on preserving Eastern Galicia as a 'viable state in expectation of her hour of emergence', he had alerted Headlam-Morley that the Poles were 'developing schemes for colonizing' the region. It was being mooted that Polish soldiers be settled on Ruthenian land. To L it looked like another trick to forestall a looming event: a manipulation of the ultimate plebiscite. As the Poles still hankered after outright ownership, F. B. Bourdillon, one of the experts on the job and a most friendly contemporary of L in Balliol, feared a possible Prussian-type colonization scheme. To prevent it, he advocated introducing into the mandate measures against any colonization; while Mrs. Edgar Dugdale, a colleague of L's since 1918, who had composed more than one memorandum on Polish settlements in Galicia, cautioned that part of the agrarian bill might be aimed at planting Polish colonists in Eastern Galicia rather than at giving land to Ruthenians. In general, the English experts variously struggled to keep the Ruthenians free enough to join a Greater Ukraine, or even Russia, at the time of the plebiscite. Once more, a paralysing conflict hardened. Learning of it, L sent an unasked for memorandum. Colonel Kisch pronounced the memorandum to be a 'masterly piece of destructive criticism'; the more guarded E. H. Carr described it as deserving 'serious consideration' on several counts. The exchange of opinions seemed likely to bear healthy fruit when the Supreme Council began to examine the commission's report. But again new factors erupted. Paderewski, invited to address the council, lamented that his government would unavoidably collapse if the whole mandate scheme were not scrapped—otherwise the whole of Poland would be plunged into disorder agreeable only to the Bolsheviks. Again the English and the French divided. But this time, after the majority had been bending this way and that, it was the American, Polk, who decided the issue, unequivocally in favour of the Poles. Paderewski had fallen, but so had the Russian counter-revolutionary forces; and Eastern Galicia was annexed to Poland outright.

At the eleventh hour Bourdillon had written to L, 'If you can act, act now.' But how could he? 'To discuss things that can no longer be altered' had from the start been 'sheer waste' to him. Moreover, Paris—not London—had throughout been the place for such efforts. And the time to act profitably had been February, March, April. Having then 'given in to the bullies and pushed the victim against the wall, how can we make a stand now or ever?' Still, 'I shall do all I can, which is not much,' he answered, and concluded his letter to Bourdillon with, 'The Polish press counts on our surrender and the Dmowski papers openly jeer' at Great Britain, certain that she 'will not be able to stand alone'. Personally, L was not yet free of Dmowski's more furtive persecutions of him either.

On 6 November 1919 Alfred Rapier, Conservative member for Islington East, acting for L's ill-wishers, asked in the House of Commons whether a Mr. Namier had been in the employ of the F.O., and if so, in what capacity; whether his father was an Austrian (Galician) named Bernstein (Niemirowski); and whether Mr. Namier had been consulted in any way whatever regarding Polish policy. Captain Guest (joint Parliamentary Secretary to the Treasury) answered,

Mr. Namier, who is a naturalized British subject and served in the army in the early part of the war, has been employed on intelligence work in the F.O.; his father was born a Russian subject in Russian Poland of a family of the name of Niemirowski, which had been resident in Poland and Lithuania for many centuries; but in middle life he assumed citizenship in Galicia under Austrian rule, having acquired an interest through marriage in estates in that country. As in the case of all Jews the Partitioning Power (Prussia at that time) imposed on the family a German name, which they have since abandoned. Under the Treaty of Peace, Mr. Namier who was also born a Russian subject, at Warsaw, now becomes a Polish subject [confusion here between father and son], and has been acknowledged as such by the Polish Government. Mr. Namier, whose knowledge of Poland and of Eastern Europe in general is remarkable, has frequently written papers and memoranda which have been of the greatest value.

Next Mr. A. Shaw (Liberal) put an illuminating question: 'Is my Honourable Friend aware that this gentleman's sympathies are entirely pro-British, that he was educated at Oxford, and that his unique knowledge has been of the greatest service to this country?' And Major MacKenzie-Wood (Liberal) added in the same spirit, 'Did he not serve in the British Army during the War?' To all of which Captain Guest replied, 'Yes, sir. The only matter I am not able to speak about with knowledge is that he was educated at Oxford. The other suggestions are absolutely true.' Two days later, when L was writing about other matters to Victor Cavendish-Bentinck, a Third Secretary at the British Legation in Warsaw, he ruefully referred to the muddle:

The answer given to the question by this office was meant to say that my father 'now becomes a Polish subject and has been recognised as such by the Polish Government'. By an unfortunate change in the order of sentences the statement which was meant to apply to him came to be applied to me, which of course is inaccurate. Today a wire was officially sent to Sir Horace Rumbold explaining the mistake and authorising him to state that I am a British subject and thus correct the mistake should need arise.

But not even this was the end of it. To L's further vexation, when on 31 March 1920 a very long enumeration of British Empire honours appeared in *The Times,* he was not mentioned. Tyrrell, Headlam-Morley, and other appreciative friends in the Foreign

Office had wished to have him on their office list, but his enemies had edged him out. And since all the men engaged on work resembling his were included, L felt the omission was a personal slight. From then on, every time he wore full evening dress, his mind's eye saw a deep hole, indeed a wound, in place of the ribbon that Dmowski and company had wrenched away. But by March, for him as for all temporary clerks, the disappointing peace talks were truly over and he was thinking of a new job.

The pre-war past had begun to thrust itself into L's present and grope its way into his future soon after the Armistice of November 1918. The first to resume interrupted relations with him was his 'American boss' Hammerling, 'the New-World *condottiere*'. L, he wrote, should join him in a grandiose scheme of East-European reconstruction. But, financially tempting and imaginative, his plans were vague on crucial points. And in a correspondence that lasted well into March, L was intent on making clear, without appearing censorious or giving offence, his own approach to easing the regional plight. 'Of relief there certainly is great need,' he said in February, at the same time cautioning that 'aggressive nationalism' continued 'supreme' in the region, and insisting,

I do not doubt that you could do much under settled conditions but fear that neither your health nor your temperament are suited to struggle against conditions as they are. I strongly advise you should wait till real peace comes out there. Meantime you might, perhaps, prepare the ground for the multitudes who will be seeking refuge in the States.

Next L cautioned Hammerling against assuming that there was only one sort of Bolshevism: 'there are many, variously dressed up'; and, 'without wishing to decry' his former employer's purpose, repeated, 'I do feel that, should you go out there now, your disappointment would be bitter.' In the final letter of this series L set out to soften his refusal by stressing his unacceptable conditions,

On the need for constructive work in Czechoslovakia and Poland I fully agree, and I realize well the advantages of your taking it up. But since I feel it my duty to continue my work of the last four years in the same capacity—as a British Civil Servant—I could not join you. Though financially unremunerative, my position gives me an opportunity to serve my adopted country, and also wide scope to help these two emerging states. I cannot leave my work for them unfinished. But shall gladly help in anything you may try to do in your own line for the good of Czechoslovakia or Poland; preserving, however, the absolute financial disinterestedness which is one of the strongest traditions of the British Civil Service. In no way—direct or indirect—could I draw any financial benefits from what I might do, nor turn to money profits any connections I have. All the same, wherever your work is primarily directed to the good of the countries which are my concern, I shall gladly help you as far as I can.

To Headlam-Morley he had written of the tempting remuneration—'easily £5,000 a year'—adding bitterly, 'My accumulated insight into statecraft will make me less fastidious about the methods of big business'; and as an afterthought, 'but I should first like to write my book on the emergence of the U.S. at the break-up of the first British Empire'.

A very different offer had come in a suitably different way during 'long talks' with the new Master of Balliol (A. L. Smith), A. D. Lindsay (a future Master, just returned from France), and C. G. Stone. Again to Headlam-Morley, L wrote after a weekend spent with his Oxford friends,

All are very keen that I should go back to Balliol for some kind of lectureship but everything is still quite unsettled. They don't even know if H. W. C. Davis [Senior History Tutor in Balliol] is coming back to take up his work, or how much work there will be to do. The College Funds are badly depleted—we have never been a rich College—and a research Fellow or Lecturer who didn't earn a good deal in tutorial fees is a luxury we could hardly afford. Put briefly, if there is a vacancy, I am pretty sure to get it. But whether there will be no one knows.

For about a year the matter lay dormant while less attractive possibilities drifted in and out of L's orbit and his preferences steadily inclined toward teaching, writing, research. Shortly before Headlam-Morley left Paris for good, L confided to him, 'Each of us now needs a rest—to get away from current politics and affairs, and do some proper historical work.' And to Kisch at about the same time he exploded, 'I really do not think I can stand much longer to sit here and watch all that is happening in Eastern Europe'.

In the event L did not leave the Political Intelligence Department till spring, his last five months there being devoted, above all, to two types of enforced drifter: Ukrainian soldiers and airmen who wrote to him—as man to man, at the office, from anywhere in the New World—letters of timid or exorbitant requests impregnated with the grief of uprooted lonely people in the grip of jagged anxieties; and East-European Jews who, having somehow slipped their hawsers, drifted about in small groups, not permitted to be joined by their dependants but communicating with them through L at the Foreign Office. On behalf of the Ukrainians he was in touch with security sections of Scotland Yard. The Jews involved him in a wide-flung correspondence with British representatives abroad. Of an evening, at home, he minutely sifted the evidence of the Peace Year's frustrations amassed in his reservoir. Analysing it, he listed significant events, carefully explained his flashes of insight, relived his worst forebodings step by step, expanded some cryptic passages in the year's correspondence, and gave point or greater precision to others. As he followed through at a ruminative pace the collaboration of iniquitous men with cussed events, Clara would sit reading a novel, or would aimlessly wander about their flat softly singing melodies he still liked, in a voice he still enjoyed. But they hardly spoke. There was nothing to say. Yet on one of his summer visits to Paris she had written him a silly little letter that he never destroyed. Years later, with me by his side, L more than once considered the round, heavy, poorly formed, untidy hand, and characterized it as that of an introspective, wayward child. The trifles Clara enumerates, rather than describes, are interspersed with funny endearments entirely her own, which make touching the few yellowing lines, and keep their spirit fresh. L, who was interested in graphology, used the letter as a specimen. But it had marked one of the better spells between them, terminated by the question raised about him in the House of Commons. Clara had been so scared by the pother that she shied away from all L's friends and never again wished to hear of his work. Between mid-winter and spring he spent many weekends in Oxford where she refused to accompany him; but where A. L. Smith and C. G. Stone—to a lesser degree Sligger too—waxed excited over the historical conclusions he was reaching on the war and its aftermath.

The collapse of the Allies' political system in east-central Europe L judged to be worse than a confined disaster. An outrage of world-wide significance, it had been blindly engineered. Its motive power had been the perverse reluctance of active men to see at the right time how unstable situations were changing and international events developing. Well- or ill-intentioned men (those resolved to wipe out a sickening immediate problem by isolating it, and the others who were eager to cash in on any favourable juncture) had retained in unprecedented situations all their preconceived notions, and had obstinately followed well-established habits of thought however obsolete. No mentor of down-trodden nations had emerged to guide them up crags of self-discipline to the dignity of a new, shared freedom. For a while L thought and wrote much about high-principled statesmen who had blindly damaged a potentially lasting peace in Europe. But of his even gloomier, more complex anxieties he no longer spoke. With fiery determination and without counting the cost he had fought for a proper, just, and therefore more stable, righting of old injustices. After the stupidest rapacities had neatly cut through many baffling complications, the rapacious had won. The general refusal to recognize men's pleasure in crushing other men, had defeated him. Adult status had been refused to an ethnic group he deemed worthy of it. A helpless bystander, he had been forced to observe a new tribal chaos obliterate the waking national dignity of a very old ethnic group; and he had seen its well-wishers turn away in disillusion or disgust. To L's already bitter sense of corporate guilt was added the dismay of personal failure.

But Balliol offered him a chance to train in perspicacity the minds of men less equivocally placed among the nations than he was. Who knew but that one day one of those younger men might redress the wrongs L had been helpless to prevent. With luck some of these younger men might even foresee other wrongs in time to prevent their being accepted as inevitable. His thirty-second birthday was approaching and, full of zest, he felt able to contain a multitude of interests. Far from letting his insight into foreign affairs dim down, he would find comfort and reward by imparting to receptive minds the experience he had gained. 'My resignation takes formal effect on 1 May, but in fact I am leaving today as term in Oxford begins on Monday,' he wrote on 23 April to a war-time friend, Colonel S. G. Talents, British High Commissioner for the Baltic Provinces. 'Do let me hear from you sometimes. Address your letters to Balliol, but it might be better to continue sending them by bag.' He was indicating what news he hoped for. Keyed to teach, glad to teach, L could not, and would not, snuff out his international interests nor his involvement in current affairs. They continued to exercise his mind; and, settling down 'to tutor at Balliol at least for a time', he was diligently keeping green his private grapevine.

CHAPTER NINE

Days Crammed Full
Spring 1920–Autumn 1921

The Oxford to which L returned was in many ways unlike its pre-war self. But for L the most agreeable and significant difference was that it had acquired yet another warmly welcoming household, the Bell-fry. His affection for Kenneth and Esther Bell went back to the year and month of his Finals. Happening to meet them 'in the garden of the King's Mound', he was introduced by A. L. Smith, and 'at once we were friends', wrote Essie soon after L's death; going on to ask, 'Did you know that he had an astonishing way with horses? There was a rather wild one in a field on our first cross-country walk together. Lewis went up to it, murmuring the while something that made it very friendly.'

From 1911 to early in the war the Bells had been much in Canada. But when in England—living in London's Hampstead Garden Suburb—they saw a good deal of him when he was not abroad. In 1919, after Kenneth Bell returned from France, and Balliol elected him a Fellow, he joined those who pressed L to take up teaching; and it was Essie who found for Clara and L a sparsely furnished flat in a small house—in a terrace across the bridge from Magdalen College. By all accounts the two settled down to a perceptibly incongruous life there. Neither was happy with the other. L—remembering well his nurse's deterioration after her marriage and his having then ascribed it to her boorish husband's effect upon her—wretchedly pondered, off and on, where he had erred in his own marriage. Even after Clara's death and despite their having come near a perfect understanding a few days before it, he never quite freed himself of a bewildered sense of guilt. Yet if their actions, and the reminiscences of others as well as his, are considered together with the whole sweep of relevant facts, some exonerating conclusions impose themselves.

A timid woman, Clara had planned their marriage in a desperate attempt to find at least a semblance of security—L had a convincing, reassuring grasp of baffling situations and was unafraid of life. As often happens with easily scared people Clara, while inclined to lean on others and seek their advice, was subject to bouts of recklessness when she could act with maniacal resolution. Her decision to marry L was an act of recklessness; her breaking up of their marriage was another. Between them stretched four years sprinkled with events which eroded her illusion of attaining security through being tied to him. Far from providing her with a solid cosiness, participation in his life was driving her to panic, till she became certain that only at a distance from him would she free herself from constant overmastering anxiety. Apprehensive, she was appalled by his erratic course, and haunted by the fear of yet another outburst of publicity which seemed to be lurking near. While he, who later analysed their incompatibilities with rueful, objective warmth, found her developing oddities even more exasperating than bewildering. Good bedfellows, they were ill-matched in courage, interests, and drive. The rest was incidental.

L's insistence, to Essie Bell, that the Oxford flat must be empty of inessentials came of his being snowed under by newspapers and other ephemeral printed matter, chiefly foreign. He would part with none before the final draft of his contribution to the official history of the Peace Conference ('The Downfall of the Habsburg Monarchy') was ready for its editor.[1] According to L the only possible place for the dust-collecting profusion was in stacks so arranged on the floor that everything was within reach of an outstretched arm, or at the bend of a knee. Some stacks grew to be as high as Clara; and she is remembered emerging from behind them, small, silent, feline, ready to bolt. She was acquiring a passion for cats, preferring females and defending their litters with a sombre rage; but most of all she would have liked to keep a flock of goats and with it roam the land. To L she confided in mock seriousness that the goats and she would marvellously protect each other from prying eyes and the evil eye.

L's analysis of the collapse of the moribund Austro-Hungarian

---

[1] *Peace Conference in Paris*, Vol. IV, ed. H. W. V. Temperley.

Empire had started to shape even before March 1919 when Headlam-Morley had written to him, 'I hope you are going on with your narrative of revolutionary events in Austria'. Obliquely, a project of the Oxford University Press had also stimulated L. In January 1919 he was asked to write for their Clarendon Press series a short History of Poland; and a couple of days later he got in touch with a leading Polish historian (Stanislaw Posner) for many years domiciled in Paris,

Before accepting the offer, may I have your opinion about available sources and material? I only propose to sum up and popularise, and would not be doing any original research. What I have in mind is to start with the origins and lead up to the present conditions and outlook —a matter of nine chapters. I know you have at your finger-tips all I want.

This was L's only project for popularizing history and nothing came of it. His mind was centred on the collapse of an empire deemed by him unworthy of survival. And 'The Downfall' has worn so well that for republication in 1958 in *Vanished Supremacies,* he made few emendations. Some rephrasing there had to be since events grown dim in the national awareness—no longer a tormenting puzzle to anyone—were being presented to a fresh public living in a new political age. Besides, L had become pointedly fastidious. And for me to observe (in 1958) how deletions and elisions enhanced the 1921 text's clarity, while it was being pared down to a new elegance, was fascinating. At the same time L, discovering by my side, that no change of argument or statement of fact was possible let alone desirable, was jubilant. The enduring quality of 'The Downfall' L attributed to the amount of energy and time he had put into it in 1920-1. But with massive tutoring and lecturing, he had little time for even thinking about his work on the phoenix empire. His frustrated urge to follow through the intricacies of the eighteenth-century cataclysm, so well weathered that the first British Empire was reborn as the second, increased, till he despaired of having leisure enough in Oxford for so large an undertaking even after 'The Downfall' was finished.

Only a temporary lecturer L nevertheless tutored many undergraduates who—directed by their elders—sought his instruction.

Mrs. Edgar Dugdale, corresponding with him on political matters almost daily in the late autumn of 1920, knew the exact number of undergraduates. 'Try to keep on feeling the savour of life,' she entreated, having learnt that a long spell of sleeplessness had left him depressed, 'it will be a sad waste if you lose it in your intercourse with the 45 pupils.' The pupils themselves remember him taking tutorials 'from about 9 a.m. at three-quarters of an hour intervals'; and that 'all wondered how on earth he could maintain such high-power intellectual activity for so many hours a day'. George Mitchell, a Queensman who was one of the very first men to be directed to him by Kenneth Bell, says,

I don't know just what it was about Lewis that made me feel he was different from the others. Perhaps it was his passionate interest in his subject, the range of his knowledge, his wit and his talk. I had the feeling at the time that his interpretation of history was not the result only of reading books but that he had taken some part in making history through his work at the F.O. and in connection with the Peace Conference. From him I learnt not to make assertions unsupported by facts, to avoid generalizations, and to try to think clearly.

This early opinion spread fast, and pupils streamed to L from many colleges though Balliol men continued to predominate. Coping with the demand, he adapted to the traditional tutor-pupil relationship of Oxford a method used by his father to sharpen L's own youthful wits. Lord Gladwyn, then Gladwyn Jebb, writes,

He liked arguing, thereby provoking his pupil into taking a contrary view and finding good reasons for sustaining it. Whenever he gave me things to read, such as books on the Ausgleich [the political agreement between Austria and Hungary, renewable every tenth year] I did my best to see whether there was some alternative theory to the one he favoured, and that in spite of the fact that I knew practically nothing and he knew everything. He never seemed to mind this and certainly never pointed out that my remarks must of necessity be completely superficial. What he wanted was a good argument.

It is in the nature of worth-while arguments that they hover close above well-known ground. But suitable books—reliable and detailed, yet comprehensive—had still to be written on recent events. To fill the gaps L typed quires of foolscap rich in detail, often recondite but always worked into a memorable coherence, and referring, more often than not, to the revolution of 1848. These pages—interleaved with short gutted reviews of relevant pre-war books—presently went to swell his formidable reservoir. They added much force to his private reference material not only on Austria, Hungary, Czechoslovakia, Poland, Galicia, Lithuania, and Belorussia but on the whole of post-war Europe, and were kept up to date for a long time afterwards.

Of all L's pupils Ivo Mallet seems to have most benefited from this particular ploy; and he sees their relationship in the light of post-war Oxford's specific quality,

Balliol after the first war was a very good place with a mixture, among dons as well as undergraduates, of men who had been through all sorts of careers and experiences, and who were therefore quite different from the peacetime senior and junior common-room types. But [L] contributed something quite distinct in his outlook, knowledge, and teaching. He brought Central-European history and the nineteenth century right into Balliol tutorials and made them live for us. . . . If I was lucky enough to get into the F.O., if all my life I have had an interest in European history and politics, and if today I still believe strongly in Europe's role and its united future, it is largely due to [L's] teaching for which I have always been grateful. . . .

Much the same effect was snappily summed up for me by Lord Samuel whose somewhat condescending attitude to the Continent—viewed strictly from pre-war insular positions—changed in next to no time by L's forcefully pushing him across the map to Vienna. Provoked into assessing the situation as seen from there, Edwin Samuel, as he then was, found to his abiding amusement that 'Europe never looked the same again'.

Not only men drawn to the fields of diplomacy and administration were significantly affected by L's instruction. F. L. Lawson, who became Professor of Comparative Law, says,

My tutor sent me to him with another Queensman for a final polish in our last term before taking the Final Honours Schools of Modern History in the summer of 1921. We went for an hour in only six weeks of the term, but I always feel that those six hours ensured my First Class in the Schools and made possible the career I have since followed. . . . What we got from [L] was an informal lecture in answer to an initial question but interspersed with other questions on his part and ours. I remember his saying that he could not start off without some sort of question to direct him. Our subject was Foreign History from 1789 to 1878, and we covered an immense amount of ground. He opened up new lines of thought of which I had no inkling previously. For the first time I began to understand the 1847–50 period of Central-European history. The books were then dull and let in little light on the subject. . . . I do not know if I can convey the extraordinary stimulus I obtained from those few hours or how I wished I could have come into contact earlier with [L]. It was like talking to someone who had lived through it all. He also gave me confidence—on the force of one test examination paper I did for him he assured me that I would get a first.

I met him only once or twice later, at very long intervals, but I never had to remind him of who I was.

An incident that preceded the writing of another test examination paper is remembered by Lord Boothby who had done hardly any work in Oxford before the summer of 1920 when, perturbed, he sought help from L. This pupil's handling of the weekly essay—on the French Revolution—had proved him an able man. Yet L was not satisfied. The multitudinous streams of French national life had not been visualized by Boothby as a meaningful impetus—a complex but homogeneous torrent of ambitions and idealisms, vices and virtues, swirling through circumstances grouped in fateful clusters. Sinking back more comfortably on the sofa, L began to talk. For two hours he unrolled before his dazzled pupil the meaning of those mighty confluences, then paused, and finished the brief review with words on Danton. August 1792: France was in peril; her frontiers were dented and Paris showed signs of a mounting sadistic neurosis. Danton knew of Verdun's imminent fall and saw how it could start a murderous avalanche rolling. The other leaders, paralysed by fear, were later to claim as a virtue their blind impotence against it. Danton alone gauged its elemental vigour and its potential uses. In a state of passionate lucidity he flung himself into its centre to become its demon. No instigator of the September massacres, he did, however, countenance them. And true to himself he accepted the label of their originator—'a monstrous dignity', but how much less abject than to rank among sheep blinded by fear. A great political figure, Danton. A man who saw the flashlight and obeyed; leaped to the burden, and carried France through a crisis potentially lethal to her. Boothby should work out the situation and write it up. If he conveyed the nature of the bond between the moment and its master, eager, with the dash of a man not given to rancour—the examiners would very likely award him a First. They did.

At least three undergraduates destined to make a mark in business and management are also aware of L's imprint. One of them, J. W. Platt, later a Director of Shell, writing in 1930 from Canton about a business matter, remarked nostalgically, 'I still remember with appreciation your capacity for putting the important things shortly and strikingly'. Another, G. E. Lavin, for more than forty years associated with engineering and timber in India, South Africa, and many parts of tropical Africa, never failed when in London to see L, and 'on many occasions profited from his sagacious advice'. And after L's death Sebastian Earl wrote:

I wish *The Times* had made it plainer how loved he was by his pupils and associates. At three or four points in my life he counselled me, always wisely and always affectionately. . . . Even in 1921 we knew he was a man of destiny and of a quite different mould from the other dons. I think he was probably the only truly great man I have known personally.

An eloquent tribute of a different kind has been useful to me of late. It is a small stumpy gold pencil-case incised *L.B.N.* '*1921*' *V.A.C.*—a token of gratitude from Victor Cazalet, later M.P. for Chippenham, to whom L had transmitted what he then could of eighteenth-century English parliamentary history, and who continued a good friend to the day of his untimely death on 4 July 1943, taking off from Gibraltar with General Sikorski.

Yet, with an even louder rasp than in L's undergraduate days, the admiration and devotion of some was outvoiced by the opprobrium of others who hated L's 'mould'. Good from the start at assessing a situation, Gladwyn Jebb had realized that L 'was not particularly popular' and tried later to explain it. 'Many people—even gifted people—refused to stand up to him because he had a habit of wearing you down and many of them found this to be a bore. I think why I got on with Lewis so well was because I was rather drawn to unpopular people.' As in the Foreign Office so in Oxford, L was either greatly liked or intrigued against. Few could long remain indifferent to him. And although Clara is unlikely to have overheard or been told about any particular wrangle over him, she was too highly strung at the time for the general atmosphere not to have contributed to her panic.

On to the thin ice that covered the confusion of friendships and enmities, affinities and incompatibilities, self-dedication and ambition, endeavour and envy, stepped Theodora. It was June 1920. From London she had bidden L come and hear about urgent family matters but he could not absent himself. And she, anyway, wished to size up this wife of his about whom he had been reticent enough for the family to fear she would be un-acceptable to them as the mother of children who would surely one day aspire to a part at least of Koszylowce. L had not seen his sister for six years, though of his parents he had caught a glimpse in January when they were recovering on the French Riviera from a surfeit of bleak discomforts and unmanageable harassments. In Paris on Foreign Office business, he had spent with them the inside of a day between two night journeys. It was not a happy reunion. Grown old and grim both parents were bitter. To his mother L appeared a craggily formidable stranger, a cypher. His father accused him outright of having done his best to make their life unbearable—at Koszylowce where all knew L to have turned into a bellicose pro-Ukrainian anti-Pole, and in Vienna where vivid accounts of his sinister intrigues against the Central Powers and his long years of spying for England ceased to circulate only when they could no longer hurt.

Theodora, lean and haughty, immediately recoiled from the timid Clara who was becoming tubby. They loathed each other at sight. And the older woman, having come for a matter of days, left after twenty-four hours, stressing that even her London hotel was more comfortable and cleaner than the house run by Clara. Moreover, she had expedited her business. Whenever her sister-in-law was out of the way—tending her cats, day-dreaming in her room, or messing about in the kitchen with the cats' food— Theodora rammed at L the unadorned implacable truth. Joseph, though now a Pole, was still tugged apart by two national whirl-pools: Poland which contained Koszylowce, the absolute devo-tion of his life since his late forties; and Vienna, his *ville lumière* since Warsaw had somehow dimmed away from him. Both were in grievous turmoil—Poland was fighting for political stability in complex bouts of maniacal fratricide, Vienna was striving after economic stability by means of too ingenious a financial policy (which had become after Otto Bauer's resignation the policy of a madhouse in L's view). The two whirlpools had knocked Joseph awry, and he was gambling as never before. The long-term position was not too bad. Some financial compensation would in time come from the new Austria, one hoped; and some from the new Poland. But every penny had to be cleverly fought for—an arduous task that kept Theodora jogging between Lwow and Vienna in ice-cold railway carriages while her parents were on the French coast. Mistress of the situation, she could vouch for Koszylowce. But for the moment—with the Bolsheviks pressing towards Warsaw—everything had jammed; yet a gambling debt of Joseph's had to be paid. What was L going to do about it? An act of atonement by him was overdue; and Joseph, recently diagnosed a diabetic, was a doomed man who had to be spared further disappointment in his son.

On her way back to the station Theodora twitted L on the women whom men of standing marry and those they do other things with. As if he did not know. L's mounting exasperation broke into laughter. With his mind's eye he saw Theodora and Edwyn Bevan in confrontation—she hot, he cool, and both laying down the law for a dummy man and a dummy woman caught up in an imaginary, stereotyped course of events. As he laughed Theodora exuded a questioning haze of frost. His laughter became uncontrollable, and the bond between them sagged further. L next saw his sister in London where she was popular among his friends. Tegan Harris remembers her as 'striking, delightful, such an amusing companion at a play'. And J. H. Paton found her a 'dignified and attractive woman'. With L she dealt adroitly and he, feeling wretched, undertook to pay Joseph's gambling debts. L had been putting by small sums of money— little enough in sterling but a substantial amount in foreign currency. It had been earmarked for a holiday in the West Country much loved by Clara; and also against the eventuality of illness. L was sleeping badly, and almost always needed sleeping pills which, as a side effect, produced in him acute hypochondria; while Clara was prone to develop any symptom she heard graphically described. Sharing the anxiety about ill-health, though little else, they had agreed to keep a reasonable sum to fall back on. With it gone, a heightened irritability soured their relationship, to sweeten which L insured his life in Clara's favour. When summoned by his family to Vienna early in the long vacation, he also encouraged her to go to the West Country, putting up at students' hostels. This cheap holiday she enjoyed so well that for a time short visits to some better appointed hostels within an easy train journey from Oxford became a feature of her otherwise desolate life.

L had been drawn into a subtle plan. With fiery drive and unshakable determination Theodora and Ann were getting ready to rebuild the gutted house, and plant near it a large orchard, which became in due course renowned in the region: over 4,000 trees of high-grade apple, pear, cherry, and walnut. Ann had chosen to supervise personally the preliminary work that needed doing before the ground froze; Theodora was to squeeze out of Lwow officialdom enough restoration money to get on with; and Joseph was to raise in Vienna whatever money he could. But in that hotbed of erratic speculation he could not be left alone. Devoted relations still dotted about the enchanting city were of no use—no one was to know, no one ever did know, that Joseph was a compulsive gambler. It was in the nature of Ann's children to keep to themselves the agonizing secret, as she had. That the inferior Clara should be the fourth to know of it, increased her in-laws' hostility.

L found Vienna in a state of acute and infectious disorientation which reminded him of a war-weary person vulnerable to the Spanish influenza. The nation's blood, its money, was in a bad way. A hectic excitement, resembling certain signals of human collapse, was aggravated by an impoverishment and a barbarization already universal throughout Central and Eastern Europe. Presently L was to observe—for three years, and on various occasions to describe—Vienna's plight: the gayest, finest, most cultivated city in that region; the centre to which people from far and wide flocked for enjoyment; something of a parasite and

beautiful as parasitic plants usually are, Vienna was hungry and
down at heel. Food no longer came to her as a matter of course
from the plains of Hungary, Galicia, Moravia. Her luxury-
industries which had largely depended for production and markets
on the highly refined tastes of her inhabitants and their frequent
visitors had decayed under pressure of isolation and of the
coarser primary needs. The Austro-Hungarian army had been
centred on Vienna but the new Austria had none, and needed a
bureaucracy different from the Empire's and much less large. The
central offices of great railways, of imposing industrial and commercial enterprises, and of the banks which had controlled—in
the German way—the Empire's industries, were become idle
giants. Of the railway lines only stumps remained in the new
Austria; and important sections of the old Austria's great industries stood in lands now alien. As the krone tumbled to nothing,
the value of mortgages and loans catastrophically fell. Vienna had
been geared to finance an Empire. Now the disproportionately
high number of pensioned officials and officers was a grievous
burden. The sustenance of pullulating small *rentiers* was disap-
pearing. In terms of money, property had been annihilated. The
lifelong savings of old people had derisively shrunk; the instinct
to save had been mocked; the economic life of the country upset,
shaken, distorted; its population debased into paupers or
speculators.

In this afflicted city L had agreed to keep Joseph under strict
supervision—a most invidious task for the impetuous son of a
mixed-up father. They went everywhere together, and Joseph
came to hate the frustrating presence. Tensions between them
increased. Both fluent men, they found themselves short of topics.
When they found one, they quarrelled; and quarrelled worst
about the 'legitimate frontier' to which the Poles in pursuit of the
Bolsheviks were ordered to withdraw on 10 July 1920 by statesmen gathered at Spa. Joseph, unable to out-argue his better
informed son, withdrew into sullen silence. And, with the business transactions dragging on, L became fully aware for the
first time of the passionate concern for Zionism sown in him by
Chaim Weizmann when they met in Paris in the summer of 1919.
Weizmann had been emphatic that only Zionism could save the

Polish Jews. L had disagreed, Weizmann's schemes seeming to him unrealistic. But now, a year later, in a state of protracted exasperation with his father, L found that he had come to share Weizmann's view, and declared himself a Zionist. Joseph froze at the first mention of it; as Theodora had when L seemed to scoff at her insinuations against Clara. First the Ukrainians, now the Jews. Was he then going to settle in Palestine and have himself circumcized? Furious, L declared that no such nonsense entered into it. Weizmann was the leader of an up-to-date Return to a Homeland suited to the new age. In a leaping cascade of eloquence L tried to put across his still incoherent ideas; and his father's hostility towards him hardened.

Assuming he would accompany his father to Koszylowce, L eagerly looked forward to reunion with the loved land. Joseph would have none of it—the memory of L's discreditable war-time activities was still fresh, his presence in Koszylowce could only cause pain. Those were disturbing statements, even if assumed to be exaggerated. More irritating still were Joseph's insinuations that Koszylowce did not lie on the road to Jerusalem. Struck with a new distress, L saw Joseph off and got in touch with his favourite cousin, Szela (pronounced Shela), who, having married Joseph's youngest brother, was also L's aunt; and, though his senior only by a couple of years, had been a widow since 1912. Rich in Austrian crowns he took her out to dinner and the theatre, and showered presents on her children who thought him very impressive in Oxford bags and with a pipe clenched between his teeth. In Szela's house he met on separate occasions, Theodor Reik, a pupil of Freud, and Marie Beer of unforgettable memories. Reik intrigued L by saying that psychoanalysis could in a round-about way cure his insomnia; Marie disturbed him with a matter-of-course, big-sister's readiness to mother him. He left Vienna unsettled, toying with unformulated wishes to return.

Either in Vienna or soon after he reached Oxford, L put on paper some thoughts about writing history. Shortly before he died in 1960, he pressed me to read and judge them. Though unable to incorporate any part of these stray thoughts in a published work, he had carefully dated the fragments. The post-dating I place in the mid-1930s because of his deteriorated handwriting. These notes, unkempt and somewhat incoherent, preserve, in trains of entwined thinking and feeling, L's earliest, spontaneous urge to bridge the seas of isolation between himself as a writer of history and those contemporaries who were ploughing up islands of a different soil from his—for example painters who were striving after a new artistic idiom. Though L never quite understood modern art, he continued to find it stimulating. And after 1942 we went together, on his initiative, to every possible exhibition of pictures, modern or established.

Since Clara and L met, they had not been separated for more than a few days at a stretch. Observing her after Vienna, he found a stranger, silent, remote, waking to his presence only to spin increasingly fantastical yarns about herself. Though uneasy, L tried to make light of it: brought home a copy of R. L. Stevenson's *New Arabian Nights,* and suggested Clara use it as a model for a work of her own, 'The Latest Arabian Nights'. As he spoke, she looked away into the distance with half-closed eyes and smiled. From such disquieting strangeness he took shelter in the buoyant simplicities of the Master's lodgings or with the Bells; and found diversion in occasional visits abroad. Reminiscing about that year, Essie Bell wrote: 'From one of his trips he brought us a marvellous Dutch doll, Peter, who was long much beloved.' But closing she said,

Clara was obviously the wrong woman for him yet I was sorry when she left Lewis. But then, I knew a side of him that very few did. He felt great pity for her; though no self-reproach. Indeed he had been almost quixotically generous. Feeling a 'responsibility' for her he paid her an allowance even when she was living with another man.

Perspicacious though Essie was, she never perceived L's sense of guilt which increased as he tried to define where he had failed Clara. Never an easy spender she was growing miserly in a primitive way. L was dismayed to find that here and there in the soft furniture she had been stuffing screwed up bank-notes. Challenged, she would don her smiling mask and walk off; till on a red-letter day she droned that casual small savings from the housekeeping money might help to cover her expenses for a course in a nearby agricultural college. Ignoring the absurdities

of her remark, L began hopefully to collect details about the
college and its courses. But she lost interest—a change that
coincided with a friend's putting at their disposal his cottage, south
of Oxford, with its two maids. L had accepted the offer gratefully,
without realizing that Clara was not pleased. She soon put him
wise to it. L, outraged to find that even in his friend's well-run
thatched house Clara still tucked away her wads of bank-notes,
blew up. She turned on him—what right had he to place her in a
horrid situation where servants were continually spying on her?
Astounded, L reminded her that she had wanted to be out of
Oxford for Christmas. Ah yes, but to stay in Somerset, at a
hostel. Surely, he protested, this was far better. But he was
rebuked. For the rest of the holiday he immured himself in work
broken by solitary walks, meals far from convivial, and restless
nights. Back in Oxford, he hopefully took up another out-of-
doors interest: 'I am delighted,' wrote Mrs. Edgar Dugdale,
'rugger matches I approve of in themselves and for you.' But it
was no good. Wretched at home, and realizing that Oxford had
come to hinder his writing the book on his phoenix empire, L
sought solace from C. G. Stone to discuss, as in the past, earnest
matters never broached in the presence of others; and his friendship with T. E. Lawrence took a new turn.

Like L both Lawrence and Stone were fascinated by words and
their usage. C. G. Stone, with his metaphysical bent, was following paths that soon led others to linguistic philosophy; in
Lawrence L discovered an inspired craftsman who treasured
words as objects made of shape and sound, and, more importantly
still, a man who had greatly suffered since 1914. Writing in 1916
about a German book, *Das Phaenomenon Dostoyevski* by Otto Julius
Bierbaum, L had contrasted the 'still-born creatures which you
[continentals like the author] call ideas', with the portentous
message waiting to be read in 'the patient eyes of a suffering
people'—the Russians in this case. 'What is spirit which neither
suffers nor rejoices but merely prides itself on an unreal existence?'
L had asked. During the remaining war years he had pondered the
reason, the purpose, the meaning, the place, of suffering in
human life. And of Lawrence, who had never caught his imagination as a military genius, L wrote between 1929 and 1939, in

166

private letters and for publication, as of a tormented man: 'He suffered as few men do, and knew how much he suffered'; 'he had the negations and instincts of a prophet and a saint without their faith'; 'there was a deep negation of life' in him; 'he had sad piercing eyes, his greatness was in them'; 'there was a stillness of soul in him and a pain that was timeless'. Most revealingly of all L wrote some years after Lawrence's death, 'there was a yearning in him for the great void where nothing obstructs the spirit' (*Manchester Guardian,* 7 January 1939). When their tenuous pre-war friendship was resumed in 1920 L realized that the much fêted Lawrence was yearning for, and yet dreading as much as L himself did, the imperative call of the haunting void.

But neither of the two resumed friendships could compensate for L's complete lack of affinity with Clara. She, having done another about-turn, was picking quarrels with him, while his phoenix-empire book seemed stuck for good. L's rare thoughts about it were the more tantalizing for his being hindered from pursuing them. Lectures and his pupils' approaching examinations kept him steadily trotting on. But, accumulating tensions and frustrations, he was restive. More than before, he wanted to study in depth the great eighteenth-century collapse which had attended a birth of good augury. And as never before he measured the immensity of the task. He knew by now that the book required stretches of unencumbered time. Spare time used fruitfully, in any sphere except the financial, is a great consumer of money; and the family home, far from any longer being a source of cash, was likely to continue a drain.

But the qualities of 'The Downfall' were already being discussed in some circles, and L's journalist friends were alerted. The *Manchester Guardian* people thought he might make a good foreign correspondent, both of their daily paper and of their *Commercial*. His earnings would not be spectacular but the position offered him useful facilities and even prestige in some quarters—which might bring from elsewhere enough money to make possible the writing of the book. With this in view, A. L. Smith introduced him in the early spring to Noel Rawnsley. With others, Rawnsley had an interest in 'shipment of cotton to mills in Czechoslovakia'. Several pleasant and informative meetings culminated in Rawnsley's declaring he wished to 'avail himself of Namier's services in connection with management of this business *now* and of any business that may be developed in connection therewith'. L's obligations would be to 'facilitate relations between [the partners] and their Czechoslovak and other connections'. He was to receive a good salary payable in sterling, and 'a bonus equal to 10 per cent on Rawnsley's personal share of the profits of the cotton business in Czechoslovakia'. Signed on 14 April, the agreement was to run for three years from 21 August. In L's calculation, by the autumn of 1924 he would have amassed enough money to devote the following two years entirely to the phoenix-empire book. He was happy as could be. He was returning to Vienna.

At every stage L had told Clara of the discussions and arrangements. In return she was outspoken about pining for a new life. But the misery of Europe's most chaotic spots repelled her. Moreover, she had come to see that their interests would never merge. A kind man, L would surely not prevent her from finding happiness with someone else, perhaps in America, should the occasion arise. L agreed in his heart that her mood and silhouette were incongruous with Vienna. And when on a later occasion she declared herself to be loved by a man who suited her to perfection and who was about to take up a lucrative offer that straddled Canada and the U.S., L accepted the situation as stated. But first Clara wished to live alone for a while, in London or the West Country. L agreed that it seemed reasonable. Who the man was she preferred not to say just yet. But she would be writing. Well aware of her unbelievable abilities for inventing plausible detail that only fringed on reality, L left it at that: bought her a suitcase and gave her some money. As she boarded her bus for the station he noted his feelings of unalloyed relief. They were to last for a couple of months while the routine of his life ran with welcome smoothness. A woman who had occasionally cleaned for them declared herself eager to serve L, tidied up the place and removed the cats, except for one kitten with which he liked to play.

Presently friends remarked on not having seen Clara for quite a while. L answered with punctilious exactitude that after he had bought her a suitcase she had left him, for where he could not say.

And one more giggly story, in several versions, went the round of his contemporaries. But the main feature by which Oxford remembered this sojourn of L's is best summed up by a contemporary of his pupils. Sir John Rothenstein who 'scarcely knew him then', has stated, 'Contacts of my generation with dons were unusually slight but a few were known and revered. Of this very small company Lewis Namier was one.'

CHAPTER TEN

Plan and Chance
Autumn 1921–Spring 1924

L remembered his second post-war journey to Vienna as a happy conjunction of plan and chance. Determined to arrive fresh, he had booked a sleeper for the continental leg: yet owing to a last minute flurry in Oxford missed the connection by minutes. Not that he had light-heartedly cut things too close. Terrorized into punctuality as a child, he had allowed plenty of time for a telephone talk with Clara about her latest plans; but finding her at none of her usual haunts, finally rang up Essie Bell, holidaying near Farnborough. By the time he was posting to her a cheque for his elusive wife, L was wellnigh speechless with exasperation. And yet, the tiresome hitch led almost at once to a happy encounter described by Mrs. Money-Kyrle, then Minora Fox:

Owing to summer time he missed his sleeper. Before I married I was much too economical to have one myself. And I was sitting, reading a novel about Oxford when Lewis rather breathlessly came in and sat down beside me. We began to talk of the book, the author and Oxford. That is how our friendship started. He told me he was going to make enough money in cotton to afford a secretary while he wrote his book on English parliamentary history. . . .

I often heard L extol the fortuitous chain of events that had led to a friendship he would have been sorry to do without. And to me he stressed the beauty of its dovetailing 'providential joints' as a good example of life's most teasing game, that of chance sequences irrupting into men's carefully laid plans.

In Vienna L stopped long enough to put through some telephone calls and see Frau Sacher, the proprietress of the Sacher hotel, about a large quiet room he wished to retain in the hotel for an unspecified period—he would be coming and going a great deal on the spur of the moment. At the very next political crisis (end of October) the arrangement paid off. He sent his newspaper short pithy reports in quick succession from Prague, Vienna, Prague again; and could add to them an important interview with Premier Beneš on Czechoslovakia's official policy. L's involvement in Czech affairs dated from early in the war when he 'was in touch with President Masaryk, Dr. Beneš and a good many Czechs'. But in 1957, turning down an exorbitant request, he denied having been 'active in the Czech Movement for Independence'; explained, 'I was a Government official'; and went on to say, 'I cannot possibly supply the answers to your questionnaire. The attitudes of the various senior officials in the F.O. is not a thing that it would be permissible for me to discuss.' His exaggerated reputation as a fighter for the Czech cause may have been due to a much read pamphlet *The Czecho-Slovaks, An Oppressed Nationality* where he claimed to speak for the silenced nation of Czechs and Slovaks—men of one race, torn in two by the harsh hands of history; men whose chief means of expression had been suppressed; and who were reduced to the position of mute victims driven to a death dishonourable for all men, that of slaves fighting to maintain slavery. This wartime enthusiasm being exceedingly well-informed, proved a good preparation for L's sojourn in Prague.

He lived comfortably enough in rooms found for him by a subordinate of Beneš; and he often visited Masaryk at Lany—a typical country house with a columned portico, but set in forest-land renowned for its game. On unofficial visits there he heard old Masaryk ponder his report to the Genoa Conference. The veteran fighter for freedom spoke much of the Russian tragedy; and about the true face of Bolshevism whose features he had seen defining themselves in defeated Russia, Germany, and Hungary. A clear-sighted witness he gave certainty to L's surmises: Bolshevism had nowhere even attempted to establish the 'constructive social revolution envisaged by Marx. Neither social nor socialist, it was entirely political.' Using Marxism as a weapon for bludgeoning the harassed Russian people—decimated by hunger, epidemics, and the deliberate massacre of those who continued courageously to think for themselves—it glibly used elsewhere its Marxist phraseology for advertising successful subversion. The inconsistency between its use of the fist at home and its use of the word abroad was deliberate. Listening, L gained a new confidence in his own political acumen, well shored up by Masaryk's appraisal of communism in action. Throughout the 1920s this led to a marked coolness between L and many of his politically minded English friends. Too benevolent towards Russia for the more banal propagandists on the Right, he was too clear-sighted about Bolshevism for the more banal propagandists on the Left. Where they admired or detested one entity, he discerned two, in conflict more often than not. Whichever he spoke of, his opponents—according to their political colour—applied his words to both. His point was missed and wrong conclusions were drawn; while he rejected with increasing impatience both fashionable stereotypes as doctrinaire and pitifully out of date.

Unlike L's reverent admiration for Masaryk, his friendship with Beneš was not free of criticism. In Prague he followed with attentive sympathy any effort to 'consolidate' the new state's policy; and found the young republic's constitutional and parliamentary practice 'extremely interesting'. Efforts to restore the economic health of all national groups who formed part of Central Europe, he deemed rightly rewarded by the high esteem shown Beneš in the League of Nations. Yet on the whole, in the Premier's special domain—Foreign Affairs, conducted by him from 1918 to 1935— L found a disturbing tendency to favour expedient measures bound to prove dangerous. And as Masaryk's correcting influence weakened with his increasing age, L saw Beneš's regrettable inclination harden till in 1925 it reached an ominous trough— Czechoslovakia was bound to Poland in a 'common front against Germany'. L's stringent criticism of Beneš on this count, led some to assume a deep enmity between them. But, answering such rashly logical suppositions, he declared himself 'both an old friend and a friendly critic' of Beneš—the sectarian mind that lumps together for approval or condemnation a man's convictions and his personality was alien to L; his powers of analysis had long since been alerted to its snares. He closed one correspondence (in the *Nation and Athenaeum*) on his supposed detestation of Beneš with the words: 'an honest reconciliation between the Czechs and the Germans who form a quarter of the population of Czechoslovakia is rendered much more difficult by Czechoslovakia's assuming a pointedly anti-German attitude along the entire line'. Again he alone seemed to have read, in his contemporaries' actions, the omens of World War II.

His third Czech friend L had not known before Prague. Yet Dr. Rašin—Czechoslovakia's first Minister of Finance and 'by far the ablest financier in Czechoslovakia'—influenced the course of L's life as neither Masaryk nor Beneš could. Founder of Czechoslovakia's currency system, Rašin soon initiated L into the financial subtleties of nation-wide industries, international concerns, and inter-state monetary operations. An eager pupil with a pragmatic bent, L objectively sized up his own situation too, and saw how favourably he was placed to supplement his earnings with hardly any additional exertion and without doing anything illegal. He started with the obvious. All his money came in sterling which, for spending, had to be changed either into Czech or Austrian crowns. He picked the right moment and the right place for each successive operation, was highly successful and acquired a taste for quick gains—a common hobby in the years of unsynchronized but interlocking monetary crises. L had in fact first learnt about the situation some time back, from Joseph; and with him in mind had written,

To keep a balance in the bank is sheer folly. The wisest thing is to get permission from the Government to go abroad with a reasonable sum of money. A man who left Poland in July taking with him £1,000 (then roughly 90,000 Polish marks) and who lived comfortably for eight months (chiefly on the Riviera but also in Italy) at the rate of £100 a month doing no work, now returning to Poland finds himself in possession of a balance of about 130,000 marks (£200). Financially Poland is rapidly becoming for anyone who tries to live a normal life in accordance with the ordinary principles of financial morality, a lunatic asylum.[1]

So were most Successor States of whom the Austrian rump was one.

Apart from leading to easy gains, friendship with the Czech Minister of Finance helped L in his journalism. Rašin introduced

[1] *Manchester Guardian*, 31 March 1920; another variant, *Skyscrapers*, p. 172.

him, as a *Manchester Guardian* correspondent, to some hand-picked Viennese financiers and bankers. L's curiosity in the movement of money no longer being detached, his reports acquired a new bite. His articles of 1922-3 describe well the 'lunatic climate' in which he was amassing capital to write in peace his book on the eighteenth century; and they reveal his accumulating knowledge and grasp of dovetailing economic and financial situations; also his observation of certain sporadic rifts that tore them apart. He observed the signs of an expectant dread —the apprehension of an unspecified catastrophe—sweep through Austria in the summer of 1922. Simultaneously he noted an unjustifiable drop of all shares to a fraction of their intrinsic value. Though traceable to nothing but the 'prevalent dread', the drop led to further muddle. Real estate seemed to some the only sound investment. But despite the incredible shortage of housing in Vienna, when landlords were at one point allowed to charge 250 times the pre-war rent, house property was a sheer loss because rents had to remain at a level which the impoverished population could pay; and only a few were able to take on so exorbitant an outlay. Incomes were reduced to about a quarter of their pre-war gold level, but the gold price of food and clothing had rocketed higher than that of anything else. Rents could no longer figure in a citizen's budget at, proportionately, the former level. Closing a long account of the involved position, L cautioned English capital against investing in such house property which, to make things worse, could not long escape heavy taxation. 'That is bound to come and its burden will not be passed on to the disastrously impoverished lodgers'—because it could not be. Dr. Ignaz ('Father') Seipel's stabilization of the Austrian krone L found 'quite remarkable'. And yet he saw the paper money in circulation increase fabulously against the gold and the hard currencies acquired by the National Bank. Though not 'inflationary' in the sense then used on the Continent, inflation it was—purchasing power had increased without any increase in wealth. As a result, the gold value of Austrian shares rose sharply between December 1922 and June 1923; shares of the Austrian banks were three or four times higher that summer than in December; and Industrials, though less spectacular, had risen by

50 to 150 per cent in five months. Everyone, wrote L, was speculating on the Stock Exchange—waiters, shop-assistants, flapper-typists. As in Prague, he was more fortunate than most; and with typical incongruity, learnt in these, his most affluent months, that for him money was no source of happiness. It was a means to an end; basically a lunatic means. Nor was it money-making, any more than journalism, that increasingly tied him to Vienna. Cast to enjoy, above all, relations with people whose interests interlocked with or verged on his, he was increasingly tormented there in his relations with some while finding comfort in his association with others.

Of L's bitter break with his mother, Joseph's sister Anna writes,

I remember well the first time I heard my sister-in-law speak against her son. It must have been the autumn of 1921. Anyway, the whole family —father, mother and sister—were in Vienna, and one of them said they would be seeing him when he got back from Prague. I had loved him very much since he was a sad little sick boy, and asked them to say I would be happy to see him. But his mother, gone very hard, said, 'Better not!' When I said 'Yes!' she strongly opposed me without explaining. But Dziunia [Theodora] honoured my request, and he came the day after he saw them. When they left he often spent the evenings with us. We were very happy to have him, and his affectionate manner to all remained for me unforgettable. He brought lovely toys for our little boy. One, a beautiful white bear, Norman fell in love with and for long took to bed with him. Lewis spoke a lot then of Dostoevski and if he saw we did not have on our shelves some good book, by or about him, would bring it round next day.

Pondering years later his mother's rejection of him, L would insist, to me, on its having been the result of a strong affection 'inverted' by the combination of at least three exasperating factors: the sullen hostility between him and his father; his incipient self-identification with the Jews; and the humiliating absurdity of his marriage which continued to shock her, not without reason. Putting together what L told me and comments on it by others, the course of events emerges reasonably clear.

Clara and John Davenport—the man she was reluctant to name earlier—had planned to sail for Canada, en route for the U.S. A little while before L had unsuccessfully tried to get in touch with her, the two had found it was not possible for them to book passages in one cabin. Maybe Davenport's having a wife and children was a contributing cause, but at the time Clara still thought him single and, perturbed by the hitch, had telephoned to L hoping he might help them. Missing him by a matter of hours, she appealed to Sir James Headlam-Morley, adapting her details to his outlook. After Essie ran her to earth, Clara wrote to L abroad, and presently Sir James did too. Yet during the months it took to sort things out and get her away—to British Columbia, then Canada, and the States—Davenport remained a hazy figure of whom Sir James, for one, may not have known. Lady Headlam-Morley, Agnes, and Kenneth definitely did not. The man's profession or occupation even in England, and when exactly he left, no one knew for sure. L supposed him to be in London till some time in 1923, but remained uncertain of his name, remarking once that as Clara always called him Davenport, he could have been Davenport John. But she sailed away at last on 31 March 1923 and wrote briefly of her joy at leading a nomadic life as near as could be to that of her Tartar ancestors.

In England only two people (besides me after 1942) knew how Clara had slipped out of L's life; Essie Bell, his confidante throughout; and Sir James who, dragged in by Clara, proved to be as discreet as Essie. In Vienna L at first spoke of it only to his mother and sister, recognizing the matter to be their legitimate concern. And as always when telling someone of an event he thought they had a right to know, he was punctiliously outspoken. Ann, a simple person all of a piece and, at heart, living outside any religious tradition, had built up her own infrangible code of honour and scale of devotions. Both were based on self-dedication to the family. She had despised her weakling son until, surviving his diphtheria—a killer in those days—he proved his stamina and guts. She then warmed to him and, as he grew robust and brilliant, her affection for him became great. But his wartime 'infatuation' with the Ukrainians started a revulsion—he was harming the family. The absurd, unhappy marriage confirmed her worst suspicions: he was not the staunch family builder she wanted her son to be; and with a sense of outrage, she recoiled from L.

To his face Ann and Theodora had summed up their dislike of his matrimonial conundrum by declaring they always knew him incapable of having satisfactory human relations. Now that he had proved it, Ann was so emphatic and Theodora so eloquent that they drove him on to a psychoanalyst's couch. Unfortunately L found his 'trick-cyclist' to be a tormentor, and also personally repulsive to him. If one of a psychoanalyst's chief aims is to channel on to himself an affection frustrated elsewhere, the treatment was a complete flop. L's anger against his acidulous father's weaknesses never extinguished his unstinting admiration for Joseph's intellect and wide-ranging knowledge of the law; while his enmity against his psychoanalyst was exacerbated by the increasing tension between L's growing faith in this kind of cure and his pessimistic superstition that a new devil is sure to prove worse than the current tormentor: better stick to the one you know however much you hate him.

Of course the psychoanalyst presently knew all L did about Clara; and also about the waxing emotional involvement between him and Marie Beer, of which the family knew nothing. In fact, he egged L on, implying that Marie was the perfect mother substitute, a subtle healer; and stating that the sooner a consummation was reached the better for his sleeplessness and her latent hysteria —she being, according to the psychoanalyst, weary of her virginity. Despite such encouragement their relationship shaped well: yet their first night together had an ominous, eerie prelude.

Marie had been unmistakably, if unobtrusively, encouraging. And when she telephoned to Sacher's at dinner time complaining of loneliness and despondency, the thought crossed his mind that if he answered her appeal he might not get back till the small hours. It was a fine night and he decided to walk. A garden thick with tenebrous trees lay in his path. He was halfway through when a hulk lurched towards him, muttering fast and vehemently. Was the man drunk or insane? It made all the difference. With drunk men L knew how to cope. Several of his contemporaries have told me of an incident in the Balliol quad that earned him their esteem. 'A wild Irishman', having got drunk, had snatched down from a wall in Philip Guedalla's room a handsome old sword and was rushing about brandishing it. Everyone moved out of his way, and this further excited the armed man. But L detached himself from a group saying something under his breath, perhaps the words—no doubt with the demeanour—he used for restive horses. Gently disarming his man, he inconspicuously handed the sword to another undergraduate who had darted over to him. Linking arms with his friend L led him away, and thought no more of it. But the proximity of a mad person cramped him with irrational dread. Minds lacking the gift of sane co-ordination reduced L to a state of acute helplessness. And as the indistinct jumble of vocal sounds gained momentum, he was overcome by panic. Asking himself if the mutterer was insane, L hurried down the deserted streets, dodging this way and that. The man stuck to him like a shadow. And listen as L would, he failed to understand what language the man spoke. With national hatreds simmering in even the most sober minds, L was reluctant to use the wrong language, that of an ethnic enemy. Yet at moments he felt impelled to respond. So he grunted—soothingly, emphatically, wearily, disparagingly. Nothing worked. Muttering and grunting they entered another small garden where the man vanished into a clump while L, bracing himself against a tornado of horror, sped on.

He and Marie must have been about the oddest lovers even in that distraught land in its worst years of distraction. L's tempestuous desire was for a phantom alive for him alone—the Marie of sixteen years before, whom he continued to call his *beau idéal*. But the power of his remembered emotions was binding him fast to an ageing woman bereft of almost all his dream-girl's endowments. The squint in Marie's right eye, that began during her attack of meningitis, had increased; her slight congenital limp was more pronounced; the dashing relatives she had most depended on, were dead; her income and capital were reduced to trifles; and there was no occasion to practise her reasonably lucrative hobby of translating English and French novels. Yet, characteristically, the incongruity between the remembered ideal, with its ambience, and the observed and live actuality added the edge of compassion to his affection for Marie. He directed to her some Englishmen who wished to learn German, and placed some of her meagre capital, with his own, in shares and currencies. Unquestioning gratitude soon riveted her to him. Their satisfaction with each other, however, was overcast from the start by two clouds: Clara, of whose irregular nomadic life Marie was the fourth person in Vienna to know; and the possibility of some stuffy relation (his or hers) guessing what turn things between them had taken. The last worry was, in the event, lightened by Theodora's demands on L. During the remaining months of 1921 and through the early months of 1922, Joseph made several visits to Italy. Since neither Ann nor Theodora could be with him, they wired on every occasion to L who, joining his father, stayed glued to his side. Only physical prostration could at the time keep Joseph away from a handy casino; yet, given the right approach, he could be restrained on the spot by a gaming, but more reasonable, companion. L who had been regularly paying his father's gaming debts, every time responded immediately to Theodora's call; and almost at once devised a plan: his route would lie through Venice, and there Marie, having vaguely spread the rumour that she was going into the Alps or the country, would join him. Such with slight variations became their routine which led to both knowing almost every stone in Venice. They sauntered about together. But in art galleries L gravitated towards the narrative masters and great portrait painters who excelled in capturing types shrewdly observed, while Marie delighted above all in emotive colour and liked to circulate among suave Madonnas.

After March 1922 the Venetian interludes lost their primary purpose. In England on Rawnsley's business early in spring, L wrote for the *Manchester Guardian* an article on the forthcoming conference in Genoa, and arranged to be present throughout the proceedings: a commitment which fortuitously led to his being neither at his father's death on 14 April nor even at the burial on the 16th, and which further increased the bitterness between brother and sister. Joseph died in Merano, at the Hotel Bavaria, with his wife and daughter there. But Theodora's wire summoning L never reached him and could not be traced. She hotly maintained that, as the end approached, she had telegraphed to his business address in Prague, having forgotten where he was staying in Genoa. Asked why she had not wired to Sacher's, she averred that, stunned with grief, all she could think of was L's first Prague address. Although unconvincing to L—deeply hurt by learning of the death through a letter of condolence from Marie—it was probably true. But psychoanalysis was generating in him a host of suspicions, often as ill-founded as they were involved. And besides, grown an obsessive stickler for accuracy, he had come to assume that most people lie, some more easily than others. For Theodora he coined a phrase, 'unsent wires, like letters never written, are most securely lost'. She did not forgive him till after World War II, if then. To my mind he was doing her an injustice. Like their mother and L himself, Theodora was inclined to be painfully outspoken, brutally so with intimates on occasion. And their silences could be stony; but all three were too proud to indulge in the mental wriggling exacted by a deliberate lie. Moreover, there was no valid reason for a lie, although he soon thought up some. At times he must have felt his accusations to be absurd: as new claims for Joseph's debts reached the ruined family, he paid them all—to save Koszylowce of course; yet, twistedly, to make amends too. Scrupulous in his thinking, L was often swayed by feelings so complex that they could be mutually contradictory.

Fortunately his luck on the Stock Exchange held—a great relief since the 'demands from Koszylowce' and his psychoanalyst's exorbitant fees were strongly sucking away at his savings. Annoyed and slightly alarmed, he resumed massive writing. Not that he had ever dropped it, but in 1921–2 his overriding concern had been with a 'special issue of the *Manchester Guardian Commercial* which appeared in five languages and certainly remains an important source for the economic history of the period'. One of his collaborators, F. G. Steiner, informs me, 'Your husband lined up the contributors and drafted the overall plan. I wrote about Vienna as the main market of exchange in Central Europe.' In the following year L began to systematize his own accumulated observations, and to record his insights into the political, economic, and monetary factors of the continuous crises. Above his regular contributions to the *Commercial*'s 'reconstruction numbers' (some of which are reprinted in *Skyscrapers*) he wrote an immense essay on 'The Problems of East-

Central Europe' (*The Round Table,* June 1923), with a long chapter on Austria omitted 'due to shortage of space', according to L's inscription on a carbon copy. He wrote another essay of about 20,000 words, on 'The Conditions and Prospects of Austrian Industry since 1918'; and several less comprehensive, more narrowly specialized accounts. He also wrote informative articles on Great Britain for the *Neue Freie Presse.* Two of them, which explain to the Viennese electorate some peculiarities of the British General Election of December 1923, contain a lucid exposition of L's own views on the three chief political parties. Mindful for once, of his readers' basic ignorance of his subject, he started from scratch and made the entire situation—not only his attitude to it—impeccably clear.

On his short visits to England since early in 1922 L had seen the country chiefly through his friends' eyes. The general election of December 1923 significantly shifted his interest to London; and a concurrent spell of work on the Newcastle Papers in the British Museum re-awakened his excitement over eighteenth-century problems. Before leaving for Vienna in the New Year he engaged, in boisterous spirits, a secretary to tidy up his accumulations of English and American material already fetched from Oxford. But while profitably summing up on the spot the knowledge and insight gained during his three years in post-war Prague and Vienna, he was hit by two blows that drastically affected his life and partly reshaped his character.

On 23 February Theodora married Tadeusz Modzelewski, by all accounts a fine and amiable man, some fifteen years her senior. Descended from an old Ukrainian family he had lost to the Bolsheviks a large well-run estate with a fine manor house in the region of Kamenets Podolsky. Having settled at the time of Joseph's death in the neighbourhood of Koszylowce, Tadeusz presently undertook to help the bereaved mother and daughter to build up their ruined estate. The shared interest and personal loneliness could hardly fail to draw him and Theodora together. Telling L, very shortly before her wedding, that it would be celebrated in the Lwow Convent of the Sacred Heart—where her future sister-in-law was Mother Superior—Theodora advised him not to be present. Casually she mentioned that Joseph had

bequeathed Koszylowce to her and, consequently, she and
Tadeusz would be living there with Ann. When the new house
was ready to receive guests properly L would be most welcome;
but not on this occasion and not just yet. Country folk had long
memories and longer resentments. Her 'screed' plunged L into a
state of aggrieved fury. On occasion it overpowered him even
after World War II. That he should have been 'dispossessed' was
outrageous enough; but that not even Ann had bothered to tell
him of it as soon as the will was read, left him glaring, speechless,
panting, choking. Had there been no will—as L had been allowed
to assume—brother and sister would have inherited Koszylowce
jointly. When, in the 1940s, with Ann and Tadeusz dead and
Koszylowce in Communist hands for good, I stressed to him the
sheer nervous waste of such fury, he was impatient of my view.
His right hand by then was wellnigh useless owing to an unspecified psychosomatic complaint. The best of his psychoanalysts (as he saw them) had ascribed the increasing rigidity to
his unrealizable desire that Hitler should be killed, by him. L did
not agree. As he saw it, his having been deprived of a rightful
inheritance had caused the nervous deterioration. For ten years
he had longed for Koszylowce as an outlet where—with a very
special joy—he would once again ride out to *his* neolithic *obuz*
(tumulus), and organize on *his* land shoots of wild boar and other
game. His right hand having symbolically become of no pleasur-
able use to him, he had let it die. L's imagination was no less
pictorial, vigorous, and constructive than his psychoanalysts';
only their jumping-off boards differed. One of the pacifying arguments I put to him was that never in his life would he have withdrawn to Koszylowce and devoted himself to building it up, as
Theodora and Tadeusz had done supremely well between the
wars. While agreeing, L insisted that he would have left them to
run house and estate as they chose; but they, by 'dispossessing',
had crippled him. He refused to be a guest at Koszylowce, and
never again saw Ann or Theodora. But letters were exchanged,
and L often looked at snapshots of his nieces, born in 1925 and
1929; both pretty girls as children.

The other formative traumatic force led L to make in 1924 a
decision entirely his own. The fees of his Viennese psychoanalyst

and the heavy demands from Koszylowce had been introducing
anxiety into his amassing of capital. The anxiety, combining with
the pleasure, had stirred up the dormant gambler in him. His
recognition of it coincided with a shift of Europe's centre of
speculation from Vienna to Paris—a pointer for many Central-
European financiers that time was ripe for world-wide speculation in shares. But the swiftly expanded field and scale jolted L
into measuring how much his primary reason for amassing money
had dimmed, giving precedence to his pleasure in devising and
carrying through lucrative financial operations. He realized also
that for some time before the assassination in February 1923 of his
Czech financier friend, Alois Rašin, they had been discussing a
variety of financial matters as experts of equal standing. Rašin had
deftly transmitted his know-how to L who, in assimilating it,
had given it a new quality that had intrigued his instructor. But
this original, personal approach to monetary operations on a
grand scale had started up a conflict between the call of L's
future book and his immediate gambling joy. The tug-of-war
lasted for as long as conditions allowed; which was also as long
as L needed to see, beyond possible doubt, that he was in danger
of drifting into a mode of life that, keeping him engrossed in a
realm of enjoyable skills, would extinguish his creative abilities.
Yet the processes of making big money were only intoxicants.
They would never satisfy his basic craving for creative
investigation.

In terms of writing, 1924 was for L, above all, a year of two
long, closely argued, valedictory articles. Ostensibly he was taking
leave of Vienna and Prague, but in fact, of Koszylowce and a
part of himself. 'Inflation at Close Quarters: a Study of its
Effects in Central Europe' appeared in the *Manchester Guardian
Commercial* on 31 January; and 'How Austria passed through her
[recent] Financial Crisis: Present-day Openings for Foreign
Capital' appeared on 20 November. Through the latter glimmers
L's decision to remain poorer than he might have been. It reflects
a maturity gained by his making, with deliberation, a significant
choice. Although his intended book was concerned with events
of long ago, in no way linked with him or his, it had scored over
concrete, immediate enticements. That in the coming venture

only the illumination of a fragment of an alien past would be entirely his, did not worry him. Eighteen months before he had written 'There is such a thing as mass delusions in economic values.' These delusions he had seen swell, breed more harmful delusions, and spread mass misery. Finding himself in a world of proliferating misinterpretations bound to culminate in crises that caused widening distress, it seemed to L pre-eminently worth while to shine a powerful light on however small a sector of man's corporate activities. If the light was strong and clear, it should burn away some of the cumulative delusions which everywhere muffled the truth and led to catastrophe. L's enthusiasm for historical research had re-awakened in a world recognized by him as lunatic. Having suffered an eclipse, it emerged more concrete than before.

CHAPTER ELEVEN

Consorting Together
1924–1929

L's secretary had found for him in Chelsea pleasant rooms well kept by a spruce landlady. Strolling round the old botanical garden he gloomed over the rootless state to which his family had reduced him. Resuming his place in London's intellectual and social life, he observed with distaste a new pervasive mood. Fresh from the Continent, he drew comparisons between it and Great Britain, finding the differences more thought-provoking than the similarities. There an abundance of new frontiers precariously held in position a clutch of states with whose self-determination he had sympathized at one time or another. Overcoming lassitude, they had behaved with the petulant rashness of young organisms. Hopefully built to prosper (actually perhaps to languish like truncated Austria) each puzzled over the ways best suited to its survival in the environment into which it was born. Here in Great Britain the ancient sea-walls stood much repaired, never questioned. Only off-shore Ireland knew territorial anguish. Yet England too was restive, her sense of insecurity manifesting itself in a hectic and nervy mood soon accepted by her creative artists as typical of the 1920s.

Most Continentals had gained first-hand knowledge of an incongruity between their nation's political drive and economic needs; and each person was aware of a corresponding tension pervading his own life. But in England, while the leading men accepted future prosperity as of paramount importance, a restive element of the population had begun to question the usefulness of any 'democratic' discussion, and the pertinence of general prosperity to their own condition. The crude simplicities of totalitarianism or dictatorship were captivating men's imagination; here as on the Continent. But here, all-out enthusiasm for Moscow or Rome was affirmed against the unique background of a well-tried, centuries-old debating body increasingly denigrated. The differences between communism-in-action and fascism-in-action appeared trivial to L. The scowling opponents' rationalized resentments clinched in resonant, barely apposite slogans—bawled rather than argued, let alone fairly debated—merely confused, to his mind, the basic post-war issues between politics and economics. And to a society tangling itself in a cat's-cradle of tense but irrelevant detestations he responded with an increase of enthusiasm for the Mother of Parliaments. His dormant book on the phoenix empire—till now a work as vast as it was vague—gained a new and narrower purpose largely because he was beginning to recognize the best way of encompassing the subject. On one of several carefully preserved half-sheets he typed,

Parliamentary government has been tried in every country on the European Continent and practically everywhere has broken down. Counterfeits of organic creations do not work: the bones may be brought together bone to bone and be covered with sinews, flesh and skin; but no breath will breathe upon them. Nations and individuals can borrow and use devices of a more or less mechanical character. They cannot usefully borrow and properly use institutions which depend for their life and functioning on the social organism which—together with its countless roots—has produced them. Guizot, in his Mémoires, naïvely remarks about the Constitution of the Bourbon Restoration: '. . . *la Charte était une machine très praticable . . . les ouvriers ont bien plus manqué à l'instrument que l'instrument aux ouvriers*'. Had he not read Faust? Or had he forgotten? . . .

Goethe's lines come next, followed by two attempts at translation. The better quatrain reads,

> How luck through merit does arise
> The fools will never see.
> Were theirs the stone to make men wise,
> Without it men would be.

To this L added a quotation from *The Vicar of Wakefield*: 'I can supply you with the arguments, Sir, but not with the intelligence to comprehend them.' And at the bottom of the page stands,

One particularly serious weakness, inherent in the reproduction of alien institutions, is that the imitation must, by its very nature, be schematic.

Certain guiding principles have to be established, and made the basis of the new and artificial creation.

Such artificiality L rejected as doomed to failure or distortion. For him the Parliament in Westminster was unique because 'organically' generated in the people's past. Even more. Mid-eighteenth-century Westminster mirrored for him, on a reduced scale, the pursuit he most valued in his adopted country. He found there men (some brilliant and dedicated others clever and rascally) together seeking workable solutions to portentous political and economic problems, as in the present, but more clearly, colourfully, intelligibly. The House of Commons became for him an 'invaluable microscopic picture of England', a brilliant expression of mankind's urge to supersede aggression by debate, and a source for sketches illustrative of efforts to find acceptable solutions to tangled affairs—private and public—by means of the word, not the fist.

When in the last decade of his life, L's work was being derided and his wasted years and energies were being deplored, he often dwelt on two courses open to a historian. The one he likened to following a stream as a diarist on the move might, noting day by day its twists and turns from the source, say in the hills, through barely billowing land to the delta that fans out to the sea. The other was to build across the river's course two dams and settle down to study that section's significant detail; which study should include analyses of the water and the river bed. Such was his choice in 1924. One dam he built in 1740 ('My own research only starts about 1740'), the other in 1783; and steeped himself there in the concerns of the British 'political nation'. In June 1928 he wrote in the Preface to *The Structure of Politics at the Accession of George III*, explaining why it had no bibliography, 'There can be none for the life of a community: I hardly remember having come across any contemporary material which did not contribute something to my information.' Pondering the change of emphasis between his phoenix empire and the book he was shaping, L measured the change in himself, ascribing this to his incurable wounds that still ached. But others saw nothing of it. Oliver Harvey well remembered lunching with him in 1919 or 1920 at a milk-bar in Buckingham Palace Road, when L was perturbed by the Polish government's exaggerated frontier claims. After L's death he wrote,

I can see now his solemn but kindly face as he warned us. . . . On my return to London in 1925, we used to meet again. I did not sense any change in the impression he made on me. He was a man of the Right and I was of the Left. . . . He was always equally earnest, equally courteous, equally determined that you should hear his reasons. He could always quote chapter and verse. At the same time he was such a lovable and earnest personality, naïve I would almost say, so that even when one did not agree with him or thought his views excessive, one could not help respecting him.

On his new preoccupations L was no less intent; yet he found time and energy to indulge the one hobby of his maturity. As he went about the country, he collected local election lists, called 'poll books' in England. To the expert they give valuable insight into constituencies, electors, and candidates. One type of man figuring on them particularly attracted L: 'men of independent character', as he described them in *England in the Age of the American Revolution*, 'who in fact supplied most of the knights of the shires' round about 1760. For them L developed an inward feeling that led to his seeking out their spiritual heirs in contemporary England. To observe a living man or woman was to him always more poignantly rewarding than the study of any amount of 'dry bones'. Splendid help towards his understanding the attractive breed through its epigones was given L by Granville Proby, joint editor of certain volumes of the Victoria County History. They had met in Granville's parents' house, Elton Hall, through his youngest brother, a pupil of L's at Oxford. Renewed after 1924 the acquaintance quickly became a friendship and, in next to no time, Granville was introducing L to neighbours—chiefly in Huntingdonshire and Northamptonshire—who kept eighteenth-century parliamentary documents. Based on a joint interest in local and national history, the friendship gained further warmth through a shared taste for good food and an attachment to poll books. 'The Guildhall have certainly *one*,' wrote Granville, almost irate on a certain occasion, 'and I think probably more poll-books which I have not had access to.' But he was taking measures to right the deprivation.

Yet above all, these years of passionate grubbing about in the eighteenth century are notable because L's old friendship with Mrs. Edgar Dugdale acquired a width and depth that made of it a permanent and most significant feature of his life. They had met in 1915 in the Chelsea house of Mrs. Hubert Walter (later Dame Flora MacLeod of MacLeod) and had soon been set to work side by side in the newly-formed Political Intelligence Department. There Mrs. Dugdale (known as Baffy since childhood even to casual acquaintances) was given the task of working on Polish ethnical and statistical problems. At once she began eagerly to absorb L's fund of knowledge and to benefit from his statistical abilities. Many who had occasion to observe them in those years, or later, have spoken of the remarkable way in which their gifts complemented each other. And the war-time co-operation formed a bond that never weakened. When L was teaching in Oxford, Baffy closely followed his success with undergraduates. Throughout his absence abroad she regularly wrote to him. After his return, a chance absence of his from London or even a weekend visit of hers to Scotland elicited from her a letter beginning at its poorest, 'I promised to write, did I not', and packed with the latest political news or rumours. She knew everyone worth knowing and had the knack of obtaining inside information. At that time she was preparing to write the biography of A. J. Balfour, referred to in her letters to L either as 'A.J.B.' or 'Nunky'. Her father, Eustace Balfour, was his youngest brother and she had been a fervent admirer of 'A.J.B.' since childhood. The prospective biography was an additional incentive for frequent visits to him at Whittingeham and for her to talk them over with L. When he later spoke to me about those years as the best of his life, L ascribed their quality above all to his discussing endlessly with Baffy the art and craft of writing English. They never wearied of it, paying equal attention to the relative weight and value of commas, semicolons, and colons, and to the flow of narrative or the clarity of expression, and the interweaving overtones of time-honoured words and current expressions that echo through a paragraph. Yet this was not all. Like Granville, Baffy was introducing L to a wide circle of her old friends now become interesting to him; and, during these social rounds she spoke so much of

Arthur Balfour that L came to share her affectionate concern about
the ageing statesman's lassitude and depression.

One of L's more childish traits was his assumption that people
whom he liked and admired shared his tastes and interests. On
the force of it, when Baffy was leaving for Whittingeham before
Christmas 1925, he asked her to give Balfour some 'rolls of free-
holders', the nearest thing in Scotland to the English poll books.
Of this present she wrote almost at once, 'It gave pleasure even
to a greater degree than I had expected. *I* feel grateful. Anything
which gives him pleasure, gives pleasure a thousandfold to me.'
She had given Balfour the book of rolls on Christmas day,

when all our presents were exchanged and the whole family were
assembled in the Library. He took it to the window and stood there
reading it for so long that the family began to grumble. . . . Finally he
came back with it to the hearthrug: 'This is most interesting, my dear.
Where did you get it?' Me: 'I didn't. Look at the title page.' This he did
and asked for explanations. A long discussion ensued. Several points of
local interest were cleared up, and one or two controversies about the
pronunciation of place-names were settled. Then my aunt ordered me
to write out—on a piece of paper to be pasted into the book—the name
of the donor and the circumstances of its coming here. So methodical
are we! The same afternoon, when out walking, A. J. B. returned to
the subject of your work. I told him something of the way you are
doing it, and he was enormously interested.

Baffy enclosed a copy of Balfour's letter of thanks which was
written 'entirely in his own hand, a rare thing nowadays . . .'.
Unwilling 'to risk so precious a document by sending it to foreign
parts', where L then was, she promised to give it him later. The
enclosure reads,

26.12.25
Dear Mr. Namier,
    Baffy has conveyed to me your delightful Xmas present. It will be a
most welcome addition to my Scottish library, and its value (so far as I
at least am concerned) is much increased by hearing that you came
across it in the course of your investigations into the obscure history of
the British Parliament in the early days of George III. This greatly
needs elucidation by someone who will really take the trouble to
examine the facts in an impartial temper. What between the Whigs, the
Tories, the King and the Thirteen Colonies an impartial temper is

almost as difficult to maintain as it is to acquire an adequate knowledge of the real facts. Your labour will be most welcome. With all good wishes for the New Year.

Expanding social intercourse was helpful and gratifying. But L was earning nothing and spending much in conditions of world-wide monetary disarray and industrial unrest high-lighted here and there by a bright sprinkling of mock-prosperity. Having spurned Mammon in Vienna, he was the more perturbed to learn of the bankruptcy of a business friend who owed him substantial sums. To be able to complete his book on politics at the accession of George III without being distracted by paid work (teaching or journalism of one sort or other) L followed the advice of Baffy, supported by Sligger and Edwyn Bevan. In August 1926 he applied to the Rhodes Trust for a grant. There was of course much rivalry and some opposition. But in the end Philip Kerr as Secretary to the Trustees and H. A. L. Fisher, a prominent Trustee and an old admirer of L's abilities, obtained for him half the sum L had named. He was grateful even for this. But Baffy, dissatisfied, strove to raise for him at least the missing half of the stipulated sum. She did so the more purposefully for L's having helped her, not very long ago, out of a financial jam. 'Many thanks for the trouble you have taken for my money,' she had written to Vienna on 27 July 1923. 'My husband was hugely impressed with the success of my "speculations". The London season is now bringing its Nemesis of Bills. If any time during August or later you start upon a new venture I would be glad indeed to join you.' She did, and was again well pleased. But when she obtained a handsome 'endowment' for L's eighteenth-century books, she wrapped up the matter in mystery. Not until his first book had made its mark in the English-speaking world was he in a position to write to Julius Rosenwald, a munificent Chicago millionaire,

I am told by Mrs. Dugdale that you and your son William [Rufus to L and other contemporaries] are the 'anonymous friend' who since September 1927 has endowed my history work. Will you accept my most sincere thanks for what you have done for me in this matter? I feel it an honour that at the time when I had as yet written and published nothing by which my further work could be gauged, you placed

On   191

sufficient confidence in me to endow it in the way you have done, and I hope that the result will prove equal to your expectations.

But not even to this did Baffy limit herself. In 1926 she arranged that L should meet Harold Macmillan, a junior partner in the family publishing house; and on 3 January 1927 in answer to a communication from L, she wrote, from Whittingeham, 'Lewis, my dear, Just a line to say how delighted I am about Macmillans. . . . I have a deep feeling of joy.' Eleven months later L told his publisher,

This is only an 'advanced delivery' of the first part (about 45,000 words) of Vol. I which will probably be called *The British Parliament in 1761*. The next volume, as I told you, will be about *The Rise of Party*. But I mean each volume to form a self-contained whole. Perhaps the entire work should be called *The Imperial Problem during the American Revolution*. But I am undecided. And for this there is time.

Not yet clear about his overall scheme, he next explained to Harold Macmillan his method of work on the particular volume,

I naturally start building from the bottom, and therefore the most general essays which will come first in the book, are the last to be written: and the introduction, which is to string together the whole collection, will be written when the last essay is ready and the order in which they are to appear is fixed.

Since the book seemed to be getting too long, he pointed out which essays might best be transferred to later books without badly disturbing the logic of the introductory book. A variant of his skyscraper theme emerges. He never speaks of chapters, always of essays—each of which he considers a self-contained unit and at the same time an integral part of the book, steadily envisaged as an organic whole. And since this composite unit could not, by its nature, be hoisted on end, he bodied forth its latent unity by shoving round the building blocks. The juggling gave him great satisfaction. But the juggling and the verbal polishing took another six months. At last, at the end of June 1928 he dated his preface, and posted it together with the last essays—to be placed first in the book. Early in December 1928 Baffy, very excited, wrote,

Some instinct prompted me to come in for lunch today—a feeling that there would be something worthy of immediate attention. And there before me your book!

How can I describe the feelings which (without exaggeration) nearly choked me when I held the two volumes in my hand ['Why Men Went into Parliament' and 'The Electoral Structure of England', bound in one book entitled *The Structure of Politics at the Accession of George III*]; no midwife felt prouder!

When I think of it all: the long talks about it we had in this room, the early times when not a word was on paper and we sometimes wondered if it ever would be, and the later stages where—I think—I had so much the best of it, for I had the excitement of seeing how order was gradually shaping itself out of chaos; how the infinity of bricks was being put together and making a truly *noble* building. I had all that excitement without any of the strain and agony of creation. And then, finally, when I was sure that it would be as great a book as I had always banked on its becoming.

When I think back on all these things with the book itself in front of me, and remember that even *this* is only the beginning—I do feel it is a day to remember! I am so proud of what you have said in the preface. Thank you a 1000 times—I like to believe it is partly true!

But even in those years crammed with shared intellectual excitement and made gay by sensible appreciation coming from an expanding circle of loyal friends, the cosiest hospitality was extended to L by Denis and Emily Buxton.

Denis had gone up to Oxford (Balliol) in January 1919 'quite exhausted and in a low state' after years of active service in France. 'I don't remember,' he says, 'how we became friends. It just happened.' And to Emily, L was 'just there' as a close neighbour in Chelsea. When they moved to Campden Hill Square in the spring of 1925, her somewhat sketchy memories of L still centred on 'his incomparable story-telling'. But after that autumn, incident and colour crowd in. On a long visit abroad she and Denis stayed at Koszylowce. He, already an enthusiast for archaeology, wanted to see L's neolithic site and to carry out there a dig of his own. From Lwow—where they saw L's pots in the Museum—they went, again by train, to Piszkowce and were met with a victoria and two horses to be driven some twenty miles. Emily never forgot the 'perishing cold' of that drive. They must have struck one of those sudden inflows of arctic air, of which L has said that in early autumn they 'will sometimes cover stagnant pools and ponds with a thin surface of ice long before winter may render them suitable for skating'. The new house, which L had not seen, Emily describes as square with two storeys,

Inside was a largish hall, also square, with a staircase going up at one side. [Tadeusz Modzelewski] like his mother-in-law [Ann] got up about six. And she, at least, was out in the farm and vast orchards soon after that. She was short and broad and had dark greying hair. I took to her at once. She had a very sweet expression and used to smile at me in a way that warmed my heart. It reminded me of L. Her daughter, tall and fair with blue eyes, I didn't really take to. The politeness of her husband astonished me. Immediately on our arrival he kissed my hand, a thing I had never experienced before.

Months earlier L had asked Emily to 'check some of his quotations from the Newcastle Papers in the B.M.'. She found them 'very amusing'; and Denis, too, made a contribution to *The Structure of Politics*, later confiding in me, 'When I first mentioned that I had a motto for L's book, he was not receptive and said he did not like mottoes. Nor do I particularly. But when he heard my Aeschylus quotation, he found it so perfectly suitable that he agreed to use it.' And here it is, in English,

I took pains to determine the flight of crook-taloned birds, marking which were of the right by nature, and which of the left, and what were their ways of living, each after his own kind, and the enmities and affections that were between them: and how they consorted together.

'Consorting together' later became a household phrase with L and me though above all it stood, in his vocabulary, for debate aimed at reaching a settlement.

Denis, Emily, and their fast expanding family were from then on so closely bound up with L's life that Emily remembered 'well the summer day when he brought to lunch Marie Beer'. That relationship was no longer what it had been. L still saw a great deal of Marie in Vienna during his 1925 visits there. And before 1927 she had stayed twice in a Chelsea boarding house run by a friend of L's landlady. But the second of these visits radically changed the character of the friendship between L and Marie. In the park late one sunny afternoon they had barely sat down at a vacant table to have tea, when Marie snatched up her spoon, raised and dropped it, slumped a little in her chair, changed from speech to incoherent mumbling, straightened up, neatly

replaced the spoon and went on speaking, unaware of the interlude. L took his perplexity to Frank (Francis) Crookshank, a good
friend and his doctor, for whom he had the greatest regard only
partly due to Crookshank's many books on the relation between
bodily and mental health. Frank's brother, Harry Crookshank,
M.P. for Gainsborough since 1924, was also a good friend, and the
three often met to talk things over. On the force of L's account
Crookshank thought Marie must have had a black-out known as
le petit mal and assured L that it need not develop into *le grand
mal*—true epilepsy. But L's horror of insanity snapped his
physical infatuation though his devotion to the unfortunate
woman even increased. And, once again, as with Clara, he felt
'a responsibility'.

In the summer of 1927, with the Austrian Republic in political
turmoil, ugly incidents frequent in the Vienna streets, and
Hitler's *Mein Kampf* already three years old, L agreed that Marie
had better come to England and settle, preferably in Oxford where
she hoped to coach undergraduates in German and French. The
Buxtons, and Emily's mother and brothers, threw themselves into
the project with their customary zeal. Soon L was visiting Marie
in Oxford where her many pupils felt they greatly benefited from
her tuition. It was as well. She had recently tried to earn a living
by translations only to prove to L that she had lost her former
verve and abilities. This had already made him wonder if her
mind and judgement were not deteriorating. Temperamentally
incapable of telling her so, he had wasted hours—urgently needed
for *The Structure of Politics*—on carefully and copiously sub-
editing her wretched translations of second-rate novels, a contributory cause of his own book's slow progress.

Confirmation of L's fears—never really allayed by Crookshank
—came at about the worst time and in the worst possible way for
him. Clara had traced him through his bank and had resumed
writing. Davenport having taken to drink in a big way and having
been placed in a hospital, had died almost at once from an acute
attack of delirium tremens. With Davenport gone, Clara was
somewhat better off—she could move about more freely and more
easily obtain work in some of the hotels strewn about the U.S.
and Canada. For the first time since she had sailed away she

communicated her address; but when she wrote again, she had moved on and, though loquacious, answered none of L's questions which were aimed at learning where and how he could best send her the money she obviously was in need of.

When L spoke to Marie about his exasperation over this reticence, which was out of character, she became agitated and presently begged L to stay in Oxford till the last train. He had work to do on his book, and would not. Sadly but firmly she then declared she would walk with him to the bus-stop. As they reached it, she stumbled and fell. It was her first fit of epileptic convulsions. A cab was hailed, L took her home, called the doctor, and did stay with her till the last train.

Some time after that horrifying experience, early in April 1928, Clara walked into L's study. She had worked her passage across the Atlantic as a stewardess; generous tips had covered her train fare to London, and would keep her off the rocks for a fortnight or so. She would be living very cheaply in Bedford Place, W.C.1; her clothes would do for another six months; and she was still indifferent to food. With undimmed candour she described, in colourful phrases, how unworthy she was of having entered L's life at any stage. She and Davenport had been pretending they were married and she still had, tucked away in her bosom, a passport which stated she was Mrs. Davenport, *née* Lefroy—a name she knew because someone bearing it had stood for an election in the eighteenth century and it had caught her fancy when she heard it from L. She rather thought that still holding the bogus passport might be an indictable offence in England. But Davenport's lack of scruples had taken time to open her eyes to L's rare integrity and its value to those he associated with. Anyway, she had come to free him of her. Could he not divorce her for desertion?

L doubted if desertion would work—with her back again, Davenport dead, and L determined not even to pretend that he wanted her under his roof. But before she left, she stood irresolute, with an air that evoked the 'waif' his heart had first gone out to. Spontaneously, he pressed on her a fiver to help her to be more choosy over the job she took. On the following morning she telephoned to say she had an urgent communication to make and that they had better meet on neutral ground. That afternoon in a dim and prim London tea-shop they enacted a scene worthy of their favourite novelist, Dostoevski.

Dramatically Clara announced that her painful, sordid confession would help L to divorce her: already she had committed adultery, in London. With whom? Oh . . . a Mr. Lewis. Who was he? She described, to the life, a good friend of L's who might have seen her but could not possibly have had the slightest sexual interest in her and whose name was not Lewis. Again Clara was spinning a tale, with the best intentions. Again L was at a loss to disentangle truth from falsehood. Besides, he saw no point in divorcing her. Though he could not hope to keep her in style, living in an establishment of her own, he would do his best to help her in a small way—if she worked, lived quietly, and handed over to him all her Mrs. Davenport papers, among which were also some American and Canadian deposit accounts run dry. Clara eagerly gave and promised him all he wished; but insisted on freeing him from the wretch she was. Finally they agreed he would consult his solicitors, though all he wanted was a formula which would discourage her from concocting any more false documents and place Oxford out of bounds for her—there was to be no clash between his 'two millstones'.

On 25 April his solicitors told Clara that L had passed on to them her letter of 15 April; that they had made inquiries at the address indicated in the letter, and had obtained sufficient evidence to enable them to 'commence proceedings for dissolution of marriage'. But the name of the co-respondent and his address had to be included in the petition, in order that the petition could be served upon him. They therefore asked for Mr. Lewis's full Christian names and his present address, and hoped to have them as soon as possible.

Five days later they were telling L they had very carefully considered the fact that he felt confident of the true identity of 'the Mr. Lewis whom your wife refers to in her letters to us, and that in the circumstances you do not feel justified in citing him as a man unknown'. But since there was no proof of the identity and they appreciated L's dislike of naming in the petition a man who was not in fact the man, and that he very rightly would not swear an affidavit containing facts contrary to those which he believed, there was in their view no course but to allow matters to remain as they were and 'to await further evidence in the future'.

On 1 May, under their guidance, L wrote to Clara,

Despite your disclosures to me, I feel it impossible to leave you short of bare necessaries, and am therefore proposing to make you an allowance of £120 a year. It must however, be clearly understood that this allowance is not in any sense a condonation on my part of the thing you have admitted to me. I am advised that I cannot at present take any proceedings upon it, as I have not received from you a confirmation of the man's identity and as you yourself do not know his present whereabouts; but I reserve to myself the right of taking proceedings on receiving any fresh evidence.

By word of mouth L had insisted on the two conditions that really mattered to him: no more pranks with documents, and no visits however short to Oxford.

In the event Clara settled down quiet as a mouse, first in the Midlands and later, when she wearied of the country, in Ladbroke Grove, London, where she remained till the outbreak of World War II. Though she still seemed genuinely distressed that her little stratagem for freeing L had fallen through, she soon proved obsessively avid for money—the one hard, material streak in her shifting world of make-believe. Yet all might have gone on painlessly in its own strange way, but for Marie: she was furious. In vain did L try to make her understand that for him to proceed against an 'unknown man' was tantamount to proclaiming Clara a tart, which she was not. On one occasion, Marie grown livid, snorted that she was just that. They quarrelled as never before. Observing her as she lashed out, spewing venom, L realized that Marie would now like to regularize their former relationship which she had carried with gaiety and dash while it was on. Also, as with Clara in 1921, L wretchedly wondered if he was not at least partly responsible for her degeneration. And since ill-health forced Marie to cut down the number of lessons she gave, L soon found himself supporting two women who could give him only memories, by no means all good ones. But the grim situation was

mostly kept to the back of his mind because it coincided with
demands on him that derived from his first book's success.

Intent on using in his second eighteenth-century book (*England
in the Age of the American Revolution*) much material, already collected, that clamoured to be handled without delay, L was being
lured aside by minor time-consuming tasks. The least trouble-
some of them came from his making meticulous corrections to
Sir John Fortescue's edition of the first volume of George III's
correspondence.[1] Though L's sensational article on Fortescue's
inaccuracies appeared only a year later (in the *Nation and Athenaeum*), his massive corrections were already causing a stir in
interested circles, and were involving him in many debates and
some correspondence. Yet this was all by the way. More protracted conflicts had followed his appointment (in April 1929) to
the Committee on the Records of Past Members of the House of
Commons. Like his colleagues on it, L had in the first place been
selected by the moving spirit of the enterprise—Colonel Josiah
(Jos) Wedgwood, M.P. for North Lancashire since 1906, whom
he had met and admired in the distant Fabian Summer School
days. On L's return from Vienna they had again met and, in a
sense, L could be described as a founder member of the Committee. In the autumn of 1928 Baffy, again at Whittingeham,
wrote,

At last I snatched a good moment to show A. J. B. the papers Jos sent
me about the M.Ps. Nunky's interest was greatly awakened. It was
your letter to Jos that did it. He kept exclaiming, 'This is a brilliant
letter! What phrases! Where did the fellow get his power of writing
English? Now look at those words in quotation marks—Political
Nation—is that his phrase? Or did he find it somewhere? Anyhow it's
a most useful one. Look at this bit about Alumni Cantabrigiensis: here
am I, Chancellor of Cambridge, but *I* never heard of this work. I am
grateful to him for that . . . What an amazing race the Jews are!'

But no sooner had the Committee on the Records begun its
sittings than L, clearly chosen for his personality and enthusiasm
not for pliability, disagreed with his chairman on the right way

[1] *Additions and Corrections to Sir John Fortescue's Edition of the Correspondence of
George III, Vol. 1, 1937.*

of setting to work. Both being highly vocal men of tempestuous devotions, their arguments generated much heat. From the start L's declared interest had been in the House of Commons as a corporate entity whose character was best revealed through detailed examination of its members' lives and interests. The History was to be, in his view, a scrutiny of the changes and continuity in M.P.s' relations with each other and of their relative position in their respective counties and in the country as a whole. He insisted that their grass roots and their financial interest should never be lost sight of.

Wedgwood, on the other hand, had grown so apprehensive of the threat coming from communism and fascism to democracy and individual freedom, that he wished the many-volumed History to be a pageant of the striving by the English political nation, through the centuries, to establish, maintain, and even extend the freedom of individuals. In consequence he favoured uniform emphasis on the democratic achievements of successive parliaments from the Wars of the Roses to recent times. Being basic, the disagreement never softened. But L's long arguments with Wedgwood—often in private, late into the night—led to his discerning a particular aspect of the House, presently seen by him as a 'very special trout-stream' where a strain of trout, vigorous in the eighteenth century, was (in the 1920s) dying out though still conspicuous in the spiritual descendants of L's eighteenth-century 'independent country gentlemen'. Long talks with Wedgwood soon convinced L that in the fifteenth century the stream which fascinated them both had been so unlike the one he knew that, loosely speaking, it was a different stream. Considering again, more narrowly, the House of Commons as he knew it (through research into the eighteenth century, study of the nineteenth, and his assiduity in the visitors' gallery) he perceived a very different, more recent, but no less important change in the object of their disputes. In the mid-eighteenth century the country's leadership had been shifting from the king—who was ceasing to act as his own 'first minister'—to the Prime Minister into whose hands the supreme direction of affairs was moving. By the 1920s, much pointed to a future when, with personal riches no longer a pre-requisite for cutting a figure in Parliament, and political achievement no longer being rewarded as a matter of course by the grander titles of nobility, England's magisterial stream would be the habitat of a different kind of fish.

Since his days at the L.S.E., the irrevocable transformations of the earth's crust had abundantly provided L with metaphors for slow-moving historical processes. That our planet's rock structure should not be the only decisive factor in surface topography—the surface being continually subjected to weathering, denudation, deposition, and actions of vegetation—satisfied his awareness of time as a cardinal factor in man's continually changing communal life. And it re-enforced his view of mankind's history as vigorously 'organic'. Changes—hardly noticeable from administration to administration but cumulatively important—were beginning to set in a new pattern. Amusing himself as always with similes, he found a pretty confirmation of his hunch in the fact that maturing streams cannot remain trout-streams; nor would Parliament remain unchanged in a political landscape the very configurations of which were no longer the same. Already aware of it in a general way, he had written two years before, 'There is wisdom in Anatole France's favourite thesis that a country at any one time is capable of developing only one type of government.' His favourites were being eased out of administrations already new in some respects. He no longer doubted it. And his blend of hunch and observation suggested to him that his finger was on the pulse of parliamentary development as Wedgwood's was not. L knew well what he was about when he wrote a 'Draft of the Third Subcommittee (1717–1832)' in 1929.

His third deflection from *England in the Age of the American Revolution* had been less noticeably insinuating itself among L's preoccupations. But, more slow to emerge, it bound even closer some of his old intellectual interests with his up-to-date emotional fascinations. As the phoenix-empire theme receded further into the background of his eighteenth-century books, it transfused his thoughts on Zionism—no longer 'entirely theoretical' as they had previously been. In 1927 he wrote an article showing why Great Britain, world Jewry, and the Palestinian Arabs would all benefit if Palestine were incorporated in the British Empire as its Seventh Dominion. He stressed the urgency of accepting in principle the inclusion of Palestine in the Empire while the British Mandate—which of course precluded its implementation—was still in force. He advocated the scheme as the only one able to foster a healthy symbiosis between the land's two distinct populations; he explained that no other scheme could make obsolete the futile juggling with majority and minority clauses; and stressed the futility of this juggling, already obvious to him but not to others. He also made clear that the one thing the Palestinian Arabs would have to give up was their unrealizable dreams of Pan-Arabism. L's enthusiasm for the Seventh Dominion was shared by Wedgwood who, having preceded him in this field too, was about to publish a book under the same title and dedicated to Baffy. But Wedgwood's book stresses the importance of imperial strategy. Symbiosis was not his concern. As to L, however much such discussions entertained or even engrossed him, he never allowed any one of them entirely to interrupt the progress of his second book, towards the completion of which the Rhodes Trust (in 1929, apparently on the initiative of H. A. L. Fisher) had awarded him the second half of the sum asked for in 1926. Yet the impact of so many contingent interests and demands was bringing about certain shifts in L's feelings.

The homeland, which the dispossessed Jews of the dispersion had long prayed to return to, was edging into the place once held in L's emotional life by Koszylowce. Characteristically though, the deprivation imposed upon him by his family had significantly modified the nature of his yearning for 'ground in which to be rooted'. He never wished to possess any patch in Palestine, though he had subscribed to the planting there of many trees. In his letters and articles as well as in his second book L demanded, not only emphatically but lyrically, an adequate staking of claims to be allowed his people in their ancestral home. His 1919 concern with a people's right to self-determination and ownership of land had re-awakened. His urge to strive after a man's right to live the traditional life that gives him a sense of stability in the political rough and tumble of nations, was blossoming anew. Men's inalienable prerogative to use in their courts, newspapers, songs and learned works the tongue in which they are most fluent once again called to be defended. Small wonder that L's ambience became highly charged, and that it lost all stability when Chaim Weizmann resolutely entered, beguiling L to help their people by accepting to work for him; and to do so at once, without counting the cost.

The cost that L was light-headedly asked to discount proved to be compounded of: a skimped second eighteenth-century book; the abandoning of a third (on the Rockingham government of 1765–6, never written); the withdrawal from editing—together with Romney R. Sedgwick—the Bute and Sandwich MSS.; a potentially brilliant career interrupted at its promising start; the loss of a stable position in a community he respected above any other; and peace of mind abrogated for many years. In short, it was to be a light-headed acceptance of self-destruction. But the time sacrificed to help a community to whom L felt increasingly bound by his gut incidentally brought him new insight into the multiple vagaries of human conduct and intentions. In addition, having studied for five years how men strove in the past to reach settlements by debate, he found himself in a good position to observe them, in the present, sweating blood to reach such settlements, and only too often failing to do so.

CHAPTER TWELVE

Reaching a Settlement
1929-1931

During the Paris Peace Conference L had met Weizmann several times in the company of two or three leading American Jews whose political abilities and manner he found far superior to Weizmann's. Yet L liked him best of all. And presently sending back (for drastic emendation) some memoranda Weizmann had hoped A. J. Balfour would peruse and act upon, L explained with the greatest regard compatible with exactitude how a précis should be written if it is to be read by anyone, let alone by an overburdened 'old and tired man'. In the course of these exchanges Weizmann had asked if L would consider joining, when free to do so, the Zionist Organization in some vaguely important and lucrative post. L thought he might. For no particular reason nothing came of it. But later that autumn L met Vera Weizmann whom he at once greatly liked; while the Weizmann entourage—all of whom went on to what was L's 'first Zionist meeting'—repelled him. After his return from Vienna, L often dropped in at Addison Gardens where Vera was warmly welcoming; and in the autumn of 1925 he arranged in his Chelsea rooms a dinner for Weizmann to meet Baffy who brought along her sister Joan. Of that evening L wrote in his Notes on Zionism,

Weizmann was in bad form and talked pathologically much. Baffy and Joan later remarked to me that he seemed overstrained and not quite himself. Still, it was a good party, and after it Baffy and I saw much of the Weizmanns and became closely involved with the Zionist Organization.

Baffy soon joined the organization in an official capacity. But L did not seriously think of doing so till asked in the autumn of 1928 by Dr. Eder, who was in charge at 77 Great Russell Street,

to come and see him. The purpose was to sound L on his willing-
ness to step into a recent vacancy. L goes on to relate,

> Eder regretted Baffy was not present as he had hoped she would support
> the suggestion. I answered that it required no support—I would gladly
> join when my history work was finished. About my proposed position
> or salary I asked no questions. After joining I realized that such
> generous trust as I had then shown is stupid.

Still unaware of the stupidity of his trust, L concentrated on his
current book while Weizmann turned on the pressure with persuasive charm. President of the English Zionist Federation from
1917 (the year of the Balfour Declaration), elected also President
of the Zionist Organization in 1923, Weizmann was intent five
years later on forming, with no further delay, the Jewish Agency
described in Article IV of the Mandate as desirable for 'advising
and co-operating with the Administration of Palestine in such
economic, social and other matters as may affect the establishment
of the Jewish national home'. In view of the diverse, vociferous,
and mutually antagonistic Jewish groups bound to be represented
on such a body, Weizmann needed there a man unattached to any
of them, devoted to Zionism, loyal to himself, with a working
knowledge of the British official mind and able to formulate in
terse clear English his chief's profound yet witty thoughts,
winning in his Russified Yiddish but puzzling in any other
idiom. L answered the specification better than anyone Weizmann
knew, and Weizmann was determined to have him.

Rumours that L was expected shortly to take up the position
of Political Secretary to the Zionist Organization quickly spread
to the States where it alarmed the Rosenwalds. Summing up a
warmly dissuasive letter, Rufus ended with,

> There seems to be a consensus of opinion that you would be making a
> great mistake to abandon your work before you have finished it, i.e.,
> before you have completed the outline you give in your preface; and I
> for one, would like to encourage you, as one who has some working
> knowledge of the material you now have in hand, to continue with
> your work. As you pointed out to me, the 'spade' work has been done
> and it but requires the writing to complete what would be as fine a
> monument to you as any man could possibly desire.

In his last letter of this fairly long exchange L answered what he took to be Rufus's 'crucial questions' and gave an account of himself not supplied elsewhere. The crucial question for L was 'how far and when I should continue the work'. His second book, due to appear after a month or two, already contained a good many fundamental points that he had intended to make about the 'Imperial Problem during the American Revolution'. A general foreshadowing of consecutive books followed. For these books considerable material had already been gathered and L had already worked on much of it. A narrower question resulted: 'Should I try to complete my work till 1783 now, before joining the Organization?' Answering, on 4 March 1929, L made a declaration which shows a remarkable change in his scale of priorities:

My primary aims were not to build a monument for myself (*aere perennius*) nor to write the history of that period: but rather to acquire a position which would enable me to work effectively for the Jewish cause, and to make certain experiments in history-writing which would be interesting and important, quite apart from the specific subject of my book.

It is most unlikely that L would have placed the Jewish cause ahead of his experiments in history-writing even a couple of years earlier. That he should have done so in the spring of 1929, in writing to a Jew who was not friendly to Zionism, is a measure of the hold Weizmann had already gained over him. Yet L continued clear-sighted enough,

I cannot tell how long I shall remain with the Zionist Organization: changes may occur in it which may compel me to go out soon, I may prove not altogether well fitted for the work, I may be driven out as an infidel by the Kosher Gang [more often referred to as the 'pi-push']; or, on the other hand, I may stay in it to the end of my life. There is no way of foreseeing or determining these matters beforehand. But as I consider it my duty to take up the work now, I have to leave the rest on the knees of the gods.

From the start he had no illusions,

I know that working for the Jews is neither enjoyable nor remunerative—every one of us can do better for himself by working, for, with, and in more prosperous and more honoured communities. Still I consider that for a Jew who sees our position as I do, it is an absolute duty to go and work with and for them as soon as he can do so to *their* best advantage. I have, I think, reached this point now. Were I not a Jew and had I private means of my own, I would undoubtedly go on with [my history work]. But as things stand, I have to consider how the urgency of this task compares with that of others, and what are my circumstances.

He gives a thorough account of his situation, explaining by the way that he had always considered the Rosenwalds' endowment as a loan and declaring that 'a loan I mean it to be'—'there is a difference between accepting money from public bodies and from personal friends', be they the best of friends. He explained to Rufus that his obligations were,

I. £500 to J. W. Wheeler-Bennett (who, by the way, asked me to let him cancel the debt, to which I naturally did not agree).
II. By the time the second year of your endowment is completed, I shall owe your Father and yourself a joint £1,200.
    £1,700 of debt is as much as I can possibly bear. That none of you three will ever press me for repayment makes no difference. My books will give me very small returns—books of this character do not pay. I shall have to repay the £1,700 by work of a different kind, and in all probability it will take me at least five or six years before I am finished with my debts. I cannot go further on this basis. If I wanted to continue my history work, I should have to take up a teaching job which would provide me with a living wage but would take up a good part of my time. Yet writing history as I do is a 'whole time' job. And if I tried to teach and write, I would have to settle down to teach practically for life.

Casting a glance back at the vicissitudes of his eighteenth-century work, he said,

In 1914 I broke it off for ten years because of a British war. Our own race is now in an infinitely more dangerous and difficult position than Great Britain was in 1914: for on a very moderate estimate half the world makes war on them, and they are practically helpless.

He concluded the very long letter with a barely veiled apology,

I hope neither your Father nor you will feel disappointed by the results of the loan whereby you have enabled me to do so much work, even though the work is not fully complete.

In *England in the Age of the American Revolution* are passages on English nonconformists and American dissenters which circuitously help to understand L's attitude to the people with whose tragic lot he was identifying himself while still aglow with the desire that they be incorporated in the British Empire. About 1770 L says, 'the modern British view of Empire' was held by 'the English nonconformists and the American dissenters alone', and they were for each other 'congregations beyond the sea', groups of brothers who had escaped or were longing to escape from unbearably degrading circumstances. Putting his last touches to his second eighteenth-century book, L found basic resemblances between the 1770 New and Old England situation on the one hand, and the Jewish situation in Palestine and the dispersion on the other. Taking the Anglo-Saxons' political achievements on either side of the Atlantic for an encouraging precedent, he gained confidence that some Jews of the dispersion would strike firm roots in Palestine. But he realized that they would have to go on striving for freedom, though no longer wrestling for it with strangers. Already he had written, 'at every stage in social development freedom has to be reconquered'. Eager to see the Jews shape a communal life based on true freedom, L wished to know better individual Jews active in the Zionist Return. He had planned to start work for the Jewish Organization on 1 October 1929 but, as August approached, L realized that impending debates at Zürich—on the emerging Jewish Agency among other matters—could introduce him into the thick of Jewish internecine strife, and that the congress offered him a splendid occasion to get in touch personally with Jews gathered from all over the world. Present at all sessions, he found especially moving the passionate pleas of old Zionists and democrats against 'junction with rich and lukewarm Jews who had hitherto kept aloof from the Zionist movement and even now would not fully accept either our name or our programme'.

When, the congress over, Weizmann—whose 'blend of eloquence, warmth and common-sense' had at last silenced the opposition—gave a small dinner party, L who arrived late found him and Vera 'much elated. She was that night a Queen in Israel.' But L, unaccountably depressed, wondered how the fate of the

Jewish Agency would develop after the enchantment of the newly-found unanimity of views about it had worn off. In fact disaster was about to strike. 'Louis Marshall—the man of absolutely first-class ability among the non-Zionist makers of the Jewish Agency—died within days. September ushered in the American financial crisis' that destroyed large fortunes from which the Jewish Agency had been promised generous help. And in Palestine itself gruesome episodes occurred in quick succession. Such was the ominous curtain-raiser to L's years of hard work for the Jewish cause.

Leaving Zürich immediately after the Weizmanns' party, L was intent on preparing for publication his first volume of essays; but before settling down to it, he went to Fisher's Hill where A. J. Balfour, very ill, was staying with his brother Gerald. Unable to see the sick man, L left in Baffy's hands his considered notes on Zürich with hastily scribbled additions. On the following morning, a Sunday, news came through to London of riots in Tishebov, when Arabs attacked Jews. The Zionist office was deserted. Some people were still in Switzerland, others at a meeting of the Governors of the Hebrew University in Jerusalem, others again were recovering in the country from the exertions of organizing the congress. Only Colonel F. H. Kisch—L's friend of 1919, by now chief of the Zionist Executive in Palestine—chanced to be in London on a visit. He rang up L and in the next days they 'did whatever could be done through the press'. On the following Sunday news reached them about Arab atrocities in Jerusalem and about the Palestine Administration's having disarmed the Jews—making of them sitting targets. As L. J. Stein was still in Baden, L acted for some days as secretary to the Zionist Organization, and found that all pleas to the authorities in London were stone-walled to the monotonous tune of heart-felt assurances about full confidence in the man on the spot. Communications between the Jewish offices in London and Jerusalem went haywire; the quickest were by telephone to Cairo and by cable from there. In an aside deploring his inability to remember those few days in strictly coherent detail, L entered in his Notes on Zionism,

I suffered from insomnia worse than usual because of the great excitement and strain. To sleep I had to take drugs, and next work under extreme pressure. When concentrating hard on some all-important matter, one's mind isn't free to take in impressions and register them for future remembrance.

Of the days following Weizmann's return from Switzerland, all L could recollect was 'endeavours to obtain for him an interview with the P.M. and the desire—which for me dominated everything—to try and stop the disarmament of our people by the British authorities in Palestine'. After L and I were married, I often noticed how, in our talks at the end of a long day, he sifted by rote those of my remarks or communications that were in some way of use to him from those that were not. The latter he never really took in. And his concluding paragraph on the unforgettable August days of high pressure and distress shows why he could not recall every detail, 'If we had to die, die we would. But there should be some difference between dying in a pogrom in the Russian Pale of Settlement and dying in our own country under a British Mandate. Here we ought to be allowed to go down fighting.' The knell of his Seventh Dominion had begun to toll; that, above all else, blocked any precise memory of less momentous matters.

Weizmann was not slow to grasp that Lord Passfield (the Colonial Secretary), together with his more active officials, intended to whittle away the Balfour Declaration. Aghast, he wished to see the Prime Minister. But when Ramsay MacDonald—due to speak on disarmament at the League of Nations' Council—was leaving London, he had as yet neither granted nor refused the interview. L, who was lunching that day with Weizmann, Lord Robert Cecil, and Jos Wedgwood, was pressed by them to go to Geneva with a 'watching brief for Weizmann', and to fix there the urgent interview. Leaving by the same train as the P.M., L had some useful talks with important members of the official party; but in Geneva he spent a week of frustrations. Weizmann, avoiding on L's advice the invidious position of hanging about to no point, waited close at hand, in Paris. One of the parliamentary private secretaries (Philip Baker) and a junior minister (Hugh Dalton) did offer to take L to the P.M., but this he declined, not because he still lacked the knowledge and authority needed to wrest from the adversary the best possible settlement, but for fear that on the force of his interview Weizmann might be refused a hearing. Full of bitterness, L spoke ironically of his first sentences for a history of the P.M.'s glorious plan for universal disarmament: 'The Arabs said there would be no peace unless the Jews were disarmed. The Jews were disarmed. They were massacred by the Arabs. They died wrapped in their praying shawls and the warm sympathy of His Majesty's Government.' Having been tantalized by several will o' the wisps, L in the end summoned Weizmann on the force of nothing but a hunch of Lady Astor's, and left on the same day unaware that her advice had actually been based on a firm promise. For a long time he considered his visit to Geneva a sheer waste, which it was not. This was his second step along the way of initiation into Jewish affairs. Founded on his Geneva experiences, and supported by his political principles, L's self-assurance acquired vigour. He developed a distinctive voice of his own. Tackling the Colonial Secretary—early in September when Weizmann was abroad—L wrote and spoke with dry restraint and courteous aplomb. Never again did he doubt his ability to deputize for his chief or to speak for his people.

The Shaw Commission's investigations into the Palestine disorders conceded that the Arabs had been the aggressors throughout. The terms used were inimical to the Jews; yet the report did not influence the P.M. adversely. And L used a lull between Jewry's multiple woes to define more clearly his already equivocal position in the Jewish Agency. Beyond doubt, he established that he was there expected to give of his best for next to no pay. The world situation was admittedly catastrophic; but so was his. It is hard to believe that Weizmann, had he cared to see L properly remunerated, could have failed to bring it about. But, though he promised to intervene when some current difficulty of his own was removed, he never did so. Strange, too, was L's persistence in blaming himself alone for it:

I ought to have carefully discussed all details and meticulously defined my expectations. The difficulties which arose between me and the absurd group which called itself 'the Executive' might have been avoided had I rammed into Eder that I was only ready to come under definite conditions. I had shown too much enthusiasm.

This he continued to do, and was exploited accordingly.

For a spell L lived on the remains of the Rosenwald endowment and the revenue from his books. In an effort to avoid new debts he also reviewed expensive books before selling them to a well-established dealer. The actual situation merely irritated him but of the future he was apprehensive. He simply could not afford to work for Zionism without adequate payment. Still, with relations between the P.M. and the Jewish Agency continuing friendly, he indulged in an Easter holiday, in Dubbiaco with Frank Ramsay whom he had found most congenial when they suffered under the same Viennese psychoanalyst. They had been to the Tyrol together at least once before, on an occasion remembered by L because he then met Frank's parents and his brother Michael (the future Archbishop) whom he found an impressively religious youth able to bear with a dignity rare in one so young the raillery of his brilliant, irreligious big brother. The second Dubbiaco visit was unforgettable for a very different reason. Coming downhill after the last climb L wrenched his back badly enough to start a complaint that never left him.

In London a cloud of anxious gloom enveloped L. The Jewish Agency hummed with rumours of secret meetings between the P.M., the Colonial Office, and an Arab Delegation. To boot, another commission was going out to Palestine, headed by a practical farmer who had gained colonizing experience on the Greek Settlement Commission but knew nothing of Palestine or the Jews. Next, even before the new commission reached its destination, the government 'declared that immigration would be suspended, restrictive land legislation would be introduced, and the authority of the Jewish Agency curtailed'. Without any consultation with or mention to a Jewish representative, the Jewish rights under the Mandate were being violated. Weizmann saw his life's work smashed and the connection between Great Britain and the Jewish Agency broken. He told his friends in the House of Commons that, having linked from the start the fate of the Jews in Palestine with the British Empire, he felt impelled to resign. The P.M. begged him not to announce his resignation: the Labour party's home politics were in a turmoil, Palestine had become psychologically very remote yet remained dangerous. Marking time, Weizmann withdrew to Geneva where Lord Lugard, who was sensitive to the Jews' plight, was Great Britain's revered member on the Permanent Mandates Commission. Weizmann, Baffy, and L, 'with a great tooth-ache in the back', took it in turns to observe the commission's mood on the spot. 'About your coming out,' wrote Baffy to L on one occasion, 'at present there seems no need.' But there was no telling what might arise, and it made her and Chaim uneasy to have no one there with sense and influence. Passing through London later in the summer on her way from Geneva to Scotland, she found L immobilized with 'lumbago'—and on 16 August she regretted that Droitwich had not done him more good. Already L's body was becoming a heavy burden but, setting his jaw, he laboured on.

In October L alone accompanied his chief during interviews with Passfield at the Colonial Office, and strove to minute them. No easy task. The Colonial Secretary's verbiage was elusive to a degree. The meaning of his first sentence in a discourse was often contradicted in the last. Such tirades—which L likened to opals: always beautiful and never the same—were no way of reaching a settlement. Could the Colonial Secretary be playing for time? And indeed, before October was out the grand scheme of land reclamation and human rehabilitation that had been steadily progressing since the end of World War I was stopped by the simultaneous publication of the Hope-Simpson Report and the Government's White Paper on Palestine. Weizmann refused to delay any further his resignation as President of the Jewish Agency. Lord Melchett resigned as Chairman of the Agency Council. Other resignations followed, and L declared he would quit when it best suited Weizmann. Their friendship had been further cemented by identical views and feelings about shared calamities.

The surging turmoil was highlighted for L by two events in his private life: one of them foreseen, but the other a blessed bolt out of the blue. Early in November he signed an agreement with

Macmillans for the publication of his first volume of essays (*Skyscrapers*). A couple of days later he received from the head of the Faculty of History at the University of Manchester a wire: 'Would you consider appointment Chair Modern History, Jacob'. If accepted and approved by the Senate, the appointment would start on 29 September 1931 at a stipend of £1,000 a year. Suddenly the persecution of him would cease—L maintained that his enemies on the Executive, an 'absurd and stingy group', had persistently treated him as 'a labourer not worthy of his hire'. If Professor Jacob's project went through, L would be free of the 'sorry crew' yet free to indulge for another ten months in reckless devotion to Weizmann; and he would be able to exert himself with gusto in the following weeks to help the Jews reach a settlement with the British Empire (as yet only slightly tarnished) at a conference of vital importance to every Zionist.

Some days before the astonishing wire from Manchester reached L, the P.M. had told Weizmann at luncheon that he proposed to invite him and his colleagues to a conference with a sub-committee of the Cabinet. Some amendments to the White Paper would be discussed and also the general situation in Palestine. Weizmann, having resigned, was in no position to accept straightaway; but the necessary authorizations were soon received, and immediately afterwards L started discussions with the sub-committee's secretary about an official Letter to Weizmann and a communiqué to be issued to the press. Only the Letter's last draft—passed by the Cabinet and accepted by Ramsay MacDonald as fit for his signature—was called the MacDonald Letter. Till then, called after the chairman of the sub-committee, it was spoken of as the Henderson Letter which—in order to satisfy the Jewish Agency, the Lord Advocate, the Colonial Office, the Foreign Office, and the P.M.—had to be redrafted five times.

To L's intense annoyance some of his more bumptious enemies among the Jews caused from the start delays so grave that the joint creative work was not terminated till 12 February 1931. The 'irrepressible and irresponsible loquacity' of the absurd group behind the scenes was damaging step by step the cause they ineptly battled for. Six years later, on 27 January 1936, L wrote to Weizmann, 'We may now obtain a proper Development Commission which we should have had in December 1930 but lost through the unwarrantable delays of the then Executive.' While the Jewish flotsam clamoured to enter the Homeland and the Palestinian Jews yearned to regain their shattered peace of mind, the absurd group persisted in throwing their weight about regardless of time. They would not see that it was vitally important for the high-pressure discussions to end, at least as regards essentials, before Parliament adjourned for Christmas; and because of their procrastination the discussions were not finished in time.

Some compensation for the group's enmity L found in the increasing confidence and liking between him and the British team, with one of whom he remained friends for life. Yet L attached far greater significance to a new quality which, during the agitated mid-winter, pervaded his friendship with Vera Weizmann. L's imaginative concern for the weak and the persecuted was riveting his latent anxiety upon Weizmann. Trapped between the sustained, clever hostility of Passfield and a manifold, irrational opposition rising in many quarters of world Jewry, the ageing leader suffered mental and emotional strain. Those who knew him well feared a physical breakdown. While the danger lasted, L's unfaltering support 'in office hours' doubled Vera's constant and unwavering devotion to her husband. The shared concern so affected the supporters' friendship, that it came to resemble an orange tree simultaneously flowering and bearing fruit. The quality of their solicitude helped Weizmann to overcome a distressed bitterness; and in his book *Trial and Error* he could look back with unclouded pleasure at the winter's work. There was indeed much to be pleased with, in retrospect. The MacDonald Letter heralded a period of 'peace, prosperity and great immigration into Palestine' (40,000 Jews in 1934, 62,000 in 1935); while the replacement by Sir Arthur Wauchope of a High Commissioner who had been most inimical to the Jews marked a temporary change in the Palestine Administration's attitude to Zionism and the official interpretation of the Mandate. Yet at the time, Weizmann's health caused grave anxiety to L and Vera.

After the Weizmanns left for Palestine late in February, L lingered on at the Jewish Agency. But his relations with the men in charge were becoming too strained to endure. Breaking point was reached when a communiqué went out, almost behind his back, to the Jewish press. Innocuous enough to the uninformed, it enraged L who wrote to the members of the Jewish Agency Executive, the Zionist Executive, and the Political Committee, a stern letter (dated 23 February), enumerating the points which proved their joint action to be outrageous. In the communiqué was a factual misstatement; it was an act of discourtesy towards the British government; it constituted a breach of a prior agreement with the government; it played into the hands of the worst Arab elements; it was bound to excite all Arabs, thus endangering the Palestinian Jews; and it disclosed an intolerable muddle between the functions of various Jewish organizations and offices. 'I am not prepared,' he wound up, 'to stay one day longer in this office if political decisions of this nature and importance are taken without my knowledge.' Copies of the letter went out to Weizmann, Kisch, and Stein. Selig Brodetsky, a member of the executive, tried to pacify him. Far from resigning L should take an active part in the coming negotiations. 'I do not want to refuse if I can be of any real service to the Jewish cause,' L answered. But he was 'very averse' to participating in the imminent talks—on specific matters that should be handled by experts. Moreover, if his co-operation was really desired, all concerned would have to comply with eight rigorous points that he clearly defined. A copy of this too went to Weizmann. Yet despite such agitation, and his other interest, L had been writing—for his chief as it were—a 'Historical Summary of Discussions Leading up to the Prime Minister's Letter of 13 February 1931'. The carefully written piece was completed late in April, after which he took it to Weizmann, by then in Merano.

An episode occurred there that revealed a great bottled up emotion of L's. Years later it was described to me by Zalman Shazar, third President of the Israel Republic. In the spring of 1931 Shazar, prominent in the Zionist affairs of Berlin, had felt impelled, by the unrest among his co-members and the approaching 17th Zionist Congress, to seek enlightenment from Weizmann on certain matters. His stay in Merano coincided with L's and while it lasted, the three men regularly went together for long walks in the hills. On one occasion their way back led past a cemetery where L—to Shazar's astonishment—left them and disappeared inside the gates. A good while later, when L caught up with them, he was so obviously upset that Weizmann asked what had happened. In a voice smothered with emotion L said he had visited his father's grave—which changed Shazar's astonishment to stupefaction: it was a Christian cemetery. The President gave a palpably exact account of L's distress which had been so manifest that the other two spontaneously engaged each other in a rambling conversation to give him time to recover before they reached their hotel. This astonished me too. But my puzzlement was due to the intensity of L's emotion. His relationship with Ann and Theodora L often summed up as 'highly ambivalent'; but his father's attitude to him, after he had grown up, L always brushed aside as unimportant to either. Joseph was in his son's view still virtually the most intelligent man he had come across but, for all that, owing to flaws in his character, L considered him a featherweight who did not and could not matter. From President Shazar's account I gathered that this flippancy was a protective delusion. And from other sources I was glad to learn that a slight clearing up of posthumous rancours followed. Back in London in October 1931 after another visit to Merano Weizmann wrote to L, already teaching in Manchester,

I visited the grave of your father. The old keeper of the cemetery has gone and there is a new man who knew nothing of the instructions (and I think of the money) which you gave to the old official. There is still the same black wooden cross on the grave which I thought you wished to have replaced.

On all following visits to Merano, Weizmann went to Joseph's grave while Vera, who did not accompany him, saw to it that a spray of flowers was sent to their rooms in time for him to take it there.

L's attachment to Weizmann reached its peak during that summer's Zionist Congress. But while the many groups in opposition were mustering forces for a vicious attack on their weary leader, L had to absent himself from Basle. In London, too, dramatic events were unfolding. Passfield, disgruntled that Palestinian matters should have been taken out of his department's control during the period of the Cabinet sub-committee negotiations, was astir; the implementation of the MacDonald Letter was being blocked by the Palestinian Administration, still unchanged; and the flounderings of the leaderless Jewish Agency had rendered it useless for serious discussions. Yet a clarification of 'the principle of parity between Jews and Arabs as national entities' had to be made: for which the P.M. wished to see at once some representative Jews. Hurriedly it was decided at Basle that David Ben-Gurion (later Minister of Defence and first Prime Minister of Israel) and L should fly to London. They did so on 12 July. A car was laid on there to take them to Chequers and, within the space of a day, they had two talks with Ramsay MacDonald in the presence of his son alone. In the afternoon Malcolm MacDonald telephoned to Weizmann, and then— together with Ben-Gurion and L—drafted a telegram affirming his father's views, as set out in the MacDonald Letter of 13 February. But there was a snag. As the Colonial Office had taken no part in the discussion, the telegram had to remain more or less secret: Weizmann was debarred from flinging it in the face of those who mocked the MacDonald Letter as useless because forgotten—still unimplemented months after its publication.

Ben-Gurion and L touched down in Switzerland just in time to reach Basle for Weizmann's address to the congress; and to witness how the distrust or dislike of him, which had long been gathering, broke out despite the fire and brilliance of his speech. The material for the address had been found and arranged by L and Baffy. But as he listened, L measured the distance between what he called the prophetic genius of the speaker and his own and Baffy's 'honest office work'. He recognized every brick and knew where it came from; but the architectural inspiration that was raising the honest bricks into a work of art, supremely enchanting to his mind's eye, L felt to be totally out of his and Baffy's reach. And again, as Weizmann expounded his policy of state-building which had remained unchanged from the word go ('man by man and acre by acre') L's heart leapt in recognition of

its similarity to his particular way of working in his own field—
the writing of eighteenth-century parliamentary history. The
affinity between their methods fanned his devotion to a bright
flame. But the groups massed in opposition remained blind to the
essential qualities of their patient, dogged leader. Addicted to
scintillation and flamboyance, they rejected him. His political
genius they condemned as weakness, cowardice, even a betrayal.
Confusing issues, they proclaimed impractical, rhetorical demands
that could not fail to excite the Palestinian Arabs when reported;
and insisted on debating at length 'the ultimate aims of the Zionist
movement'—totally irrelevant to the burning issues of the day.
Defeated, Weizmann left them to it.

L, on his return home, wrote on 20 July to Brodetsky a letter
of condolence for his continuing in the same position as before
which now involved him with 'those frogs born of the slime of the
Seventeenth Congress'. L's vituperative abilities had reached
heights that he never surpassed. His startling, surrealist word-
pictures fascinated his victims themselves. They could not desist
from using his imagery and repeating his words, out of context of
course and usually garbled. As they circulated, the approximate
quotations did not make him any better loved by the sorry crew.
But rid of them, since they had rejected Weizmann, he threw
himself with zest into preparing lectures and seminars for the
autumn term. Not in his happiest dreams nor wildest fantasies
had he seen himself Professor of Modern History in a redbrick
university. It was a totally new situation.

CHAPTER THIRTEEN

A Confluence of Torrents
1931–1939

In later years L enjoyed using Professor Jacob's November wire as a fine example of how one man's life can be unpredictably affected by a sequence of events in another's, a man who was almost a stranger at that. Describing the circumstances that prompted him to send the telegram Professor Jacob says,

I was having tea in the old staff common room one afternoon and reading a now obsolete periodical *The Nation*. My eye lit upon a review by G. Trevelyan of Lewis's *England in the Age of the American Revolution*. It ended by lamenting the probability that so fine a historical scholar would, for economical reasons, shortly be lost to historical studies. I thought of our Manchester situation. . . . After the resignation in 1927 of Professor (now Sir John) Neale from the Chair of Modern History, the Senate made no new appointment, and when I came in 1929 I found that the work was being done by a reader and a lecturer. . . .

I ran downstairs, got a telegram form and wired Lewis. I had no warrant or any authority for doing this. But I told the Vice-Chancellor (Sir Walter Moberly) that it was a unique opportunity to lift the whole teaching of modern history in Manchester on to another plane, and he . . . immediately consented to the summoning of a Senate to interview Lewis and report.

On 4 December 1930 the Senate Committee invited the prospective professor to come and meet them. Meantime L—determined not to be imposed upon as he had been by the 'absurd group'—inquired into his likely leisure: he wanted enough of it to do 'massive historical research', in the first place for the book on the Rockingham government of 1765-6. Reassured, he became elated. Professor Jacob writes, 'as a matter of fact, Lewis interviewed the Committee! The result was a recommendation to the Senate for which I can never be sufficiently grateful. He had impressed even the most hard-bitten.' But changes in L's routine and habits had to follow his appointment to the professorship, and some perplexed him. Insignificant decisions easily raised in his mind hosts of possibilities, each weighted down with obstacles. Where should he live during term, in Manchester or in the country? If in the country, how far out? And if he did live in Manchester within walking distance from the university, how would the well-publicized dampness, so good for cotton-spinning, affect his breathing and his heart? And where would he go for his daily walk? Above all, how would the change affect his sleep? Recognizing the absurdity of such trepidation even while succumbing to it, he ascribed this tiresome state of mind to the fact that he had not been allowed any say in the management of his nursery which he would have liked to have seen run on certain lines. Instead, no account had ever been taken of his views on schooling. Whether L's interpretation was true or wide of the mark, he was sorely in need of help when in anguish over trifles. Baffy, ever resourceful, came immediately to the rescue. From the Buxtons she knew of Koszylowce scintillating for most of the year in a bracing brilliance; from L she knew that he had found, by contrast, the muggy gloom of Oxford most depressing. Since Manchester was bound to be worse, he ought to get out, she said, into the country at least for the weekends. Opportunely her youngest sister, Alison Milne, was living near Bridgnorth in Shropshire in a large house curiously misnamed 'The Cottage'. With its many spare rooms, well-kept garden, and well-run home farm, it was just the place. And Alison, approached by Baffy, agreed to let L join the household when it best suited him.

At the end of November 1930 he spent one night at The Cottage; but may have been there before. A new friendship that was to prove most rewarding had already taken shape. Elizabeth, the sixteen-year-old daughter of the house (later Mrs. Jocelyn Gibb), had named him with typical spontaneity 'Clumsy Boy' almost at once reduced and mystified as 'C.B.'. In The Cottage visitors' book, following a blank half-page unintentionally skipped by him, is an entry in L's hand: 'C.B. November 28–29. Misplaced—living up to the name.' Baffy's signature follows, and the rest of the page like the previous half, remained unfilled. On another visit L formed a no less sound friendship with a singularly humanized sheepdog. Addicted to long walks he and Cherry would disappear together into the hills. And when his intelligent, sensitive companion was getting old their concord was still perfect. Acutely aware of any creature's disabilities, L on his way out would stop at a cross-roads where a decision had to be made— to go further uphill for a long walk or to turn aside and rest content with a short walk. Having made up his mind, L asked the collie what suited it best: to follow him and stick to him and bear the hardship of the decision, or to run back alone, now. After a moment's pause the collie would either nip at the edge of his sleeve and streak ahead, or turn round and wend its leisurely way home. But, owing to the Cabinet sub-committee and L's visit to Merano, half a year had to pass before he could stay at The Cottage for three weeks at a stretch (25 May–13 June 1931) and ponder his autumn lectures and seminars. His next visit of considerable length followed the Seventeenth Congress—when he travelled several times to Manchester in search of suitable rooms; and to Sussex where, on one occasion, together with Mary Piercy he snatched away from a grand gardeners' bonfire in the grounds of Stanmer (till recently the home of the Earls of Chichester) some of her ancestors' eighteenth-century documents which were soon to help them both in their separate spheres of history writing.

The Stanmer holocaust was no isolated case. Complaints of varying merit were reaching L from alarmed or distressed eighteenth-century scholars, while universities or their libraries— English and American—sought his help for rescue operations. Typical was a request dated 10 June 1931 from Howard Corning of the Baker Library (Harvard University):

I have many times come just too late to save valuable material and, fortunately, sometimes in time to save it. . . . It occurred to me that you might come across sources of information. . . . If the owners don't want [their ancestors' eighteenth-century business correspondence] and there is no place to keep it in England, and it relates to America, we would be glad to get in touch.

Answering, L stressed the sorry financial position 'especially of the old landed families'; and asked, in the name of some, if the library was prepared to buy such business correspondence primarily of interest to America. But on the whole he was against the dispersal of family papers, and was optimistic about finding more. In an amusing exchange of letters with Lord Clifden, whom he knew since 1918, L says, 'Of course collections of papers are sometimes lost; but more often they have a queer knack of hiding themselves. There are forgotten cupboards and garrets. One favourite hiding place for political correspondence is in estate offices and old boxes of family solicitors.' His keen desire to dig out such treasure had lately increased: new finds—their owners willing—might help to enliven the tasks he would be setting the young as he trained them in research.

His room in the Arts Building of the Victoria University, Manchester, was across the corridor from Professor Jacob's, who remembers him being

constantly in and out, talking about reviews, articles, etc; or about his students who, from being overawed at first, came to admire and prize their new mentor. He never rode rough-shod over them: always encouraging when he criticised, never allowing any slight or sloppy judgement to be made, and insisting on a (to them) wholly new standard of historical thinking. . . . With A. J. P. Taylor fresh from Vienna a most powerful combination began to revive modern history in the university.

Soon it was clear that, once again, L's imprint would be strongest on his more gifted and enthusiastic pupils. One of them, Ninetta Jucker, a keen observer, writes of the

sort of flutter produced among the city worthies by the announcement of his coming, and the extraordinary impact he made on the rather priggish Liberal and Fabian circles in Manchester. . . . He appeared very exotic. Not on account of his Jewish and East-European origin. The percentage of East-European Jews among the local merchant families was about one in three. It was Lewis's ties with Balliol, the F.O., and the aristocracy that made him seem different. . . . There was at the time a municipal patriotism in Manchester and a jealousy of London rather like the Milanese attitude towards Rome. People were truly astonished and hurt that Lewis did not sever his bonds with the South when he came to live in our town. . . . For his part, he could not understand why there was so little contact between the townspeople and the county. But he settled down and, in time, came to feel less of an exile. He even lived down an early-on answer to a very rich lady at a grandiose dinner: she, making conversation, had asked what he considered to be the purpose of primary education. 'To keep the children off the streets, I suppose,' he had murmured pensively.

Ninetta, who vividly remembered many such situations, was one of the few whose home address appears in L's pocket-diaries. With certain pupils he wished to keep in touch during vacations in case they passed through London where he intended to show them the best way of tackling research in the Manuscripts Room of the British Museum. The initials B.M. appear alongside the pupils' names on various dates in the next few years; and in this connection Ninetta says, 'The pains he took over us were extraordinary.' 'As a teacher,' she goes on to say,

he was immensely stimulating. In his essay class which I attended in my first year, there was an essay on what is and what should be in a newspaper; it determined my future career. . . . To his most receptive pupils he could communicate a vast amount; above all, I think, his appreciation of what England stands for in European culture; and his quite unsentimental feeling of the pathos of human endeavour and the fragility of mankind. His great merit as a teacher was that he taught us never to take anything for granted, not even the moral values.

Naturally enough his students' memories cluster round examination papers, seminars, and the weekly essay; as do some of his colleagues'. When setting examination papers he was pernickety about the wording; the examinations over, he was scrupulous in awarding marks. One of his students stresses L's insistence at seminars 'upon clarity of thought being coupled with conciseness of expression'; and recalls, as typical, L's comments following a long and tedious essay that had started 'Ever since the dawn of human history'. When the drone stopped L evoked a senior man in the Foreign Office who, in L's hearing, had declined to read any document longer than a typed foolscap page. For the weekly essay L preferred any student who had vividly experienced something to describe that experience rather than write up a historical subject based on the views of others. Explaining this, he said that the best way to learn to write well is to try to convey events which affect one deeply as an individual. He wanted his students to be free from the generalized and stereotyped thoughts and phrases which schoolchildren must needs pick up, but which the young should discard. At the university they should be helped to acquire the knack of observing and of accurately recording their observations.

His early Manchester pocket-diaries are packed with university activities and social engagements. Civic dignitaries as well as the *Manchester Guardian*'s top people entertained him to lunch and dinner, and induced him to put in an appearance at bazaars and fêtes. Yet he also found time for lecturing outside the university to sixth-formers, students, teachers, and historical societies; and to address historical conferences and a variety of meetings. Married colleagues invited him to their houses and drove him into the country in fine weather. Margaret Taylor—a staunch friend whose eldest child was to be named after L—considered him with a humorous but kindly eye. In her opinion their immediate circle—of men and women a generation younger than L— 'looked up to him as a father figure and a *grand seigneur*'. His anecdotes about the old Vienna conjured up in her mind 'the world of the Merry Widow. He was a fund of fun about himself and had a fund of older stories remembered from childhood.' Many remain fresh in her memory owing to some off-beat phrase. 'His conversation, though a bit heavy and monolithic, always had, hidden somewhere, a pearl worth waiting for. All his stories were rewarding.' With such younger people L enjoyed associating. Yet whenever possible he spent the weekend at The Cottage and went, whatever the weather, into the hills for long walks with the Milnes' sheepdog. Vacations, divided between Shropshire and London, were interspersed with frequent short visits to the Royal Archives at Windsor and several country houses which still harboured eighteenth-century documents of continuing interest to him. For one long stay in Somerset he went with Romney Sedgwick to work at Chewton, each on his own period among the Waldegrave papers. They stayed at an inn well remembered because they were 'reduced to live on cheese there'. In Manchester, too, food was a source of annoyance. To quote again Margaret Taylor, 'Fond of good cooking he suffered in those days from landladies and seemed often to be in digs trouble. We would motor him around prospecting, and always he made a point of saying, "for breakfast I wish to have eggs and bacon"; as for my home-made jam, he fairly wallopped it.' The decorative and cosy

England that L had enjoyed up and down the country was acquiring the superimposed image of an England also long established, but bleak: mean streets of back-to-back houses with groups of unemployed at the corners—an England blighted with monochrome grime and the monotony of idleness; even more depressing than the Bloomsbury which had appalled him in 1907. Years before the Welfare State was thought of, the Midlands made of L an advocate of welfare.

His correspondence with English and American historians had become voluminous. Owing to his many reviews of their books on the eighteenth and nineteenth centuries, L's opinions were much discussed on both sides of the Atlantic. And now that his reputation as a meticulous, original scholar was established it was crowned by his election to the Ford Lectureship. On 30 November 1932 R. W. Chapman of the Clarendon Press wrote of the Delegates' satisfaction with Oxford's recent choice, and informed L of the general expectation that the Ford Lectures of 1934 would be published by the Clarendon Press as soon after their delivery as possible. But the first to benefit from his election were L's pupils. On them he tried out during the next three terms—in what he called 'preliminary trots'—the results of his research, his synthetizing and formulation of matters germane to their classes. And yet four years later, although the Ford Lectures had been given and had won L considerable acclaim, he was still (on 13 April 1937) preparing the six lectures for publication. From the spring of 1933 extraneous work had forced him to refrain from fixing anything much in writing. Even with the help of two secretaries (one in Manchester, the other in Bridgnorth) writing had become too slow, too cumbersome a process.

When Hitler's wish to exterminate the Jews solidified into a feature of German policy, new entries appeared in L's pocket-diaries: Refugee Relief, Refugee Fund, I.S.S. (International Student Service). Scores of German scholars and scientists, deprived of their jobs owing to their origin, entered L's sphere of awareness and bound him afresh to Weizmann. Together they strove desperately to push through schemes for help wherever possible; and almost at once their friendship began to crack. In their hands was the destiny of persons, indeed personalities, whose 'roof' had suddenly been 'burnt over their heads'. To decide who should win, among several men doomed by an insufficiency of funds and posts to compete against each other for survival, was nerve-racking. Cumulative strain, irritation, exasperation, began to erode with startling speed the ties that had formed between L and Weizmann since 1928. Their conflicts were not intellectual; nor were they political at this stage; that came much later, when it no longer was important. The earliest and significant clashes stemmed from an incompatibility of backgrounds and temperaments which began to tell under the new stresses. When the incompatibilities irrevocably surfaced, the friendship broke up. Its destruction left L more deeply scarred for its coinciding with another grave psychological readjustment. Enmity between a certain type of Jew and some Englishmen was increasing, and it distressed L greatly.

The 1939-48 persecutions of the Jews in, or seeking to enter, Palestine by the abdicating Mandatory Power failed to make of L a hater of England not because of any merit in the fading Mandatory's Occupation Forces: L's love of England finally won because—when the war was almost over and he was about to resume his professorship—he saw with indescribable horror some older Palestinian Jews incite Jewish boys and girls to murder individual Englishmen in the name of a 'romantic' message to the world at large which could not have cared less. At the same time his assessment of the British system of education as the best available (in the higher reaches) was reinforced; and it appeared to him to be well suited to its 'livestock'—mentors and pupils alike. The basic qualities of the mentors L had gauged when his harrowing human salvage work was greatly increased between 1933 and 1939. As the Jews' perplexities accumulated, Weizmann began regularly calling L to London for two or three days tacked on to the weekend, and not one of his colleagues protested. All agreed to rearrange their timetable to suit the new humanitarian demands on L.

With his schedule changing, L's decisions about teaching and rescuing had to be worked out, elaborated, and co-ordinated, on long train journeys. The stops at stations he used for jotting down notes in a shorthand largely his own. His right hand was cramping up. The finer movements of wrist and fingers were becoming lost to him. Having diagnosed the deterioration as psychosomatic, and as his doctor, Frank Crookshank, had died, L once more sought help from a psychoanalyst. As in Vienna, he found the interpretations interesting but the sessions of no therapeutic use. Still, those personal preoccupations, too, bound him closer to London; and during one of his longer stays there his morale was boosted by a request that reached him from Winston Churchill, the contemporary he revered more than any other.

Maurice Ashley (then Churchill's research assistant) brought round one day a copy of the first volume of *Marlborough*, and acknowledging it on 15 December 1933 L wrote, 'I am most grateful to you for the inscribed copy, and hardly can tell you how much I appreciate your kindness and your remembering me after all these years.' They had met several times in the early 1920s at lunch with Victor Cazalet.

I can say without flattery [continued L] that I have always been an admirer and follower of yours and, in view of the European situation, am more so now than before. I shall read your book with the greatest interest during the Christmas vacation—I have not been able to do so before as I had all my time taken up with University work, German-Jewish relief, and the Ford Lectures.

On 6 January 1934, as L had not yet given his criticism of the book, Churchill sent a reminder, 'I should be grateful for any advice or reflections which reading this book may have stirred in your mind.' L explained at once,

Even during the Christmas vacation, I found I had to go on with the work on my Ford Lectures and refugee relief. As a result I have so far read only about half of your book—and as I mean to give you a full and honest reply to your question, I shall refrain from answering as yet.

A month later, on 14 February, he wrote a lengthy criticism that reveals much of him, not only his mature views on history-writing.

...I hardly need to tell you how much I admire [your book]—it is a work of art and at the same time a masterly analysis of the historical material. You have succeeded in proving your thesis, and yet have not overdone your case for Marlborough. You have re-examined material previously used in an uncritical manner, and discovered new and important documents; and you have given a comprehensive picture of the transactions.

But I feel sure you would not like me to go on with praise . . . and that what you want from me is frank criticism. Here I must start by warning you that I speak as a layman in so far as your period is concerned, and that I have not the knowledge of it which you seem to ascribe to me. . . . I look at the age with which you deal somewhat like a neighbour, across the garden wall, not as one inhabiting the house. My criticism therefore touches only either fundamental matters or small points of detail; but with petty detail I do not mean to trouble you—corrections which I have to suggest of that nature I have communicated to Ashley.

My first criticism concerns your preoccupation with Macaulay. I have heard it said in Whig circles that you are forcing an open door in tilting against him. With that view I do not agree . . . the Whig mind is not an open door; it is a rubber ball which speedily regains its previous shape. I therefore think you had to deal with Macaulay; but it seems to me that by paying too much attention to him in the body of your book, you have impaired your own picture of Marlborough, whom you seldom discuss without turning aside and engaging in an argument calculated to expose the caricature which Macaulay had drawn of him. As a result, having finished reading your book, I am fully convinced that Macaulay's account of him is wrong, but I have nothing to put in its place nearly so impressive as the picture you have given, e.g. of William III. Had you gathered all your criticism and exposure of Macaulay into a single appendix of, say, fifty pages, and ignored him otherwise, you would have destroyed him just as effectively, or perhaps even more effectively, without distracting the attention of the reader from your own portrait of Marlborough, and you would have avoided giving the book the polemical touch which is disturbing in a great work of art.

My second criticism is that you do, perhaps, especially in the first part of the book, too often engage in imaginary pictures of what *may* have happened, or what some people *must* have felt. Perhaps it is a professional 'malformation' with me; but such passages leave me cold. It is better to stimulate the reader's own imagination than surfeit it with imaginary stuff—to open windows onto the starlit night and let his thoughts roam in the unknown rather than to try to supply him with a fanciful description of life on a distant planet. Human nature and life are so complex that it is wellnigh impossible for any one to guess past scenes or events with any degree of probability; just as it is impossible for us to foresee scenes and events through which we ourselves are about to pass. Therefore any such imaginary accounts always throw me into opposition. Our conjectures must always be rational whereas neither men nor events are rational and there is seldom a real correlation between a so-called historic moment and what people feel or do on the occasion. . . . My third criticism I can hardly call by that name, for it is merely asking for more of a good thing, of which, to my mind, you have been too sparing. You will remember what Gibbon said about the experience of the Captain of the Hampshire Grenadiers and the historian of the Roman Empire. There is no one alive engaged on history work with your experience of politics, government, and war. Please do not try to write history as other historians do, but do it in your own way. Tell us more how various transactions strike you, and what associations they evoke in your mind. When studying the detail of government at a distance of almost 250 years many comparisons must have occurred to you, which you seem to have suppressed. Too much history is written by don-bred dons with no knowledge or understanding of the practical problems of statecraft. In this first volume you had less occasion for such discussions, although even here you seem to have imposed on yourself a restraint which I regret. But as Marlborough moves more and more into the centre of government and politics, I do hope you will let your own experience bear stronger and more visibly on your account of past transactions. Even in polemics one quiet thrust like that at the top of page 248 carries further than where you engage in them in a more academic style.

Now as for materials: I see you have used a good many collections of papers published by the Historical Manuscripts Commission, and I wonder whether you have had the original collections examined for you once more. In my experience the people who did the work for the Historical Manuscripts Commission, especially during the first forty years or so, were past masters at missing important documents. To be quite frank—the work has been done, and is still often done, by underpaid hacks who have neither the time nor the knowledge to do it properly. After all, they were expected to calendar whole collections extending over many centuries, and in the earlier volumes of the H.M.C. had to get reports into so short a space that their remuneration could only have been very scanty. Wherever such a report indicates the presence of Marlborough papers I should advise you to have the collection examined once more.

There are still many things concerning 18th-century history which I should like, if you can spare the time, to talk over with you personally. I shall be in London soon after Easter, and if you will allow me shall call on you at the House of Commons.

The letter is above all valuable as an expression of L's belief in the importance of man's involvement in human affairs if he is to understand events. His appreciation of this was not new, but it had developed. In his first spell of teaching, in Oxford, L had enlivened his tutorials with relevant accounts of his own back-room boy's experience during World War I; and had communicated even more useful anecdotes 'after history tutorials' when 'many matters were discussed very freely'. Teaching his Manchester pupils to write essays he raised the habit into a principle, adapting it to their needs. By 1934 he was sure enough of his ground to press his principle on a distinguished statesman and writer. The reaction was satisfactory. In a letter dated 18 February 1934 L was thanked for his cogent comments; his arguments against imaginary passages were accepted; pleasure was expressed about his request that more of the author's personal experience in military and political affairs should be woven into volume two; and L's hope of meeting in the spring was echoed.

The sequel was an interview in the Churchills' London house. By this time a tentative offer of a possible future collaboration had been delicately hinted at and L had been preparing a carefully worded, politely evasive little piece. But this he never had the opportunity to recite. Preliminaries over, Churchill turned out of position a fire-screen, rested his arms on its top and proceeded to deliver a fascinating oration on the writing of history. When he had finished, it was time for L to leave. On the way to his club for lunch, he clearly saw why the collaboration could never have worked. Had the parts been reversed, L would have acted almost exactly as Churchill had. Neither was a ready listener. Both needed additional hands to do their work. In any joint venture Churchill would be the head. But in history-writing L could only follow his own lead. Thoughtlessly to build up a collision with a national leader whom he revered would have been silly.

L's delivery of the Ford Lectures had enhanced his prestige no less than did their contents. But he congratulated himself chiefly on escaping two perils, either of which could have brought disaster. Throughout the preparation he had in his mind's eye an audience seated in a circular hall; but on arrival in Oxford he found that he would be speaking in a long, rather narrow hall. Although a trifle to most academics no doubt, the sudden reorientation could have easily upset L. The second danger came from

Marie's insistence on being present. By now it was more likely than not that she would have an epileptic fit at one or other of the lectures, probably at the first, upsetting L beyond recovery. Any break in his concentration, which alone could release into the hall at the right time and in the right sequence every one of the strands of thought tidily kept in reserve in his mind, would have knocked him off course. By lucky chance, he was midway in a run of quiet, sleep-filled nights; and during the critical weeks Marie never once had a fit.

With the last Ford lecture delivered, and the prompt publication of the series still hoped for, L nevertheless threw himself again into rescue work. The dramatic result was discord with Weizmann so serious that when he, in Palestine, wished L to come out and take on a new task—in 'haavarah', which involved banking trans-actions in and with Germany—Weizmann approached L gingerly, through Baffy. A reconciliation followed among the orange groves where both men tried to live up to the sentiments which L had already expressed in a letter. 'Our position is such that if I can be of service, we have no right to quarrel, or part com-pany in Zionist work,' he wrote to Weizmann on 18 December 1935. But both found it hard because of other currents re-emerg-ing in L's lifestream, some of which became turbulent owing to the rise of the Nazis. Providentially though, before the truly ominous events experienced by their generation began implacably to unfold, a stabilizing influence had entered L's life.

Norman Maclean, who had been Moderator of the General Assembly of the Church of Scotland during 1927–8, came to The Cottage for a three-week Easter visit in 1935. His daughter Helen remembers him meeting L and their 'making tremendous friends at once'. Brought up on the Isle of Skye by his stern, Calvinistic, schoolmaster father, Maclean had broken through as a small boy to an unrestricted belief in the love of God as a unifying power that makes all men one. Other 'inner visions of God as Love' followed, there and in Inverness. Possessed of a brilliant mind which he used to full capacity when the need arose, Maclean com-municated to L his spiritual experiences and transmitted his impressive interpretations. Helen remembers them 'going up and down The Cottage drive, up and down for hours talking and talking', so much in earnest that no one dared interrupt. Later in the summer Helen's stepmother (Iona, *née* Macdonald) invited L to stay at Armadale. Again, for about a fortnight, the two men talked, mostly alone; and the happy days on Skye established a new interest of L's which steadily grew. Prompted by Maclean he relived his childhood's enjoyment of the ritual in the old Ruthenian churches of Galicia and, under expert guidance came to see the purpose of ritual as a purification of man's inveterate bent to dabble privately in magic; also to accept it as a man-sought opportunity to make good those runs of chance which irrupt uncalled for into carefully laid plans. After Skye, the links remained firm; and in 1942 Maclean asked L to come north to help read the proofs of his book, *His Terrible Swift Sword*. Responding immediately, L stayed with him and Iona in Edinburgh for equally memorable days. 'Again there were important talks, interspersed with much gaiety and fun,' remembered Helen. But Maclean's stabilizing influence remained hidden from most, while disruptive influences and their sequels noticeably affected L's demeanour. During a hurried, harrowing visit to London in the spring of 1937 he felt several sudden jabs of pain in the back— reminders of the Dubbiaco trouble that Droitwich had not cured. A jab of pain immediately caused an awkward, jerky movement. Jumping off a bus on his way out of London, he made a false step, stumbled and twisted an ankle, but continued his journey. In Manchester a sprain was diagnosed and a week of complete rest prescribed. Learning of it Baffy wrote, 'How glad I am! For some time I have been longing for something which would give you complete rest. It was Providence that led your idiot steps to Manchester—you could not have been nearly so well looked after in London.' But too soon L's rest was over. He was back, on crutches, listening, observing, talking. Europe was drifting into moral disarray. Spain's fratricidal war, reaching a peak of ruthless intensity, had turned the way England, France and others had banked on its not going. A flaccid nervousness was spreading north of the Pyrenees. L's anger against himself and others flared up more quickly, had more bite to it and more often lingered as a bitter resentment; while Marie was becoming an ever-present numinous horror to him.

In the spring of 1936, restless and no longer able to teach, she had decided to re-settle in Vienna where a relative had left her some real estate and a goodish sum of money. L felt in honour bound to restrain her; only to learn that any close-argued discussion brought on a fit. She had deemed herself master of her own life and had refused to be influenced; but some months later, with the Anschluss situation on the way, she had begged to be got back to England for good. Always eager to see things for himself, L had made a fleeting visit to Vienna, and sealed his fate. Coming together out of a doorway at dusk, he and Marie had chanced upon a handful of loitering Nazi-minded youths. Despite her limp, Marie had deftly placed herself between L and the gang, drawing their attention to herself—a cripple of 'definitely nordic looks', and with an air of imperious effrontery that any one of them could have envied. It had worked; in more than one way. On his return L pulled all the necessary strings to get her to England, which this time involved his declaring himself responsible for her actions and upkeep. 'Lewis dined alone with me [wrote Baffy soon after] and discussed the affairs of his life till 1 a.m. He is pushing alone into an arid desert. One can do nothing. His hand and mind alike refuse to help him. Poor Lewis.' Marie had first stayed with friends in the country, then with the help of other friends she had moved into a room not far from Gloucester Walk (L's new home), and kept dropping in to make scenes. The latest had been over Baffy whom Marie was referring to as 'our Egeria'. Induced by her alarming condition to bottle up most of his disgusted reproof, L went about in a state of sombre rage. The true cause of it he felt unable to tell Baffy; nor did he speak of the crucial Viennese incident, no matter how Baffy chided him for bringing over the tiresome wreck of a woman and making himself legally responsible for her. Not till two years later was Marie certified insane and removed to Friern Hospital, in north London. To L insanity was man's ultimate degradation; a madhouse, however well appointed, was hell. But his hand had been forced in the end by the local landladies. Among them Marie had become a legend. Some refused to have her for lodger because she was known to be abusively quarrelsome; others because they dreaded her fits. L, having accepted her incapacity to live on her own, had to face the practical issues it raised. Time and Dr. Moore's eloquence at long last made him see that to shut up Marie in a private room in an exclusive nursing home would be far more cruel than to place her in a suitable ward of a large institution where she would have ample opportunity to quarrel with divers inmates, but where she was more likely to continue on tolerably good terms with the staff. In agonizing turmoil he gave his written consent, on 3 March 1939; and for years expiated it by frequent visits. Travelling underground to Friern and back he pondered in paroxysms of self-hate if he was going mad. Years before, on the way from Koszylowce to Oxford in 1911, he had considered the likelihood with immediately grievous results. Since then the same menace seemed to have crept in on mankind as a whole. Was it not degenerating into madness? Still, even half a year after his difficult dinner with Baffy, on 8 September 1937 she entered in her diary—at Caponflat, her daughter's home in East Lothian where L was staying for a few quiet days—'Poor old L. He is at his best here; and devoted to the children.' A happy home situated in untamed country could even then restore his equanimity in a matter of hours. Anxieties, personal and general, were steadily eroding his magnificent powers of resilience but had not yet destroyed them. Foreseeing the end of an era, he passionately wished to fix on paper his seething thoughts and emotions. He resumed shaping his book on the Cabinet, based on the Ford Lectures of 1934, which required more steady reference work in and near London; he spoke to Baffy of wanting to write on secret diplomacy,[1] and also on Tory Radicalism in the past. Dropping in to tea in June 1937 he read out to her the opening paragraphs of a book 'recently begun—Vienna and Versailles. Very good it will be', she thought, 'if he can keep his nerves in order'—more precisely if he could sleep by night and be less stormy, distressed, irritable by day. Concentration of thought on Europe's past was not easy in the prevalent mood. 'There may be a European war,' wrote Baffy at the end of the month. 'The Russians have shot all their generals; Blum's Government has fallen.' In the event, 'From Vienna to Versailles' did not appear in print till February 1940—as an article[2] so concise that the theme echoed on through

---

[1] This article appears in *In the Margin of History*, p. 3.   [2] Reprinted in *Conflicts*.

much of L's later work, notably throughout his Creighton
Lecture—'Basic Factors in Nineteenth-Century European History'.[1] But he did manage to bring out his second book of essays—
more exactly articles 'republished with a minimum of change'—
before the outbreak of war. (The preface to *In the Margin of
History* is dated June 1939.)

Conspicuous among the political manifestations that appalled L
as World War II rolled in, were the effects communism-in-action
and fascism-in-action were having on two numerically great
nations. Of these effects he wrote,

Nazism, from the very outset as far as the Jews are concerned starts
with the worst characteristics of what is usually described as Bolshevism—disregard of the rights of persons and of property, and the joy of
humiliating people of higher standing and education than their
tormentors.[2]

Haunted by premonitions of an 'early break-up of Europe as we
know it', he explained to Baffy on 10 May 1938 the inevitable
magnitude of the impending Polish disaster, and later told her of
the likelihood of 'a widespread Bolshevization', by which he
meant the deliberate strangulation of our hard-won, more cultivated modes of living. In early spring 1938 his dejection, like that
of many, had been aggravated by horrified thoughts about the
fate of his Austrian relations and friends trapped, by concerted
complacency, into being victims of the Anschluss—unopposed
incorporation with an octopus. 'We have breathed on a house of
cards which was the peace of Europe,' commented Baffy on this
first step in the 'mopping up of the new little states', with whose
affairs she had been concerned after joining the League of Nations'
Union in 1922. Distressed and disapproving she yet admitted that
in view of 'the Western Powers' infirmity of purpose, joined to
inadequate defences, nothing could be done about Austria'. 'But
what about Czechoslovakia?' Soon she knew: it was her second
'little one' to go as a propitiatory gift to the octopus. In May 1938
the Foreign Office were saying to Jan Masaryk (the son of L's old
friend Thomas, and Czechoslovak Minister in London) that they
knew nothing about the Sudeten-German leader Henlein visiting

[1] Reprinted in *Vanished Supremacies*.
[2] 'Vienna Jewry' reprinted in *In the Margin of History*.

London. In September—with French Ministers flying in—Jan remarked to L, '*we* have nothing more to sell'. There were rumours of an exchange of populations. An enormous influx of German refugees into Czechoslovakia coincided with these rumours, soon followed by a further exodus of Germans, and of Czechs. Baffy housed a few new paupers at Roland Gardens while they waited to learn what to do. Alison offered shelter to as many as The Cottage could hold. 'In a grinding rage' Baffy could detect 'neither honour nor courage anywhere in Europe'; felt 'oppressed by the misery of utter helplessness'; and reeled under the 'fearful impact of the world's anguish'.

As London filled with men engaged in diplomacy—secret or open, honest or devious—L's passion for studying history in the making, was renewed. Awakened in the U.S. by General Huerta's 1913 Mexican exploits, this passion had established itself between 1915 and 1919 as a current in L's probing mind. London in the late 1930s offered splendid opportunities for him to renew the study of the nations' ways of using exchanges of words to affect the pattern of things to come. If on the spot, he could easily bring about casual or contrived chats with or about international intriguers. Data gathered with acumen, and sifted with his usual care, could open up startling vistas of linked causes and effects. And once again his Manchester colleagues chose to help him. Alive to the likely fruitfulness of his obsessions, they decided in Senate to give him a sabbatical year from September 1939. Immediately grateful for the boon of time granted him to satisfy his curiosity about diplomatic history in the making, and to complete his book on the Cabinet, L realized in due course how the Senate's decision had contributed—despite the quirks of fate —to three books: *Diplomatic Prelude*, 1948; *Europe in Decay*, 1950; and *In the Nazi Era*, 1952. As they appeared, presentation copies went out to his helpful colleagues.

L's colleagues were not alone in being stirred to act during the war scare that preceded the Munich Settlement. Nor were they alone in being uneasy about the peaceful agreement reached in Munich on 29–30 September, which left a truncated, discredited, devitalized Czechoslovakia dangling, attractive to vultures. Air-raid precautions were soon being discussed in the English press. And Clara, alerted, got it into her head that, as in the previous war, she would feel safe only in Oxford. Since Marie was no longer there, L lifted his ban. But Clara lingered on at Ladbroke Grove. Among the things he never knew was which Church she had originally belonged to. During their few years together she had declared herself, in conversation with members of the Russian Orthodox Church, to be a Roman Catholic; but to Poles had firmly said she was a member of the Eastern Church; while to L's questions her sincere if irrelevant answer had been 'I don't mind'. In fact she minded so little that, soon after her return from the States, she joined the Islamic Community in Woking. On this 'conversion' L—by the time I knew him—had two opinions. In friendly mood, he thought it admirable that she should have dropped her pretence of being whichever Church member she was not; also that the re-established link with her Tartar ancestors might possibly 'anchor her'. But when feeling resentful, he snorted, saying that he well saw through her attempt to make him look ridiculous: her enthusiasm had coincided with a peak in his Zionist work. Nor did her attachment to the Surrey mosque of Shah Jehan prevent her leaving London hurriedly for Oxford when, early in 1939, gas masks for babies were first discussed in the House of Commons. At the time L was again in London, on Zionist affairs which were further embittering relations between the Jewish Agency and the government, and for which he had again been given leave of absence from his university.

On 7 February 1939 the Prime Minister, Neville Chamberlain, opened in the Picture Gallery of St. James's Palace a tripartite Conference on which *The Times* newspaper drily remarked 'conferences rather than Conference'. The obdurate Palestinian Arabs, refusing to meet the Jews, built up a situation rich in comic incident as the English delegation hurried hither and thither in the same building to see each of the other two in turn. With the grim days of disappointment rumbling on, L first found delight in the eighteenth-century way of describing voyagers as 'lying' here or there overnight. He 'lay' at Gloucester Walk—but slept only if he took a good dose of sleeping tablets. The anguish of tussling daily with phrases which, said or written in the right context, might

9a. At Dunvegan Castle in 1935. Left to right: Flora Walter (later Dame Flora MacLeod), Sir Reginald MacLeod, L, Helen Maclean

9b. On the Isle of Skye, August 1938, with the Macleans and friends

10. Outside the Zionist Organization. Left to right: J. Linton, Berl Locker,
Moshe Sharett, I, L. Bakstansky

ease the desperate lot of some at least of his co-racials, drove him to take an equally strong dose of pep-pills in the morning.

The sixth session, lasting into the night, was hardest on L. Over-excited, restless and depressed, he hurried towards the Ritz, hoping to pick up a late bus; yet wondered if he had not better walk home—there would hardly be time enough left for him to sleep off his tablets' effect before morning. As he approached the stop an old acquaintance, on leave from abroad, hailed him. Boisterous greetings over, L was introduced to an attractive young woman whom I shall call Deirdre. She was a friend of L's acquaintance's family and was waiting for L's bus, which they presently boarded waving goodbye to their mutual friend. Sitting by her side L liked Deirdre's quiet, self-possessed manner and when, getting up, she suggested he should see her home, he accepted. Her flat was well furnished and, at the moment, she lived alone. Having made love, they were fortifying themselves with some food when Deirdre explained her tiresome situation. Some six years ago her husband had been struck by an incurable complaint. The family fortune was sufficient to keep him in a comfortable nursing home and their child at a good school. Deirdre, too, was not unprovided for but, from time to time, was desperately short of ready cash. Sexually starved and having a good business mind on the level of advantageous barter, she steered the conversation where she wanted it to go; clearly not for the first time. Before L left they reached an agreement which for a number of years worked to their mutual satisfaction. And yet, despite his psychoanalyst's approval of the affair, L continued to slip steeply into misanthropy. At one of the last sessions at St. James's he saw himself stuck on a perilous ledge, the only 'quick' man hobnobbing with hollow men, stuffed men, in a vast emotional and intellectual Waste Land. The surrealist vision superimposed itself on three-dimensional reality more than once; and L wondered if it was not opportune to accept personal insanity as normal in a world he saw slipping into a nightmare where the unthinkable was imposing itself on the ordinary: a policy that came to be known as 'Operation Coffin-Boat' was starting up in the Mediterranean.

In May 1939 the MacDonald White Paper was published. The

Mandate was being twisted out of all recognition. Pretty well all Jewish immigration into the Homeland was to be henceforth illegal. The Zionists' friendship with the White Paper's avowed author was severed; and the scope of Operation Coffin-Boat gained amplitude. As the cancer of man-made hells infected vaster stretches of the Old World—from the Russian Arctic to the Gulf of Cadiz, from the eastern shores of Asia to the western shores of Europe—the greatest maritime power of the day started using the most up-to-date methods in order to push back into the limpid blue a straggle of Jew-laden unseaworthy boats, to flounder in the Mediterranean with their obnoxious 'illegal' cargo. As elsewhere, the exigencies of security, even justice, were put forward to explain this criminal action. It was symptomatic of an epidemic of cruel behaviour, which generated more suffering in its course. Its inception can be traced to the year of the Paris Peace Conference, and it was to reach its utmost extension towards the end of World War II. Hitler's peculiarity was to use chiefly the pretext of race where others before and after him chiefly used that of ideology. But on the Palestine coast, expediency seems to have been the first avowed incentive.

For L the nightmare reality lifted only for a few days, in August when, suffering from a sensation that he described as a contraction in the elasticity of time, he resumed his Notes.

Wednesday, 23 Aug. 39. I had been entirely out of touch with the [Zionist] Congress at Geneva; but in view of the German-Russian bombshell felt that immediate action was required, and that this was the psychological moment to take it. I 'phoned up Walter [Walter Elliot, then Minister of Health], asked him to see me. He said I should be at his house at 10 a.m. I told him that in my opinion, at such moments one had to assume that those with whom one worked would react in a manner similar to oneself, and that I considered myself, therefore, as representative. I declared that the Jews—I mean in the first place the Jewish Agency—would stand unreservedly and unconditionally by Great Britain; that we would wish immediately to raise a Jewish Army from volunteers in neutral countries and all countries that would not introduce conscription; that the Congress sitting in Geneva gave us an exceptional chance of immediately arranging for action with the key men from various countries, and that if H.M.G. made up their minds quick enough I would fly out to Geneva immediately. . . .

Thur. 24 Aug. Moshe [Shertok, later Sharett] arrived at the office with instructions from Geneva to do in a concrete form what I had already started. . . .

Nothing came of it. Evasive thanks were voiced for Jewish readiness to help the British war effort. Suitable individuals were anyhow expected to do their duty. Concerted action by any large body of foreign Jews was a tricky business, to be handled carefully some day.

More gloomy than before L returned to the lecturing he had undertaken earlier in the summer up and down the country, to young people drawn into divers groups under the service ministries. Much of it was on obscure aspects of World War I. Despite the shortening days and the blackout, the lectures continued in full spate till he was called to Manchester for two interviews. First his sabbatical leave was cancelled, and then he was given leave for the war's duration at the request of the Foreign Office, for liaison work between them and the Zionist Organization. As the documents he needed to complete his book on the Cabinet had been whisked away to Wales, Intelligence and Liaison claimed most of his time during the phoney war—London's winter of tranquil discomforts. His lecturing to the young, though become less widespread, never stopped entirely; not even when, with Hitler's attention fixed on Norway, Liaison and Intelligence were stepped up. But when the Continent started falling to Hitler piecemeal, certain readjustments were again carried through. When the French Army was breaking, Vera Weizmann—twice qualified as a doctor, in Berlin and in Manchester—went the round of chemist shops collecting three lethal doses of veronal: for herself, her husband, and L. When under a summer sky smooth as silk, Londoners listened for the boom, rumble and crash of a Nazi invasion, she handed L's vial to him. 'The possibility of a German invasion of this country is doubly terrible for Jews,' wrote Baffy on 17 June 1940.

Vera told me of the veronal casually, in a relaxed, reminiscent mood, on the last night of my stay with her at Rehovoth in 1965. For once we had dined alone and no one had dropped in for a game of bridge. I said L had spoken to me soon after we met of a lethal dose of some drug he carried on him since the 'invasion days' but that he had felt unable to disclose who gave it him. Vera, never having made a mystery of it, was perplexed. But then, she and her husband had thrown away their vials as soon as the likelihood of an invasion was over. When she learnt from me that it was weeks after we married, in 1947, that I at last persuaded L to flush his vial down the drain, her eyes—as she sat opposite me —widened. 'Why?' she wanted to know.

After I had spoken, she sat on, upright and taut, repeating in a voice raucous with unshed tears, 'But why?' I had not found the right words in which to convey the horror, strain, and temptation to destroy himself that L's haunting void had been to him from boyhood to old age.

PART III

TOWARDS MATURITY

CHAPTER FOURTEEN

Agonizing Reappraisals
1940–1945

The Churchill government's take-over, in May 1940, gave L satisfaction untinged by hope of speedy relief in Palestine: a country's long-term policies cannot change overnight. Still, he anticipated considerably fewer and more intermittent acts of destruction. In the Jewish Agency's London offices he picked up echoes of afflicted Jewry's sighs of deliverance that had rustled through their ranks at Churchill's elevation. With Baffy he devoted himself to squeezing the juice of hope out of the most unlikely documents published or drafted during the preceding year; and concentrated especially on immediate help to the most threatened individuals and groups. Devotion to them pierced what Maclean called L's 'true texture' and filled him with a poignant attachment to the planet whose surface he saw churned up under his feet, as well as to Jews who were being made to die for presuming to have any place on it at all. As in 1929 L ardently battled for just pacts; but owing to increasing daily rigours he was plagued with a variety of ailments all termed 'the flu'. To his fury, and Baffy's recorded distress, one or other infection forced him to stay at home when it seemed least opportune. Undernourished and overworked, he was haunted on such days more than ever by the patient eyes of suffering people turned to him in mute appeal. By the time common-sense humanity entered the ghastly Palestine situation (in 1942), the marks left by the preceding three years could no longer be deleted. L had grown chary of adverse changes in administrative personnel. Continually apprehensive, he had stepped up his relations with editors and deputy editors of newspapers and periodicals. The English press was still an open channel and a reliable weapon.

Since he took up his professorship L had met weekly the editor of the *Manchester Guardian* for a working lunch. When seconded for liaison work in the south, he centred his attention on the editorial staff of important London papers of whom Baffy still managed to entertain at home a chosen few. The publication that year of her earliest memories of Inverary, Whittingeham, and Hatfield (*Family Homespun*) had strengthened her literary connections; and when the presentation copies of *Conflicts*, a collection of essays L had written since the outbreak of war, were going out in 1942, he had reason to expect favourable reviews. But before the main appreciations appeared in high summer, he had gone into the National Temperance Hospital for a major operation, the first of many. For close on a fortnight he was kept in bed, too ill to dictate or read. Dozing dopily, he stared inward at interlacing coils of his past. A season of exasperations was being superseded by a season of reappraisals. In a state of abiding grief he froze into the stance of an observer meticulously attentive to humanity's murderous antics.

Baffy, the first friend to visit him in hospital, brought a batch of laudatory letters thanking L for his new book. The longest and most exciting was from C. G. Stone who rejoiced to see 'the powerful mind as powerful as ever' and to recognize 'some of its products'. In *Conflicts* he had found the 'hyperbola'—a favourite term borrowed from geometry and long since used by L (and Stone) to express the attraction of extreme opposites to each other. Both men had adapted to their ends the concept of two lines for ever gravitating towards each other yet unable to merge owing to an inherent repulsion bound to dominate their relationship before fusion could be reached. Stone had detected it 'incognito' on page 205. On page 53 he had found the 'mono-methodism of the individual', of which Machiavelli had written in the sixteenth century but few people took into account even in the twentieth though L had introduced it into his 1914 W.E.A. lectures. And on the 'very first page' was 'that idea of the freely expanding ends and cramped middle of Europe' also given by L to the W.E.A. while the nations were gliding into World War I. Stone's twenty-two large pages, covered in a minute hand, dissected L's preoccupations 'in so far as you are a student of the way the world is going' and commented on those preoccupations in philosophical terms. But the brilliant, close, elegant, at times perverse arguments were also the bricks of a wall built to provoke L into leaping over it. Stone, too, was figuring out what actions he should carry through now that his former scale of values had broken down. In search of a new one he argued obsessively about the post-war world's being in need of a new logic, free from the inherent self-contradictions of the old. Had L been less preoccupied with his own reappraisals, he might well have recognized Stone's appeal for help, and might even have presently travelled all the way to Cornwall to meet again the one philosopher whose thought intrigued him. But feeling groggy, he could make nothing of those close-argued, abstract phrases, and took at their face value Stone's words, 'There will be nothing . . . that I shall expect you to answer; nothing . . . will need your immediate attention.' L always took at his word a man whom he respected; and the thirty-year-old friendship lapsed through his silence; to be broken only by me, after his death. During what remained of the summer of 1942 L continued in so bad a shape that, when I first saw him, in the autumn, he gave me the impression of a great ship trapped in some fabulous polar solitude, creaking slightly as it moved—or let itself be pushed—further into the ice. Not wholly unaware of it, he had remarked in print on the little warmth there was about (*Conflicts*, p. 127). Yet warmth steadily came to him from at least three quarters; from Baffy, the Buxtons, and Tegan Harris, the oldest friend of them all, by now a widow living, for a time, in a cottage near Robertsbridge in Sussex. After leaving hospital L regularly stayed with her. 'It was restful for him . . . he revelled in picking blackberries, did exactly what he liked' and thought how best to formulate his disturbing reappraisals for C. G. Stone, who was an indefatigable seeker for the words best suited to a particular context.

L and I met on Sunday 25 October at an afternoon party of the Kullmanns. A League of Nations expert in International Law, Gustave Kullmann was a Swiss whose Russian wife's family had settled in France in the early 1920s. Recently transferred from Geneva to London in connection with the expanding refugee problem, he kept open house at Ladbroke Grove throughout the war: Marya Kullmann excelled at parties ennobled by some worthy cause which she cleverly introduced into each occasion. This particular party was intended to find common ground between enthusiastic Christians and persecuted Jews. Because of it L had gone that weekend not into Sussex but to the Buxtons who had moved to Ongar in Essex within easy reach of Chingford, the north London district where Denis was in charge of Barrage Balloons. To help Denis get back to his duties shortly after noon, the sparse Sunday lunch finished early; but Emily and L lingered over their coffee in the garden. In a brilliant burst of sunlight she noticed how worn he looked, and said so. L acknowledged being weary, but refused to stay another night: something of use to some Jew might come of the Kullmanns' party—one never knew.

Entering their drawing-room about tea-time, I saw Gustave standing in my path with a man of his own stature, tall but thick-set: 'My old friend Namier.' Presently, sitting in an irregular circle, we heard of rumours and reports about atrocities committed in Eastern Europe chiefly against Jews. Since I had been imprisoned in Russia and was kept for a while in a concentration camp east of Moscow in the early 1930s, Kullmann put some questions to me. Answering, I noticed the glint of L's spectacles turned on me. Asked by Kullmann to elaborate I found myself addressing L— the person who listened most attentively and with even greater understanding than my host. There followed an argument of great heat, with L attacking some Jews who sentimentally descanted on the contribution to mankind's spiritual regeneration bound to come from the Jewish mass-suffering in Central Europe and further east. L's attack against them, scathing and bitter, made a pleasing change—no trace of saccharine there. When the party was breaking up, he asked if I would read an article by him on Russia; could we perhaps settle on a date as we walked away? But Gustave, intervening, drew him into the study. The weather had changed; rain clouds were gathering fast. I left. After dinner L telephoned about his article on Russia. The inflection of his voice was questioning and reproachful. We fixed a date for him to come. Having brought his article with him, he took it out of his brief-case, put it on the table and settled down to talk of himself. To clarify events, situations, experiences, he drew distinctions between the Galician Ukrainians and their Polish persecutors, the

Jews born free in Palestine (the Sabras) and ghetto Jews, the Russian people and their communist tormentors. I listened fascinated. Of the first two matters I knew nothing; but I was amazed that he should be so perceptive about the last. Views on Russia were often being aired before me; some by accepted experts. Whether coughed up in a true-blue drawing-room or round a pinko-red supper table, all were to me like gobbets of undigested dream, of which there was no trace in L's words. Before leaving he asked me to read his article with merciless care, gave me three days to do it in, and suggested he should then come round for my opinion—it would save my writing. On his following visit we meticulously dissected his article on the U.S.S.R.'s 25th anniversary,[1] which I thought remarkable, as it showed no sign that the author had never been to Russia let alone the U.S.S.R. The only possible improvement was a slight shift of emphasis here or there.

In those days I was living in the flat of a friend, Prue Barrington who, having met me in the peak months of my vagrancy in this country, had pressed me to share it with her. After some unsuccessful efforts at war-work she had settled down as part-time secretary to an almost blind vicar of a near-by church. Having been very ill shortly before the war she usually got home extremely tired at the hour of our evening nibble, which no longer could even be called supper. When L began coming regularly, I insisted that he should leave before she was due back. But there came a day when he was so dilatory that in the end I rather hustled him out, opening the front door for him. Outside, on the gallery the night was pitch-black. Changing his reading spectacles for another pair he swayed a little, feeling the floor before him with his feet, for a step or threshold, explaining the while the disconcerting mysteries of 'bi-focals', easily dangerous in the black-out. Somewhat alarmed I took him by the hand saying I would lead him along the gallery to the lifts, well enough immured never to have their permitted regulation-blue lights switched off. Almost shouting, L repeated with great vehemence, 'Yes, lead me to the light, lead me, lead me,' and clutched my hand as in a vice. With dismay I realized that he was not in full control of the pressure he

[1] *Manchester Guardian*, 7 November 1942.

was exerting with his right hand. He was unaware of its force. Having left him at the lifts, I walked back wondering what I had let myself in for.

One afternoon not long after, L became unmanageably turbulent, indeed aggressive, and we had a blazing row. Fed up, I said that unless he mended his ways I would ask him to leave and not return, which would be a pity. His reaction was instantaneous and spectacular. Dignified, he rose to say he would not come again till I asked him to; at which I realized I never had. Pausing in the doorway, L revealed one of his most puzzling characteristics. He stopped to mention the best hour for my telephoning to Gloucester Walk in the morning, and to the Athenaeum later in the day. I gasped. Totally unaware of it, he had toppled his melodramatic exit into a farce. Similar episodes were to astonish me till I realized that despite L's great sensitivity for style in writing and in the actions of others when seen against a vast background, he had none at all for his own relatively unimportant actions in the narrow confines of particular situations. Not a result of his being in any way insensitive, it sprang from his utter spontaneity when confronting another person. Most unusual except in very young children, it seemed incongruous to a degree in a man of his intellect and worldly experience; but it was typical. I had already sensed this and intended to play the sequel as L had planned it. Aware of his unhappiness, though not yet of its burden, I would not have wished to add even a twinge of pain. But once he was gone, I forgot about him. There were two reasons for this.

I had been selecting and translating some letters of direction to lay people by a Russian monk whose vocation distantly resembled that of a guru. Finding the best English twentieth-century words and expressions to convey the flavour—not the mere dictionary meaning—of Russian nineteenth-century monastic speech, was my least worry; the cardinal one being to bridge the chasms I saw yawning between Anglo-Saxon religious and ethical assumptions stemming from centuries-old disputes between Protestants and Papists, and Russian Christian assumptions stemming from Byzantine theological disputations of about A.D. 300–900. Soon after the Kullmanns' party a publisher had shown sufficient interest in my typescript for me to become absorbed in tidying it up. This temporary state of mental isolation was aggravated by my lack of a normal sense of time which had been destroyed during the months I had spent in solitary confinement in Moscow. When I reached England, in 1934, the subtle internal computer that checks the passing hours was easily restored to working order; but I had not yet regained any sense of the number of days that slipped by. L's voice, stifled with depression, pierced my cloud of forgetting: 'You didn't telephone. I had to.' While silence held between us, he had read a book, published in 1938, which I had written about my Russian prisons and concentration camp. The conclusion he drew was that I could, and should, be taught to write English properly; and be taught by him. The suggestion delighted me but my consent did not close the incident. Good at remembering dates and celebrating occasions, L wished our restored friendship to be marked by my lunching out with him and by our going on to an exhibition of nineteenth-century pictures at the National Gallery. From there I intended to go to Vespers at the Russian church near Victoria Station, and I wanted to reach it in time to make my confession before the service, in preparation for taking communion on the morrow—the anniversary of my son's birth. Since the child had died in infancy, it was for me a rather ambiguous life-and-death date, not to be scrapped because of current interests. When L continued to linger in the National Gallery, doing once again the round of the pictures he most liked, I told him I had to leave and why. At once he moved with me to the exit, mentioning a building he wanted me to notice on the way. As we turned off Buckingham Palace Road into a crooked little street, where the Russian church then stood, I did what is customary among us before going to confession: asked L to forgive me if I had caused him any hurt. The question and answer are conventionally turned, which does not prevent sincerity but makes for verbal smoothness and simplicity. Both are so short and obvious that I foresaw no hitch. But L stopped in his tracks, grasped me by the arm and shouted several times, 'You, me!', causing a commotion in a run of little old ladies who bumped into us from behind. Taking his answer for given, I threw a comprehensive smile over my shoulder and nipped into the porch. Total oblivion of all but ourselves became usual with

L in moments of stress and never failed to disturb me, perhaps because his display of this oblivion in January 1943 marked the bomb-shattered crooked street as the place of my irreversible first step on to the quicksands of his anguish, while the world around us alternated between swoops into gloom and flights into hope.

Britain's gains in Africa (coinciding with those of her Allies on other fronts) were stirring up a speculative effervescence. Baffy enjoyed many 'lively arguments on the future of Europe', above all at weekend parties in country houses accessible by rail. But to L they brought scant comfort—any easing of tensions between an abdicating England and Jewry in peril of extinction seemed unlikely. Still, right outside the shattered framework of his former aspirations, he found comfort in the opinions held on the 'Semitic region south of the Mediterranean' by a politically neutral and scientifically scrupulous American. Dr. Walter Lowdermilk in his book, *Palestine, Land of Promise,* written before the war and published in 1944, indicated that an ultimate symbiosis between Arab and Jew would surely be a boon to those vast stretches of the earth's surface which had been allowed to degenerate throughout the centuries of Jewish eviction. Though L foresaw the process as slow and painful for both groups uncared for by a mellow, fair-minded empire, he accepted the snail's pace of political change as part of our inescapable frustrations. To the discrepancy between the speeds of surmise and events he referred intermittently while pressing on with my education and drawing into my orbit some carefully selected friends.

Edwyn Bevan—who with his eldest daughter lived near both of us—was chosen for the brilliance of his casual talk, perfectly expressive of his gracious personality. Wyndham Deedes—another older man whom L thought typical of the England he loved—was also chosen and he brought with him a pressing invitation for me to join a Palestine House committee chaired by him with fabulous skill. And immediately after, L arranged a luncheon at which I met Margaret Rhondda, foundress, pro-prietress and editor of an independent weekly. L wished me to review books for her, as an exercise in clear thinking expressed briefly, in paragraphs sweeping along with consistent drive from start to finish. Soon I was not only writing reviews for *Time and Tide* but spending most weekends at Margaret's Surrey cottage. Yet each introduction came about for such obviously good reasons that I only realized how many of L's friends I already knew when he once again went into hospital, in June 1943, to have his hopelessly infected tonsils removed. I then totted up how many friends we shared because he asked me—and no one else— to carry out certain instructions regarding his books, typescripts, and sheaves of rough materials should he not survive. It struck me as the more odd because he also mentioned, very casually, that he had made a will in my favour; not that he had much to bequeath; nothing for me to fuss about; but the extraction of his tonsils—trifling compared with the operation he had taken in his stride the year before—had evoked the wretched tinkering with his eyelids and nose bones in early boyhood. He was full of apprehensions, which in a sense proved justified. Besides the mismanagement of the whole thing, he suffered a severe blow upon returning home to convalesce.

The fabric of 15 Gloucester Walk had been damaged in September 1940 by the blast of a 500-kilo bomb of high explosives. In 1941 its condition had been worsened by oil bombs, a profusion of incendiaries, and a German bomber that had crashed a quarter of a mile away. In the summer of 1943 the authorities found the weakened structure likely to crumble, and L was ordered out. If picked to spite him, the time could hardly have been more cruelly chosen. Engaged on writing the essays later collected and published under the title *Coloured Books*,[1] he was about to start planning his Raleigh Lecture for the British Academy which had elected him a Fellow. To protest against eviction was of course useless. Having asked me to house most of his books and papers, he moved with the indispensable ones to Roland Gardens, three doors away from Baffy; and at the same time the heavy bombing switched to that neighbourhood. In October he had to move again; and was kept on the hop all winter by near misses, or nightly yapping of lapdogs. His former landlady in Gloucester Walk had told most of his friends a story to dine out on: cowering under the stairway with her niece, she envied the Professor's

[1] Published in 1948 as the first part of *Diplomatic Prelude 1938-9*.

indifference to raids and sirens; he was, she knew, sound asleep at the top of the house, oblivious of din and danger; but when, after the all-clear, she crept out stiff and thirsty and, on her way to the kitchen, heard the neighbours' doggies shrilly greeting each other on their walkies, she knew the Professor was suddenly wide awake and furious—he would sleep no more that night. From the yapping he fled deliberately. From blasted buildings he was made to move. Yet before his itinerant months ran out, L's bomb found him. Unhurt himself, he lost clothes, books, and papers. Having enrolled from the start as auxiliary Air Warden, he scrambled choking and groping into blast-damaged clothes and, having done what he could for his landlady, walked diagonally across the street to a house of which the door had been wrenched away. In a theatrically perfect set of desolation he found an old acquaintance, Mrs. St. John Philby—wrapped in a dressing-gown, her bright hair flecked with plaster—being helped by her daughters cheerfully to hand out cups of tea to their rescuers. For some time L was reduced to begging a bed, no longer even a room, from anyone who would kindly put him up for a night or two, in or near London. Not till spring 1944 could he settle down to his Academy lecture, in a boarding house that had been started up by some enterprising refugees in Brondesbury Park, north London. He was, of course, not alone to suffer distressing upheavals. A couple of days before his lecture I heard a typical V1 crash, and from my balcony saw smoke and dust billow up into a smooth sky of tender blue. Some thirty minutes later a friend of ours, Agatha Forbes Adam (whom I had known for about five years, and L since she married Eric immediately after World War I) was brought round by an Air Raid Precautions man on whom, bruised and tattered, she leant heavily. Her house, within fifteen minutes' walk from where I lived, had received a direct hit. Severely shocked she could remember no name or address except mine when asked at the first-aid post where they should take her. All she needed, the man assured me, was to lie quietly for some days in an airy, darkened room; which we could organize for her though the situation did make me doubt whether I would be able to hear L's lecture. It was a summer of continuous traffic disruptions caused by night and day raids. I might be a full hour on

11. L

12. L in 1958

the way to the hour-long lecture, and a third hour on the way back. Agatha should not have been left unattended that long; but she insisted I should go.

Most of L's lecture, *1848: The Revolution of the Intellectuals*— given on 12 July 1944 and described by Baffy as 'very Lewis-ish, packed with new stuff'—I had already heard or read. But L's delivery astonished me. There was no trace of the brilliant impersonator. He kept his voice level and allowed himself no gesture, only a telling change of facial expression now and then. His mind was communicating with other minds by the sheer power of words flowing freely yet chosen with meticulous exactitude. The result was in Baffy's words 'a tearing success'. I was telling Agatha about it when L arrived, intent on having my candid opinion. Pleased by my praise he ordered, rather than asked, me to join him in a prayer of thanks during which I gauged the quality and receptivity of the soil on to which Dr. Maclean's fiery reasoning about ritual and liturgy had fallen. L's prayers were to the point, fervent yet brisk. The liturgical shape he gave their sequence was a gem. Rising from his knees and nodding a message of encouragement to Agatha in passing her door, he hurried off to a dinner Baffy was giving at the Carlton Grill 'for a very few of his oldest friends'. 'Such evenings do one good,' she noted later that night.

The success of L's Academy lecture was no less important to him as a recognized historian than had been the achievement of his Ford Lectures when he was still establishing himself in academic circles. But he was only too well aware that his delight sparkled under a lowering sky. Increasing acts of terrorism by young Palestinians coincided with the approaching end of his wartime leave of absence. As the days shortened, his mind dwelt expectantly on the young people he would be returning to in the new year; and wretchedly on the young people who were being misled in 'the Semitic region'. Never a pacifist, he felt outraged that young Jews should be corrupted into stalking and killing individual Englishmen, selected by Jewish splinter-group leaders, in the name of some spectacular 'Deed'. No amount of grim provocation by the occupying power was for him a justification for older Jews to be wrongly conditioning such splendid, fresh human material. With sombre fire he spoke to me about the iniquity of deflecting the young into errant ways; and of his dread that Palestine Jewry might perish through internecine strife between the stalwarts of the Jewish Agency and the anarchical romantics. But he also sat very still for a long time, staring at me as I bent over my needlepoint.

He broke one such spell by saying his move to Manchester would be a good opportunity for tapering off his arrangement with Deirdre. Reluctant to express my indelicate thoughts on the difficulties which might arise between us if he carried his intentions through, I launched out into generalizations about its always being rash suddenly to break a relationship of long standing. But when he went on to complain about the tedium of visits for so narrow and definite a purpose, I had to agree that it must be pretty revolting. L did not return to the matter but on his first weekend in London after the beginning of the Lent term 1945, he said he had reached the certainty that we must get married despite the tiresome legal preliminaries which his divorcing Clara would entail after years of harmonious separation. All my feelings were against it. Of course one accepted the laws of the country one chose to live in. But for either of us to get embroiled in the sordid farce of an English divorce suit, was to me unthinkable. L hotly retorted that he knew it to be God's will for us and that nothing else mattered. Besides, only so could he retain his sanity as Palestinian Jewry committed suicide by internecine strife. Helpless to stop it, he would need my hourly support to face the dreaded situation. His arguments sounded very convincing, but I still could not admit that the act of sordid lunacy which he now favoured was compatible with divine wisdom; and, wearied by a heated argument that led nowhere, made the mistake of scoffing at his certainty about God's intentions for 'us'. Never before or after did I see L fly into such a frenzy. Flinging himself on his knees he clutched me by the legs with his beautifully shaped but unmanageably strong hands, commanded 'pray' and, resting his chin on my knees, proceeded to do so. I, born into a community of church people who prayed a lot and variously, had never heard the like; and his manner was to me highly distracting. Time and again L punctuated his words by giving me a great shake up, which I felt to be intended not for me but for God himself, whom L was shaking into action. In a mixture of English and Russian, of biblical phrases and everyday words, he demanded that we be led to see eye to eye in this, the greatest crisis in his life. Quietening down he declared, to the Almighty, that it did not matter which of us was led to see the situation as the other did. But see it in the same way we had to. Somehow this was to be brought about. His frenzy having spent itself, L rose, courteously took his leave, and asked me to pray again, in the same spirit, at 10.30 when he too would be praying. He laid great store by the simultaneity of prayer.

I knew he was dining with someone but would be careful to reach Brondesbury Park no later than ten. In the meanwhile I occupied myself with domestic trifles which were interrupted by L telephoning. He had picked up his mail at the Athenaeum where many people still wrote since he had left Gloucester Walk. In the batch was a letter from Clara which he read at once. She was in hospital dying of cancer. Would he come and say goodbye? L paused. I could find no words; and he hurried on to remind me how pathological a *malade imaginaire* she was and what an inventor of tales. He would see her of course, but first thing in the morning he would telephone Margaret Taylor in whose Oxford house Clara had recently been staying.

When he saw her, incredibly thin and tiny, Clara thanked L for having consistently been the one person she could in all honesty love and respect; and asked him to give some money to the Moslem cemetery where she wished to be buried. On 11 February she died, leaving him in her will £3,000 odd—a good portion of his allowance to her which she had hoarded for years while living in a state of penury verging on squalor. The Woking Imam suggested a pleasing, austere monument to mark her resting place, and expressed the wish to see engraved on the stone, 'For God we are and to God we go'—a quotation from the Koran. L's solicitors advised him on a fitting donation to the mosque and in about a year the matter was closed. I never ceased to marvel that L should have had his fit of frenzy when he did. Had he not had it, I doubt if Clara's death would have substantially affected my life. I was satisfied to leave things as they were. Yet the effect of her death on L perturbed me almost as much as had his behaviour before it.

On his return north, he resumed his duties in a condition of sombre self-hate bordering on a nervous breakdown during which he wrote to me sometimes twice daily, and occasionally telephoned.

A committee appointed to ferret out suitable quarters for staff and students in war-scarred Manchester and the neighbouring country, had found for L pleasant rooms in Alderley Edge, a Cheshire residential area at the foot of a long narrow hill, some ten miles out. As he roamed the wooded Edge and breathed in the frosty air, he brooded on all the pain he had caused his fellow humans without meaning to. Had I then known of the state in which Weizmann and Shazar had seen L after he had visited his father's grave in Merano in 1931, I might have better understood why a man utterly indifferent to the thought of dying should have been so deeply affected by the death of one to whom he imagined himself completely indifferent. I did not yet know how the fact that he could no longer make amends, for actions done or words spoken, increased L's self-hate. In the next weeks he told me much about it. Early on 16 February 1945 he typed, 'My heavy cold, much travelling, much excitement, wch, all-round, went even deeper than it seemed to, account for much.' In the evening he added,

I was unable to write any of my 1848 today. Too tired, stiff in the head. How much I wished I could talk to you, tho' it is hardly necessary; you have come to understand me w-out explanations.

Things were going through my head all day. My life falls into queer numerical patterns. I've noticed another: I was 28 when I married. I am now 56; half of my life I hv spent in that legal union wch ws real for only five years. What a mess I've made of my life. How weary I am. Write. [And in Russian] The weight on my heart is great.

On the following day he typed, 'I feel like after a long illness—and perhaps nt altogether after.' Determined to accept my decision about our marrying or not, in the spirit I wanted him to, L concluded, 'How strange that in the one thing wch now matters to me I can do nothing except wait. But I shall obey.' Next day he typed again,

I hope you didn't think me simply mad this morning. I had to talk to you: nervous panic came over me in the night, such as I can hardly remember. I felt as if you were in danger. And then I felt guilty, so guilty, toward you. It was hell. Bt the talk with you put it right.

That I should have helped him I was glad. But that he should have felt any guilt towards me was most odd. Think as I would, I could find no rational reason for it. Nor was there any clue in what he typed later in the day,

I was much more ill than I admitted. The last talk with C moved me to the depths. With me it always is delayed action, a 'slow motion' film. I still hear and feel all she said on her deathbed, the words of love and thanks and recognition after 22 years of separation, and then the prayer she and I said together [the Lord's Prayer recited in Russian by L]. The journey back ws v. peculiar. I shall tell you. Write.

During the first fortnight in March L typed, 'Worst are the days when I can think quietly: then the tension and horror come up. I am terribly tired; or, rather, weary'; and three days later, 'my hurried note ws a cry of pain—a pain wch gnawed me, day and night till I could bear it no more. It fastened on a detail'—Vera's lethal dose of veronal, always kept handy. A knock at his door stopped his swallowing it and, of that, he typed a further explanation,

The preceding Saturday I hd bn fighting hard to keep down a feeling of despair, and to adhere to the line we had agreed upon. Then something snapped. . . .
  The word horror does express what I hv bn passing thru'. Do you remember 'the clawing horror'? it hs come back in an intensified form —there is nt even the 'frozen hell' for protection any more. In these last ten days my life has bn passing before me with a clearness as if I were in the agony of death [a Russian expression, written in Russian]. How I hv ruined everything for myself! How little there is left! And what shall I make of it? I go about the Edge and think which way I shall lead you up so that you should nt tire. I feel as if soon we were to share things 'where rock and light are one'. Then comes the reaction: 'point de rêveries'. And I feel how poor I am—'roses red and roses white brought I for my Love's delight'; but I hv no 'blue roses'. And so it goes on, till I weary and cannot think or feel any more. It is my fate that during these crises when we should go through things together, we are, each time, separated.
  In spite of all this, I hv of course bn doing my full work, and hv even pushed on w 1848. . . .

My greatest pleasure during these last few days has bn reading at night *War and Peace* in Russian.

On 15 March L arrived in London for six weeks and we stepped into a new season. The war's increasing ugliness, grim enough when we met, was bogging down into squalor. Though VE day was already being mooted, V2s could still cover a street ankle-deep with the houses' shattered window glass. But even this nuisance dried up at source before we heard of Parliament's being dissolved and a Caretaker Government's being formed (prior to the Labour Party's resounding summer success). In memory the season is inseparable from our long saunters in Kew Gardens to enjoy the flowering cherries, magnolias, and the lilacs budding and then in full bloom; and during a cold or wet windy spell, inseparable from visits to the big art galleries where the returning old master-pieces were on view; or visits to the smaller galleries—offering us new delights, Epstein's Lucifer for one. But Kew predominates. Allowing for England's climatic vagaries, it was a hot, bright spring; which helped me quietly to consider the gist of L's recently disclosed sense of guilt towards me. Subject since child-hood to paroxysms of self-hate he had reached the conviction that every such paroxysm was a betrayal of those to whom he felt most attached at the moment. Only frenetic work, time and energy consuming, could keep an approaching paroxysm manageable; and he had learnt to take precautions against letting a paroxysm move to its logical end: our leisurely walks in the less frequented stretches of Kew Gardens culminated in his solemnly promising to throw away his veronal whenever we set up house together.

Other self-disclosures occurred when L spoke of the Raleigh Lecture that he was preparing for publication. In its printed version there are no impassioned words like those written in the late 1920s, on the native land being a man's lifegiving Mother and the state his lawgiving Father. Nor is there anything resembling that 'wellnigh mystical power' with which he had then endowed 'the ownership of space'. The opening up of lands occupied by Hitler had brought L news of his mother's death in Lwow from an incurable internal complaint, and of the almost miraculous survival in northern Poland of his widowed sister and her daugh-ters. Koszylowce was in communist hands. Lost for good, it was

moving into the realm of dreams recurrent long ago, now recol-
lected wistfully, and calmly except for occasional outbursts of
bitterness. L's considered view of national sovereignty had become
almost Olympian. He now thought it a principle 'as unsuited to
living organisms as chemically pure water'. Following through the
nineteenth-century collisions between constitutional articulation
(which he recommends) and the contemporaneous national movements, L sides on the whole with W. N. Senior to whom, in 1850,
the feeling of nationality was 'barbarous'—'the curse of Europe'.
Elected by Magdalen College, Oxford, to be Waynflete Lecturer
1946–7, and expected to speak at other 1848 centenary engagements as well, he could not drop European nationalistic embroil-
ments. But his tormented enthusiasm had been replaced by an icy
scrutiny. On the other hand, the strand of thought started up in
1913 by Mexico's General Huerta, was reaching its natural term
in the essay 'The First Mountebank Dictator';[1] while at the same
time Baffy noted, 'L is pulling out of Zionist work' which was
anyway moving to the States. It seemed L's life was being
rearranged to allow for a preoccupation which was to demand his
full, agonized attention.

L's adult interest in Christianity had been aroused in Balliol by
his reading the Gospel in Greek, the Old Testament in English,
and Calvin's *Institutions* in Latin; Edwyn Bevan's books on pagan
classicism's surrender to devotional Judaism had for a time fixed
L's interest on the early centuries of the Christian era; Dr.
Maclean's books and conversation had transfused L's intellectual
interest with warmth. In Manchester, after World War II, L drew
near T. W. Manson, Rylands Professor of Biblical Criticism and
Exegesis, who pressed him to read *The Influence of the Synagogue on
the Divine Office* by the Rev. C. W. Dugmore. Finding here
Dugmore's definition of worship: 'Man's evaluation of his growing understanding of God', L grafted it on to Maclean's arguments
on the possible psychological restorative virtues of ritual; and
soon shattered me by declaring an insuperable wish to drop
eighteenth-century English parliamentary history and the investigation of nineteenth-century European social convulsions, so as

---

[1] Included in *Facing East*.

to study in depth the most significant theme in man's development
—the emergence of Christianity on the shores of the Mediterranean in the ambience of the last century B.C. and the first two
A.D. He maintained that the situation had been misinterpreted and
misunderstood because never researched into as he would have
done—he would have attempted to detect the message of the
real church, lost when the Christian Synagogue was crushed
between conservative Jews and converted barbarians.

To dissuade L from pursuing his declared folly was not easy
despite his agreeing that total ignorance of Hebrew and insuffi-
cient knowledge of Greek and Latin as used in those centuries
were grave handicaps. Only when he began to relent did he reveal
he had been first activated by an urge to ritualize his allegiance and
self-dedication to Jesus Christ, of which allegiance he had written
in 1941,

Whether the 'tables were the work of God and the writing of God', or
whether they were the work of the People; whether the Sermon on the
Mount was spoken by the Son of God, or by a son of the People: these
events occurred in our midst, are part of our history, have determined
our fate, and through us the fate of the world. Nineteen centuries ago
our people divided: one branch, the Hebrew Nazarenes, carried into
the world our national faith coupled with their new tidings, the other,
as a closed community preserved the old tradition. Yet both were part
of one nation, and both are part of our national history.[1]

L's friends, Jews and Gentiles alike, had acclaimed the article; but
all had missed his intended implication—that baptism into Christ
was the proper development for a Jew aware of his people's
history in its worldwide significance. Recently he had realized
with horror, that as things were, no baptism into Christ could
come about unless a man penned himself into one or other
exclusive Church. Yet all such enclosures—from the most conventional group in the Catholic Church to the most anarchical
nonconformist sect—repelled him for some concrete reason.
Stressing to me how gradual and inevitable had been his desire for
baptism into Christ, and how impelling it had become, L was
exasperated that there was never time enough to go thoroughly
into matters that lay nearest his heart. But he found a way out: we

[1] *Conflicts*, p. 134.

should both spend Christmas at Wern-y-Wylan, a comfortable small hotel in Anglesey, overlooking Red Wharf Bay. It would do both of us good and we might at leisure discuss important matters which he only had time to raise in London.

I had been to Wern several times since the proprietors had invited me to stay as their guest for a long summer holiday in 1943. On 18 December 1945 L and I started out early in the morning to be greeted hours later with rare cordiality in a twilight exalted by an opaline brilliance. In the train he had told me we would presently be joined for a few days by Stanley Morison whom L had known for long but to whom he had recently drawn much closer, partly owing to Morison's appointment as editor of the *Times Literary Supplement* to which L was contributing important articles; but chiefly because Morison was a man of their generation for whom L felt a rare, active respect and who was, in fact, the only person besides me to know of L's intention to be baptized. A passionate convert to Roman Catholicism Morison had retained much of the sectarian intolerance of his Calvinist upbringing, and throughout his days in Wern spoke to me a great deal of the Church L ought to join. Recognizing that the Russian Orthodox Church was almost as good as his own, Morison insisted that I should bring L into it. But I did not think it right to do so, chiefly because L's burning desire was for 'baptism into Christ', not for being accepted into any particular community however congenial. In my view L's correct course was to consult his own conscience, prayerfully attuned to the divine will. L listened to our arguments with rapt attention but without commenting on them; and Morison's presence so dominated us that when he left, L and I were plunged into the state of cosy bereavement that draws those who remain closer together.

In the following days we spoke of all that seriously affected either of us. But one special theme of L's and one of mine predominated. His he called The Torn Out Pages, mentioned in the *Manchester Guardian* article on the U.S.S.R.'s 25th anniversary, on which he had sought my advice when we first met. The significant passage is,

Individuals and nations have to read the great book of life, in which the road traversed by mankind is recorded, before they can safely advance;

if parts are missing they turn back again and again in search of the torn out pages; and pay in suffering.

When 'the torn out pages' are many, their absence forms a 'great void and burden', which L detected in Russian history and suffered from in his own spiritual life. The Torn Out Pages had long been intended as the title of a novel to be written by him one day. When Clara drifted away from him, when Joseph disinherited him, and at other crucial moments in the intervening years, he had sketched out the novel's plan and fixed in his mind useful highlights and turning points. But only recently had he perceived that the void was the non-ground of an unmanageable sense of guilt.

In return I told L of my irreparable tragedy, which stemmed from my first deliberate and sustained effort in self-education. Having been taught from infancy to chat pleasantly in several languages, I had realized with a shock in the 1920s that I knew none well and could only ramble on in a haphazard way about frivolities in Russian, English, French, German, and Italian. Since my husband and I were trapped in the U.S.S.R. with no hope of getting out, and since he was being arrested and released with monotonous regularity, I settled down to learn Russian properly between enforced bouts of teaching elementary English and translating into Russian, from various tongues, technical and scientific reports and papers. It is a characteristic of the Russian language that profound knowledge of it incites one to write verse. I reached this stage while we were forbidden to live in Moscow or Leningrad. During my term of solitary confinement in a Moscow prison I learnt to compose verse without writing it down (there was nothing to write with or on). In a concentration camp I absorbed—through association with colourful criminals and heart-broken peasants—a crudely bubbling tongue new to me, which I could understand and appreciate but had never before heard. For a year I composed verse copiously, still without writing it down. Between my release and my departure for England, a friend typed as I recited them, the pieces she and I liked best. Presently some of the leading 'repressed' poets read the typescript. One said I had invented a new 'form' which, ripe to emerge, should catch on; another that the texture of my language had astonished and delighted him. Boris Pasternak sent me a message: if I left Russia that spring, a Russian poet of considerable promise would be committing suicide. What he never knew, since we no longer dared to meet, was that for me the choice was between the suicide of an emerging poet and the suicide of a mature person. My true choice in 1934 amounted to either my severing all links with the subsoil of a language I had made mine and my consequent floating about linguistically rootless; or my accepting cumulative degradations of body and mind before death came at the hand of a zealous servant of the regime, while I recited to myself—though to no one else, of course—poetry that I knew to be good. When I told L of my problem as to how to live for ever incommunicado on any but the most superficial levels, the drumming of a subsidiary thought warned me that I was being silly: L could no more understand what had befallen me than the rest of them, not one of whom had been anywhere near my wilderness of numb detachment. But I was doing L a grave injustice. The moral support he at once gave me was bestowed with the simplicity of perfect understanding.

We travelled back to London on 8 January, a few days before he went north to be tangled once more in his regular occupations and preoccupations.

CHAPTER FIFTEEN

Hindered Recovery
1946–1949

The Waynflete Lectures needed all the spare time L could give them. But twelve months later, on 22 January 1947, he confessed, in a letter to Alec Randall, a former pupil,

I have produced two books [on contemporary diplomatic history]. One consisting very largely of first articles in the *Times Literary Supplement*, which you may have read without knowing they were mine, will appear in March under the title *Facing East*. The other is a book which you specially wanted me to finish: *Diplomatic Prelude, 1938–39*. The instalments of *Coloured Books* which you read as they were appearing form only a small part of it. This book very nearly killed me. I had hoped to have finished it by November '45. Then the Nuremberg Trial came on and I realised that I would have to rewrite it, making use of the enormous material provided by that trial. And next, books of memoirs started appearing. Ciano, Noel, Bonnet, etc; collaborationist books which have come to our notice only since the liberation of France; a great deal of material from Polish sources, etc.

The Nuremberg trials mattered the more to L since surviving Jews, prevented from entering their forbidden land, were kept languishing in or near the exposed death camps of Europe. Besides, his father's legalistic approach to all complexities had left its mark. A careful study of *The Times* newspaper's Law Reports had long since become L's favourite recreational reading, and of the Nuremberg hearings he absorbed all one could. Gothick-ally fascinated, he was piecing together mankind's bestial leering face. And though intellectually and artistically stimulated by Sir Maxwell Fyfe's performance on the War Crimes and Crimes Against Humanity Tribunal, L was quickly disappointed in the general drift. His hope that mankind was about to recognize itself as a criminally-inclined species evaporated. The German

266

culprits—reasonably educated and well trained each in his own speciality—had not only been supported by millions of Germans but sympathized with, in the formative years, by further millions belonging to various nations. During the hearings the 'human instruments that managed the regime' for Hitler, were proved to have been hollow men whose emptiness only too easily reverberated to words emphatically repeated. When the detainees' turn to speak came, Baldur von Schirach, analysing in court his own misdeeds after listening to an account of them, declared that 'if on the basis of racial politics and anti-Semitism an Auschwitz was possible, then Auschwitz must become the end of racial politics'. His concern for the young whom he had long misled was sincere. And Hans Frank—a recent convert to Christianity—was heard cogitating on there being evil in all men. As early as January 1946 the disclosed network of organized atrocities had been subsumed by the French Prosecutor as 'a crime against the spirit'. But by mid-May Hans Frank feared that the Trial's 'moral purpose' was getting lost in the mass of evidence. Since the publication of *Mein Kampf* L had followed with compulsive attention the Nazi-type profanation of words—a set of lies plausibly strung together and repeated *ad nauseam* in the belief or hope that, working magically, they would generate the desired truth. Five years later he was to broadcast *A Study in Tyranny* on Hitler as 'the prophet of the possessed' to whom conscience was a Jewish invention and who, with hardly any conception of truth, became the spokesman of his nation's 'gutter elite'. In 1946 L observed how, week by week, minds as honest as they were brilliant let mankind's emerging sense of shame be smothered by the accruing weight of carefully worded circumstantial evidence. Soon the sheer bulk exacted concrete conclusions which could no longer be deferred. The Tribunal never entirely lost awareness of its basic significance. At the close Sir Hartley Shawcross reminded the court of what he had said earlier about the need for every misled follower to choose sooner or later between his leader's orders and the dictates of his own conscience; he continued to see the Trials as a milestone on the way to the recognition that the individual has more value than the state. But still, the reappraisal dear to L's heart was submerged. The legalistic mind is conditioned to apportion blame. At

Nuremberg blame was apportioned with scrupulous fairness. But once the blame is justly affixed, most law-abiding people shrug off any further concern. Pockets of persecution continued to simmer; and sequels followed of necessity.

It had been agreed that L should return for the Christmas vacation to Breams Farm, Tegan Harris's house in Essex, where he had worked well and had relaxed happily during much of the summer. Over Christmas he hoped to push on with his diplomatic books and put final touches to his Waynflete Lectures; but it had also been agreed that he should stay at the Athenaeum when the need for more details drew him for longer than a day to the British Museum or the London Library. On 30 December, having secured tickets for *The Family Reunion*, he fetched me after dinner. We did not have far to go, but all the way he complained of feeling ill, of having difficulty in dragging himself about and not knowing where to turn for advice—he was between doctors, as it were. I too had no regular doctor in those days and as I listened to the play—which I had seen more than once—wondered what to do. To my distress L insisted on seeing me home afterwards. By a stroke of luck though, as we approached the house, a taxi-cab drew up. While the passengers were getting out, I persuaded L to get in; and, thoroughly alarmed, I completed, before I fell asleep, a list of people to get in touch with the next morning. But before I had achieved anything worthwhile the Egyptologist Stephen Glanville telephoned: he had lunched beside L at the club, had been shocked by his ghastly mien and had driven him to his own doctor. Acute appendicitis had been diagnosed and a perforation was suspected. By another stroke of luck, one of the best surgeons was available and L was to be operated upon at once. A little later he telephoned from the London Clinic, gave the number of his ward and said he had entered me as his next of kin—the Sister would give me all the possible information whenever I telephoned. The doctor's worst fears proved correct. For some time the issue was uncertain. But next, pepped up by the post-operational drugs of the day, L was almost too cheerful; exasperated only at having stupidly lost so much of the time he had allocated to the Waynflete Lectures. On 17 January the Dugdales, Baffy and Edgar fetched him in their car and drove him to the Athenaeum. On the following day, he

was picked up by his senior assistant Eric Robson, accompanied
to Alderley Edge, and handed over to his most efficient landlady
who had been housekeeper for twenty years in a big 'Cottentot'
house, in the former grounds of which her husband still was head
gardener.

After Clara's death talks about our getting married had taken a
new turn. Well aware how I revelled in solitude L avoided nagging me, but jutted out his jaw to state he would never let go.
However long I dragged the matter out, he would be there. My
chief argument he dismissed out of hand. It was that I had been
too severely damaged by Stalin's men in body and mind ever
again to lead an active social life. L countered that others could
put right any misdeed those men had done; and my subsidiary
lines of opposition he never knew since I thought it best that he
should not. With and among people kindly disposed to L I was
meeting others who spread around, as authentic, injurious inventions about him which I could already recognize as false. In the
U.S.S.R. I had been surfeited with plausible lies often started as
mere jokes with a barb, then deftly used by someone as darts
dipped in lethal poison. From any such development of an invention L was safe in England. But I could not unlearn what life had
taught me about twittering men and did not relish mixing in
circles where the favourite pastime was the secreting of poisoned
words. When L fell ill, we had reached a dead-end, which he
unintentionally cut through by writing—in January from Alderley Edge—that after much torment his cardinal problem had
melted away. He would seek baptism into the Church of England
which could accommodate Calvin's austere intellectual integrity
together with L's own devotion to the mother of Jesus as a 'poor
little Jewish girl' good enough, because sufficiently pure in heart,
to be uniquely elected by her Maker and revered by multitudes of
men. When reverting somewhat later to this solution, he remarked,
'Simple things should not be made complicated, and things which
are of a passing nature should not be allowed to deflect those who
go to the rock-bottom things,' his words fell on to the ready soil of
my anxiety for him, and my course now became simple. On his
next visit to London we disposed of two matters, closely linked

but not causally connected—his baptism and our wedding. A couple of days later, on 16 March 1947, Baffy wrote,

L came. He intends to be baptised and is going to marry Julia de Beausobre. I never thought he would make up his mind to the first. [L had been accompanying Baffy to Sunday Service at Crown Court for years.] I knew he would not do it simply in order to marry her. He spoke with great dignity and simplicity. He is more Zionist than ever, convinced that Judaism and Christianity must in the end be reconciled, and that this can only happen in Palestine. I never felt so warm to him, he is now my oldest *great* surviving friend. He deserves to be very happy.

But from another quarter L got no understanding. Having arranged to see Weizmann before he left for Palestine, L started in much the same simple sentences as he had used to Baffy and me. But Weizmann cut in to advise categorically against our marrying —bound to be an all-round disaster. In loud-voiced irritation he talked for a long time, tightly knotting together the two strands of L's thought, and he finished by insisting that if L perversely wished to be baptized, he should keep it absolutely secret. L protested in vain that he was not asking for advice. Mental anguish, springing from one source or another, there had been, but that was over; his mind was now untroubled, his decision firm. As for keeping dark an event of paramount importance to him, why should he? 'Chaim behaved like a frustrated prima-donna,' L said to me several times, succinctly formulating the impression I had gained when I first saw the two men together soon after the Weizmanns had reached London in 1943, following a long absence abroad. Yet for L it clearly was a new observation; and it shook him. Later he brought me some character sketches of Weizmann, jotted down through the years. Warm, outspoken, meticulous, they capture the Zionist leader's most exasperating features as well as the most endearing and elusive ones. 'To understand the devotion people have felt for Weizmann,' wrote L, 'one has to hear him and somehow get under the magnetic spell which he casts when at his best' —'cold type cannot convey his words' effect. All written records fail to capture the spirit.' But he goes on to say, 'if Weizmann somehow gets across [a person] there is no way of putting things right. The situation will as likely as not lead to bitter hostility'.

Such hostility there was between Chaim and me from the start, though known, apart from him and me, only to Vera who did all she could to soften it. In the years to come L often regretted I had not known his 'old chief' at his best; the dim, often distorted shadow I knew was nothing to go by. Could be. But from that spring, all L's work for Zionism was ignored by Weizmann as if it had never been. While L's reaction to Weizmann's muddled obtuseness might well have been even milder had their talk at cross-purposes not coincided with worries over that most ill-starred series of events, L's Waynflete Lectures.

When he was brought back to Alderley Edge in January, every one of L's lectures on the German problem in 1848-50 was clear in his mind. For a unifying feature he had chosen a 'demographic analysis' of the Frankfurt Parliament. His aim was to disclose that parliament's character by carefully examining who 'the chaps', its members, 'really were and why each was there'. Every lecture formed a homogeneous whole yet also an integral part of the series, and their dovetailing was smooth. But no section was properly written out, and several minor issues were not yet cleared up to his satisfaction. As always, Manchester University proved sensitive to L's plight. His colleagues reduced his official attendance to as few hours as possible to encourage the husbanding of his strength for the weekly journeys to Oxford. But he remained unpleasantly aware of the after-effects of his operation and of having 'got into rather low water' before it, when 'desperately overworking for two years'. Besides, as for most of us in that outstandingly harsh and difficult winter of 1946-7 everything, even the daily routine, was an effort. L's train journeys between Alderley Edge and Oxford—wearisome at the best of times—were calamitous. Bitter frosts, heavy snowfalls, driving sleet and blinding blizzards started in January and continued well into March. Once L reached Crewe only to find the line to Bletchley blocked. Another time Oxford put him off at the last minute owing to a hopeless disruption of communications between Oxford and Bletchley. In the end, the last lectures—intended cogently to restate the problem perhaps grown diffuse through elaboration, and to suggest answers to it—were botched owing to examinations. His delivery was by many accounts 'brilliant', 'fascinating', 'spell-binding', 'unforgettable'; but he had spoken without notes and was left only with carefully typed lists and quotations. Separate lectures he still thought good, but—'due to the unfortunate conjunction between a harsh winter and the fixed course of academic life'—the last two or three had perforce been over-compressed. The ensuing deformity distressed him: his carefully traced line of thought had been damaged and blurred. The only thing left to do was to spend much time preparing the lectures for publication. How to find it? Far from well, he went off at the end of term to recuperate at Wern. But I could not go.

In the family of Prue Barrington, whose flat I shared, there had been serious illness which affected her general situation. Often absent in the last twelve months, and inclined to move back into the country, she had suggested I take over the flat, thus reversing our position there. After I had done so, the bitter winter imposed upon us acute discomforts. There were even drastic power cuts which led to our heating system's breakdown. By the time L was going to Wern, repairs were in progress, Prue was moving out in stages, L slowly moving in; furniture was being replaced and I—incapacitated by prohibitions and restricted by coupons for every-thing imaginable—scoured London for decorators. But to this tense bustle L returned in a mood of relaxed tranquillity, grate-fully to approve of everything, and to be 'baptized into Christ' on 15 April, in St. Faith's Chapel (Westminster Abbey) by the Dean, an old friend. Yet here too, L met with incomprehension.

Later the Dean told two of my close friends on different occasions that he could not make out why a man of such intellectual calibre should wish to join any Church when dozens were streaming out of whichever Church they belonged to. He also found odd L's dismissal of the conventional question about accepting Christ for the true Messiah. The hot retort had been that the question never arose. The term 'Messiah' was too fly-blown to make sense after all the Messianic pretensions voiced by European nations in the nineteenth century. For his own part L had, foolishly, as he later thought, risked communicating the trend of his thoughts and feelings that had made him a convinced Trinitarian. As he spoke he felt he was not getting through and quickly dried up.

Meantime a strong sense of universalism was penetrating into scraps of drafts for his Waynflete Lectures. Writing on nationalism —he says,

In between the Habsburg and the German national bid for European and ultimately world dominion intervenes that of the French, started by the proudest national King, resumed by a revolution national yet supernational, and consummated by an un-French Emperor of the French. That second bid for world dominion differs from that of the Habsburgs in that in its second phase it assumes a popular character and is borne by the masses; in that it bears throughout a national character and yet is universal through its high cultural values. The French language and civilisation had spread a French veneer over Europe before the French armies went outside their French-speaking country; and when these armies, revolutionary and Imperial, overran Europe they carried a human message and creative values which started the modern development of many a country.

The contrast with Hitler spreading abroad a form of Teutonic barbarism was obvious, but L did not stress it here.

His mood of benevolent universalism continued when I accompanied him to Alderley Edge, early in May, to be introduced to his Manchester colleagues and entertained by their families. The generosity on a shoe-string that I observed everywhere eloquently spoke of north-countrymen's abilities to be hospitable even in acutely adverse circumstances. Not only did I enjoy the visit, but my pleasure appears to have been shared. Eric Robson, in his letter of congratulation after our wedding, told L how happy, indeed relieved, the whole body of his assistants had been to see L was not marrying the highly unsuitable flibberty-gibbet that gossip had made me into.

The Russian priest in charge dissuaded us from being married in the big church off Buckingham Palace Road. Waiting to be demolished, it stood boarded up, dejected, dark and bleak. The light, cosy chapel attached to the priests' house off Fulham Road suited our occasion better though it was not entitled to keep a registration book; because of this 4 June 1947 began with our going to Hammersmith Registry Office and was a long, patchy day. To recover we went into the country almost at once; and spent most of what remained of the summer staying with several of L's oldest friends. Many lived in sections of their down-at-heel

houses, much frequented by L in the days of style and splendour.
Worst off were people whose houses and grounds, having been
requisitioned, bore the scars of a heavy siege. Even the stairway
balustrade had been ripped out of one. Many owners, while
bargaining with the authorities about derequisitioning, compensation and repairs, camped in a gate-house, an agent's house, or
some village house that had fallen vacant. But there were signs of
indomitable creative adaptability. Pre-war talk about eighteenth-
century papers was resumed between L and owners pondering
what best to do in the straightened circumstances. Depositories in
county towns were much discussed. A new era was dawning for
the custody of family papers. We examined on the spot as many
concrete possibilities as we could before L was due to return north
where I would probably join him. It was not to be. His kind and
efficient landlady had a son, who, demobilized and about to be
married, had failed to find a house near his post-war job. Forced
to live with his bride in his parents' home for a year at least, he
was moving into L's rooms and the one I had hoped to occupy.

Before the end of Michaelmas term L transferred himself to
Disley, postally still in Cheshire but geologically part of the Peak
District. The village, formerly all built of local stone, stands 2,865
ft. above sea level, and L's bedroom—to his intense delight—
commanded a northward view across sweeps of ruggedness to
the majestic, seemingly close at hand, Kinder Scout. After Easter I
joined him in the 'crisp air' he praised; and I have seldom shivered
so much. But at Disley I found a new pleasure. It had become clear
to me that L could no longer count on owners of important
documents regularly fetching him from their local railway station.
Not only was petrol rationed but chauffeurs were being snapped
up, as they were being demobilized, by various Boards. The
obvious thing was for me to buy a car and learn to drive it. I
found a competent instructor not far out of the village, and we
soon looked forward to moving about regardless of railway
tracks. Together it seemed we could overcome the adverse circumstances heaped up around us; but we were soon reminded of
our vulnerability. On the eve of 'English-Evacuation Day' Ben-
Gurion proclaimed the emergence of an independent Jewish state
on to the international scene, and named it Israel. L was irradiated

with a new joy, but it was pierced with new apprehensions. The tiny malformed state was woefully insecure, like every new-born thing whatever its ancestry. Could it be that any birth was a fool-hardy hazard? Such cogitations were cut short by Baffy's death at Kilkerran—her daughter's eighteenth-century Ayrshire home—on the day of Israel's self-affirmation. As we briskly walked for the last time to and from L's favourite haunts, he stopped now and then with his hands resting on the crook of his walking stick of which the ferrule was pushed far into the turf. And with eyes see-ing beyond the accidents of landscape, he murmured, 'No Baffy, I can't believe it, I can't take it in.' Yet we had known for more than a year about the serious condition of her heart.

A few days earlier the university had suggested L take up at last his sabbatical leave, cancelled by them at the outbreak of war. To do so suited him well. Requests for articles and lectures on the centenary of the 1848 revolution had been pouring in and demand-ing prompt attention. To Alec Randall in Copenhagen he wrote on 15 January 1948, 'I have accepted to address the Academia Nationale dei Lincei in Rome. The invitation is not merely an honour but a great pleasure now that we cannot easily travel unless invited.' Neither of us had been abroad since before Munich. Although keen to go, we had been prevented by the stringent currency regulations which continued for years.

Habitual Italian hospitality, lavish without ostentation, en-veloped us on the outward going aircraft and remained with us till we arrived back at London airport a fortnight later. As for the Congress, planned by the Fondazione Volta and the Academia, it proved an eye-opener and indisputably rewarding though exhausting.

The business of the conference was kept in hand by a request that all papers be sent in at an early date, for the translator's benefit; and that the summary, spoken in the original tongue, should last for no more than a quarter of an hour. Here some failed. L's turn followed two men who had outstripped their limit by an hour or so. When he closed on his fifteenth minute the spontaneous applause was deafening. For a second his eyes, as they met mine, registered an urchin's amusement; and when he rejoined me he murmured that the acclamation must have been due to the learned audience's grateful relief not to their approval of what he had said, which few could have grasped before the translator had spoken.

The Rome Conference offered the opportunity of bringing Italy into L's work on 1848. Mazzini and Cavour had fought under one banner with their French, German, Slav, contemporaries, but in an Italian way, consonant with their own background. In the last sentences of his Lincei lecture[1] L was able to call on his own experience of the nations' interlocked conflicts and mutual dependence not only because Europe was a homogeneous though variegated entity, but because for him the Paris Peace Conference with its aftermath had provided the occasion to see the same basic situations at work in a way typical of the years 1919–24, a period which formed for L a bridge between 1848 and 1948.

Looking about for means to break L's sleeplessness, which was troubling him greatly even after our return to London, I spoke of moving to more spacious quarters, easier to run. He bade me wait: all his essays on contemporary diplomacy would have to be finished before he could bear my shifting him and his papers whose sheaves grew weekly. Moreover, he liked his bedsitter: tranquil as no other place he remembered sleeping in, it captured every sunbeam that broke over London and it opened on to his well-sheltered 'reading balcony'.

But the composition of the Waynflete Lectures was proving itself a nagging harassment. He had found aggravating gaps in his nineteenth-century material, and in moments of distress was inclined to exaggerate their importance. The documentation he lacked could have survived in Frankfurt or Vienna. Yet the mere thought of going into lands which had so recently flourished as Jewry's hell, nauseated him. He never went; and increasingly detested himself for not going. Fortunately his other two involvements entailed obligations he enjoyed. The finishing touches to his last essays on pre-war diplomacy required our entertaining to lunch or dinner people, chiefly recent émigrés, whose first-hand knowledge of the 1936–40 diplomatic transactions had to be extracted and absorbed before they moved away or lost touch with their past. Resolutely wearing in public their most light-

[1] 'Nationality and Liberty'.

hearted masks, these men and women nevertheless spread a feeling of impermanence akin to despair. Consorting with them intensified L's awareness of mankind's fragility, and intensified his compassion for the young to whom he was due to return in the autumn. The young were to the fore in his mind when we drove out of London to further L's third concern, eighteenth-century parliamentary history. On the whole we found little solid fare for his own book, on the Rockingham government, but many tit-bits for his research students.

CHAPTER SIXTEEN

Malgré Tout
October 1949–August 1952

After L's sabbatical leave his relations with colleagues and pupils remained much the same as before. But his deafness had grown much worse and his determination to catch the meaning of elusive sounds was moulding a scowl into his heavy-featured face. Desperate concentration made him look fierce even when he was at his mildest. To my suggestion that he should be as frank with others about his deafness as he was with me, he simply said he could not bear to be. But those who liked him well did not seem to register the scowl. The Buxtons' eldest child has written, 'He might have been an awe-inspiring figure but I don't remember him like that—he always took us seriously and was completely himself'. A granddaughter of A. L. Smith held the same view. Consuming in her mother's Oxford garden a plateful of ripe plums when this 'niece by adoption' was about to become an undergraduate, L read her 'first piece of history writing'; and casually made of it her 'first lesson in essay writing'. But L's regular method of teaching his pupils to write by making them write on any subject they cared about was not always appreciated. One pupil explains that a certain essay class 'did not see how writing on "any subject" would help their degree course'. It was not that L had changed his ways. But the ambition of university students had been re-orientated. The average undergraduate was already developing the rat-race mentality and felt irritated by L's whim. 'I was struck by his intolerance and impatience', writes the same pupil. 'Remarks made by members of the class were summarily dismissed. I could understand why he was not popular.' Yet an undergraduate who found L congenial says,

To my knowledge he was the perfect teacher for he encapsulated you with himself on the same footing so that his concentration was directly experienced and his restless omnipotent mind moved you also. The sheer loving-kindness of the man spellbound me as much as my admiration for his astonishing mind.

In accord with this student's sense of being encapsulated, a psychiatrist who knew us well wrote to me after L's death, 'he belonged to those rare people who intensify those they meet'. Through years of work, thought, and caring, L had evolved a way to discover, draw out, and exercise a pupil's thinking abilities much as a musician training voices discovers, draws out and stabilizes a voice through guiding and exercising it.

His approach to examinations had by now taken a new turn. Towards the end of a Lent term he told one of his classes that he intended shortly to give them an exam. John Brooke, another of his pupils in these years, writes,

Its real purpose was to test the quality of minds and the students' understanding of their work. He would have been prepared to let the candidates use any books they wished so that they should not be bothered with trying to remember dates and quotations.

One of L's tenets was that memory is best trained and can best be profitably exercised in childhood. Consequently, not bothering about that, he raised the matter of some more suitable innovations with his colleagues. They turned them down, and he devised the following compromise:

His method [says Brooke] was to set about half a dozen stock questions which were pretty much the same from year to year, and to ask the candidates to choose two and write upon them fully. He said we would not be invigilated during the examination, that the senior student would collect the papers from his secretary beforehand and return the questions afterwards. If you talk to one another, he said, you will only waste your time, and if you help one another I shall know about it. . . .

After the examination he saw each one individually in his room and commented upon [the] papers.

Even more than previously L's teaching was aimed at spotting teachable minds. When he found one, he cherished it. Elected Honorary Fellow of Balliol in July 1948 he wrote to the Dean, A. B. Rodger, in a letter expressing gratitude and delight, 'What I really like is to train the young in research.' Though his open lectures—to which the avid came from near and far—were L's most spectacular contribution to academic life in the resurgent Midlands, J. R. G. Tomlinson wonders how many of those present were 'of sufficient intellectual distinction' to appreciate 'LBN's off-beat conglomeration of cultural backgrounds which was his hallmark' and could 'trigger off new insights into history'. His 'insight into humanity' and his ability 'to speak with deep emotion and yet avoid sentimentality' did tighten L's hold on large audiences. But for all that, his 'immediacy of historical experience' came over most tellingly in seminar and private discussion. There, writes Tomlinson, 'One often felt one had been talking to someone who had heard Townshend's champagne speech and seen Pitt carried into the Commons with his crutches and red flannel. This I am sure made more sensitive our antennae.'

A strange enough character when he first appeared in Balliol, L's chequered career, ill-assorted interests, and especially his unpopular (post-1930) political views and enthusiasms, stated clearly and expounded with vehemence, had built him up into a controversial figure. Seldom merely liked, he was either much loved or ardently detested. As time went on, the dislike spread by contagion to less scrupulous men who knew next to nothing of him and based their attacks—if not on hearsay—on some phrase, chapter or, at best, a long essay, picked out of the context of others. Such cavalier treatment of his meticulous research and careful phrasing enraged L. And yet, in keeping with his hallmark of oddity, the mounting adverse criticism made him more widely known than had his useful actions or brilliant techniques. The irreconcilable impressions he made and the misinterpretations they fostered are perhaps easiest to grasp in the light of a report on a Rorschach Test which he subjected himself to in December 1942:

Intelligence superior and concrete. Approach often intuitive. There is also evidence of imagination. The number of details is too small to say he is a practical person. In fact he can hardly be bothered with details however important. He is most interested in the crux of a problem (Proof: of 25 responses, 9 were focused on the centre of the plate).

Originality striking as well as convincing (original answers were of a superior quality).

His experience range is ambiequal—he is capable of introversion (inner life) as well as of outgoing interests. There is no preponderance of the one side of his personality. In view of his high intelligence and originality, he could be described as intelligent in a general way rather than gifted in some particular manner. He might undertake various tasks with good prospects of success and is not tied down to any one specialised interest.

But his being ambiequal is strenuous and, due to his compulsive neuroses, has led to considerable ambivalence. Often he is uncertain whether to pursue his original inner life or to lead a life that is active.

Some of his feelings allow him to develop intimate contacts. But unrelated impulses of a more egocentric quality are in marked evidence. Well aware of these impulses, he keeps rigid control of them. Yet not stable enough to be always in control of particularly strong impulses, he can erupt into sporadic explosions.

Danger fascinates him, and he is quite capable of getting nearer to it than he can stand. The strangest fact is that he knows all this well, since his capacity for introspection is remarkably high.

His powerful tensions require of him rigid self-discipline, and his demands on himself may be exaggerated; from which result frequent feelings of failure; also a cautious shyness that ill suits the occasional aggression against himself or others.

Capable of sympathy and tact, he has social interests, but not much love of people. Most of his interest is directed to his own ego.

Remarkably versatile for his age, he is perhaps even too distant from any stereotyped approach. Which is not to say he is unmethodical but, rather, that his method is his own, ingenious and intuitive, not one of organized routine or regularity of procedure. In fact he tends to despise the usual care of formality. Still, his originality and lack of set ways leave him enough common ground with others for him to be in close touch with reality.

Capable of considerable anxiety (the sources of which are known to him) he is also liable to worry unduly.

Though he does not love others much, sympathy can be roused in him against his wish. Also he is generous and tactful.

His fate is to bear the brunt of his being ambiequal. This middle line forms the connection between his inner and outer potentialities, which adds to his marked interest in it.

An intellectual in the sense that his range of consciousness is wide, he is also an intellectual because this sphere is strongly emphasised in him. His extreme repressions and inhibitions are not always maintained; and his unrelated impulses can be overpowering.

Controversies between L's well-wishers and ill-wishers, grown shrill, brought him unsought, and unintended, publicity. His name was being bandied about. Its syllables were soon used for

conjuring up new concepts. The Vice-Chancellor of his university esteemed him one of its brightest assets; and we were
presently bidden to our first Royal Garden Party. The courtesies
of entertaining transatlantic academics—who once again reached
England in droves—followed as a matter of course. We gaily
paddled about in scintillating company; while lost currents of L's
life-stream were surfacing and others, for long vigorously conspicuous, were silting up in the sands of his past.

During one of our more impressive social rounds L was
sounded, by an habitually reticent friend, about a possible revival
of Jos Wedgwood's defunct, or dormant, History of Parliament.
Asked if he would take part in shaping it, L gave a noncommittal
answer. Two such schemes had already faded out; until he knew
more of the third scheme's exact purpose (and who were to be his
colleagues) he had nothing to say. Sworn to infrangible secrecy,
he assumed nothing would come of it. Yet the seed began to
germinate. Over a cup of tea at the Athenaeum, while encouraging
a former pupil to push on with a particular piece of eighteenth-
century work, L mentioned that 'he himself would soon be
returning to eighteenth-century parliamentary history'; and he
started to bring home road maps, carefully to plot excursions into
the country. Late in the summer we left on our first 'cross-
country paper chase', as L came to call the expeditions which in
the next seven years took us all over England, and also into Wales
and Scotland, to locate the whereabouts, and assess whenever
possible the usefulness, of parliamentary papers still kept in private
muniment rooms or already deposited with local Record Offices.
His old interest in local history—a contributory factor to the new
project—was falling into its last resting place.

Contrary to L's supposition the revival of Wedgwood's
enterprise was again spoken of in strict confidence round about
Christmas. L's response was to take driving lessons when he
returned to Disley—he would share with me the strain rather than
the pleasure of cross-country motoring. He also pressed me to
apply for additional petrol coupons. But to his chagrin L had to
give up his generous intention. What with jerky movements,
deficient hearing and an increasingly stiff neck, he could never

make a safe driver. Acceptance of the disappointment was softened only by his becoming instead a most accomplished 'navigator'. First of all he would pore over his maps to trace the most direct route to our goal; then he would puzzle out the pleasantest secondary roads. And since few of the sign-posts or place names removed when Hitler threatened invasion had been put back, he rejoiced that his 'sense of direction' equalled his powers of observation. And indeed, our expeditions could not have been better managed, not even our tricky drive north when the Disley household was breaking up and L again had nowhere to live.

His Vice-Chancellor—a graduate in medicine though he early took up a teaching and administrative career—realized the effect Manchester's damp gloom was likely to have on L's chest and strongly advised his settling in Buxton, some 1,000 ft. above sea level. The department's secretary found for us a hotel from which to reconnoitre, and L hoped he might arrange to stay there till Christmas at least. It proved too noisy and pretentious, with food fussy yet meagre. Despondent we walked about the town and drove about the immediate neighbourhood till at last the owner of the garage where I kept the car at night, and the newsagent at the corner, told us of a house perched high above a steepish slope leading to the railway station. Not exactly a guest-house it was run by an amiable enthusiast of the theatre and had within living memory been packed with actors. As it had fallen on empty days owing to some crisis among its chief clientele, its landlady could at once let L have two lofty, rather bleak rooms for as long as he wished, and I could have a smaller, warmer one for a week. We liked the landlady, the crisp air, and the view. The food we were served was neither skimped nor untasty. But I wondered to myself miserably how safe that winding slope would be in winter for a preoccupied old man decreasingly sure of his movements. L, however, had no misgivings. His mind was on other things. Before we drove south again—aiming to reach London during the first week in October—he fetched from his room in the university a slim file with old papers, for me to read attentively after he had returned north by train.

First in the folder came L's 1928 letter to Wedgwood which, taken to Whittingeham by Baffy on that distant Christmas, had impressed A. J. Balfour. Having stated that the House of Commons was a 'microcosmos of the British political nation', L explained why and how a 'careful analysis of its personnel throughout the centuries' would 'show the rise and decline of classes and interests, and elucidate the inner structure of British politics'. His own work on 1761–84, had proved to him that the 'survey of one single period must needs be more or less static, movement being shown by comparison only'; a number of consecutive surveys should correct this and establish the factor of change. Next in the folder came an undated four-page memorandum according to which a departmental committee of M.P.s and historians (L among them) was appointed by the Treasury in 1929 to examine Wedgwood's scheme. In 1932, having issued an Interim Report and having thereby served its purpose, the departmental committee was discharged. Its historian members had given their support, L wrote, 'to a particular scheme, to be carried out in a particular way'; soon after which the History of Parliament proper emerged; with a new committee consisting of Peers and M.P.s gathered 'for the purpose of raising funds; and presumably also to exercise a general supervision over the work'. The new entity 'had the good-will of the historian-members of the departmental committee but none of them was asked to join it. In the summer of 1935 a group of distinguished historians was got together constituting an advisory sub-committee.' Except for an American scholar, 'the sub-committee included none of the parliamentary historians who had served on the departmental committee; nor was it a committee of parliamentary historians'. Its scope was extended to include the House of Lords and 'many subjects which the expert historical advisors would have warned the committee against'. A prospectus and one volume (Wedgwood's) having been produced, the venture drifted into abeyance. Third in the folder came typed jottings for a character sketch of 'Jos'. Some of these are incorporated in L's review[1] of Wedgwood's *Testament to Democracy*—a glowing tribute to a deceased friend. Incompatibility of opinions on the History's purpose and organization had been obvious and differences vehemently expressed. But neither L nor Wedgwood lost his warm regard for

[1] Reprinted in *Avenues of History*, p. 171.

each other. L admired the 'champion of unpopular causes' in whom burnt a light, 'a fire, more valuable than logic and precision, and far more sacred than mere intellectual achievements'. Wedgwood admired the steady flame of L's unpopular Zionism and his scrupulous examination of historical evidence followed by an imaginative drawing of conclusions. The clash and struggle of two characters basically attractive to each other, and captured within a slim folder chock-a-block with facts, fascinated me. None but the participants could have known more of the relevant data than I did by Christmas; and as the third attempt to launch a History of Parliament gained momentum, L's most cursory allusions made sense to me. In February 1951 the 'Government announced their decision to give support' to a History of the House of Commons and L was 'put in charge of the modern period covering the 18th and 19th centuries'. Told of it, my first thought was that the government had served me a trump card. I would play it to speed up L's retirement from his professorship— at sixty-five not seventy. If he did he would leave 'Boo' (as we had come to call those slippery slopes) in the summer of 1953. Two more perilous winters were better than seven. On the plea that his pension would be larger if he stayed on, and because he wanted to steer some of his new undergraduates towards their theses, L had been resisting my pressure. Now my arguments prevailed; and six years later he wrote, 'a man like Fox is not determined by his wife—except when she voices his own unavowed thoughts and feelings'. In this case at this time L was in this matter a man like Fox.

But L's students still were his chief concern. The History of Parliament seemed to offer senior scholars a remarkable opportunity for training young historians through a new mode of supervision. Men of his stature L saw directing the initial work of able but half-ripe historians into channels which would be profitable to the nation and also a contribution to mankind's evaluation of its past; while they, the experienced historians, should remain mindful of the young careers that they were inconspicuously shaping. He deemed that sensitively co-ordinated work should leave each one free to reach conclusions off-beat perhaps but, owing to the agreed framework, restrained from being unprofitably wild. He surmised that in some ten years the nation could be enriched by a considerable body of vigorous historians both meticulously exact on facts and daringly imaginative in conclusions. Of it he spoke to me with emotion in Balliol on 20 April 1951. His honorary fellowship could at last be marked by a small celebration. Despite all hindrance, redecorations had been completed in the Master's Lodgings and as I helped L—in the new guests' suite—with his black tie that he could no longer deftly manage with hands increasingly deprived of their cunning, he spoke of A. L. Smith, and also of Sligger whose enduring friendliness had made accessible to L the Bute papers in the late 1920s. L acclaimed the two great teachers' tradition of nursing and fostering their pupils' careers and hoped never to fail in vindicating their opinion of him as a proper successor. But for how long would he be able to bear the strain of constant travelling between London and Boo which was noticeably sapping his energy? Communications by rail between the two places were increasingly complicated and tedious.

Largely owing to his mounting physical disabilities L presently felt 'obliged to take leave of pre-war diplomatic history' at least till his main task in the History of Parliament was completed, as he explained in the Preface to *In the Nazi Era*. Actually he never returned to it; and rightly. Seen in the full context of his life the three books written between 1940 and 1951 are the summary of a lifetime's observations transfused with close thought and based on a vast output of official and personal records going back to 1915 at least. He had started *Diplomatic Prelude* as a comparative and critical analysis of official collections of documents, and it remained anchored to L's 1915–19 involvements in European affairs. *Europe in Decay* goes on from there to dissect the Continent's political and moral disintegration between 1936 and 1940, doing so chiefly through the scrutiny of memoirs written by statesmen whose policy of inveterate compromise had failed to preserve peace in Europe. *In the Nazi Era* considers the responsibility of two groups of men—Germans who served Hitler, and Europeans who served his purpose by surrendering to fear of him. As the momentous events of the 1930s—experienced and cogitated, ferreted out, and recorded by L—ceased to be his concern, they joined other strands of his past from which he readily drew advice when it was asked for. At the end of 1951 he gave an old friend, Sir Walford Selby, who was trying his hand at writing contemporary history, his 'very frank opinion' on it: 'A difficult and invidious job.' 'Beware,' he cautioned, 'of suppression, exaggeration, *obiter dicta*, and excessive repetition.'

Oxford had meantime invited L to deliver the Romanes Lecture —one of its highest honours. In perfect accord with his prevalent mood he chose to speak on Monarchy and the Party System, spotlighting the ability of both institutions to accept and use life's shifting challenges. But he was frank about having felt unsure of himself. 'I have never been so nervous, for a reason you may think curious,' he presently wrote to Dr. Enid Starkie.

It was the first time I had thoroughly prepared [a lecture] and written every word of it. Then I wondered if this would not work like tangle-foot for a fly; or if by speaking some and reading the rest, I would not make it sound like a comic opera where parts are sung and others spoken. If I escaped all these dangers, I am thoroughly glad.

To his immediate satisfaction though, he had made of the lecture a bridge between his past (notably the Ford Lectures of 1934) and his future. To describe significant changes in the re-shaping relationship—the adjustments made by sovereign and parties—L had of course chiefly examined the second half of the eighteenth century; but, on occasion, had ranged outside his 'narrow field', turning intrusions into opportunities for mentioning collective research. Of the scholars whose domain he had entered he named fourteen (in the published text) but acknowledged his indebtedness to many more, with whom he also hoped to work on the History of Parliament 'as a team, exchanging ideas and information'. Coincidentally, admirers of his work were getting his past services rewarded and, unawares, affecting his future.

A few days before L delivered his Romanes Lecture he came into my room wearing an expression of utter consternation. In his hand was a stiff official-looking letter. At the request of the Prime Minister he was being informed of a suggestion that his name be submitted to the Queen on the occasion of the forthcoming list of Birthday Honours—with a recommendation that she may be graciously pleased to approve that the honour of knighthood be conferred upon him. Waving the letter, L advanced towards me repeating, 'Why? But why?' till a smile had wiped out his look of bewilderment. Leaving the house to consult someone who knew how officially to express joy without betraying naïve astonishment, L bound me to absolute silence on the matter till it was announced, in a month's time if ever; and neither of us spoke of it to anyone before his name appeared in the Honours List of June 1952. After his lecture, agog with uncertainty at first, but next aglow with delight, L concentrated on marking examination papers which were coming in by the stack. Finished with that—and having set me to acknowledge the remaining pile of congratulations on his Honour as well as to destroy a swelling trickle of the usual unsigned abuse that accompanied the publication of anything by or about him—L amused himself with planning our next expedition, to Newcastle.

The University of Durham had invited him to come and be awarded his first honorary D.Litt. Though a long drive, it could have been a simple one, were it not for L's passion for dovetailing things. Despite his having been given leave of absence, expressly to help start the History of Parliament, he wished to be in Manchester for some viva-voce exams and, between times, insisted on putting in a good deal of work on the 4th Duke of Devonshire's papers at Chatsworth. Moreover, on our way back he chose to stay with his old friend, and former colleague, Professor Edward Hughes who was writing a book L greatly cared about. Based on the manuscripts of Northumbrian and Durham families, it pieced together north-country life as lived between 1700 and 1750. L's enthusiasm detained us at Hinchcliffe Manor so long that we reached London barely in time for his investiture.

As I prepared to drive him to Buckingham Palace I wondered how I would acquit myself of my dual function. Where and when should I cease to be L's driver and become his family? I need not have worried. By the police of the inner court I was told—as if by a benign, firm, experienced nanny—where to drop L, what to do with the car, and how to rejoin him. Fittingly poised and under different guidance, we branched away from each other on the stairway; to meet again on the way out. By L's side stood Arnold

Lunn, who had devoted himself to ski-ing since they graduated. L introduced us and went off to fetch his hat and gloves, while I heard moving words on the spontaneous friendship that had sprung up between them in Balliol, never to weaken though they seldom met. Before the day was out we were having champagne with Bob Boothby—the first of many celebrations that kept me gyrating by L's side till we left on our autumn paper chase that was already taking shape in L's mind despite his being engrossed in an address to a conference of parliamentary historians. The immediate purpose of the conference was to discuss the shape and contents of the History of Parliament in its third embodiment. In this address L expressed the hope that the assembled scholars would use the provided opportunities fully in order to establish enduring contacts; he then proceeded to expound his ideas about the History presented sketchily, as 'dry bones', in the previous summer to the Anglo-American Conference. A surviving note for that, 1951, address says,

A planned piece of historical research must start with two inter-connected questions: what will be its component materials, and what its purpose? For the purpose will determine the processing of the material; and the material, formless at first, will give substance and solid outline to the design. The History of Parliament on which we are now engaged will be based on the biographies of members of the House of Commons who sat at Westminster (or thereabouts) from the second half of the 18th century till 1901; and nothing shall be made part of the structure we are trying to raise but what is contained in those bio-graphies, or emerges from them. It is therefore not our task to write constitutional history, nor to record the work of Parliament, not to deal with its procedure, nor to compile debates which are unreported or inadequately reported; although each of these subjects bears closely on our studies, and will in turn be affected by them, directly or through byproducts. Our interest centres primarily on the anatomy of the House; but inherent in anatomy is physiology—and a proper study of living substance cannot be oblivious of its functions. In short, our History of Parliament will be a dictionary of parliamentary biography grouped, stratified and analysed in a number of self-contained, manage-able sections to form in the aggregate a motion-picture-film of the House of Commons: it is, especially in the last few centuries, the most important single corporate body in the State, and as such supplies a most significant cross-section of the political nation.

In 1952 he expanded his theme to state that the History was not envisaged as a 'mere' dictionary of parliamentary biography,

The biographies collected in each section are the raw material for analytical work which will extract and sum up whatever can be distilled from it. . . . From the analysis of the House through the ages will emerge a social and economic history of the nation such as has never yet been attempted. . . . The way in which men became Members, their political birth, will be [a] basic aspect of our History. . . . The individual biographies when strung together will supply a pattern of the history of families and classes; of their rise and decline. . . . In terms of country houses, and manor houses and vicarages, and counting houses, and finally of workshops and factories can be written the history of this country.

Much of the nation's past could be

documented through the membership of the House, the goal—at least in the last 250 years—of all who could hope to reach it. The great representative value of the sample is that it is not the researcher who has selected it; it has selected itself.

The sample was widely serviceable too: take the political aspect,

Only through the study of the individual Members, the interest on which they sat in the House, and the nature of the groups which they formed can [you] trace the rise and the history of party formations: the basic elements in modern British constitutional history.

As for 'the cultural and educational side: you can trace it too in the sample. The average even more than the outstanding.' At the back of L's mind was a constant readiness to weigh the significance of averages. In adolescence he had been trained to use statistics whenever possible and appropriate; the analyses of parliaments which he had made in the 1920s had stirred up an interest in their 'average' Members—elusive, pale, public figures yet often rugged or flamboyant men, more enigmatic, and so more attractive to him than those with a well-defined (almost obvious) public image. He had of course valid rational explanations for it. Already in his letter to Wedgwood seen by A. J. Balfour, he had written,

In scientific work the last ten per cent are the salt one has to put on the bird's tail. This last ten per cent of rather obscure Members . . . is from the social point of view the most interesting part of the House.

Forecasting in a wide sweep our future paper chases L had also said to the parliamentary historians,

There can hardly be a political correspondence which does not enter into our purview. Few studies on economic history do not touch on parliamentary biographies. A very large proportion of the history work in this country bears in one way or another on the work we are attempting to do.

The work of hundreds of scholars in ever widening concentric circles can and will contribute essentially to our work.

How to organize co-operation among so many?

When going through a collection of manuscripts each must do the work for all of us grouped together. If I know that A is working on the history of a county or a borough, B on the history of a family, an estate or of an individual, C on the history of a trade, or D is editing a certain correspondence, I shall make it part of my task to inform them whenever I come across material of interest to them, naturally on the supposition of due reciprocity.

At last L had found (or was founding?) a group to which it seemed he could whole-heartedly belong. The lone worker was attempting to use men—himself in the first place—as builders' blocks *and* as builders of a new-type living skyscraper, or, rather, of what the skyscraper had signified to him before World War I. But as he affirmed himself part of the fabric and one of its builders, I wondered how long my strength would suffice to carry him from site to site. Into these despondent meditations L himself injected hope. Before our autumn excursions started, the last act of his knighting still had to be performed. Its several short scenes were staged in the College of Arms. Based on his Jewish ancestry and his English career, a coat of arms was being pieced together for him. As the delicately elaborated sketch grew, the words used and the symbols chosen fascinated L. They formed an arresting, concise synthesis of him. He sat absorbed; silent till asked to suggest, if only in general terms, a suitable motto. Springing to life, L blurted out, '*Malgré Tout*'! It pleased and was at once accepted. Later I took it as a comforting sign that, for all my inefficiencies and deficiencies, I would not fail him.

CHAPTER SEVENTEEN

Treadmill by the Void
August 1952–December 1956

I would have continued reasonably self-confident had L limited himself to including in our expeditions the concerns of other scholars engaged on the History. Such 'concentric circles', however widened, would not have overstrained his capacious mind. But when he succumbed to the temptation of being deflected from English parliaments in the eighteenth century 'or thereabouts' into nineteenth-century Europe, I was alarmed. In Manchester he had obtained official permission from his Vice-Chancellor to deliver the Creighton Lecture at London University in Michaelmas term 1952. In May, officially accepting the invitation to lecture, he wrote to the Principal of London University suggesting for title 'Some basic factors of 19th-century European history' and, carried away, had expatiated on the 'definite change in the conception of the political nation' which took place far and wide in the nineteenth century owing to the 'rise of the lower classes to full citizenship and political action'.

In these islands it was exemplified by the 'protestant ascendancy' in Ireland breaking down. Grattan's Parliament thought themselves representative of Ireland, when in reality they merely represented the Anglo-Irish. The same process can be traced all over Europe: in Finland, the Baltic countries, the eastern borderlands of Poland, in Hungary, Bohemia, Upper Silesia, the Adriatic littoral, etc. It is probably the most important source of international conflict in the last hundred years.

He made out a brilliant case. But I failed to see how so vast a subject could be compressed into one hour by a mind not free to be centred on it; and L himself confessed, 'I am harder worked at present than I have ever been—which is not altogether good at the age of 64. I wish I could take some time off and go to Spain,

France, Italy, and Scandinavia'. Former pupils now in the Foreign
Office were pressing us to stay at this embassy, that legation, or
some exotic consulate general. 'But,' explained L, 'when I am not
in London or Manchester, I go the round of Record Offices,
Muniment Rooms and Universities. I cannot deny that it is most
enjoyable but it is tiring.' In fact he relished our exhausting
pleasures,

Soon there will be few people who know England and English architecture as Julia and I do. We go by car; and I—with a curiosity perhaps
not quite suited to my years—want to stop everywhere and look more
closely. But Julia, in the kindest way, mostly says, 'Next time, darling'.
Sometimes I wonder if we have that many times ahead of us.

All very amusing and gratifying, as were the results summed up
by L to the Dean of his faculty when our days were devoted to
'MSS-hunting with satisfactory results' and he could write, 'Last
week I discovered magnificent and plentiful material at Lord
Rayleigh's place in Essex for the elections on which Pickersgill is
working (for an M.A. thesis).' On such occasions L easily bubbled
over with joy. Yet his over-stretched mind was again refusing to
relax. Wherever he 'lay' that autumn—at home, or in a canopied
historic four-poster, or on a well-sprung Trust House bed—he
remained out of touch with sleep. The hours of darkness, slipping
by, reduced him to a throbbing nerve teased by the elusive
Creighton Lecture drumming round the rim of his dreadful void;
round and round; till, tantalized beyond endurance, he almost
simultaneously invited and rejected sleep. All that could be done
to ease his nocturnal wretchedness was done, but nothing worked
and he could not come to grips with his torment. One hope
remained: at 1,000 ft. above sea-level sleep would probably return
and he would be able to shape his lecture in snatches between
university duties. Not so. His first letter from Buxton shook me.
The relentless course of an ill-starred event was gaining momentum.

Outspoken as ever, he had told his landlady he would be leaving
for good before high summer 1953. Recently some of her actor
friends had returned, and she now sweetly but firmly asked L to
fall in with her new arrangement of rooms, which he found to be
deplorable. Yet the mere thought of moving house was even more

distracting; and he went down with shingles. A local doctor undertook to give him a treatment that would keep him going. It did and L missed few of his university duties; but dead-beat, he continued to sleep fitfully, and the true shape of his lecture still eluded him. Some fragments of his Buxton efforts survive. Challenging but scrapped because out of scale they begin,

Since the time when I was very young the tenets of the classical bourgeois economists have achieved their apotheosis in the materialistic conception of history obligatory under the Soviets. And now the life of Everyman is dominated more than ever by inter-state conflicts. . . . In the 18th century such conflicts were conducted mainly in terms of dynastic possessions; in the 19th, increasingly in terms of national territory; now we hardly know in what terms to discuss them. To us the game seems much the same by whomever, or in whosoever name, it is played. . . . In 19th-century Europe, instincts and concepts, territorial in origin, were developed—denatured rather than sublimated —by uprooted urban intellectuals into the ideology of strident nationalisms, and as such were communicated by them to the semi-educated both below and above their social strata.

At one point L's mind nostalgically wandered to our cross-country drives, 'How much forgotten history there is in the squiggles of an English country lane, and what disproval of attempts to explain them rationally in a neighbouring Old Roman Road!' At another point, being a devotee of life's diversity, he tilted against the 'primitive *Gleichschaltung*' which

a dictator can conceive in his pragmatic mind and ruthlessly carry through, but which cannot gain ready assent from a living community composed of many groups yet comprising them all, each with its own heritage of rights and claims. . . . No one principle is ever absolute except in the mental void of doctrinaire radicalism.

Early in November L began to shift his university duties. He wanted several comfortable days in London before delivering his lecture on 17 November, a Monday. Buxton was having its first sharp night-frosts. Hurrying down the odious slopes in the early morning on his way to London L slipped on a patch of frozen milk or beer, and sent what remained of a broken bottle clattering downhill. He only just stopped himself from falling, wrenched his back and arrived at our London flat in a lamentable state. A variety of treatments was prescribed. The pain eased but never again left him; and his nerves long remained jangled. At this stage the smooth delivery of his lecture hinged on two wall maps, showing the linguistic divisions of Europe. They were being specially prepared for him, and were to be hung on blackboards somewhat to the right of where he would be standing. Having been promised this aid, L visualized himself pressing his wide-open palm to one region after another from east to west then back again, following migrations old and new, pointing here, fluttering a hand there— establishing the basic pattern of conflicts between ethnic groups whether they had pushed on or stayed behind. Having made visually clear the consecutive stages of the process that had 'formed the essence of European history since the French Revolution' but had 'now reached its term', he would be free to get on with telling incidents, often rather funny and all leading to his peroration.

But the sequence of misadventures continued. Stepping aside to let me enter the lift ahead of him on the way down to Beveridge Hall, L took a false step and, blanching with agony, reeled against the lift wall. In Beveridge Hall, we found no maps—and never knew if they had been forgotten or mislaid. While being comforted for their absence by a hopelessly vague young man, L was shown a brand new lectern with a glass top illuminated from inside; and found that—in the lift—he had firmly rolled up his notes. They would no longer lie flat. He floundered on for his appointed hour, increasingly depressed. The well-intentioned chairman asked for questions. Far from hearing them distinctly, L could not even catch their drift; confusingly, they revolved round India—a topical matter but alien to him.

Before returning north on the morrow L wrote to a friendly doctor, 'I had been unwell for two months'; 'downright ill for the last fortnight'; 'dead-tired I barely got through'. Was there still no drug that could help? To me L made no excuses, offered no explanations. A period of dumb self-castigation set in, aggravated by letters of appreciation. One expert in modern history claimed to have been launched by L 'upon new, more promising lines of thought' than he could have imagined; for another historian 'the social and economic development on the continent' had, during that one hour, 'acquired a convincing inevitability'; a third declaration described L's Creighton Lecture as an 'overarching synthesis which assembled many historical strands and made of them a fabric of historical understanding'. But L ,in sombre mood, deflected his mind from it and himself to young scholars seeking his guidance and to his pupils' careers. Attending in Paris a session of the *commission Tocqueville*'s editorial Board, he discussed with two professors of the Sorbonne 'electoral surveys from the sociological point of view'; learnt that a great amount of work was 'being done on this subject in France'; and that a good deal of it was 'as yet unpublished'. But he was promised 'a list of what is accessible', and when it reached him, he would forward it to the Assistant Librarian at the L.S.E. who, under his supervision, was working on 'the representation of the large towns in Parliament during the second half of the 19th century as reflected in two or three particular elections'.

L's Christmas vacation was marred by three spells in bed; first with a general type of 'flu; next with gastric 'flu; finally with bronchial 'flu; and he continued with an aching back and a great patch of shingles across the ribs. In the intervals between high fever he prepared his Creighton Lecture for publication.[1] In the grip of a feverish attack he spoke volubly. The lecture had been conceived on the wrong scale for an hour's talk. He knew too many detailed facts which hung together 'organically'. Only in the aggregate could they justify his snappy statements. These sounded hollow to him when insufficiently supported. As he enounced them, they clamoured for detail to raise them from statements to conclusions. Details, tempting him to digress, had damaged the over-all design of his spoken piece. The written version—compact, sand-papered—was being worried into cool brilliance; but could not be taken in by ear. Every paragraph has to be read slowly. Drawing my attention to its brevity, L contrasted this with his British Academy lecture, the published text of which was more than double the length of its spoken version. He was seeking an up-to-date relationship between the spoken word and a written text.

Depression finally eased off after the president of the Royal

[1] Reprinted in *Personalities and Powers*.

Academy asked L (the accepted expert on 'our Patron, Protector and Supporter') to give a lecture on George III. The Royal Academy of Arts had decided to mark the Queen's coronation by showing portraits of the kings and queens of England in the Diploma Galleries from March to the end of June. A series of lectures was being arranged for the duration of the exhibition. L's was finally fixed for 27 May. His interest in George III had developed slowly. Some time before *The Structure*'s publication, he had insisted in the press that 'the nursing of constituencies (or of patrons) was a long and more or less continuous process of which the cost could hardly be calculated'. Being unable even in the 1920s to consider a dramatic incident without pondering the characters fascicled in it, he had insisted that neither the king nor Lord North should be summarily condemned for the financial mess they got into over the election expenses for August 1780. Well aware how 'truly tore to pieces' the king's mind was over the ensuing conflict with his minister, L was still siding with North—'a broken man' whose 'moral obligations' L was at pains to present 'in rather a different light' from that flashed on them by Sir John Fortescue's articles in *The Times*. All the same, L's commiseration with North as a systematically self-degrading man, was soon eclipsed. The mental and emotional predicaments of the king out-shone it when L traced to the king's home background the psychological malformations which prevented his living up to what was demanded of him. In 1953 the Royal Academy of Arts lecture prompted L to probe the deep of his own personality for better understanding of the conscientious king boxed up in a hard political situation; and unexpectedly L hauled up the answer to a marginally related problem, relevant to his Creighton Lecture. His own basic aversion to studying the Austro-Hungarian Empire with perfect coherence was due to his having smelt the stench of decay when considering in boyhood the political concepts and practices of moribund Austria-Hungary. Loving life he had averted his face as far as circumstances allowed. By contrast, when applying his mind to the second British Empire, he breathed the ozonized air of a general predisposition to resurgence *malgré tout*. (Some years earlier, in a review of Arnold Toynbee's *Civilization on Trial* he had written, 'The unfathomable mystery of life and creation attaches to origins.') No less importantly, analysis of the course that had been followed by Great Britain heading for the unexplored seas of commonwealth, had enhanced L's own courage to work and to live.

His Easter vacation was devoted to a scrutiny of the king's monarchical and personal problems. Bitter-sweet enjoyment enveloped L as he considered the mishandled opportunities of a man whose portraits on occasion stressed intimate characteristics only too well known to L. And the incurable sadness of the afflicted old king dutifully mounting the futile steps of his tread-mill, wrung L's heart. A new perceptiveness entered his approach to the subject. Several passages on George III's boyhood in *Personalities and Powers* startle because obviously autobiographical. We saw the exhibition twice. Between the two visits L's insight became profoundly compassionate. After the second visit, he felt and looked remarkably relaxed. Of 27 May he made a delightful afternoon.

For the rest of the month through early June, L's last examination papers arrived by every post. Coming into my room to snatch a rest between desperate efforts to mark with absolute fairness papers often very poor, he talked of our approaching marathon paper chases, the first of which was to include a twelve-day expedition to Manchester for vivas and our leave-taking from his colleagues. He also wondered aloud what to do with the books which had for years lined the walls of his room in the university. I again broached the matter of our moving house. But L, prefer-ring to expand without moving, had written on 12 March 1953 to the management of the block where we lived,

My wife is a tenant of yours. . . . I have hitherto held a professorship from which I am retiring. I shall henceforth be resident all year round in London and shall require a study. It would be most convenient if I could have it in this building. I should like to take a two-room flat. The higher the better.

No vacancy was expected in the foreseeable future but L did not lose hope and I gave up trying to budge him. His recent experi-ences of moving had been too catastrophic. It was best to leave him in peace; especially in view of an extraneous unpleasantness that sorely unsettled him.

At considerable inconvenience to himself L had agreed to meet in Oxford an élite eighteenth-century group. The discussion they sought he had squeezed between his marking of examination papers and the lecture on George III on the one hand, and our last drive to Manchester on the other. To the organizer of the group he had written,

I shall do as you suggest and step off with a talk of 10–15 min., about the further work which my Romanes Lecture suggests. I have become a regular recruiting sergeant [for the History of Parliament]. The number of vacancies is enormous.

In his few opening words L intended to draw distinctions between historical work 'best done collectively and once and for all; and work that everyone has to do for himself'. By and large the difference was this:

basic preparatory work usually lends itself to, and calls for, a collective effort; but the superstructure must ultimately be the work of the individual historian. . . . Individuals can deal with individuals and with individual transactions, anything approaching demography can better be done by teams.

Such statements L intended to interweave with much older, more general ideas formulated in 1944 to answer the *Strand Magazine*'s query on the possibility of historians ever reasonably viewing World War II. Dismissing any 'basic difference between those events and any other set of historical happenings', L had affirmed that

The bias is in men not in events. Nothing is intrinsically beyond the range of aggressive controversy [often prompted by a] breathless curiosity which can attain the pitch of intellectual sadism. . . . Accuracy I would associate with statements rather than with views.

The *Strand Magazine*'s cautious doubts about our ever knowing 'anything worth knowing' he thought justified; yet to the Oxford dons and research students he planned to stress the happy coincidence of the historian's indomitable urge with his chief obligation —to find out and make public the closest possible approximation to what happened and how it happened. To L's amazement hardly had he paused to draw breath when he was subjected to harsh abuse. Dons who had clearer insight into his methods hotly defended L's aims. But the altercation deafened him and the hostility bit deep. L answered the convenor's written apology with spontaneous courtesy, 'I am sorry that for all the trouble you have taken, you should have been repaid by unpleasantness. For my part I only want to thank you for your kind and cordial hospitality and for the trouble you have taken'. Unfortunately, in L's mind, the incident merged with an issue already placed by him in the hands of his solicitors and the consequences of which dragged on till they fizzled out.

Increasingly deaf, with a wellnigh paralysed right hand, alternately wearing long-distance and close-work spectacles, L had been finding his regular railway journeys between Buxton and London a great strain since the winter of 1950-1. To shorten and simplify them, he had ingeniously worked out an unusual route which, though odd, was fully permissible. Yet in March 1951 a ticket collector at London Road station, Manchester, refused to let him pass the barrier, forced him to put down brief-case, suit-case, walking stick, and to fumble in his pockets for small change. Outraged (having all but lost the train chosen to get him in the nick of time to a vitally important organizational meeting) L complained to the railway authorities; and months later the trifling surcharge was refunded with apologies. For a year all went well; till in February 1952 the same ticket collector repeated his manœuvre. In L's view, this was manifest persecution and he instructed his solicitors to get in touch with the railway authorities. In due course the Railway Executive expressed regrets, refunded 24*s.* 10*d.* and promised to give the ticket collector instructions which, a little later, he denied having received. Still later, the Railway Executive agreed to pay L's legal expenses in a hushed-up sort of way. To him this was not good enough. The sacrosanct principle he had battled for was the freedom of any citizen—however crippled, old, or foreign-sounding—to proceed on his lawful occasions unmolested by vigorous young chaps eager to throw their weight about. But the principle was never openly re-asserted by the railway authority. And the Oxford incident, following afterwards, seemed to confirm L's unhappy suspicion that the self-discipline which, in the last resort, is the one power adequate to hold in check the cruelty inherent in every member of the human race, was breaking down among the young, and that its collapse was being condoned by officialdom. Were not his recent Oxford antagonists and the ticket-collector representative of the New Vulgarian whose advent had been forecast in Eastern Europe but L had never thought to see surfacing in England? Of the New Vulgarian it had been prophesied that he would differ from the older type by not caring a rap even for amassing money, only for throwing about his weight to the detriment of the weak within range, and to the destruction of urbane living. That the taint should have spread to Oxford saddened L to the point of his stating it was providential he should not have taught there after World War II. Such bitterness about the collapse of the civilization he loved—into the ghastly drumming void, during his lifetime—persisted till we flew to Italy late in the autumn. We were taking up a standing invitation from friends near Florence; and the slightly raised travel-allowance made possible our remaining some ten days at a Fiesole hotel.

In 1907 L's first visit to Florence had imbued him with a throbbing enthusiasm for its humanistic past. Almost half a century later, the still lovely city suffused him with new hope that 'spontaneous barbarization' could, indeed would, be resisted if only in pockets where genuine appreciation of the Renaissance coincided with a healthy faith in Europe's future. Two very old men contributed to it: Bernard Berenson, as a repository and dispenser of the Renaissance gift of enjoyment brought up to date; and Gaetano Salvemini as an intrepid fighter, against great odds, for valiant personal opposition to tyranny, whoever was being tyrannized. Yet L's resurgent faith in Europe's urbanity's survival against all odds, harboured no seed of illusion that individual happiness would accompany the survival. His juvenile enthusiasm for Machiavelli's analysis of contemporary events had left L aware of the murderous intentions and actions of men fired with the will to preserve mankind's heritage and with the ability to build beautifully. His acceptance of the discord between their conflicting impulses, to preserve and to destroy, had engendered in him a cheerful indifference to his own death, which had recently developed into a genuine indifference to *our* death, provided we died together. As we were approaching the Alps on our return flight he once again expressed it in his lapidary way. A storm broke round us. Mirrored in the tip of a wing that we could both see, a flash of lightning gave us a visual illusion of the wing having been hit. The craft shuddered. L leant close to my ear remarking, 'cremation free'. The pilot's voice ordered the fastening of seatbelts—already he was rising above the storm. 'Not yet, after all,' was L's comment as we returned to thinking of his next flight, to Dublin where I would not be accompanying him.

In March Miss Holloway, the Principal of Alexandra College, had conveyed to L her council's invitation to be their Lady Ardilaun Lecturer for 1953. The girls—aged sixteen to nineteen gained more she said from 'hearing about personalities than about political movements'. Having decided on France 1815–75 for subject, L replied that he would 'prefer not to give the lectures a purely biographical character', but to 'group' his material round Napoleon, Talleyrand, Louis-Philippe and Guizot, and Napoleon III. Working out, before our Italian visit, a detailed syllabus for publication in Dublin, he hit upon an ingenious way of highlighting events by pinpointing some characteristics of the personalities involved, and high-lighting some personalities by pinpointing certain events. The tight-knit lectures soon were so limpid that the hard work involved in their composition could no longer be felt. A master strand—important to L but not allowed to protrude—was an adaptation to modern French politics of an old and favourite theme: the bond between men and the territory they inhabit as of right. When I drove him to Northolt Airport on 10 November, the four lectures lay ripe in his serene mind. If only he felt on the following three days as he did that morning, all would be well. Once again the lectures' shapeliness hinged on how he would sleep. Luckily, he was whisked away that night into the country by a member of the college council related to the lectures' foundress. To the sensitive hospitality given him at Knockmaroon L ascribed his Dublin lectures' success; and characterized it on his return as 'an achievement collective in a marvellous sense'. Dostoevski was right: many are implicated in what an individual pulls off, fails to pull off, or does wrong—however obliquely they are involved. But for his part, L had again been guilty of unavoidable yet 'absurd overcrowding'.

Soon after accepting Miss Holloway's invitation, he got in touch with friends in Trinity College, Dublin and Queen's University, Belfast. The upshot was that, in Ulster as in the Republic, he saw everyone he could have wished to, had he flown over on History of Parliament business. In Dublin the emphasis was on collective research; and though firm about not dining out while under the stress of daily lecturing, L's Dublin luncheons and the whole of the Saturday were packed with useful encounters. As for Belfast, his letter to the Vice-Chancellor of Queen's University about coming over from Dublin 'in order to get in touch with your historians, and examine collections of MSS. in the Record Office or in other libraries bearing on parliamentary history', brought an invitation to meet at lunch 'a few people who might be able to help in providing records'. A short communication followed from the Vice-Chancellor, 'Am asking the P.M., the recently retired head of the Civil Service, the University Librarian, and J. C. Beckett' (Professor of Modern History). Despite L's remarkably smooth run of luck in Ireland, he reached home in a state of acute and lingering over-excitement which led to his rejecting a most tempting invitation when we presently lunched with the Robert Oppenheimers.

For some time Sir Llewellyn Woodward had been luring L to join him for three months at least at the Institute of Advanced Study at Princeton, N.J., where Oppenheimer was Director. Then on 16 October 1953 Woodward wrote more urgently, 'R.O. would much like to see you'; 'you will find him attractive and interesting'; 'it is a good thing that—if you ever find time to come to America again—you should be able to write to him personally about a stay at the Institute'. But over lunch L firmly told Oppenheimer that he would not be able to go to Princeton before he had finished his section of the History of Parliament. And at about the same time he told the editor of *Foreign Affairs* (an American quarterly),

I am absolutely determined for the next three years at least to eschew anything which could divert me from my main work. Within the last few weeks I had therefore to refuse a very tempting invitation from Bryn Mawr to deliver the Mary Flexner Lectures, another invitation from the Princeton Institute of Advanced Study, and a third from the S. African Universities.

Of the reasons that forced him 'regretfully to refuse' the Mary Flexner Lectures of 1955, he wrote,

I would have had either to deal with British 18th-century parliamentary history, which would hardly be fair as I might be forestalling what I should reserve for our own publication, or I should have to lecture on 19th-century European history which would divert me from the work I have to do here.

'Even the administrative side,' he was discovering, 'takes up a great deal of time.' Besides, the lesson or moral of the 'Creighton fiasco' had been learnt. And L's attractive Ardilaun lectures proved to be a valedictory salute to years of 'breathless curiosity' about the continent of Europe.

In the previous spring L had been put in charge of the History's 1679–1901 stretch (twelve volumes); he had accepted editorial responsibility (as 'Author') for his period's middle section (1750–90, 3 volumes); the Board of Trustees had expressed the hope that the manuscript of this section would be substantially completed in the course of 1958; and L had offered the gerancy of the sections flanking his 'narrow field' to experts avowedly sharing his views. In L's thirty-six-year section alone there were almost 2,000 M.P.s to be dealt with—a powerful disincentive to any indulgence in mental diversion. Had not the economic life of the country been easing up and the world's technological achievements advancing, the demanded pace could not even have been contemplated. Henceforth the gigantic task of garnering data was to be done more thoroughly and systematically than it could have been by us alone, two old things in our jalopy. More often than not L's young men took with them, for photographing documents at speed, a Graphlix camera. Yet for another few years he and I still had to carry through some marathon paper chases which for whatever reason the others could not undertake. During one which kept us steadily at work for more than a week in Powis Castle—poised among delectable hanging gardens just inside Wales—I measured the distance between my appreciation of L's abilities and his own assessment. As the owners lived elsewhere, we were looked after all day by an admirable caretaker; but we slept at a hotel situated high above Church Stretton, some thirty miles away.

304

On our first day at Powis Castle L had calculated that his task (to finish with the Clive Papers for good) would exact seven steady hours every time we were there, and he decided to cut each seven-hour stretch into unequal halves by a hot lunch at Welshpool. Only on our last day did he realize that his pace would have to be stepped up. Back from lunch, he put a huge letter-book on a lectern with a seat like a miserere joined to it, gave me a job to do, and said I was on no account to interrupt his photographic reading. About mid-afternoon, looking up, I saw L's face more than usually pink. Next time I looked, it was turning purple and I wondered if he would burst a blood vessel. In another half hour he was puce. I sat still, observing. He closed the book, wriggled out of the seat, opened the door into the library and, still engrossed in thought, paced the long room between the bookshelves and the centrally positioned tables. When he came up to me at last, every word was engraved on the tablets of his memory; but he complained of its not having been easy. There was a time when such mental exercise was child's play; all he then needed after many more hours of it was a gallop on Kashtanka, his chestnut mare. Now, after a mere three hours, he was fagged out; his body ached, his head throbbed. While I continued amazed by his achievement, he lamented this further sign of mental decay. To me his flushed face and throbbing head were not signs of decay but the result of a continuous rash squandering of powers and abilities. Nor was I astonished when he paid for it by more ill-health during the winter.

On 27 January 1955 L wrote of having been laid up with a bronchial cold which he had 'not yet shaken off'; and of finding 'great difficulty in carrying on'. By mid-February his doctor insisted that I pack him into the car and take him to Bognor Regis. There, sitting in a shelter and staring out to sea, L began to elaborate his opinion on a biographer's moral obligations and clinched it with a warning. If I survived him, I should let no self-important biographer get hold of those scraps of information about him that only I had. There could be no preventing an enthusiastic distorter or misinterpreter from saying what amused him or writing what he thought profitable. Against exploitation by that crew I should be on guard, bearing in mind that even solid facts, when wrongly grouped, could bolster up untruth. A smear cleverly coiled round correct facts makes of the combination a heinous lie. An honest biographer should above all serve the truth hidden in his subject's unobtrusive self. Lacking empathic insight into it, a writer should keep to his own impressions if any, to thumb-nail sketches, and to a straight chronicling of verified activities. Attempts to write biographies without empathy for the subject of the work, the 'empaled butterfly', are schoolboys' jokes or exercises in sleight of mind. Such wording was the result of the acceptance for publication by a highly reputable publisher of a 'biographical enquiry' on T. E. Lawrence. Because rumours about its being offensive had reached Professor Arnold W. Lawrence (a brother of T. E. and his literary executor) before he left Cambridge in 1951 for Achimota (Gold Coast), he had asked L to act for the family should the need arise. Like any other experience that came his way, the details of the case proved immediate grist to his mills. Even in Bognor the case was falling into the context of his wider concerns. But I was wrong to reckon it a sign of regained health. His doctor continued dissatisfied. And on 20 June L wrote, to yet another friend active in the T. E. Lawrence affair, 'I am off to Oxford tomorrow for the Encaenia and after that for the Balliol Gaudy. Immediately on our return we start for Switzerland, myself under doctor's orders.' At that Encaenia L was to receive the degree of D.Litt.—an honour which had special significance for him. His not having been elected a Fellow of his college when tutoring and lecturing in Oxford after World War I (despite warm approval of him by the Master of Balliol and the Senior Tutor) had been in his eyes an act of corporate rejection no less wounding than his mother's contempt for his offering of pink daisies at the dawn of his conscious life. He saw his Balliol Honorary Fellowship in 1948 as an act of reparation, deeply moving yet almost his due. His 1955 university honour astonished him nearly as much as had his knighthood. And because it blended with a rise in his ever-latent self-deprecation, started a new chain of events; not obtrusive, however, till well after our Swiss holiday. Montana, at 1,500 metres above sea level, imposes its own way of life. While L's heart and mine were getting acclimatized, we slept deep all night and dozed on our long-chairs between meals. The lullaby of cowbells on the high pastures never annoyed but rather comforted us. After a week of somnolence we began to wander about; then went for walks up or down hill; and returned to London so vigorous that a long paper chase well into Northumberland— broken at many country houses and almost as many hotels near Record Offices—told on neither of us. L's self-deprecation vigorously resurfaced only with the spring.

Sixteen representative English historians had written a book of essays to express their admiration of his work.[1] His seventieth birthday was still two years off, but the originator of the scheme was a dying man, and A. J. P. Taylor, the co-editor, was set on the presentation taking place while Richard Pares, though immobile in his wheel-chair, could still take part in the occasion. It was a vivid day. Pares, with whom we lunched in All Souls, was no longer able even to eat unaided yet his every remark was worth remembering. At the close of the late-afternoon presentation by the Master of Balliol, L, thanking him, the editors, and the contributors, spoke of the formative forces directed into his life by A. L. Smith—the elder scholar of L's youth—who in days of acute need generously gave more solid and subtle encouragement than could be defined. After nightfall we dined with A. J. P. Taylor in Magdalen, quite a celebration. But as I drove L home on the morrow he bitterly questioned—in view of Pares's qualities and fate—there being any sense in any group stressing L's own worth. We were about to fly to Rome, whose university was awarding him an honorary degree. During our few days there L's gloom steeply increased, largely due to circumstances inducing an over-indulgence in sleeping tablets and pep pills. The suite we occupied in a well modernized hotel on the Pincio was for once isolated from road and hotel noises; but on our first night we realized that almost adjacent to its outer walls stood a small church attached to a Benedictine convent. A bidding bell regularly summoned the nuns and us out of sleep. The raging irritability it built up in L got out of hand when only one night more remained to be slept there, after which we were due to go to Montana, passing by I Tatti to catch a glimpse of Bernard Berenson. That last day in Rome, a Sunday, we had no official

---

[1] *Essays Presented to Sir Lewis Namier*, 1956.

engagements, only a private luncheon with the Professor of Diplomatic History, Mario Toscano.

Having thoroughly enjoyed the previous night's send-off supper to all honorands in the underground cisterns of ancient Rome refashioned into a restaurant, and having successfully ignored the bidding bell, I woke at the usual hour. L lay still but awkwardly, and his breathing was irregular. Before drawing back the curtains in the living-room section of our open-plan suite, I noiselessly adjusted those round his bed. When silent and frowning he went through to the bathroom, I had long since finished my breakfast. Some ten minutes later I ordered his tray and had mine removed; but when L, having stayed in the bathroom unusually long, rejoined me at last, he looked ghastly. Flopping on to an easy chair he said, as if thinking aloud, that he had nearly killed himself; would have, had he not been stopped. In a quick staccato he told what he had been through. Buffeted by waves of self-hate as powerful as in earliest childhood, he stood naked before one of the pier-glasses, shaving. Suddenly yet not unexpectedly, an insuperable desire possessed him to slice across his jugular vein with his cut-throat razor. Staring at the point where razor and vein touched, he saw in the looking glass a swirl encircle his wrist which went rigid. Simultaneously, at the back of his mind, he saw himself sprawling on whitish tiles in pools of blood and me opening the bathroom door to remind him of our luncheon engagement. My image continued framed in the doorway as the turbulence, still seen by him in the looking-glass, coiled round his hand and arm while a voice asked 'Can you do this to her?' As L told me of it, his words—the more impressive for being disjointed—evoked a very old tradition traceable to Ezekiel and transmitted, through Byzantine channels, to the Russian Orthodox Church. It says that the angel of death bestows the gift of cherubic insight on a mortal who has met him face to face and survived. Never again will such a man see a situation as unequivocally as before. For him every situation will shimmer with multiple significance, and every problem will summon round it a choir of solutions. In the past L's inherent ambivalence had often tormented him, though it sometimes provided him with quiet amusement during an argument. But that Sunday he sat through most of lunch in beatific silence. When the rest of us argued, he saw the point of view of each one complementing the others. When we were alone he spoke of the enjoyment the all-round insight had given him. And some weeks later, when the re-issue of his eighteenth-century books was being discussed, he drew my attention to a passage on 'every man' attaining freedom at a point in his life called, by L using biblical terminology, his 'ford at the stream'. There a man who is reaching spiritual maturity wrestles as never before and never again. If he prevails, he is henceforth 'free and at peace'. That peace L claimed to have found on our last Sunday in Rome.

On the morrow at I Tatti Nicky Mariano, hospitable as ever, was waiting for us. But there were shadows near her eyes and mouth. Though Bernard Berenson had recovered from a recent accident as well as he ever would, he had shrunk and grown pitiably frail. No more walks for him in his favourite gully where, on a previous visit, we had been driven to see him, a few minutes later, leaping toward us like a goat from crag to boulder on his way back to the car. Because of the complicated train connection between Florence and Sierre, we took our leave of Berenson before he had risen. In his ordinary-sized bed, and wearing striped blue and white flannel pyjamas, he looked even smaller than he had downstairs—an eleven-year-old perhaps. But against the pillows rested the much lined waxen mask of one who had outlived all ability to drink at his chosen sources of enjoyment. Jogging away towards Milan, L and I agreed we were unlikely to come that way again while life still flickered in the maker of I Tatti. As we crept up the alp by funicular train, L mused on the difficulty of finding a reason to go on living when you have lost the incentive of greed and the handicap of fear—the panic about this or that greed's possible frustration. With their tug-of-war over, what incentive, of what different order, could support a man disenchanted with himself and the world?

In Montana only the weather disappointed us. A wind locally called Mombra kept the sky overcast and the view misty as in a Chinese print. Although after a while we went out twice daily, picking our way between soggy stretches of gentians indigo dark, there could be no sitting about as in the previous year of abundant sunlight. Instead—having found shelves with a fine collection of paperbacks in our hotel's public rooms—we read long; I lying, L sitting, swaddled in rugs on our balcony. Many Herman Melvilles were among the books L had not read. On my advice he started with *Moby Dick* and was enraptured. In Ahab's persistence, perversely intensified to an obsession, he recognized a tendency of his own, indulged for most of his life. His Maker's purpose in making him—out of nothing, and what the devil for?—was L's Leviathan. To capture it—to master the ghastly void of his radical nothingness—he had laboured incessantly, often rashly. Having reached a point where insight was beginning to glimmer, he retraced with the glee of intimate recognition his steady descent, seen of a piece thanks to the unifying web of Melville's private symbolism. The impression was lasting. Among the preliminary sketches for his Introductory Survey (to the three volumes of the History written under his direction) is one typed by L a few weeks before his death. It reads,

We have to say with the narrator of *Moby Dick*, 'Small erections may be finished by their first architects; grand ones, true ones, ever leave the copestone to posterity. . . . This whole book is but a draft—nay but a draft of a draft. Oh Time, Strength, Cash and Patience!'

True things, he concluded, moved away from us open-ended. But there was one blot on our muffled exhilaration in high altitudes. L developed symptoms suggestive of cystitis, pronounced enough for him to be sent on our return to London into a clinic for observation and tests.

Restive, I put off resuming the social work I had taken on at the end of his sabbatical leave. It had originated for me at tea with Agatha Forbes Adam. She spoke of the 'Borstals' her brother-in-law had long been involved with, and I learnt that the Governor of the Boys' Prison at Wormwood Scrubs was in need of women social workers to help interview sixteen- to twenty-one-year-olds either on remand, or, if they had received Borstal sentences, waiting for allocation. Rendered usefully mobile by my car, I quickly joined the volunteers; to find that my urge to understand how people tick and collide and how their collisions affect easily widening circles, was even better satisfied during visits to the boys' homes than in chats with the culprits themselves. Every social worker was of course instructed to tell no tales. But talking to L of the social conundrums I faced was easy without betraying anyone or anything. Eager to listen, he enthusiastically went to the root of every situation: those were English circles he did not know even marginally. As for my reports, their purposeful conciseness greatly benefited from our exchanges. And yet, as I brought L home—reassured by extensive examination and negative tests— he asked me to give up my prison work.

That summer he had defined his Introductory Survey as his section's guide to readers of his M.P.s' 'political birth', their biographies. In the coming months he would be discussing with me Survey and Biographies; moreover, he wanted me to come in on the revision of his two big eighteenth-century books; but above all, pondering his likely death, he had been appalled to see how little he knew of my mind, of the way it worked. This should be remedied: we must see more of each other and I must do most of the talking. In accord with this, I shortly afterwards suggested L should accompany me on a short visit to Holland where two great exhibitions were currently on view—Rembrandt's engravings in Amsterdam, his paintings in wellnigh obliterated Rotterdam noisily re-emerging out of its wartime rubble.

Of all pictures L still liked portraits best; and those of Rembrandt even more than most Titians. After some humming and hawing he agreed we should spend a few days at The Hague; and he switched his mood to one of visual enjoyment. Moving about mostly by train, we saw much of the low, flat land whose overhanging clouds, torn by bursts of streaming sunlight, turned the sky above it into the peaceful landscape's dramatic feature. For good measure, on the second day, L initiated a pursuit of Franz Hals. In the old almshouse of Haarlem he compared the great group-paintings with English 'conversation pieces' and drew distinctions between the English and the Dutch choice of points to stress in the sitters' relationships. At night, drawing even closer emotionally and intellectually, we strolled round the ingeniously floodlit Mauritshuis. And on our return flight I shared with him, as a matter of course, a sudden visual impression that had whisked me back to early childhood. The days by now being short we came in over London after dark. Reclining by a window, with L between me and the gangway I was wafted into a long since for-gotten mood and state. As a child I had often flown in a recurrent dream, reclining just so in what I took to be a railway carriage without compartments and with someone on my right of whom I was cosily aware but whom I could never identify. I always woke after I had been looking out of a window on my left, down on to an unforgettable pattern of lights—red, green, blue, yellow, white. And there it was, drifting in below me. When it had gone I spoke. L, having often been struck by fleeting, but unmistakably sub-stantiated, flashes of foreknowledge, had never speculated about their nature, not being equipped to do so usefully. But he had every time felt the event reinforce a scale of values that bolstered up his will to live. My communicated foreknowledge was helping him to return not only refreshed, but steady, to battle with those among his colleagues who thought his 'perfectionist' approach, to the multitudinous biographies that spellbound him, was dragging them all on to a treadmill of his construction. The intensifying conflict was between minds differently cast. There could be no compromise. Something would have to give.

CHAPTER EIGHTEEN

Maturing Out
1957–1960

Dreaded, but almost unnoticed in the general bustle, the financial year 1957–8 had crept in on the scholars and secretarial staff engaged on the History of Parliament. The Trustees—chosen from Members of both Houses, and responsible for a treasury grant-in-aid spread over twenty years—were counting on some biographies of L's section (as well as some of an earlier period) being available for the printers before April 1958. Neither section lived up to the expectations; and the perennial apprehension of questions raised in Parliament slithered round board-rooms and between office desks. To close friends L wrote that every hour of his day was taken up by the job on which he worked against time; and that the relentless daily pressure kept him in his office 'day after day from 10 a.m. to 7 p.m., usually with only 40 min. for lunch'. Consulted on how much political and biographical material it was best to collect before putting pen to paper, he spoke from experience: 'Up to a certain limit the power of the researcher multiplies enormously, like combinations and permutations with the increase of the units involved; but in time a degree of saturation is reached; and further accumulation proceeds along the curve of diminishing returns.' For L's section of the History the curve of diminishing returns was reached during the summer, and none too soon. I was beginning to find utterly depleting our long drives that alternated with our sitting upright, hard at work, in Record Offices; and this interspersed with scintillating social occasions or important academic functions.

On 12 June 1957 we drove to Cambridge in time for tea with the Provost of King's College. There we dined in splendour and stayed the night. In the morning L was awarded an honorary Litt.D. Afterwards there was a luncheon with long speeches;

then we changed into driving clothes, packed, and sped away to other engagements further north. As always the pomp continued well sequined over with spots of light comedy that blotted out fatigue. And I had drilled myself never to flag at the wheel. But in Lincoln, and at last in bed, I closed my eyes only to find sleep killed by the day's road relentlessly driving in through my closed eyelids. How to keep properly alert on the morrow and the morrow nagged me. L came to the rescue. Resourceful, he fetched for me a good tot of neat whisky and supervised my drinking it as fast as I could without choking. I barely remember the last sip, and slept till breakfast was placed beside me. Well rested, I was in command of nerves and mind. But there was no good reason to think I would not be muzzy with cumulative fatigue even before starting on the long drive home in a fortnight's time. Re-examining the situation, L decided our part in the paper chases should be tapered off. Others could complete most of what remained to be done; besides, owners were generously depositing their documents at the Institute of Historical Research for unencumbered perusal by him; and this flow was likely to increase. As for the other object of our complicated expeditions—the hope of finding collaborators by the dozen—it had long since been dashed.

L's idea that the 'basic preparatory work' for the vast enterprise would lend itself to 'collective efforts' with advantages to all, had not caught on; nor had his idea that the 'superstructure' would be well suited to individual historians helped by material chanced upon by other researchers. His excitement over the marvellous opportunities provided by the History for senior scholars to help young ones through a new mode of supervision was pooh-poohed. The highly vocal, utterly uncomprehending hostility displayed by the Oxford eighteenth-century group was to become a stereotype. L was being accused of exploitation, of filching other men's ideas, of a sinister determination to drive them as slaves to his own further aggrandizement. With denigration of him and his work growing fashionable in academic circles, it looked to me that lesser men were projecting on him their own most shaming aspirations; which contributed to the drying-up of voluntary and part-time help. This was followed by pleas for financial retrenchment, while to the consternation of all involved, the work was observed to be inexorably expanding as it slowed down. Brought to life, the History of Parliament had acquired its own momentum. But the situation though serious was not disastrous; offers of financial help were coming from the U.S. Traditionally disposed to support worthwhile ventures, Americans had noted L's circumstances; and on 14 May 1957 the Rockefeller Foundation had assigned to advanced research under his direction the sum of £4,000 a year for four years. Despite the echoing and re-echoing sneers, L's scope expanded; and the joint interest, snowballing, eventually contributed to an American's participation in one of the History's earlier sections with no call on the gratified and grateful History of Parliament's resources. Yet at the time, the mooted aid increased the harrowing of L, forcing him to define more closely his views on and intentions for his section.

Pressed by the board—for reasons of prestige or kudos—to write his Survey before the biographies and the summaries of constituencies were ready, he refused even to consider the suggestion. His biographies—inseparable from the constituency accounts —were no 'pebbles strewn about a beach' but an integral part of a vast 'interlocking study of the political nation' in the second half of the eighteenth century. Only when all the biographies and accounts were well advanced, would he know at all what to put in the Survey. His main discovery had been, so far, the 'independence' of his Members after they were elected. This he affirmed to be of universal interest as well as of local significance. But to assess it he had to look closely at every individual biography, which irritated the uncomprehending, and increased the burden carried by his team. Early in 1957 L pleaded with the board that his full-time and part-time assistants be helped to feel that the section's goal was within reach; to which end their remunerations should be stepped up and their share in the great work marked in every reasonable way. The re-adjustment he initiated made feasible to his team—who were progressing in exemplary harmony among themselves and with him—L's long contemplated visit to Israel.

He had been approached, from Rehovoth, some months after Chaim Weizmann's death, by Boris Guriel prompted by Vera. They sought advice on gathering in and arranging the Weizmann papers. In the autumn of 1956 Vera's legal adviser invited L to join a board of trustees (ultimately, the Chaim Weizmann Archives Board). Vera was its president, Meyer Weisgal its chairman, Boris Guriel its secretary general. Seven months later, in June 1957, Chairman Weisgal invited L to be present, in Rehovoth, at an inaugural meeting of editors. After some hesitation about dates, our visit was fixed for the spring of 1958. L was by then one of twelve members on the Board of Editors for the Weizmann papers —six members being resident in Israel, six elsewhere. Leaving London on a raw March morning we reached Lod (Lidda airport) in about fourteen hours. The Weizmann car was there to meet us and we were driven through long pitch-dark avenues balmy with the scent of orange blossom. As Vera had retired to her rooms, we tiptoed beyond, up a winding stairway, and fell asleep to the music of jackals loping through the night in search of water. Next morning our eyes dilated on to a view of the Judean Hills swimming in a sunhaze. Before us stretched a schedule as tightly packed as any planned by L to serve the History of Parliament.

Our visit fell into three parts. The first part, spent at Rehovoth, was encumbered with documents emerging out of chaos and still to be put each into its place; the second, in Galilee redolent with a numinous past and thrusting with confidence into the future; and the third, in Jerusalem—a dignified city of robust administration and daring scholarship. But owing to the minute country's size and shape, none of the components was of a piece. Compression made for fluidity. During our week at Weizmann House we were driven about a good deal; even to Sodom by the Dead Sea for a day. And we were flown over the Negev to Elath for another day packed with delights: a stroll through weirdly shaped ancient copper mines for one thing; a cruise over coral fields darted through by shoals of unimaginably colourful fish for another. Everywhere we met L's old friends or made new ones. Yet whenever possible, he worked with Guriel in the cellars of Weizmann House chock-a-block with stacked papers. Our second week was chiefly spent criss-crossing the malformed strip between Tel Aviv, Jerusalem, Haifa and the Sea of Galilee, with me taking copious notes. L had undertaken to write a couple of articles on Israel after Ten Years for the *Sunday Times*; I to give a Third Programme talk on my reactions to a land, community, and way of life totally unknown to me. With note-books bulging, we returned to Rehovoth's '*cité universitaire*' for the winding up of the Editorial Board's business; and for talks with army educationalists busy transforming men and women born and bred, say, in Germany or the Yemen, Holland or Iraq into members of a homogeneous Hebrew-speaking community. But every one of those educationalists was fired with a determination to steer their pupils—boys and girls in revolt against mankind that they knew to be vile—away from the twin perils of crime and psychosis, along ways of easy yet firm discipline. The directness of approach and the subtlety of method were heartening. Still, the event which affected us most occurred in Tiberias, on the eve of some visits to neighbouring settlements where L had old friends characterized by him as Russian Jews of the best type: hard-working, level-headed, unostentatious free-thinkers; practical, tolerant, and kind.

A drive more than usually long, with many interruptions for closer examination of a particular site, landscape or ruin, had predisposed us to have tea in the quiet of my room when we had at last reached the Galey Kinnereth. In need of a thorough rest I suggested we part to meet again for dinner. Some time after cool darkness had settled on the lake cupped in its crouching hills, I went in search of L. Having scanned every room alive with voices I found him on a deserted, hushed, star-lit terrace that overhung the lake. His bulky shoulders and well-rounded head were stamped against the paler grey of the smooth water. With hands resting on the balustrade, he stood motionless, gazing out. He did not stir at my approach, but when I had stopped beside him I heard him murmur, 'Of course he walked on these waters. Could again.' We pondered the lake's past, present, and future, turned simultaneously and went in to dinner. The night being too lovely to withdraw from, we strolled out into it again after coffee, and went along the lakeside towards Magdala. Almost at once L began to speak: of religion as a feat of reciprocity between God and man; a reciprocity so inclusive yet so intimate that it could only be known through a personally discovered union with the Creator who suffered as the most receptive and vulnerable of his creatures must. The enduring bloom of that evening enveloped with its serenity two talks—or rather public chats—given by L before we

317

flew home. Their shape was so easy that it eluded his spellbound audiences, who failed properly to record them. The first was set among Professor Talmon's undergraduates in Jerusalem; the second among the research and teaching staff in Rehovoth. Two interweaving themes held each together, firmly yet inconspicuously. The spinal cord of one theme was the message of Karl Marx—a genius who had vigorously drawn thinking men's attention to the significance of economic factors in mankind's social life. The spinal cord of the other was the message of Sigmund Freud—a genius who had elaborated the importance of the hidden yet potent psychological factor in the interlocking private, communal and political life of every man. Distortions, exaggerations, misapplications of either man's lifework should not be allowed to obscure the new planets they had steered into our ken. The exploratory genius of each had enhanced our understanding of ourselves, others, the group we belonged to and the groups with whom we joined issue. Both men had helped L to understand the predicament of an observant generation aware of living and working in a world panting for redemption—a personal need. Yet redemption was not among the words used by him, while Marx and Freud he named only in passing. In Jerusalem he put slightly more stress on Marx, in Rehovoth on Freud. Both chats were essays in his newest method of communication. Much of value, though barely mentioned, held each together. And the spirit in which they were conducted never left L.

Back in London, while he worked at home on his *Sunday Times* articles and I worked on my broadcast, L lingered much in my room. He had been confronted in Israel by the incalculable factor of history, unimaginably active there. The ingathered oriental Jews—fleeing from a variety of degrading laws and practices in the Moslem lands of their birth—were already outnumbering the 'Russian' settlers. Those 'Yemenis', 'Moroccans', 'Iraqis' were as artistically gifted and as fanatical about religious customs as were their hosts of yesterday, and as traditionally prolific. How soon would they bring about the Arabization of Israel's finest achievement: the 'Jew who has never known unfreedom'? Would not the new country emerge out of our world in flux a typically oriental land, monotheistic like most in the Middle East though

still rigorously keeping to its own most ancient form of mono-
theism; otherwise barely distinguishable from its neighbours. L
wished the emerging nation immensely well. Having striven 'with
God and men' in the Sinai Campaign, it had won through; as he
had in his ludicrous Roman bathroom, hung with all those
looking-glasses. But the Israelis were not the people he had
sacrificed so much to; and his distress for every one of them was
over. 'Who is a Jew?' had been fiercely debated while we were in
Israel. L hardly was one in the emerging sense. Yet he continued
a Semite, of course, for what that was worth—a sport of the old
stock; as were no doubt other Jews, and Arabs; of whom too
many were being deflected from the true task of every inhabitant
of the region—the reclamation of deserts, exacted by our planet's
circumstances. In the same re-assessing spirit L considered the
Oxford incident. Had not those vehement, obtuse young men
been better in touch with their day than he was? Emotionally aware
of having come in at the death of an era (aware of their position in
time rather than in space) were they not destined to be the mere
scavengers of a dying thing? L, having long since accepted the
French precept not to arraign history (*on ne fait pas le procès à
l'histoire*) was beginning to see the point of their being scavengers
—to be replaced soon by a more imaginative, creative lot able to
forge the new times. The same theme—of destruction preceding
resurgence but being tragically destructive for all that—made the
success of L's first public engagement after we had recovered
from the acute phase of upsets caused by our 'oriental jaunt'.

The publishing house of Macmillan were marking with a
luncheon in the Dorchester Hotel the issue of a book on the later
Churchills by A. L. Rowse, and L had been asked to give the
address. Called upon to speak, he rose in good voice to deliver a
lament for the English way of life which, having perceptibly
begun at the Restoration, as A. L. Rowse showed in *The Early
Churchills*, had undergone a series of remarkable modifications in
the eighteenth and nineteenth centuries, and was fading away in
the mid-twentieth. Already it could be summed up. And what a
brilliant, brave and fruitful way of living it had been. L's appreciative audience loved his plucking at their heartstrings in an unconventional, minor key. Smiles were wistful, eyes were moist.

But as I drove him away to his office, still excited he talked of the ease with which an opulent group on the crest of its wave had roped in the poor and the destitute to slave for it. By contrast, in our dawning day of self-help and do-it-yourself, human dignity could best flourish on the astringent soil of personal frugality. Harsh soils produce some of the best wines. Greed was an anachronism, inappropriate to the reshaping social fabric. Mankind appeared to be moving out of an era of ravenous prosperity and countenanced greed into an era of tentative welfare and countenanced waste. Waste he abhorred, but frugality was enjoyable, and he found pleasure in our own life being, on the whole, frugal. So saying, L had inadvertently shone a new light on matters we had frequently been discussing. Our capital, though small had increased almost dramatically owing to luck and the good management of our stockbroker. I wanted to spend every possible penny on making L's remaining years as comfortable as could be; but he insisted on our making further capital gains, so that I should never worry over money no matter by how many years I survived him. As I dropped L at his office that afternoon, I knew I would no longer push my view. Since his enjoyment of our frugality had surfaced, nothing would come of my doing so; yet my justification remained valid: it rested on a situation at his office that fiercely tormented him.

At the History of Parliament's inception the Institute of Historical Research had taken L under its wing and provided him with a small, unheated temporary office. There, in close proximity to a built-in sink with a tap, he had worked at weekends and during vacations, cheek-by-jowl with John Brooke and Valerie Baum, another former pupil and at the time his private secretary. After two years he was winkled out from between sink and desks to be placed in a fine large room open to sunlight and with something of a view. Immensely relieved he had spread himself out, with his books on shelves round the walls. But the University of London's Senate House (where the Institute had its quarters) was scheduled for considerable reconstruction; and all too soon L together with his staff had been moved down into the basement. His young people were pleased: at last they were next door to their chief, and most of his books (already bequeathed by him to the

Institute) were now close at hand. Moreover, their office was reasonably large and light. But his was not only small to the point of being poky; owing to a wall rising high at a few feet outside the only window, it was lugubrious. Feeling wretchedly hemmed in, he dubbed it to me his Black Hole of Calcutta. Since there simply was nowhere else to put him, the only thing for L was escape into the library for a breather every now and then. When the lifts were out of use, it was a very long trudge up many stairs, and the routine was wearing him out. Hoping to entice him to work at home as much as possible, I had reorganized the place and myself to this end. Beginning to relent, he had promised seriously to consider my suggestion after a particular ploy that tied him to the Senate House was completed in essentials.

The biographies of 'rather obscure Members'—'from the social point of view the most interesting part of the House'—were pretty well finished. L's attention was on a disreputable handful of them. His old friend Thomas Newcastle—that 'dim fellow' ensconced in ducal splendour and caught in the field of history's magnifying glass—had been to the rank and file of negligible M.P.s what another, equally odd, politician appeared to have been to Members balancing on the edge of respectability. Less elusive than they were, the gifted but freakish Charles Townshend—bewitched by more than one rogue—seemed likely, if probed, to reveal a specifically eighteenth-century drift into evil ways; and to pinpoint at least a presage of the second British Empire's crumbling away. No Manichee, L found that the trends of history, or the purposes expressed in it, were better revealed to him on the fringes between light and darkness, rather than in the eye of light or, for that matter, the eye of darkness. To him the shadowy grey fringes were worth exploring on many counts; thirty years before he had traced back to the Age of the American Revolution certain origins of contemporary historical phenomena; a mere eight years before he had thought himself engaged by the Trustees to raise a living translucent skyscraper in which to cherish the roots of contemporary parliamentary history; now L perceived he was building an era's mausoleum. In pensive mood, he quoted a Russian nineteenth-century poet's (Nekrasov's) rhetorical question to a street walker: 'What was it that brought you so low?' When and how had decay insinuated itself into the second British Empire? Invited by Trinity Hall, Cambridge, to give the 1959 Leslie Stephen Lecture, L chose for subject Charles Townshend: His Character and Career.

I drove a rather jumpy L to Cambridge on a fine afternoon in May. No sooner had the road emptied of traffic than he said the thought of dinner in hall greatly troubled him. Strangers would indistinctly speak against a humming background. Much of what they mouthed he would guess wrong. None of the hearing aids he had tried out was of any use to him. The only thing to do was to say what seemed appropriate, then sit smiling and feel a perfect fool. Very chastening. But the sensitive warmth of our reception by Sir Ivor and Lady Jennings dissolved his bitterness. 'We will leave you in peace,' Sir Ivor had written, 'until just before the lecture', which they did. It went well and was liked. L enjoyed his dinner after all; and I mine with my hostess, the wife of the Vice-Chancellor, and a tableful of their women-friends. Our way home was leisurely. Yet after a couple of nights spent in the house of his oldest and dearest friends L sadly remarked that for him any stay away from home had become an ordeal. Having already planned for that summer a long holiday in the Haute Savoie, at Talloires on Lake Annecy, I felt uneasy; but I had no time to distress myself over the possible effects on him of a strange bed and irresistible food: the yearly influx of American scholars was on.

Last thing before we left, a professor from California entertained us with a fateful garland of legends about L. We had ceased to wonder at any such legends after a former Manchester colleague told of an American girl-student who had marvelled, over a family dinner, at people there speaking 'of Namier as though he were alive'. Assured that he was, she retorted that in her country he was far too famous not to be assumed dead. For all that, L found the new crop outrageously fantastical. Why could not people exercise their imaginative abilities in the legitimate fields of fiction and leave facts to others prepared to verify them? I wondered if some people were not acting out of frustration, as L had turned down all requests to write even a short autobiographical sketch. What would some not invent after his death? L pounced: I was the one person able to write the truth about him with the understanding that any biographee deserved. In the same breath he undertook to help me while he was still here. I was dumbfounded.

On the third day at Talloires L began to tell the consecutive story of his family background, childhood, and youth. I took notes, and read most back, as we sat isolated under our favourite pergola above the lakeside. Constantly he pressed upon me the importance of my writing the truth about 'everything, everything'; by which I knew he meant all that he and I judged significant. He spoke slowly, with deliberate precision, often dwelling on a single point till satisfied its quality had sunk in. But at other times, sitting on some rustic bench or at table sipping wine between the dishes, he silently looked at me with a meditative kindness cut across by a hovering, shy, almost guilty smile not entirely new to me. I had been puzzled by it on occasions separated by many years. In May 1946 I had been sent by the literary editor of *Time and Tide* a book of folk-poetry, *Gold Khan*, said to be immemorial among the Turkic-speaking tribes of south-east Siberia. The independent weekly had been allowing me great latitude in the articles and reviews they wanted from me. Though not subject to nostalgia I was deeply stirred by the slim volume and wrote a long and rapturous review. The legends had evoked the earliest impact on me of rhythmic prose rich in traditional rhymes and impelling alliterations; they told of magnificent or diminutive or malformed (three-eared, six-legged, hunch-backed) horses as the prime protectors of persecuted heroic children immensely vulnerable in the steppe. Aware of having been carried away I posted my review to L asking if, in his opinion, my praise was extravagant and should be toned down. In next to no time he arrived at the flat and, in a flurry of lyrical excitement, asked for the book, to take to Manchester with him. The sequel which Norman Cohn—the translator of *Gold Khan*—inadvertently brought about, left me even more puzzled three years later. In the summer of 1949 he and his wife were passing through London and the four of us met. L deployed his best winkling-out technique and we quickly learnt that the basic MS. used by Cohn had been left to his wife by an uncle, a Siberian Jew who had roamed the steppe collecting folk-

poems still recited, chanted or sung in his day in the local nomads'
Russian idiom (no longer in the original tongue of which only
echoes, tags and jingles remained). After we had parted from the
Cohns L—strangely shy, and smiling in a puzzled, guilty ecstasy
new to me—incoherently said he would tell me all about something or other when there was time; it needed time. Eight years
later he came into my room one weekend with a book *The Fountain
Overflows*, recently sent us by the author, Rebecca West (Dame
Cicily Andrews). Pressing me to read it he said triumphantly, yet
with the same hovering, guilty, shy smile, 'Cicily understands
about horses!' and again mumbled something about telling me all
one day. Under the Talloires pergola an hour came when he spoke
of life at Kobylowloki. There, at the age of about three, L had
been visited by a gigantic white mare and had loved her visits to
the point of entering into a bond of complicity with her. I realized
that I was gaping in utter stupefaction when I saw L's shy smile
change into sombre chagrin. Reacting violently to my bewilderment he rose. It was unbelievable that I should not have understood. Facing me he whispered, 'It was idolatry, blasphemy.' An
idolater by nature, his earliest recollection was of blaspheming:
acts of obedient adoration inspired by a creature are blasphemous.
As he resignedly sat down and talked on in a different key, my
amazement increased. Only a year later did L sweep my bewilderment away by enacting an explanation in a typical, almost fortuitous manner. On one of London's most lovely summer evenings
we were due to dine with Professor Robert Walcott and his wife,
who were once again over from Ohio and were again staying for
the summer in a pretty Hampstead house. Before L left for his
office that morning we agreed he should be back in time to dress
comfortably after I had finished with the bathroom, at about 5.30.
Having done my weekend shopping by the late morning, I took
the car back to the garage where a man, busy sloshing vans,
offered to wash it for the usual fee. Assuming him to be known in
the mews I agreed, stressing that I wanted it ready no later than
3 p.m. when I would drive it to the front of our block ready for
use. But at a few minutes after three, I could find no trace of car or
man, and discovered that no one in the mews knew anything of
either. Having looked here and there I went to the local police

station; to be good humouredly assured that the lad must have taken my spruced up car for a joy ride and would no doubt bring it back before night unless he had an accident, of which they would hear soon enough. Walking home I figured out the best rearrangement of my timetable. Alone, I would have light-heartedly taken a taxi to the Walcotts though the chance of getting one back from Hampstead on Saturday night was slim. With L in tow, the situation was calamitous. He would be inordinately upset, over-excited and depressed by the possibility of the car having been stolen or smashed, and our being immobilized for long. Sadly I unlocked the door of the flat, to be confronted by him—returned more than an hour too soon. He had sat in the Black Hole after lunch extracting for his survey the essence of several biographies, when apprehensions about me assailed him. Having phoned and got no answer, he hurried home; found I was out; had gone to the garage and found neither me nor the car there; had returned home—my car was not before the house and I was still not in. As he spoke with mounting agitation, the telephone rang. The proprietor of the garage, with whom he had been in touch, had once again looked out of the window: there at last stood the car, apparently undamaged. We agreed to get ready for our evening out and that we would then walk together to the mews and drive on from there. As always with Daisy Walcott the dinner was delightful and L a courteous contributor to the stimulating conversation. On our drive there and back, being well drilled, he was monosyllabic. But when we had put away the car, he exploded into despair. Never again would he know peace when I was out of his sight. Our walking in circles round the flat and garage without our paths crossing would incapacitate him. It had been his hour of dereliction such as no man could survive for long. The dread of losing light and air by slow compression, through loss of me, was ineradicable. As he clutched my arm I understood what he had meant in Talloires by idolatry and its being blasphemous. Late into the night he spoke of the price a man pays for putting a creature where only the Maker should be—on a throne or pedestal, in the sky above or the mind within. When fagged out we parted, there was nothing I did not know of L. I had accepted his declaration that, ambivalent as he was towards all and everything, there had never been any trace of ambivalence in his attitude to me; and he had resigned himself to our not dying together. In less than six weeks he was dead. But when we were leaving Talloires, in the summer of 1959, a curtain of mystery had flapped between us to increase L's disorientation as London sucked him into a whirl-wind of anxieties.

The financial year 1958–9 had ticked away with not even 1,700 of L's section's 1,966 biographies ready; of the 314 constituency accounts fewer than 200 were completed; of the Introductory Survey not a page was written though a vast amount of preparatory work for it had been done. Some time previously, all concerned had reluctantly admitted that the nexus of time and cash stipulated early on, had been 'an unfortunate guess'. L's section for one thing, could not possibly be ready for the printers before the end of 1961. Inflation and other social changes were largely account-able for it. Besides, there had been serious illness, even death, among assistants, and in their families; some staff had left; most offices of the History of Parliament had been moved to another building; the usual clashes between men at work had become frequent, regional jealousies had come out into the open, humdrum frustrations and tensions had increased. National life was at last seen to be the true regulator of the scheme's scope and pace. Retrenchments had become imperative, as well as an extension of the time limit and a supplementary grant. Even the Trustees on their Olympus were torn between genuine enthusiasm for the board's determined stand on 'unimpeachable scholarship' and their own traditional rules of admirable rigidity. Joint meetings were held. And L's section—the middle one of the History's last period—was singled out as the venture's first-fruits to be hurried to its date of issue even at the cost of slowing down others. On L's stooping shoulders the weight of haste without damage was heavy when I added to it a burden beyond all reason.

Having been instructed that L's easy chair should be resprung in a particular way, I had sent it to the upholsterer. Meantime the most suitable of mine was placed by L's reading lamp, but he did not care for it. At long last his was returned and left in the passage outside our door when I was out. My first thought on catching sight of it was that no porter would be immediately available, the next thought was that L was due home from the office any minute. (And I had also been instructed that L should on no account put any strain on his arthritic back by moving or carrying things.) In rather a flurry I pushed and pulled my chair out of his room into mine, got his into the flat, and into the corner where it belonged. But at the last jerk, an indescribable, incapacitating pain shot through me. After an agonizing weekend, I was taken to an orthopaedic surgeon. And six weeks later, in February 1960, L, cancelling a traditional stay with some friends in Dorset, wrote,

Shortly before Christmas Julia dislocated a bone in her back which lacerated her sciatic nerve and started up a bad inflammation of the nerve sheath. After weeks of fever and pain she is only beginning to move about in the house. As for me, my lumbar osteo-arthritis gravely limits my movements and energy, and contributes to my crippling insomnia.

Our one gain was that we could at last figure out the origin of my 'lumbago' that I had been advised for years to grin and bear.

It would seem that when I lay for nine months some thirty years before, wellnigh unfed and immobile in a Moscow prison, a bone in my sacrum had partly perished; from then on it had tended to slip out of place but had been righting itself unaided. Now, repeatedly clicked or shoved into place, it would not hold. While a physiotherapist visited me daily I lay stupefied by pain, beyond speaking or being spoken to, writhing or afraid to stir lest the ache that had dimmed down increase again. Some years earlier L had written of a cousin's condition, 'For my part I would prefer being dead to half paralysed.' My state seemed to him worse even than partial paralysis. He spent much time in my room, silent, observant. Gradually a tormenting thought dominated me: had I failed L after all? A further leap by him into serenity reassured me that I had not. The old criteria no longer applied since a new tranquillity had stabilized below the movement of his hourly agitations.

Our minds had for so long been in accord that I followed step by step his reorientation of purpose. Considering himself of no further use to me, and thinking that he had become an acute problem in the History set-up, his proper course was to leave without fuss. Under the impact of economic and political events, and under the strain of adverse publicity, an apprehensive bitterness had tainted even L's team. Generalized dissatisfaction had waxed into impatience, to harden next into destructive acrimony well fed from outside. Opposition to his 'perfectionism' had crystallized. His assistants were expounding views contrary to his, and insisting on his formal acceptance of them. Whenever eloquent dissent blocked agreement, he firmly put off the solution. His opponents assumed that he counted on being more fit on some morrow, which by then was unlikely even in their eyes. No one seems to have understood that his intention was to leave the 'opposition' free to carry through, after his death, the solutions they favoured; or that his conscience having become, if possible, even less conciliatory he could not flaccidly subscribe to decisions that went against it. When the opposition blindly pressed round to force on him their views and will, he chose neither to impede nor to acquiesce, but to abstain. Because any simple mention of death as a concrete, impending moment, ranked at the time among unmentionable improprieties, L's certitude that he would not live beyond Christmas 1960, coupled with his awareness of being involved with a task bound to survive him, created an absurdly difficult situation between him and everyone but me. He had to wrestle tongue-tied with the dilemma of harmonizing imminence of death with a concrete job of work still to be done. His chronic fatigue increased and, too weary to argue, he avoided all exhausting, repetitious disputes. It is not possible to say if L's decision to die started the tiny cancer in his pancreas which after half a year bit into his aorta and quickly bled him to death; or if once again subject to an impelling flash of foresight he had merely heard and welcomed the order to quit. For most historians of his stature L's task would have been more easy. Anyone who had elaborated his own historical formula could easily have gathered round it the chief facts, giving them a smooth coherence by using as a main stem the favourite formula of a lifetime. But L's method was radically different. He had always aimed at contemplating the multitude of gathered facts and letting their coherence emerge out of the strivings, writings and sayings of the men who urged on or impeded the interrelated bulk as it moved, subject to the specific vagaries imposed by that time and that change. The period of gestation needed for such emergence was always long; in old age his ill health and lack of tranquillity had further prolonged it; and he felt that he was being induced to substitute the usual 'any other historian's' method for his own. Once or twice, in moments of deep depression, he was tempted to give in, with open-eyed cynicism, but succeeded in resisting; to the salvation of his intellectual and moral integrity. To me, he was so clearly expanding into death that I readily accepted his new criteria that were changing all along the line. Between us at least all was outspoken; and a few others had an inkling of what was afoot.

An account by J. R. G. Tomlinson, L's former pupil who now seldom saw him but was perceptive and had visited him that spring in the Institute's basement, has well captured the impact he made.

I knocked on the door and heard his gravelly, half-foreign, half-Oxford voice call 'Come in'. I pushed open the door and as he looked up and saw me he smiled, brought himself to his feet and stretched out his hand. His eyes which were always both analytical and sympathetic at the same time searched my face for signs of 'how things were'—he had a wonderful way of using slang when nothing else was better to convey a meaning. I assured him I was well and we relapsed into chairs. This may sound a very ordinary greeting and it was similar I suppose to many others I had had with him. But there is much more to convey before those who had never known him can realize the old-world courtesy and the warmth and the consideration that all this amounted to. . . .

LBN had been ill of chronic over-work and insomnia for years, sustained only by incredible stamina and conviction—which must also have been there in the '20s when, detached from academic historians, he was quietly working on an entirely new kind of history. The act of rising to his feet, when sometimes even reaching for a book seemed an unbearable effort, was symbolic of his kindness to a person so much his inferior intellectually yet in whom he recognized perhaps some honesty. And the offering of the hand which had been half-crippled for many years, again through over-work, was a gesture made only when friendship was secure. One took it and marvelled at its grip. . . .

Like some other rather deaf people he seemed to listen to you with some inner, more sensitive organ than his ears. When you were speaking his eyes would watch you intently, not to follow your lips but to tell from something about you the truth and significance of what you were saying. I always found it easier to express myself simply when confronted by this intent, listening gaze. . . .

For him there was no elaboration of parting: as soon as it was understood you should go he assumed you had gone and returned to his work without even watching you leave. But the manner of his bidding you go compensated overfully—a sudden smile lighting the whole face and revealing the man.

Soon L was to take his leave of many with equally little fuss; but meanwhile our life went on.

Doctors advised us to take a course of waters, mud-baths, and underwater massage at Montecatini in Tuscany, near Pistoia. No sooner were the involved arrangements made, than L was told of the Prime Minister's (Harold Macmillan's) intention to confer—at the first Encaenia after his election as Chancellor of the University of Oxford—an honorary doctorate of Civil Law on him. Deeply moved by one more official recognition of his efforts to serve Britain to his best ability, L ordered our plans to be recast. That our stay in Italy was considerably shortened mattered little as things turned out. The doctor in charge doubted L's being strong enough to benefit from the usual succession of treatments and drastically cut down his course. After a few days, true to himself, L was busy working out, like a schoolboy allowed off lessons, trips to Siena, San Giminiano, Sinalunga, Montepulciano—the places he had visited in a flurry of enthusiasm over fifty years ago. Refusing to be driven there alone, he laid his plans against the day when I would be allowed to skip some of my intensive treatments. On the first occasion—a half day—we took the local train up to the old fortified town (Montecatini Alta) and sat outside its walls on a bench shaded by broad-leaved trees. Looking down the abrupt hill on to the Tuscan plain evocative of many centuries' political entanglements, L mused on the strangeness of a man's outstripping his contemporaries. What they could understand he no longer cared to say; what he could now say they would not understand nor wish to hear.

The only entire day I was allowed off, saw us speeding by car to Siena because of its cathedral and museums, and having lunch on

the way back at San Gimignano. Gazing out at another aspect of
the great Tuscan plain which stretched away mile after green mile,
L recaptured, as we ate, his dominant mood of 1907. With the
wisdom of half a century's involvement in human affairs, he
judged the Italian Renaissance's impact on him and its significance
to the human race. But his customary sparkle kept breaking
through all earnest meditations on universal themes. After what
was for him an 'enchanting period of Tuscan leisure' we flew back
from Pisa barely in time to repack for Oxford where we stayed, as
usual, with the Principal of Lady Margaret Hall, Dr. Lucy Suther-
land—one of L's special friends whom he wished inconspicuously
to take leave of while the year's good driving weather lasted. In
the next few weeks he sought reconciliation with a couple of
people towards whom he had harboured bitterness; and brought
together, over dinner, others who had long wanted to meet each
other. But he was easing himself out of boards and commissions
on the excellent plea that he could no longer hear the drift of discussions. At home he spent much time tidying up masses of papers
stuffed into drawers or stacked on shelves. Yet when more alert,
he busied himself with revising *England in the Age of the American
Revolution* or bringing the biography of Charles Townshend
nearer completion.

To get *England in the Age* out of the way, we devoted to it about
an hour every morning, before he left for the office where he
worked almost entirely on the Survey; and we agreed, on 18
August, to push on with it in the evening too. In the early afternoon L confirmed his keenness by telephoning to say I should not
expect him to supper: he wanted me fully rested, to work on
England in the Age the moment he reached home, at about seven;
he would keep me steady at it till nine. Whenever I undertook to
help him, I carried out L's instructions with meticulous care
knowing that he would reach me too soon rather than five minutes
late. But fifteen minutes and more had passed the hour when I
heard his key strangely fumble at the lock. When an unusual
shuffle followed, I leapt to it. L stood livid, speechless. He had
been strap-hanging all the way. An extraordinary ache in his
lower back made sitting down unthinkable. The doctor, quick to
come, gave an injection to loosen the cramp indicative of some as

yet indefinable affliction. I was to telephone if the pain returned. It did not, and at about one L sent me from his side, to sleep. At five he summoned me with gentle tapping on the wall alongside his bed. I coped with symptoms of internal bleeding. But he would not let me call the doctor: too early, let the man sleep. Curbing my impatience I waited till eight, on that morning which L knew to be 'Russian Transfiguration'. I had intended to go to church. Rather astonished that I should put it off, he spoke of the lovely day being appropriate to so marvellous a feast, and savoured the word 'transfiguration'. His decades of rationally inexplicable anguish and self-hate were being compensated for by hours of stupendous joy, equally lacking in any rational cause and aglow with an all-embracing sense of reconciliation, even with himself. The doctor confirmed my suppositions, said an immediate operation was imperative, engaged for L a private ward at St. Mary's, Paddington, and ordered an ambulance to take both of us there; he would rejoin us soon. As we waited to be fetched, L spoke with a new assurance about having realized, when the unbearable pain was sweeping in on him, the true shape of his Survey. It would take no more than a fortnight to write and should be ready for the printers well before Christmas. Since the History could no longer be a living skyscraper but had to be a mausoleum, his Survey would make of it a Testament projected towards future generations unaware perhaps of the grand English effort to rule by consorting together—the greatest achievement of the time called the second British Empire. L's love of the Old World, proclaimed to his readers in Oxford's *Blue Book* in 1912, had become beautifully caught up in a commemorative work larger than any man could have tackled alone.

The ambulance men sized up the situation at a glance and the driver, before mounting, said he would go like the wind. He did, clanging his bell all the way. As I bent over L, placed on his stretcher below the hospital steps, he roguishly smiled up to say 'Some driving!'. After he had been put to bed I was allowed to sit with him. His mind had been dwelling on practical details at home and in the office. He told me what precisely to do before the day was out. When the surgeon came I was sent away till 3 p.m., visiting time. Having reached home by taxi, I thought rest more important than lunch, and lay with closed eyes till it was time to tidy up and walk to the garage. The telephone rang. L's doctor had bad news for me: with two nurses getting L ready for a test and still laughing at a joke he had made, he suddenly died. I was wanted at the hospital to make decisions and sign papers. Badly dazed I walked to the garage, but, once in the driver's seat, the well ingrained habit of concentrating on immediate vision and instantaneous decision took over.

The amount of detail to be coped with for the disposal of a man's remains is astonishing. I was drawn into strings of discussions by word of mouth and on the telephone. Between times I managed to visit the chapel where the body was already laid out. As I first knelt then stood by what had been Lewis I knew beyond a flicker of doubt that none could have gone more gentle into that good night. But his having lived and departed left a great deal strewn about to be dealt with at speed.

It was early evening before I returned home, dog-tired. Having eaten a scrap or two, I lay down on the divan in Lewis's room, with a writing pad in one hand and a pen in the other. I had done so for years, ready to draft his letters or jot down a sentence that had at last jelled; or keen on helping him to formulate a stray thought which, if netted in evocative words, might some day prove useful. I had now to plan sensibly the morrow and the following days. But tossed about by a febrile energy, I could not concentrate. Despairing, I closed my eyes; and did not open them when my hand began to jerk, blindly doodling. 'Automatic writing?' I wondered with lazy consent. When my hand jerked to a final flourish and relaxed, I read: 'I'm filled with wonder. God is indeed love life eternity. I've loved disastrously little. My void waited for love and called to be filled with it which alone can. Thank you for being lovable. Because I love I live.'

It seemed to have been an open-ended life.

UKRAINIANS AND RUTHENIANS

(based on material written by Namier between 1916 and 1926)

Centuries after successive Mongolian hordes had destroyed the old all-Russian centre of Kiev and devastated extensive tracts of Kievan lands, Muscovy, far to the north, became aware of itself as the dominant Russian centre, and of the wastelands to its south as the Ukraine or 'Borderland'. When, in time, miscellaneous groups of fugitives started re-populating the wastes, the new settlers were called 'Ukrainians' after the place they disappeared into. 'Ruthenian' is the Anglicized version of a Polish term that came to be used locally for 'Russian' after the Polish ascendancy had established itself in a part of the Ukraine which itself came to be called Eastern Galicia.

In 1919 the territory that intervened between resuscitated Poland's eastern ethnic border and her eastern political frontier of '1772' (as it was known because it was the eastern frontier of her imperialist era at its peak) consisted of three main regions. Of these, two (Eastern Galicia and Western Ukraine) were ethnically Little-Russian; the third, to the north of them, was ethnically Belorussian and Lithuanian.

Eastern Galicia, starting on the eastern bank of the river San, covered about 18,000 sq. miles packed with some five million inhabitants of whom 64 per cent were Greek Catholics and spoke Little-Russian at home; many of them knew no Polish. The economically and politically dominant Polish minority amounted to hardly more than 24·5 per cent of the population; the difference between the two being made up of Jews and some Germans. After the partitioning of Poland the Western Ukraine formed three Russian governments (Volynia, Podolye, and Kiev), together extending over some 60,000 sq. miles, with 12,337,000 inhabitants (1911 figures). Here, about 80 per cent were Little Russians, 13 per cent Jews, 4 per cent Poles. During and after World War I, aggressively nationalistic Poles regarded the existence of a Belorussian nationality and a Ukrainian nationality as variable factors in Polish policy, not as stable facts. L, too, considered that the existence of the two nationalities was still unstable, but already arguable. On occasion he called them nations *in posse*. Despite differences of dialect, the Belorussian and Little-Russian peasants called themselves 'Russky', like the Great-Russians. In antiquity, when Kiev was the centre alike of Great-Russians, Little-Russians, Chervono- (or 'Red') Russians, and Belo- (or 'White') Russians, there were no fixed dialects. The later typical linguistic variants largely arose owing to 'the Tartar-Lithuanian-Polish partitionings of Russia'. But either way, whether the Belorussians and the Little-Russians had or had not become stable nationalities by 1919, Poles they certainly were not. Only the topmost layer of the population in these regions was Polish or Great-Russian; while the numerous traders and artisans had long since been Jewish. At a Belorussian Peasant Congress held in Minsk in April 1917 the indigenous peasant population insisted, 'We don't want autonomy. The Polish lords have invented this autonomy thing to rule over us and cheat us out of the land.' The whole of the Ukraine was emphatically peasants' country and the chief concern of every peasant there was to possess himself of as many acres as he thought his due.

BIBLIOGRAPHY OF NAMIER'S PRINCIPAL WORKS

The Structure of Politics at the Accession of George III (1929, 2nd ed. 1957). London: Macmillan; New York: St. Martins.

England in the Age of the American Revolution (1930, 2nd ed. 1961). London: Macmillan; New York: St. Martins.

Skyscrapers and Other Essays (1931). London: Macmillan. Contains essays written between 1914 and 1929.

Additions and Corrections to Sir John Fortescue's Edition of the Correspondence of King George III, vol. I (1937). Manchester University Press.

In the Margin of History (1939). London: Macmillan. Contains essays written between 1925 and 1939.

Conflicts: Studies in Contemporary History (1942). London: Macmillan. Contains essays written between 1918 and 1942.

1848: The Revolution of the Intellectuals (1946). London: Oxford University Press. First published in Volume 30 of the British Academy Proceedings.

Facing East (1947). London: Hamish Hamilton.

Diplomatic Prelude: 1938-1939 (1948). London: Macmillan.

Europe in Decay: A Study in Disintegration, 1936-1940 (1950). London: Macmillan; Gloucester, Mass.: Smith.

In the Nazi Era (1952). London: Macmillan.

Avenues of History (1952). London: Hamish Hamilton.

Personalities and Powers (1955). London: Hamish Hamilton; New York: Macmillan.

Vanished Supremacies: Essays on European History, 1812-1918 (1958). London: Hamish Hamilton; New York: Macmillan.

Crossroads of Power: Essays on Eighteenth-century England (1962). London: Hamish Hamilton; New York: Macmillan. The essays include 'King George III: A Study of Personality' (1953), and 'Charles Townshend: His Character and Career' (1959).

With John Brooke, *The House of Commons, 1754-1790*, 3 vols. (1964). London: H.M.S.O.; New York: Oxford University Press. Published posthumously, these are the first three volumes of the projected 'History of Parliament' dealing with the House of Commons from 1264 to 1832.

With John Brooke, *Charles Townshend* (1964). London: Macmillan; New York: St. Martins.

INDEX

Adam, Agatha Forbes, 254, 255, 310

Adam, Eric Forbes, 115, 254

Alexandra College, Dublin, 302

Allsop, Henry, 76

All Souls College, Oxford, 99, 100ff., 104, 307

American Leader, 114, 119

American Revolution, 105, 188, 199, 201, 208, 220, 321, 331

Andrews, Cicily. *See* West, Dame Rebecca

Anson, Sir William, 104

Archaeological finds, 59ff., 66, 84f., 107, 193

Ashley, Maurice, 228, 229

Ashmolean Museum, 85f.

Astor, Lady, 211

Atkinson, Mabel, 97f.

Baffy. *See* Dugdale, Mrs. Edgar

Baker Library (Harvard), 222

Baker, Philip Noel, 210

Balfour, A. J. (later Earl of), 144, 189, 190, 199, 204, 209, 284, 290

Balfour Declaration, 205, 210

Balfour, Gerald, 209

Balliol College, Oxford, xi, 71, 76, 81ff., 91, 100, 101, 111, 123, 142–57 *passim*, 177, 193, 261, 280, 286, 307

Bancroft Transcripts, 107

Barrett, Rachel, 70, 76

Barrington, Prue, 249, 272

Bauer, Otto, 161

Baum, Valerie, 320

Beckett, Professor J. C., 303

Beer, Marie, 43, 48ff., 164, 177, 178ff., 194f., 195, 198, 232, 233ff.

Beit Prize Essay, 104f., 106

Bell, Esther, 153, 154, 165, 170, 176

Bell, Kenneth, 153, 156

Beneš, Eduard, 171ff.

Ben-Gurion, David, 218, 274

Berenson, Bernard, 301, 307, 308

Bernsztajn, Balbina (LBN's paternal grandmother), 4ff., 7, 13, 18

Bernsztajn, Jacob (LBN's paternal grandfather), 3ff., 6

Bernsztajn vel Niemirowska, Ann (LBN's mother; *née* Sommersztajn), 16, 19, 20, 27f., 38, 42f., 99, 143, 217; education and home life, 6; religion, 6f., 35; marriage, 7; daughter Theodora born, 8; LBN born, 10; moves to parents' home, 12f.; life in steppe farmhouse, 13ff.; miscarriage, 33f.; death of father, 34; in Italy, 36f., 66; plans children's education, 37f., 45; befriends Marie Beer, 48ff.; her advice sought by many, 52; appearance, 72; reveals his father's gambling to LBN, 85; heart-to-heart communication with LBN, 93, 94f.; in France, 160; post-war plans (after 1919), 162; breaks with LBN, 175, 176f., 182

Bernsztajn vel Niemirowski, Joseph (LBN's father), 14, 15, 19, 33, 42f., 45, 46, 53ff., 58, 72, 75, 99f., 143f., 160f., 163, 175, 217; personal appearance, 5f.;

339

Wingate, Sir Reginald, 91
Wingate, (Sir) Ronald, 91f., 95
Women's Social and Political Union, 70
Wood, Major (Sir) Murdock McKenzie, 147
Woodward, Sir Llewellyn, 303
Workers' Educational Association (W.E.A.), 103, 115, 246
Wyndham, Sir Percy, 143

X, Mme de, 63ff., 92

Yale University, 110, 111, 112

Zaleski, August, 60, 69, 129
Zionism, 108, 142, 164, 201ff., 240, 241, 270, 271, 285
Zionist Archives, Jerusalem, xii
Zionist Organization, 204ff., 209, 241, 261